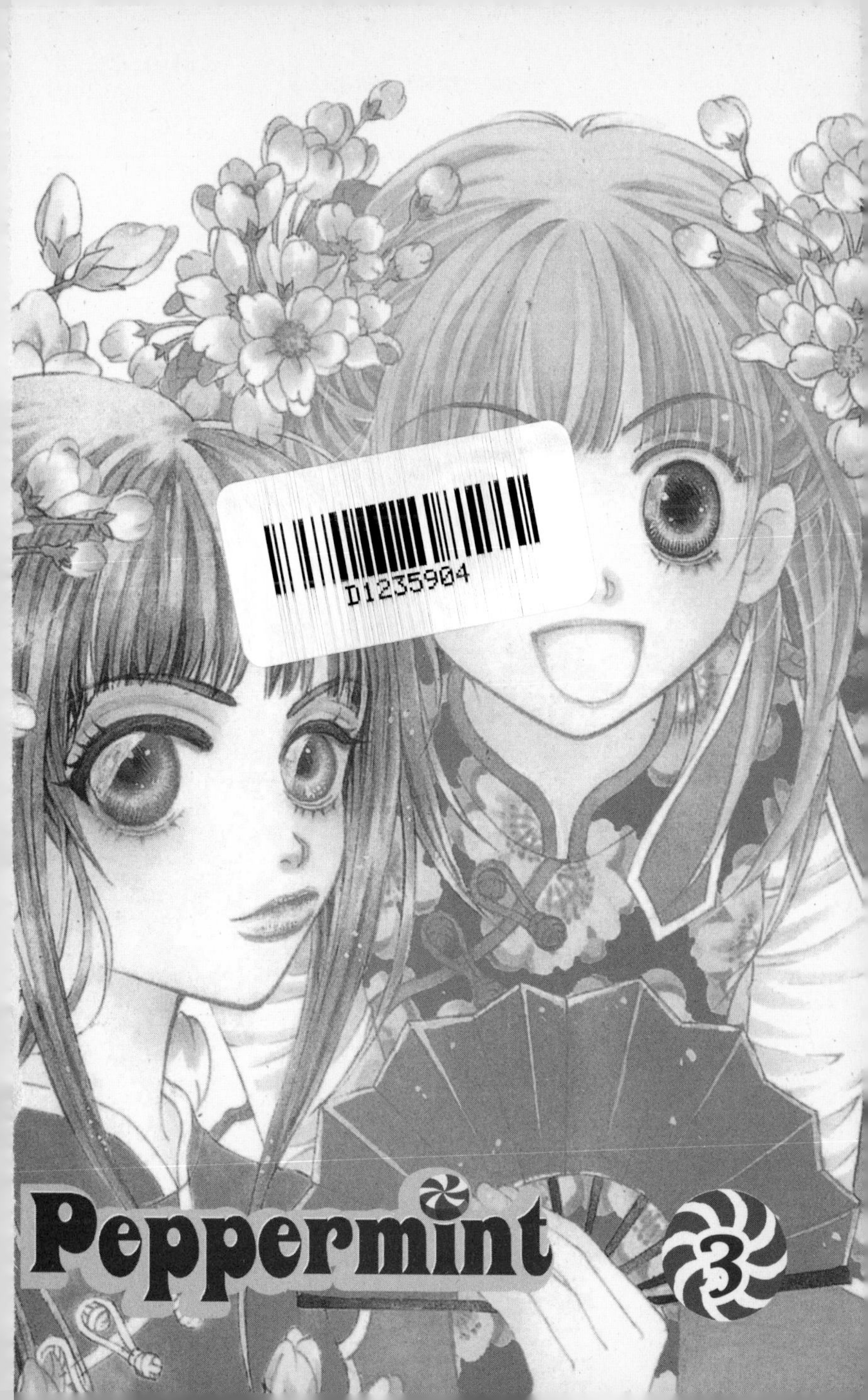
Peppermint
3

***Peppermint* Volume 3**

Created by Eun-Jin Seo

Translation - Jennifer Hahm
English Adaptation - Marc Goldsmith
Retouch and Lettering - Jennifer Carbajal
Graphic Designer - Al-Insan Lashley

Editor - Katherine Schilling
Digital Imaging Manager - Chris Buford
Pre-Production Supervisor - Erika Terriquez
Art Director - Anne Marie Horne
Production Manager - Elisabeth Brizzi
Managing Editor - Vy Nguyen
VP of Production - Ron Klamert
Editor-in-Chief - Rob Tokar
Publisher - Mike Kiley
President and C.O.O. - John Parker
C.E.O. and Chief Creative Officer - Stuart Levy

A TOKYOPOP® Manga

TOKYOPOP and [logo] are trademarks or registered trademarks of TOKYOPOP Inc.

TOKYOPOP Inc.
5900 Wilshire Blvd. Suite 2000
Los Angeles, CA 90036

E-mail: info@TOKYOPOP.com
Come visit us online at www.TOKYOPOP.com

© 2003 EUN-JIN SEO, HAKSAN PUBLISHING CO., LTD. All rights reserved. First published in Korea in 2003 by HAKSAN PUBLISHING CO., LTD. English translation rights in North America, UK, NZ, and Australia arranged by HAKSAN PUBLISHING CO., LTD.
English text copyright © 2007 TOKYOPOP Inc.

All rights reserved. No portion of this book may be reproduced or transmitted in any form or by any means without written permission from the copyright holders. This manga is a work of fiction. Any resemblance to actual events or locales or persons, living or dead, is entirely coincidental.

ISBN: 978-1-59816-683-5

First TOKYOPOP printing: March 2007

10 9 8 7 6 5 4 3 2 1

Printed in the USA

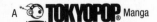

Peppermint

Volume 3
Eun-Jin Seo

HAMBURG // LONDON // LOS ANGELES // TOKYO

Peppermint

*Your heart flutters and you're overwhelmed
with the absolutely wonderful feeling of your first kiss.*

Table of Contents

Get To Know Your Neighbor...

Hey

YOUR REGULAR HIGH SCHOOL SOPHOMORE WHO'S DOWN ON HER LUCK WHEN IT COMES TO A LOVE LIFE. HAVING A CRUSH ON THE UBER-POPULAR SINGER/ACTOR EZ CERTAINLY DOESN'T MAKE THINGS ANY EASIER, BUT SHE'S DETERMINED TO STEP INTO THE SPOTLIGHT OF HIS LIFE.

EZ

HANDSOME, FUNNY, RICH... AND DID WE SAY HANDSOME? HE MAY BE A LITTLE NAÏVE, BUT THIS TEEN IDOL'S GOT WHAT ALL THE GIRLS ARE LOOKING FOR, LENDING TO HIS ALREADY HUGE FANCLUB!

EO

WALKING TROUBLE, WITH SKATEBOARD MOVES AS SHARP AS HIS TONGUE. HE HAS A STRANGE ALLERGIC REACTION TO GIRLS, EXCEPT FOR WHEN IT COMES TO HEY. HE ALWAYS MANAGES TO POP UP WHEN HEY IS IN A JAM.

Mary

EO'S CLASSMATE WHO'S GOT THE HOTS FOR HIM, AND WILL DO ANYTHING TO GET HER MAN. SHE'S A MASTERMIND AT LAYING TRAPS, AND RIGHT NOW SHE'S GOT EO AND HEY AS HER TARGET.

Chung-sik

SMOOTHER TALKER EXTRAORDINAIRE, HE'S A MEGA-PLAYER THAT'S GOT ALL THE RULES DOWN WHEN IT COMES TO SNAGGING A GIRL.

Our Story So Far...

FOR THE FIRST 15 YEARS OF HEY'S LIFE, SHE'S HAD HER HEART SET ON ONE MAN AND ONE MAN ALONE, THE INCREDIBLY POPULAR TEEN IDOL, EZ, WHO ALSO ATTENDS HAKSAN HIGH SCHOOL. AND THOUGH EZ ONLY SEES HER AS A RELIABLE CLASSMATE TO HELP HIM REHEARSE HIS SCRIPTS, HEY'S FALLING FASTER FOR HIM EVERYDAY!

THIS ALL CHANGES WHEN EZ'S YOUNGER BROTHER, EO, STORMS ON STAGE! WHAT FIRST STARTED AS A SERIES OF INNOCENT TEASES HAS TURNED INTO SOMETHING MORE, AND IT'S CLEAR EO'S GOT HIS HEART SET ON HEY. HE'S WILLING TO FIGHT OFF SCHOOL TERRORS AND EVEN HIS OWN BROTHER TO STAKE HIS CLAIM, BUT HEY'S NOT ENTIRELY SURE HOW TO HANDLE THIS BALL OF TERROR.

A FEW NOBLE ACTS ON EO'S PART MAY BE SWAYING OUR YOUNG HEROINE'S HEART, BUT SHE'S STILL GOT A LOT OF ISSUES TO OVERCOME BEFORE SHE'S READY TO SPILL HER FEELINGS.

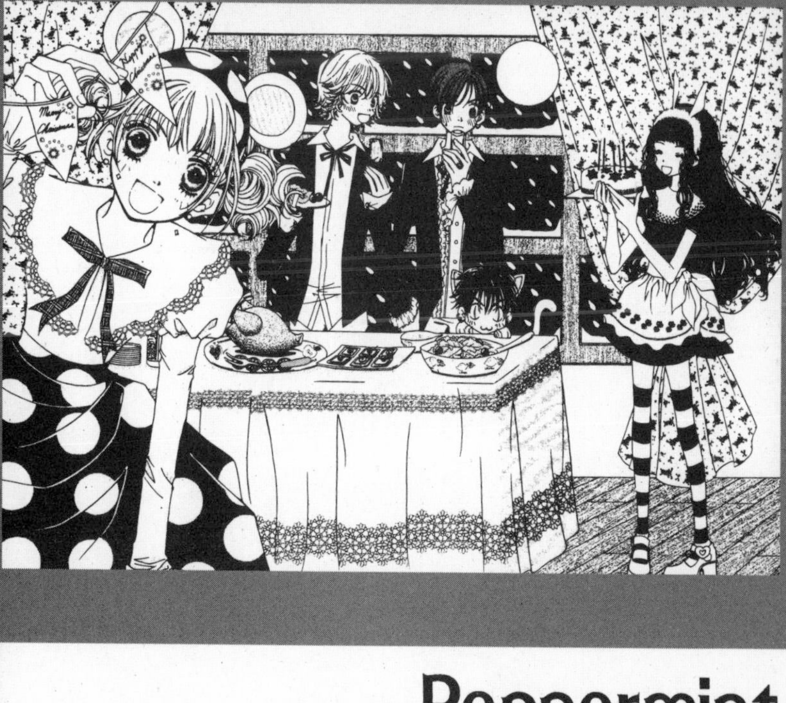
Happy Christmas
Merry Christmas

Peppermint

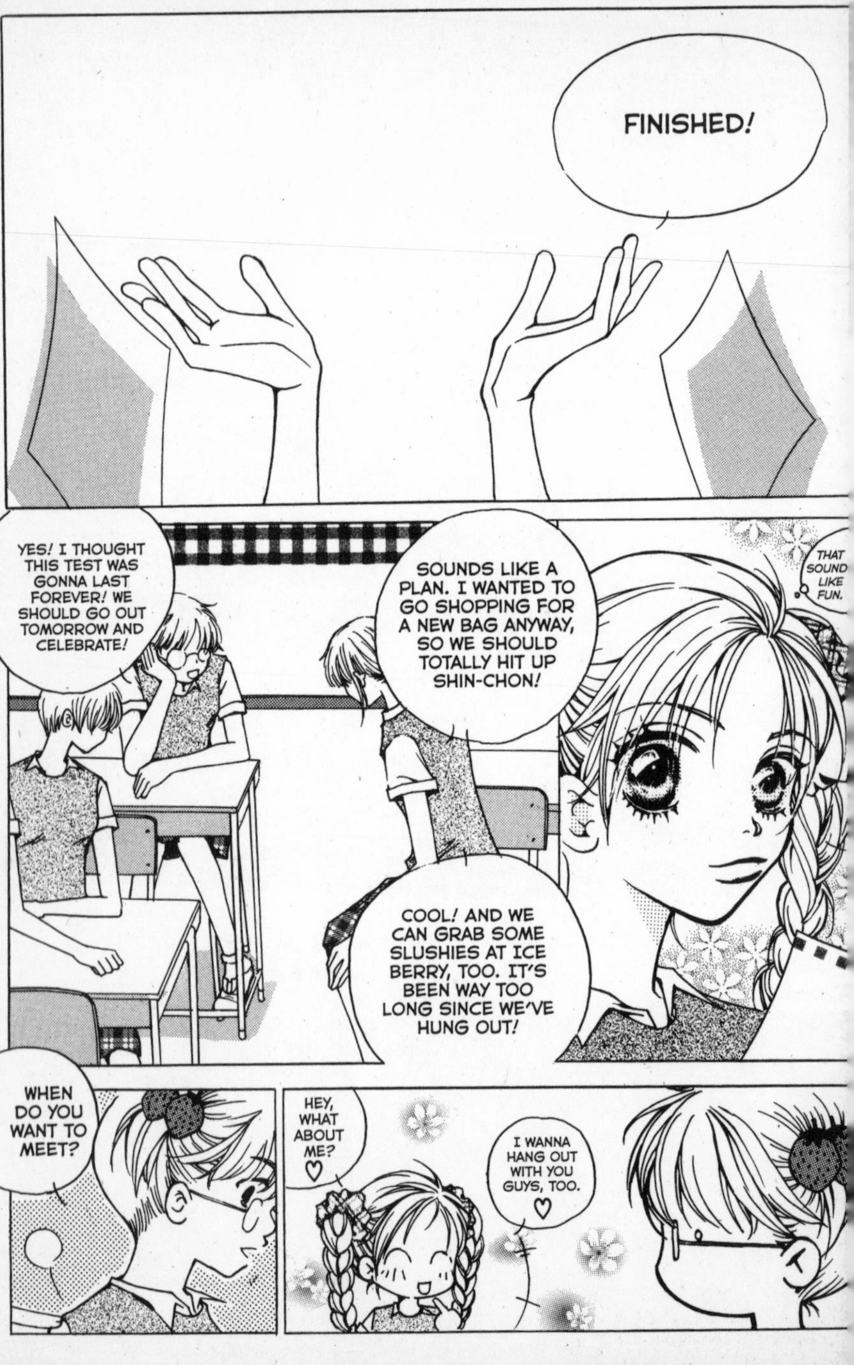
FINISHED!
YES! I THOUGHT THIS TEST WAS GONNA LAST FOREVER! WE SHOULD GO OUT TOMORROW AND CELEBRATE!
SOUNDS LIKE A PLAN. I WANTED TO GO SHOPPING FOR A NEW BAG ANYWAY, SO WE SHOULD TOTALLY HIT UP SHIN-CHON!
COOL! AND WE CAN GRAB SOME SLUSHIES AT ICE BERRY, TOO. IT'S BEEN WAY TOO LONG SINCE WE'VE HUNG OUT!
THAT SOUND LIKE FUN.
WHEN DO YOU WANT TO MEET?
HEY, WHAT ABOUT ME? ♡
I WANNA HANG OUT WITH YOU GUYS, TOO. ♡

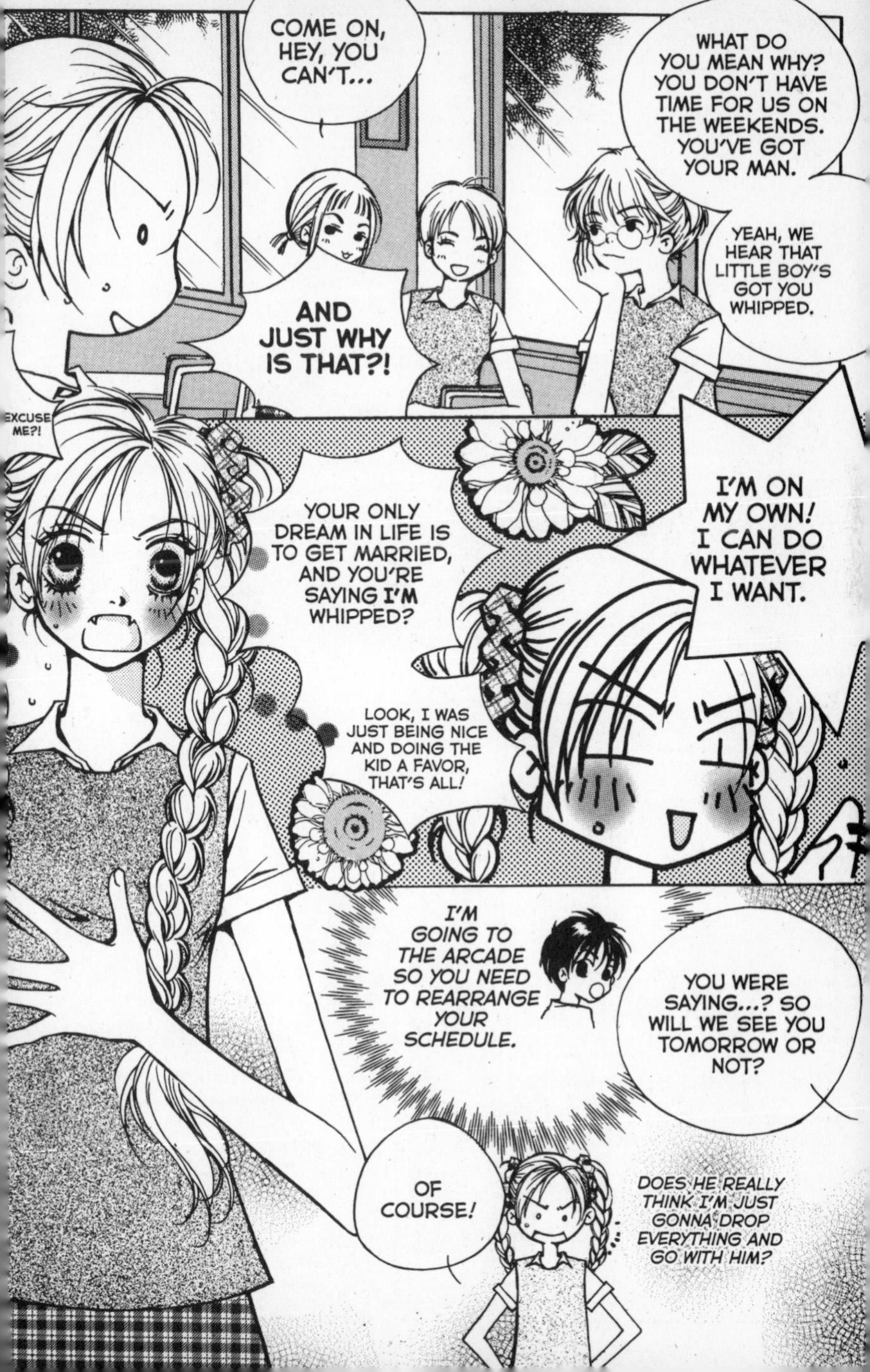
COME ON, HEY, YOU CAN'T...
AND JUST WHY IS THAT?!
WHAT DO YOU MEAN WHY? YOU DON'T HAVE TIME FOR US ON THE WEEKENDS. YOU'VE GOT YOUR MAN.
YEAH, WE HEAR THAT LITTLE BOY'S GOT YOU WHIPPED.
EXCUSE ME?!
YOUR ONLY DREAM IN LIFE IS TO GET MARRIED, AND YOU'RE SAYING I'M WHIPPED?
I'M ON MY OWN! I CAN DO WHATEVER I WANT.
LOOK, I WAS JUST BEING NICE AND DOING THE KID A FAVOR, THAT'S ALL!
I'M GOING TO THE ARCADE SO YOU NEED TO REARRANGE YOUR SCHEDULE.
YOU WERE SAYING...? SO WILL WE SEE YOU TOMORROW OR NOT?
OF COURSE!
DOES HE REALLY THINK I'M JUST GONNA DROP EVERYTHING AND GO WITH HIM?

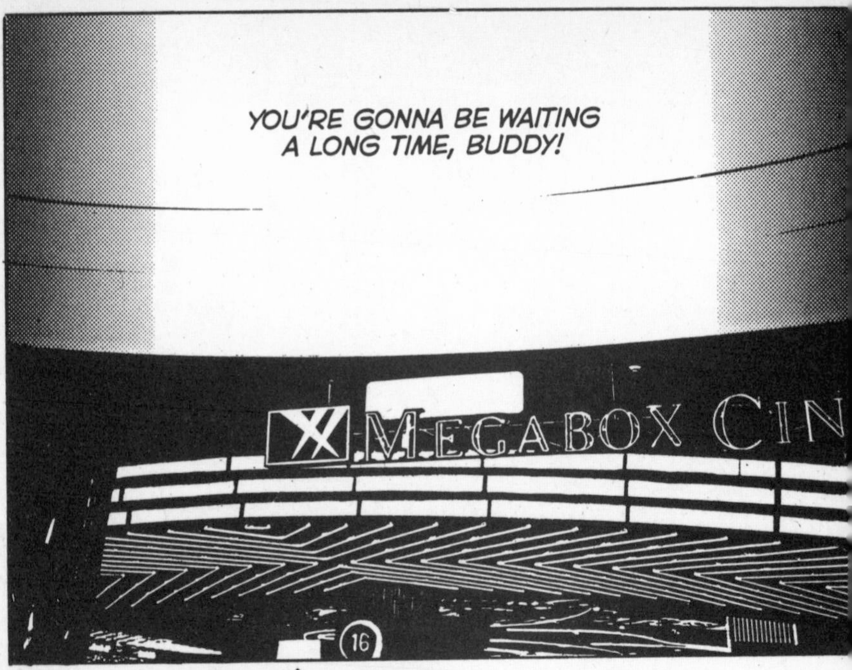
YOU'RE GONNA BE WAITING A LONG TIME, BUDDY!
MEGABOX CIN
16

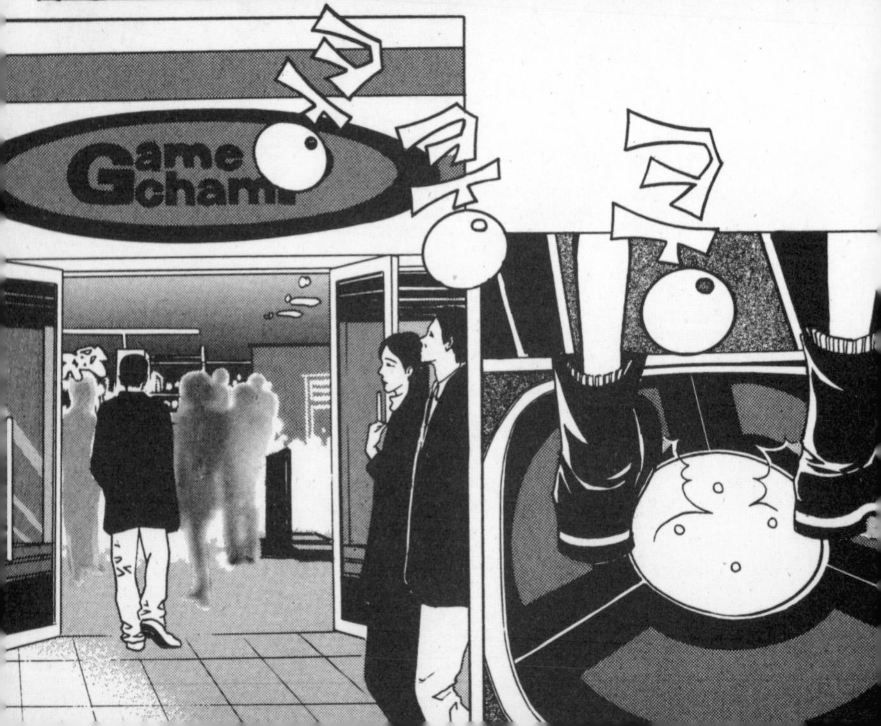
Game
cham

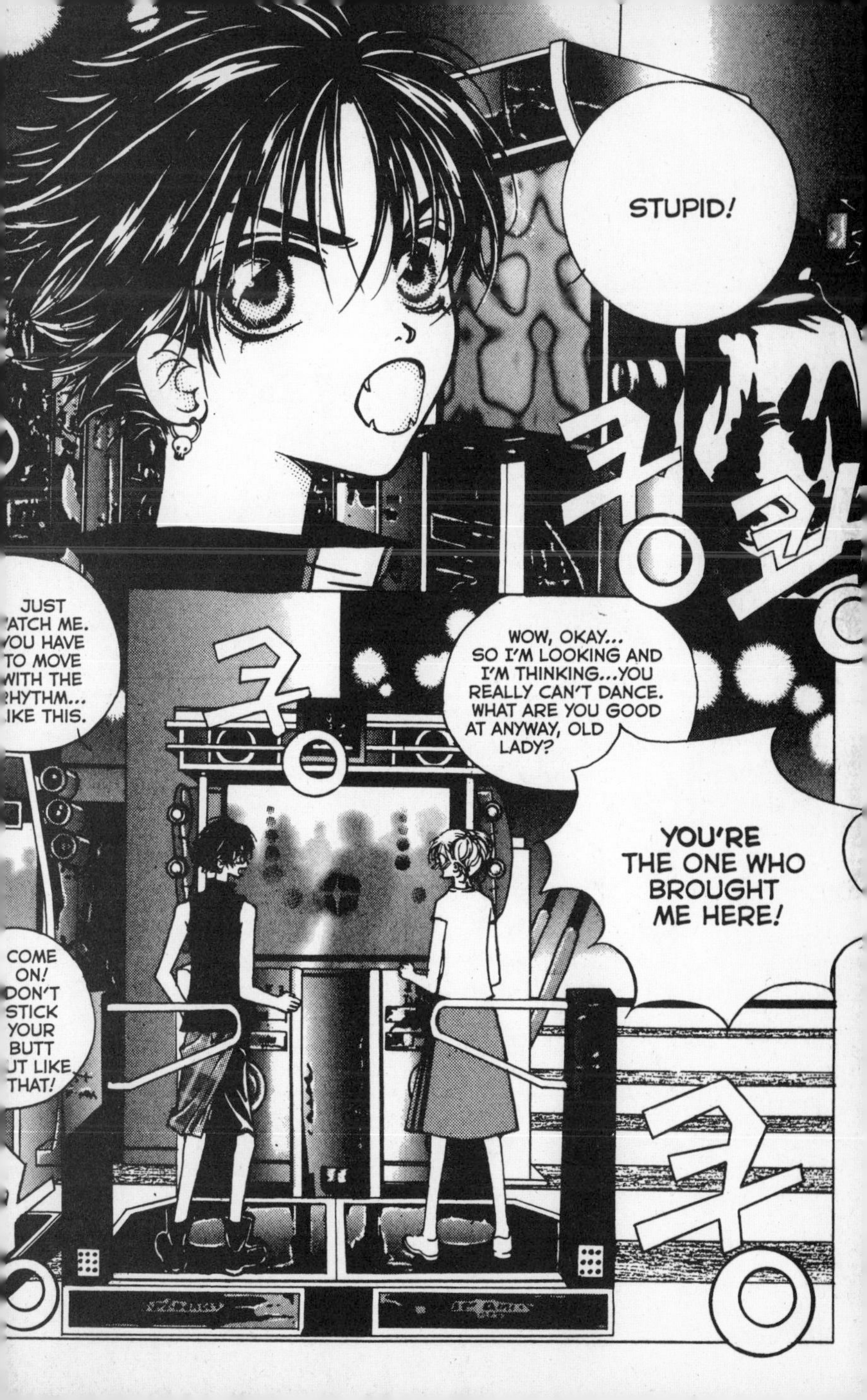
STUPID!
JUST ATCH ME. OU HAVE TO MOVE WITH THE HYTHM... IKE THIS.
COME ON! DON'T STICK YOUR BUTT UT LIKE THAT!
WOW, OKAY... SO I'M LOOKING AND I'M THINKING...YOU REALLY CAN'T DANCE. WHAT ARE YOU GOOD AT ANYWAY, OLD LADY?
YOU'RE THE ONE WHO BROUGHT ME HERE!

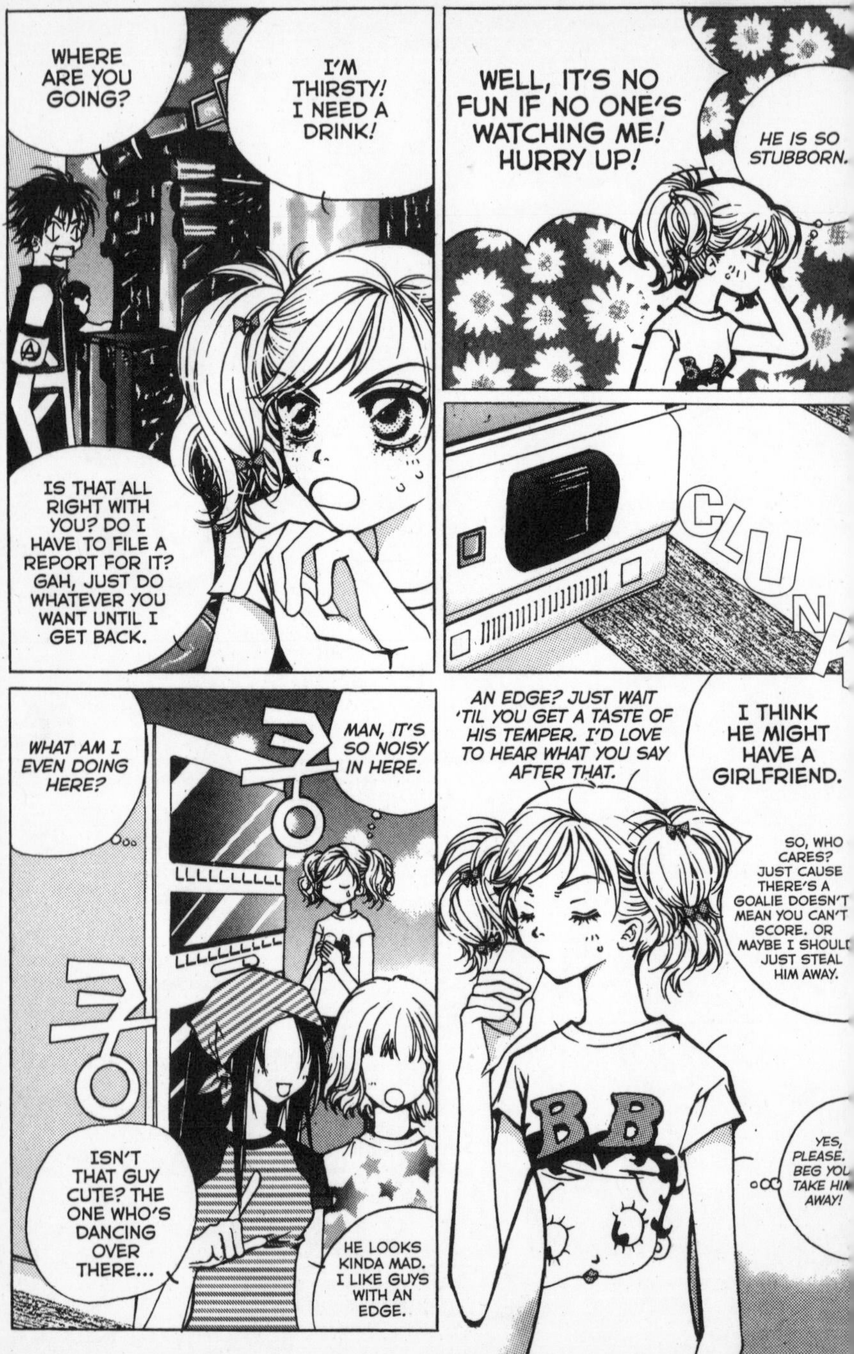
WHERE ARE YOU GOING?
I'M THIRSTY! I NEED A DRINK!
IS THAT ALL RIGHT WITH YOU? DO I HAVE TO FILE A REPORT FOR IT? GAH, JUST DO WHATEVER YOU WANT UNTIL I GET BACK.
WELL, IT'S NO FUN IF NO ONE'S WATCHING ME! HURRY UP!
HE IS SO STUBBORN.
CLUNK
WHAT AM I EVEN DOING HERE?
MAN, IT'S SO NOISY IN HERE.
ISN'T THAT GUY CUTE? THE ONE WHO'S DANCING OVER THERE...
HE LOOKS KINDA MAD. I LIKE GUYS WITH AN EDGE.
AN EDGE? JUST WAIT 'TIL YOU GET A TASTE OF HIS TEMPER. I'D LOVE TO HEAR WHAT YOU SAY AFTER THAT.
I THINK HE MIGHT HAVE A GIRLFRIEND.
SO, WHO CARES? JUST CAUSE THERE'S A GOALIE DOESN'T MEAN YOU CAN'T SCORE. OR MAYBE I SHOULD JUST STEAL HIM AWAY.
YES, PLEASE. BEG YOU TAKE HIM AWAY!

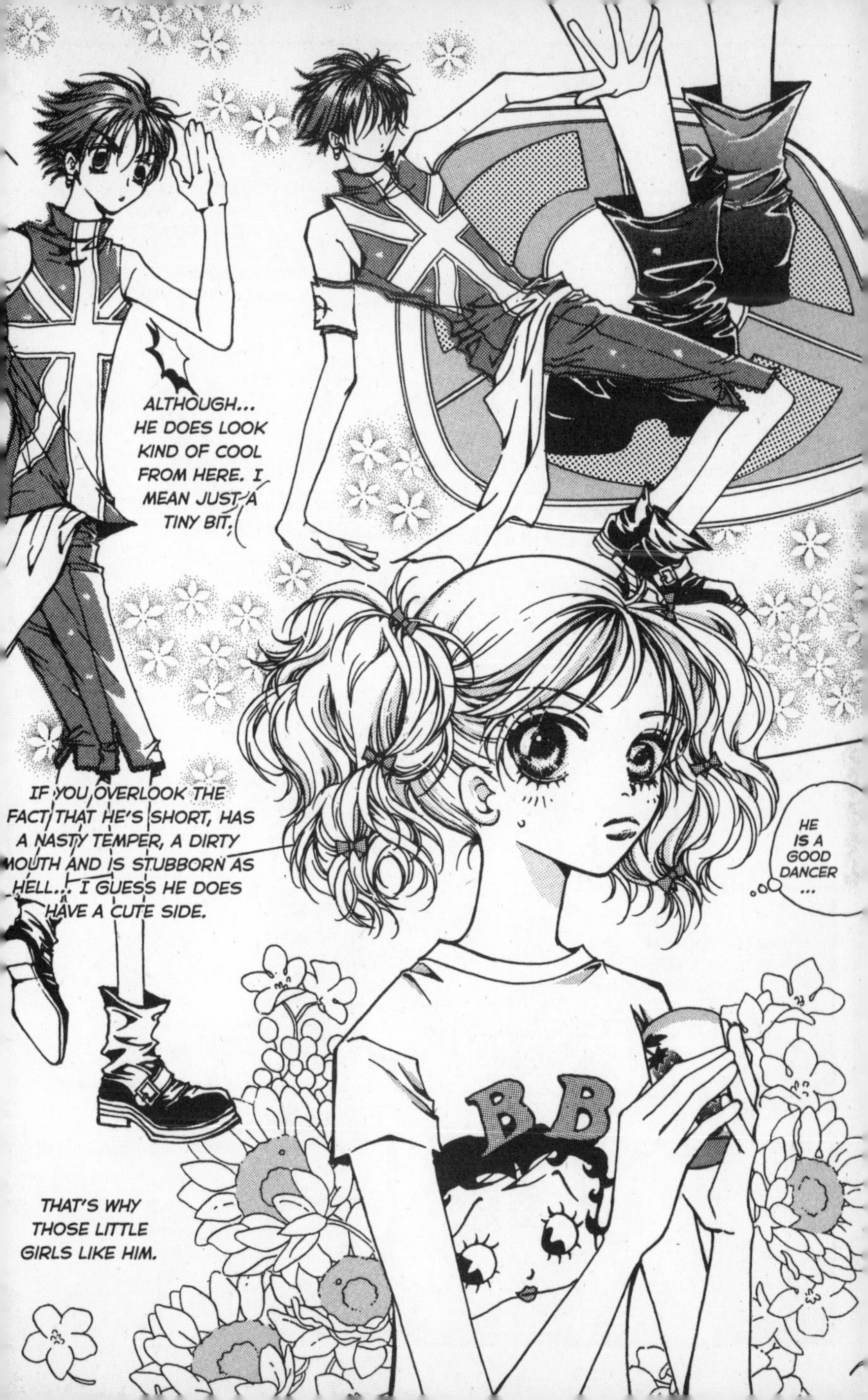
ALTHOUGH... HE DOES LOOK KIND OF COOL FROM HERE. I MEAN JUST A TINY BIT.
IF YOU OVERLOOK THE FACT THAT HE'S SHORT, HAS A NASTY TEMPER, A DIRTY MOUTH AND IS STUBBORN AS HELL... I GUESS HE DOES HAVE A CUTE SIDE.
HE IS A GOOD DANCER ...
THAT'S WHY THOSE LITTLE GIRLS LIKE HIM.

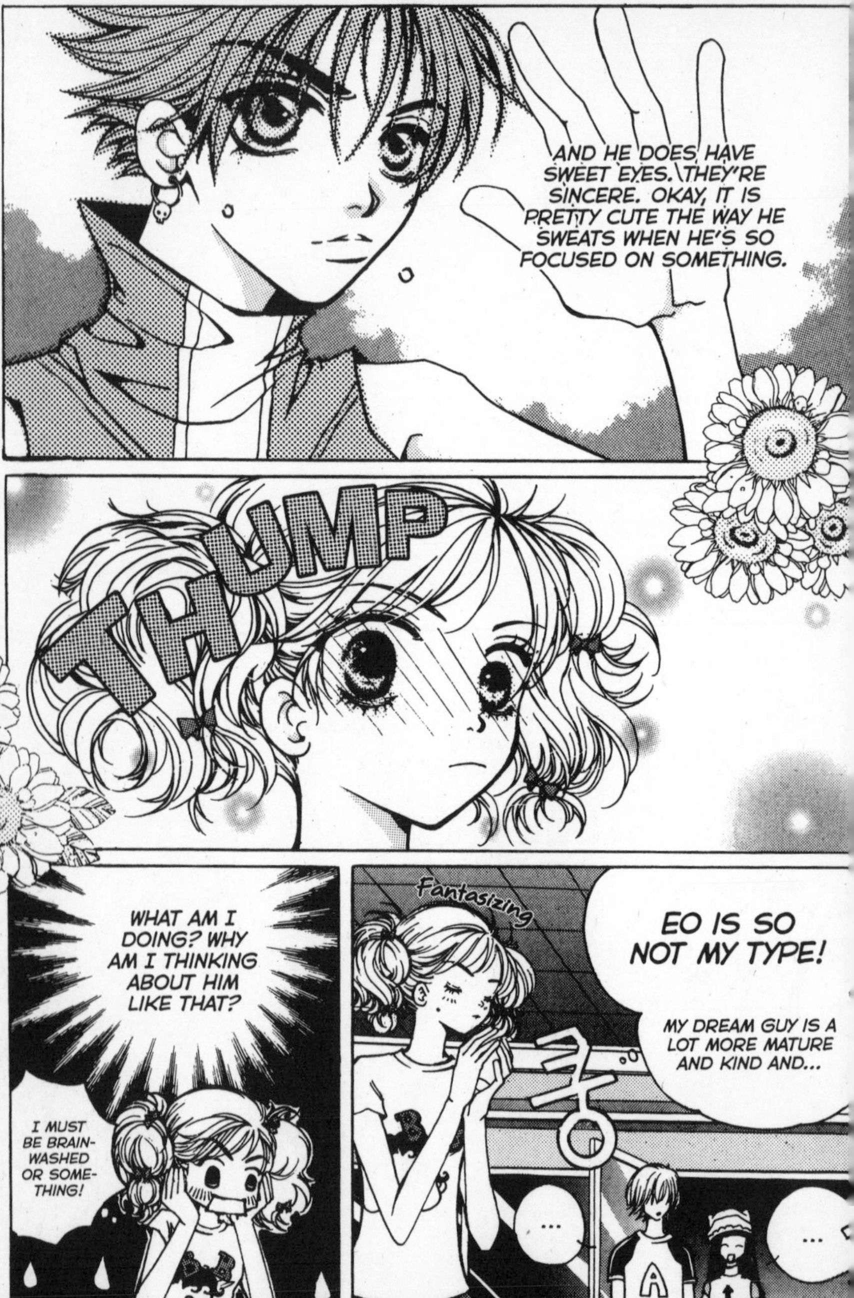
AND HE DOES HAVE SWEET EYES. THEY'RE SINCERE. OKAY, IT IS PRETTY CUTE THE WAY HE SWEATS WHEN HE'S SO FOCUSED ON SOMETHING.
THUMP
WHAT AM I DOING? WHY AM I THINKING ABOUT HIM LIKE THAT?
I MUST BE BRAIN-WASHED OR SOME-THING!
Fantasizing
EO IS SO NOT MY TYPE!
MY DREAM GUY IS A LOT MORE MATURE AND KIND AND...
...
...

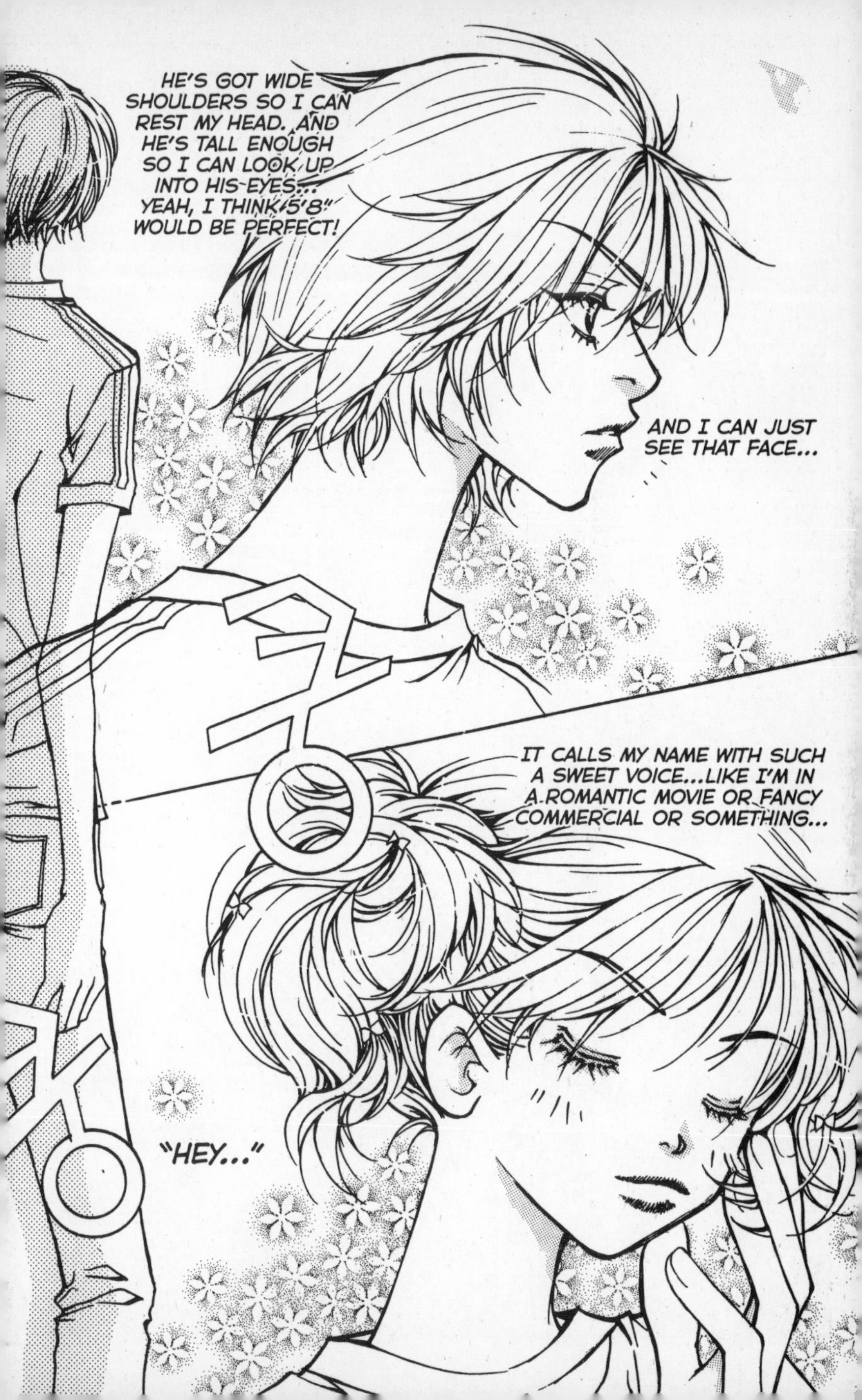
HE'S GOT WIDE SHOULDERS SO I CAN REST MY HEAD. AND HE'S TALL ENOUGH SO I CAN LOOK UP INTO HIS EYES... YEAH, I THINK 5'8" WOULD BE PERFECT!
AND I CAN JUST SEE THAT FACE...
IT CALLS MY NAME WITH SUCH A SWEET VOICE...LIKE I'M IN A ROMANTIC MOVIE OR FANCY COMMERCIAL OR SOMETHING...
"HEY..."

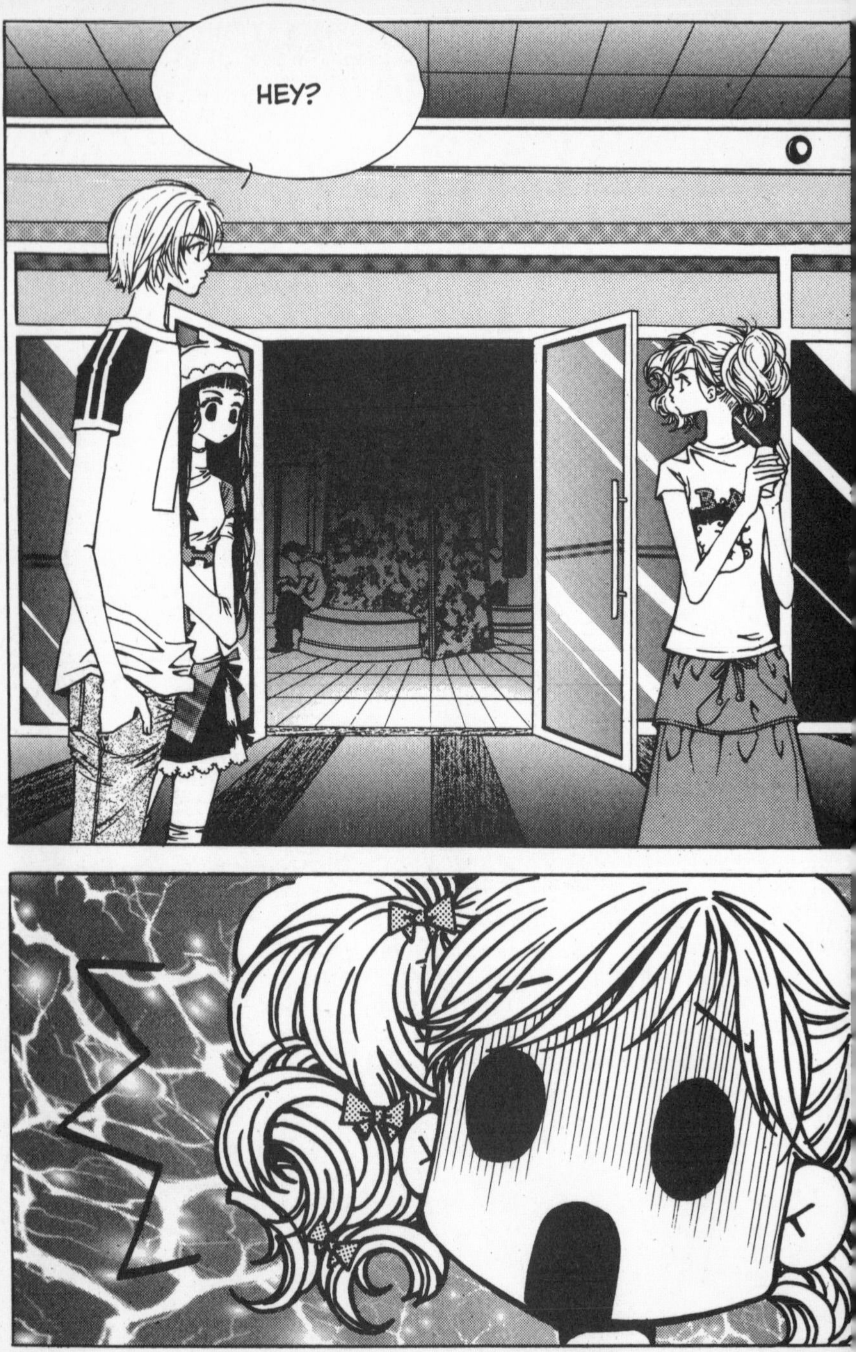
HEY?

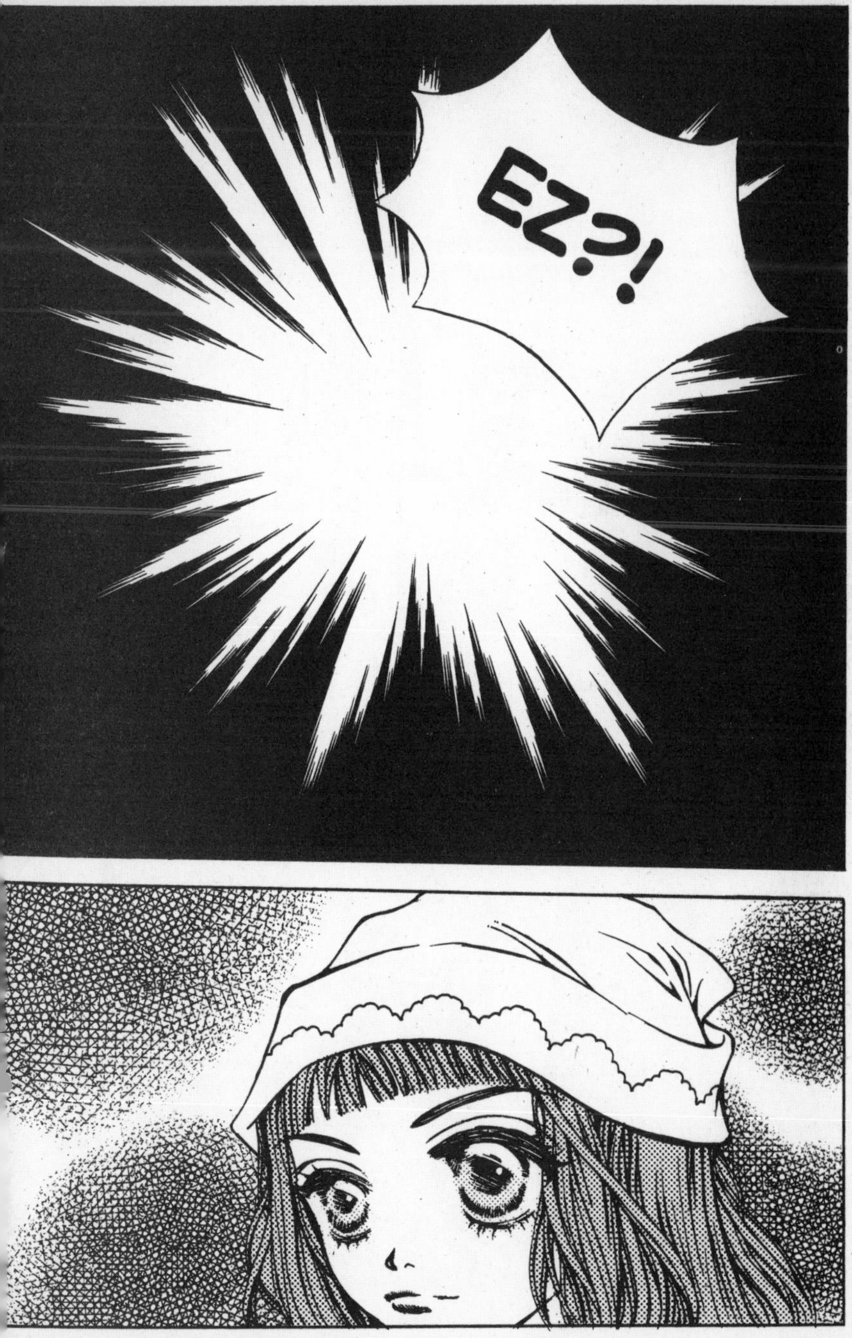
EZ?!

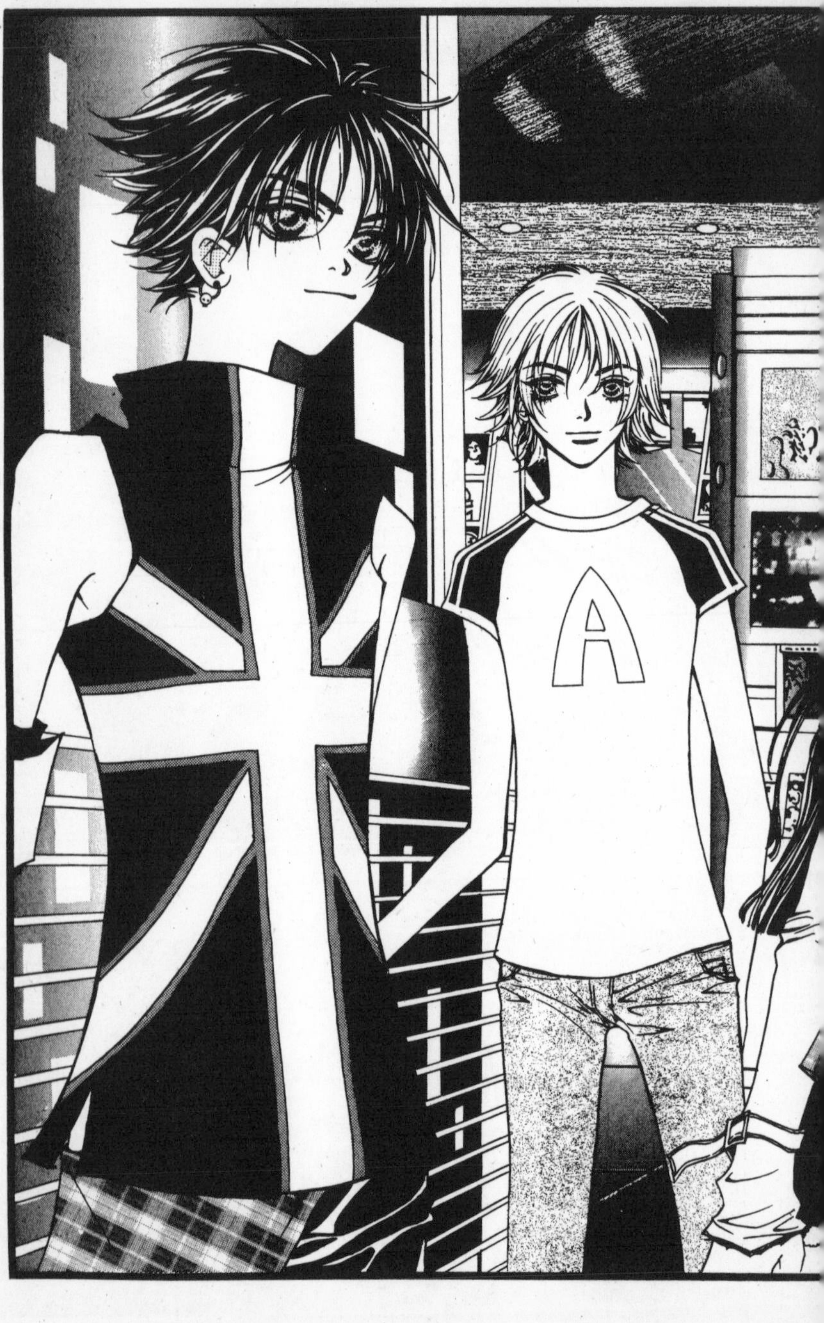

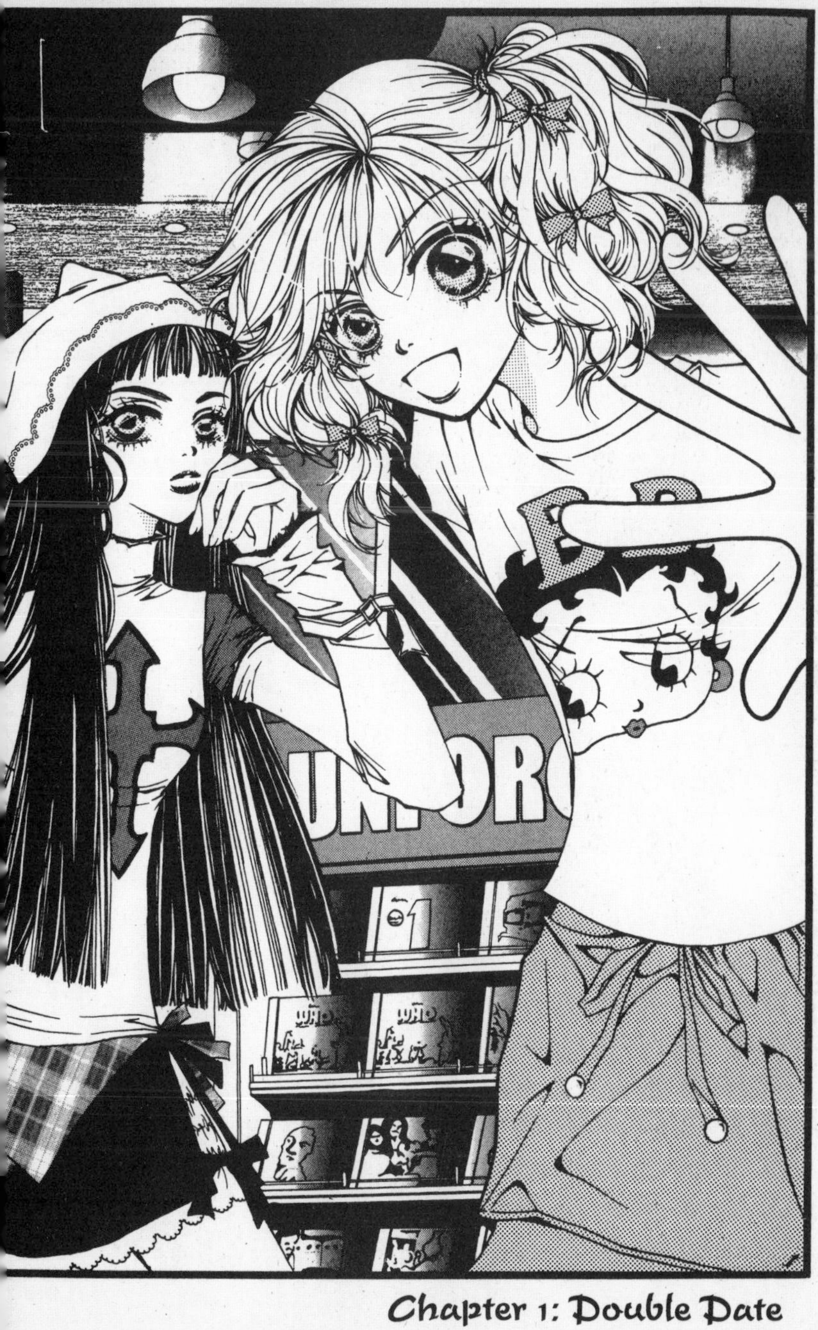

Chapter 1: Double Date

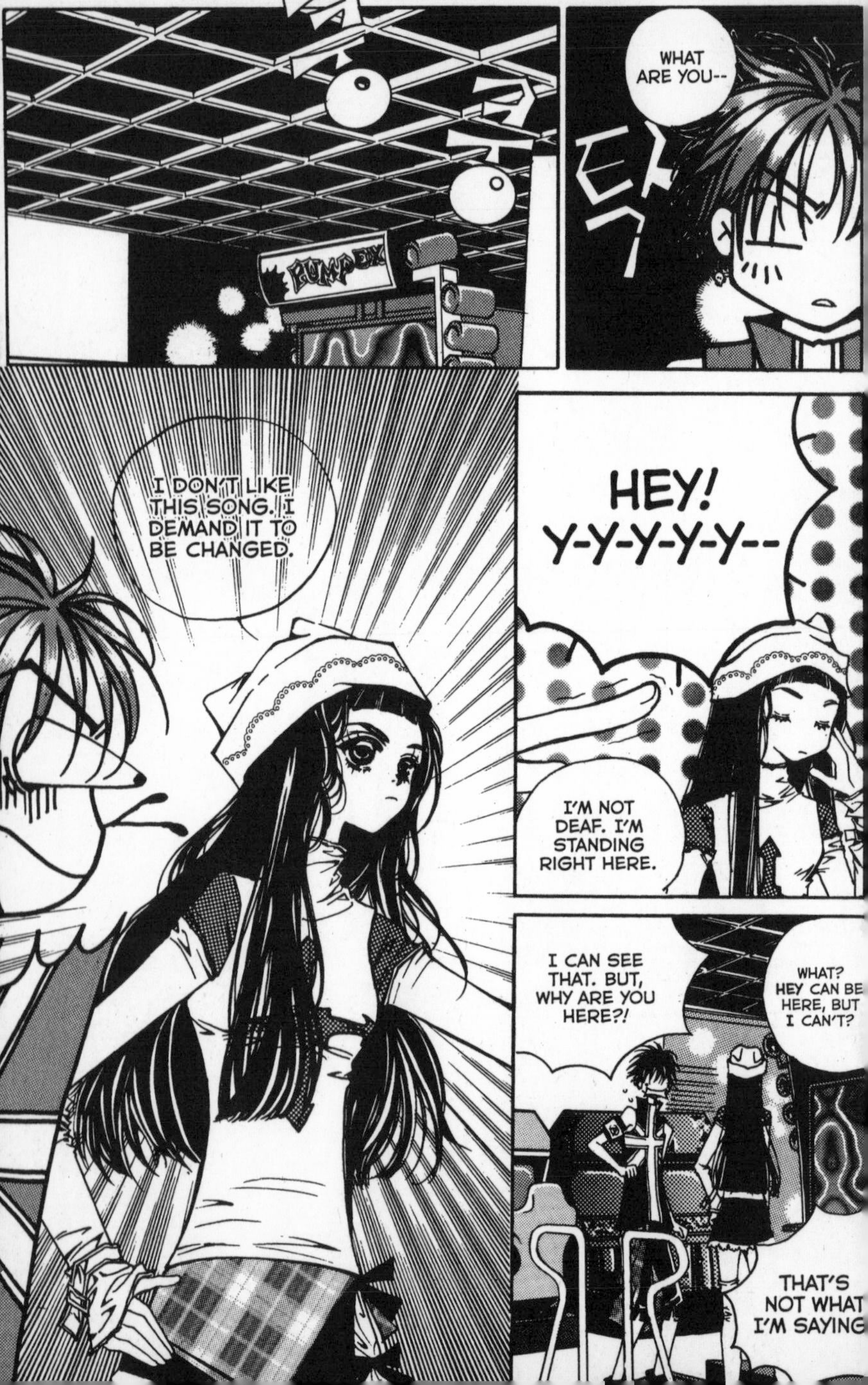
WHAT ARE YOU--
I DON'T LIKE THIS SONG. I DEMAND IT TO BE CHANGED.
HEY! Y-Y-Y-Y-Y--
I'M NOT DEAF. I'M STANDING RIGHT HERE.
I CAN SEE THAT. BUT, WHY ARE YOU HERE?!
WHAT? HEY CAN BE HERE, BUT I CAN'T?
THAT'S NOT WHAT I'M SAYING

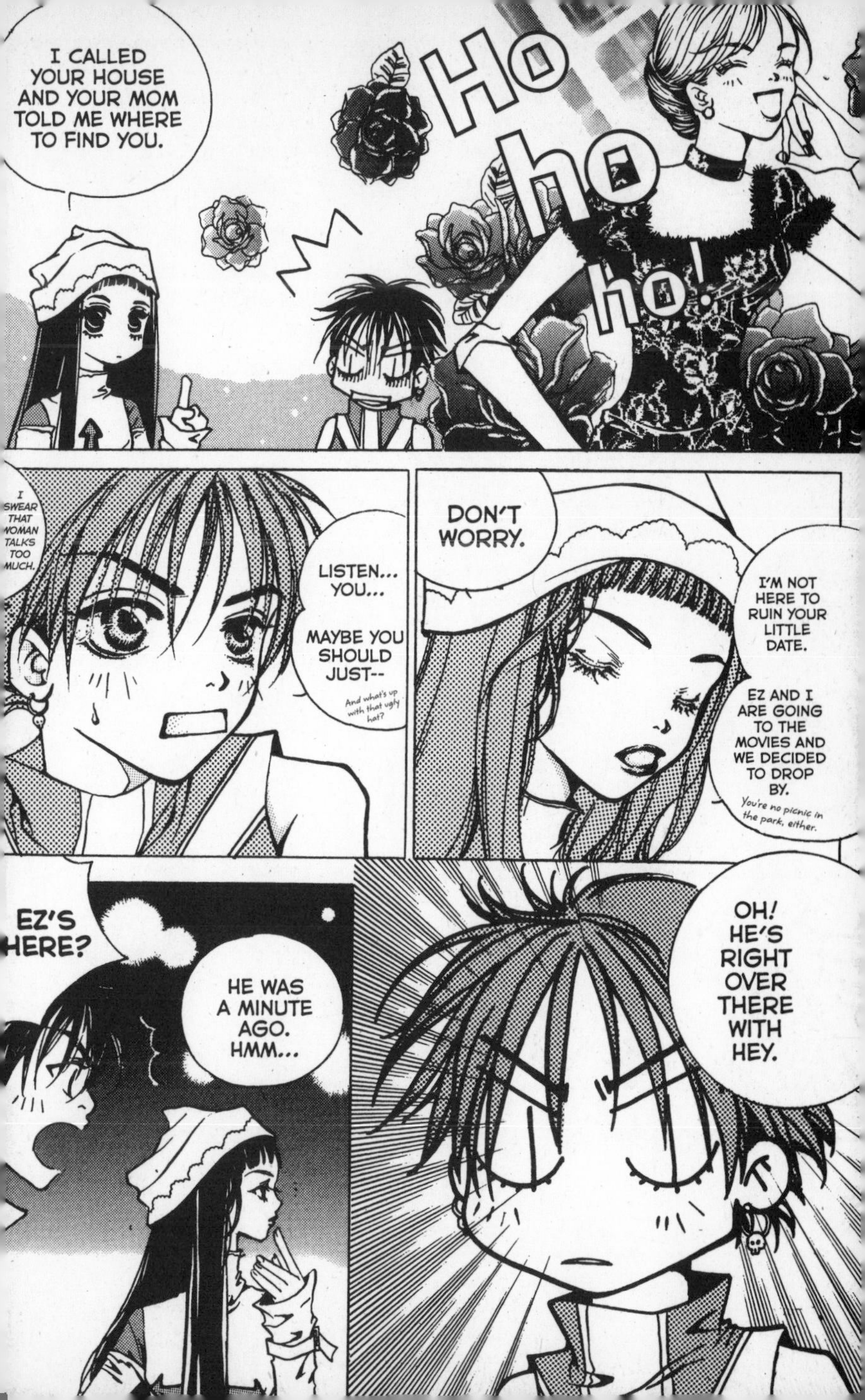
I CALLED YOUR HOUSE AND YOUR MOM TOLD ME WHERE TO FIND YOU.
Ho ho ho!
I SWEAR THAT WOMAN TALKS TOO MUCH.
LISTEN... YOU...
MAYBE YOU SHOULD JUST--
And what's up with that ugly hat?
DON'T WORRY.
I'M NOT HERE TO RUIN YOUR LITTLE DATE.
EZ AND I ARE GOING TO THE MOVIES AND WE DECIDED TO DROP BY.
You're no picnic in the park, either.
EZ'S HERE?
HE WAS A MINUTE AGO. HMM...
OH! HE'S RIGHT OVER THERE WITH HEY.

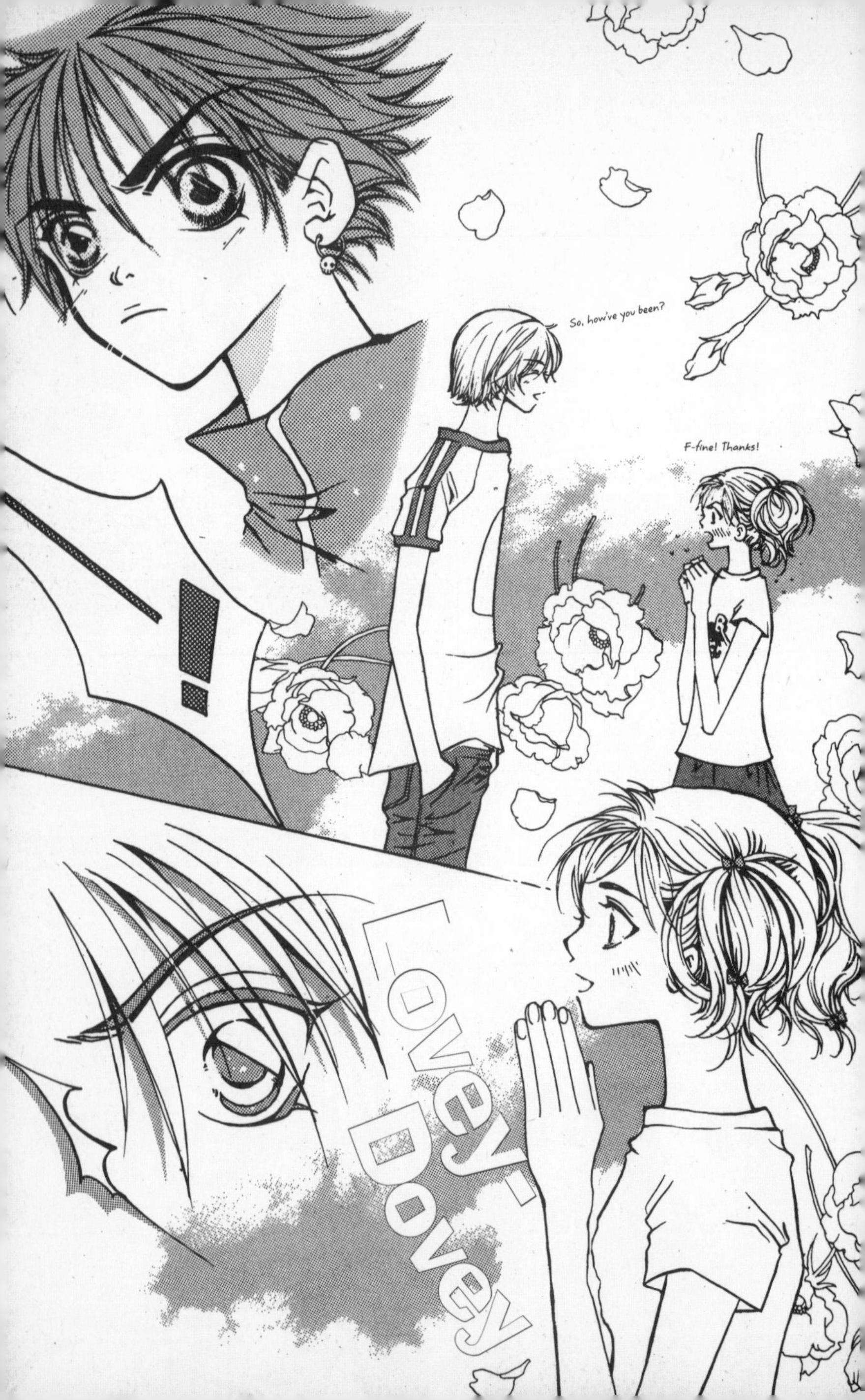
So, how've you been?
F-fine! Thanks!
!
Lovey Dovey

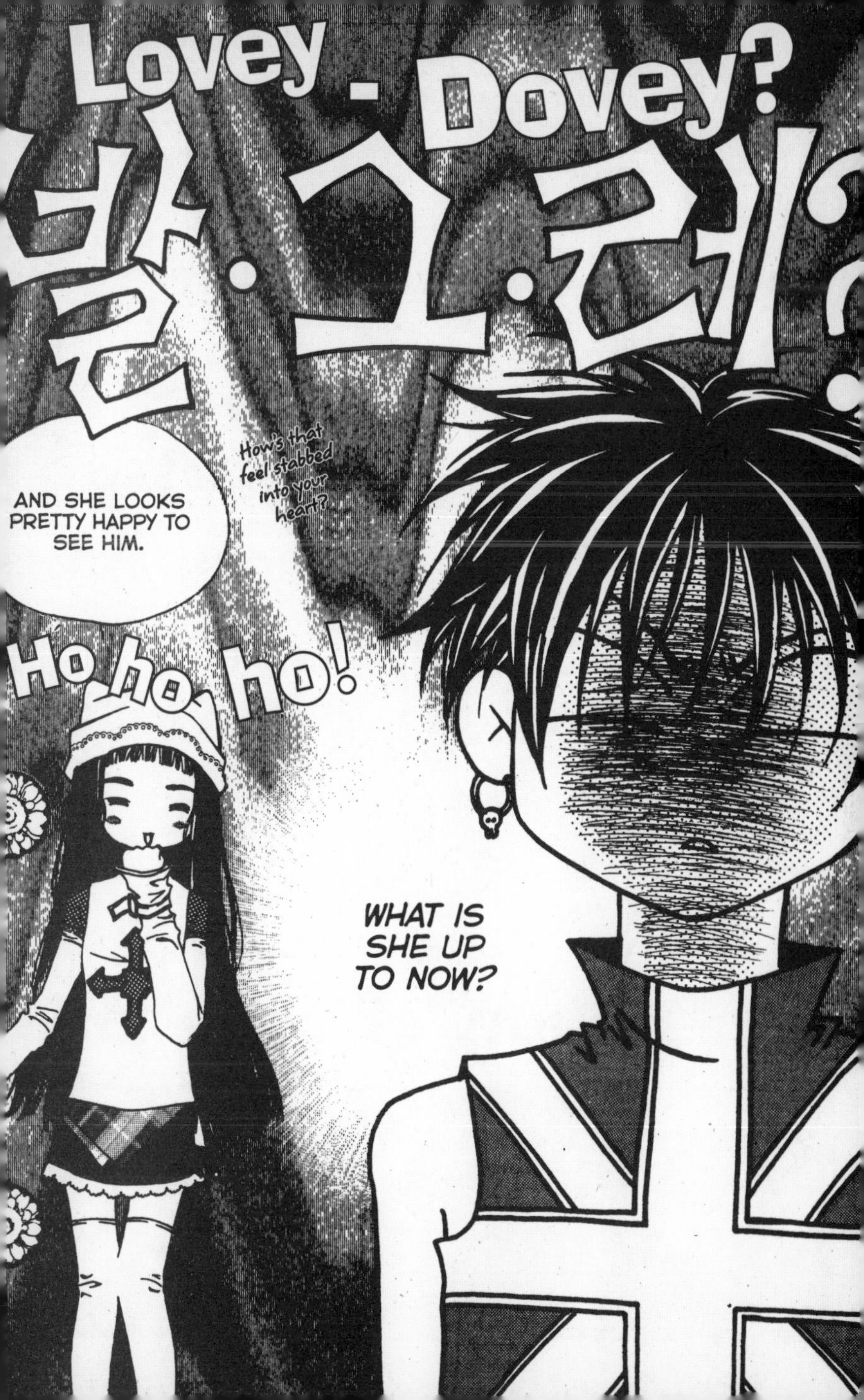
Lovey - Dovey?
AND SHE LOOKS PRETTY HAPPY TO SEE HIM.
How's that feel stabbed into your heart?
Ho ho ho!
WHAT IS SHE UP TO NOW?

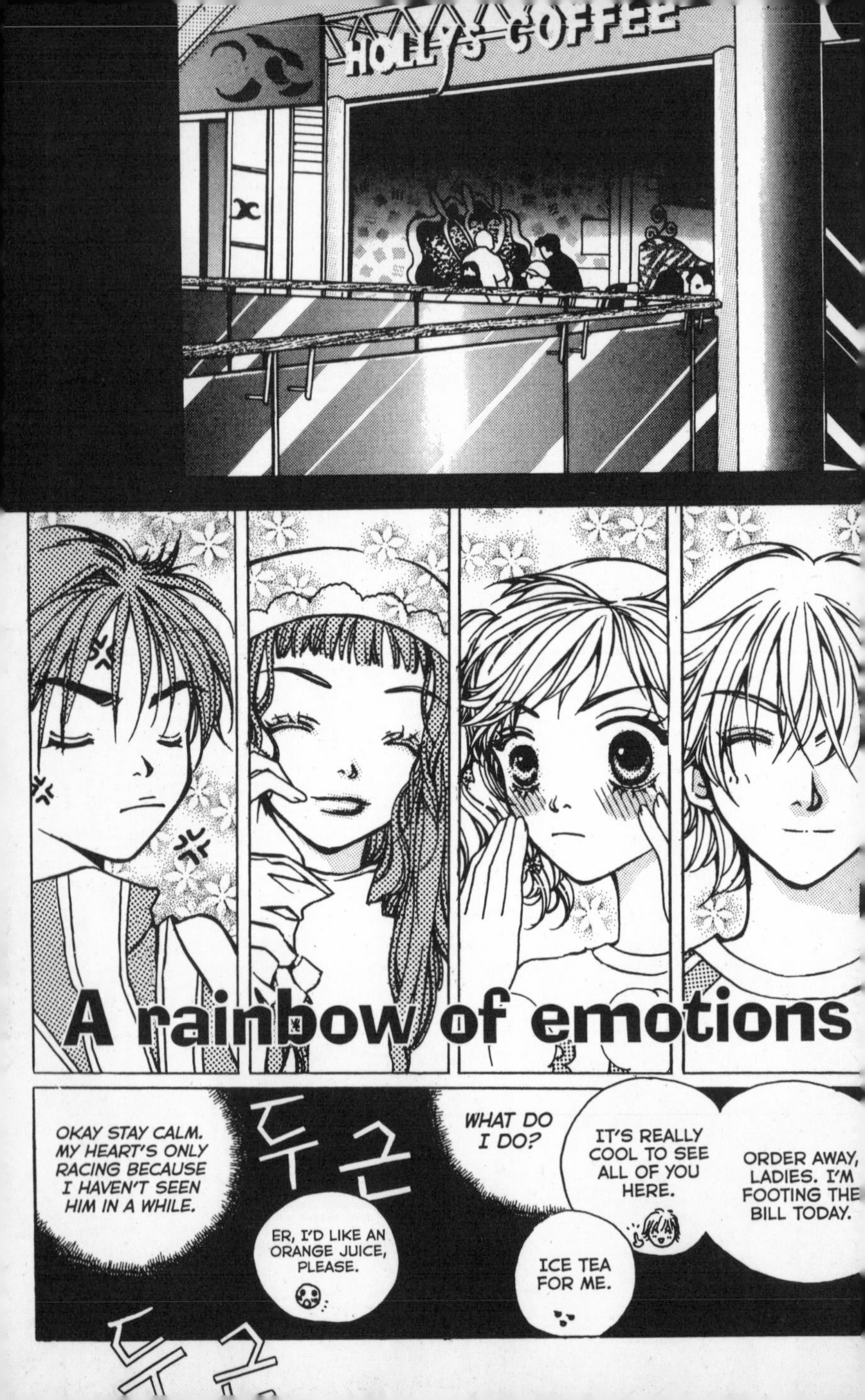
A rainbow of emotions
OKAY STAY CALM. MY HEART'S ONLY RACING BECAUSE I HAVEN'T SEEN HIM IN A WHILE.
ER, I'D LIKE AN ORANGE JUICE, PLEASE.
WHAT DO I DO?
IT'S REALLY COOL TO SEE ALL OF YOU HERE.
ICE TEA FOR ME.
ORDER AWAY, LADIES. I'M FOOTING THE BILL TODAY.

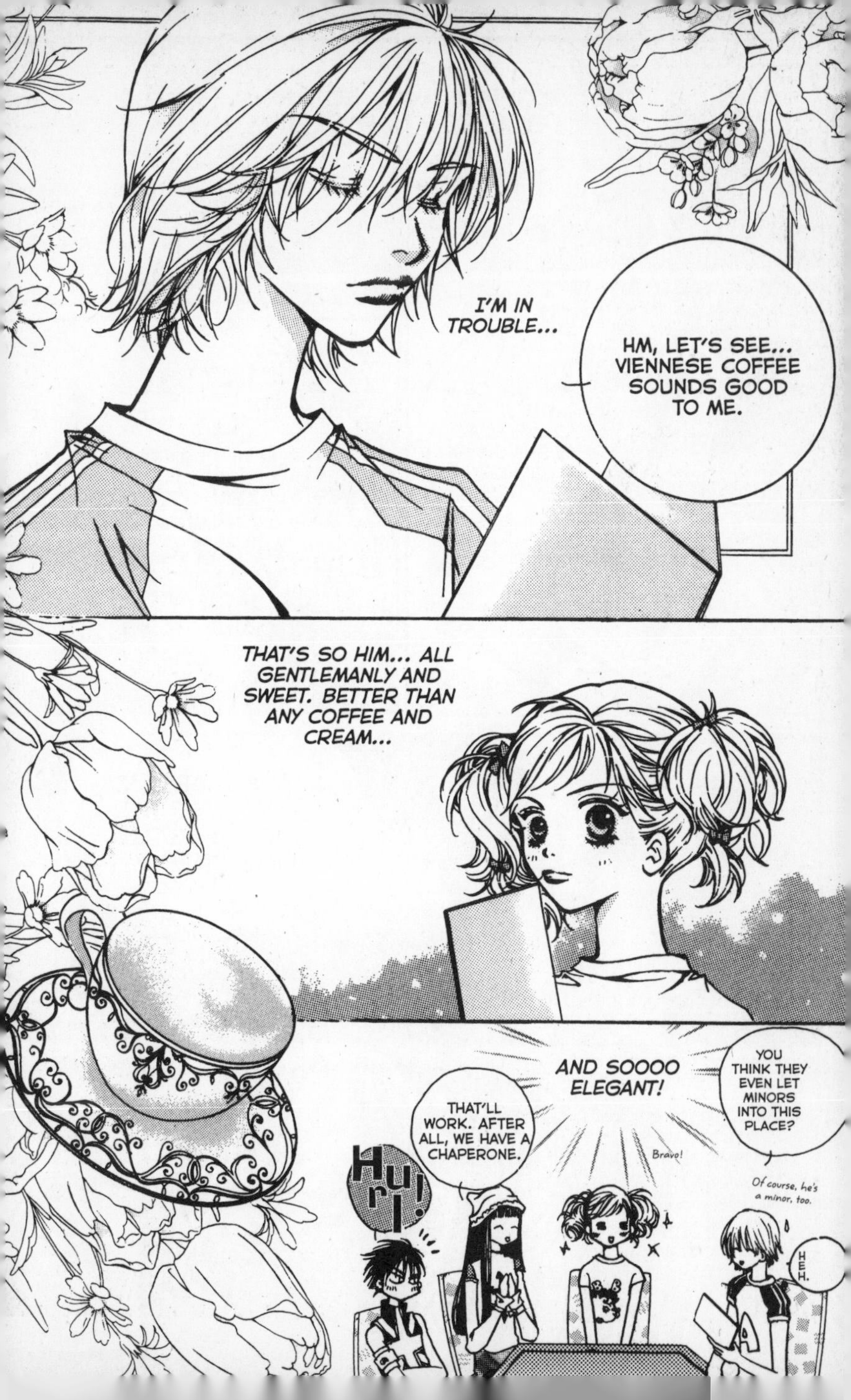
I'M IN TROUBLE...
HM, LET'S SEE... VIENNESE COFFEE SOUNDS GOOD TO ME.
THAT'S SO HIM... ALL GENTLEMANLY AND SWEET. BETTER THAN ANY COFFEE AND CREAM...
AND SOOOO ELEGANT!
Hurl!
THAT'LL WORK. AFTER ALL, WE HAVE A CHAPERONE.
Bravo!
YOU THINK THEY EVEN LET MINORS INTO THIS PLACE?
Of course, he's a minor, too.
HEH.

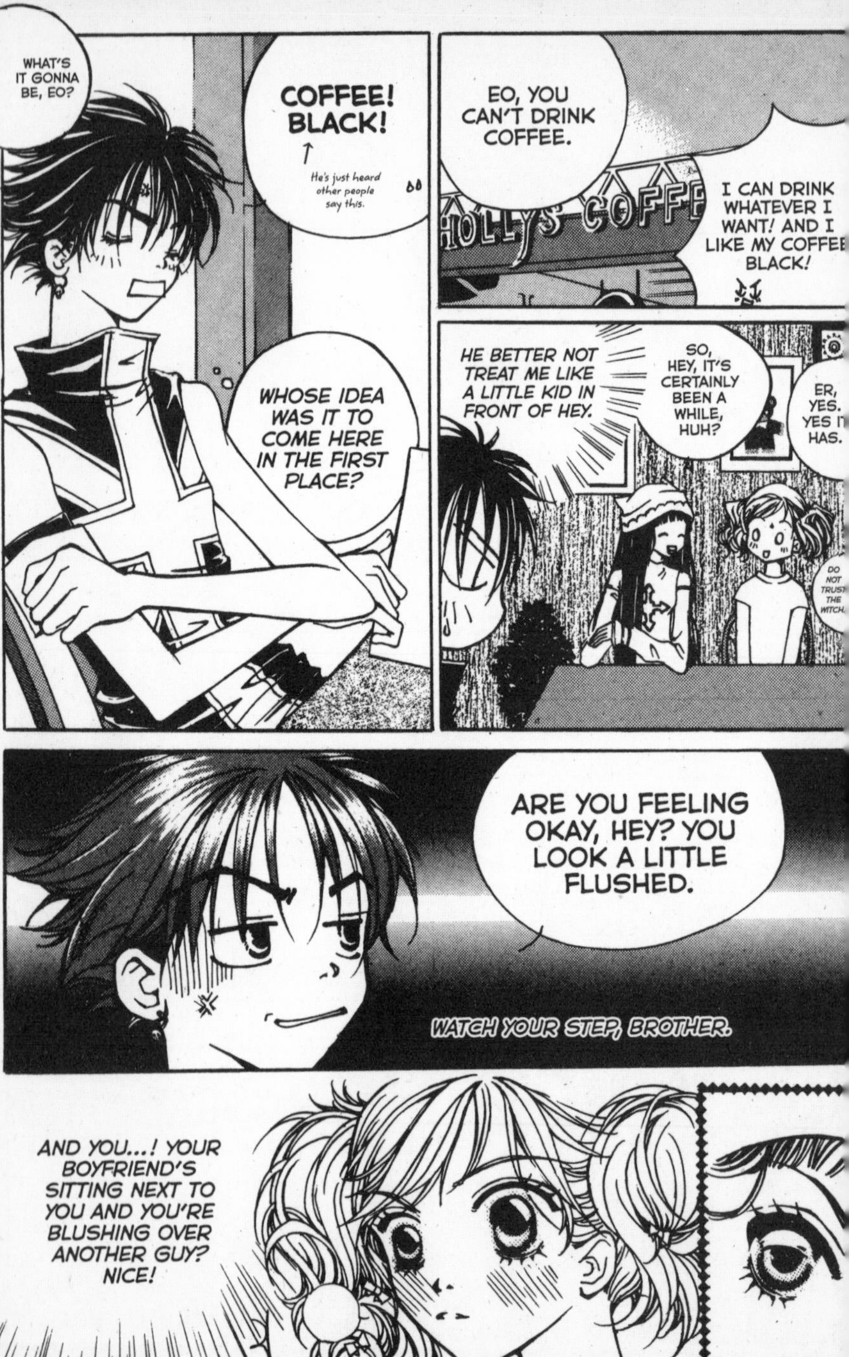
WHAT'S IT GONNA BE, EO?
COFFEE! BLACK!
He's just heard other people say this.
WHOSE IDEA WAS IT TO COME HERE IN THE FIRST PLACE?
EO, YOU CAN'T DRINK COFFEE.
HOLLYS COFFE
I CAN DRINK WHATEVER I WANT! AND I LIKE MY COFFEE BLACK!
HE BETTER NOT TREAT ME LIKE A LITTLE KID IN FRONT OF HEY.
SO, HEY, IT'S CERTAINLY BEEN A WHILE, HUH?
ER, YES. YES IT HAS.
DO NOT TRUST THE WITCH.
ARE YOU FEELING OKAY, HEY? YOU LOOK A LITTLE FLUSHED.
WATCH YOUR STEP, BROTHER.
AND YOU...! YOUR BOYFRIEND'S SITTING NEXT TO YOU AND YOU'RE BLUSHING OVER ANOTHER GUY? NICE!

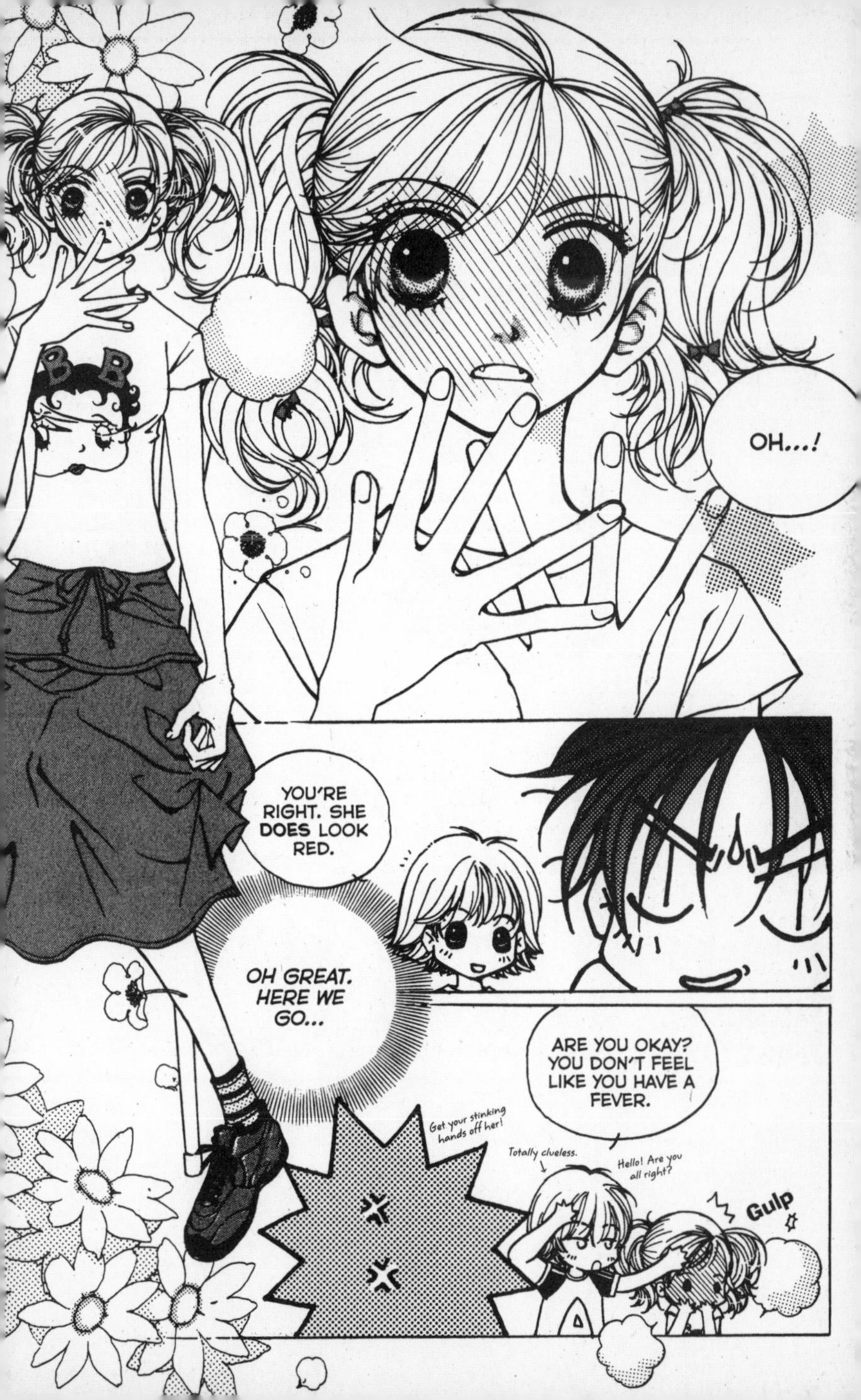
OH...!
YOU'RE RIGHT. SHE DOES LOOK RED.
OH GREAT. HERE WE GO...
ARE YOU OKAY? YOU DON'T FEEL LIKE YOU HAVE A FEVER.
Get your stinking hands off her!
Totally clueless.
Hello! Are you all right?
Gulp

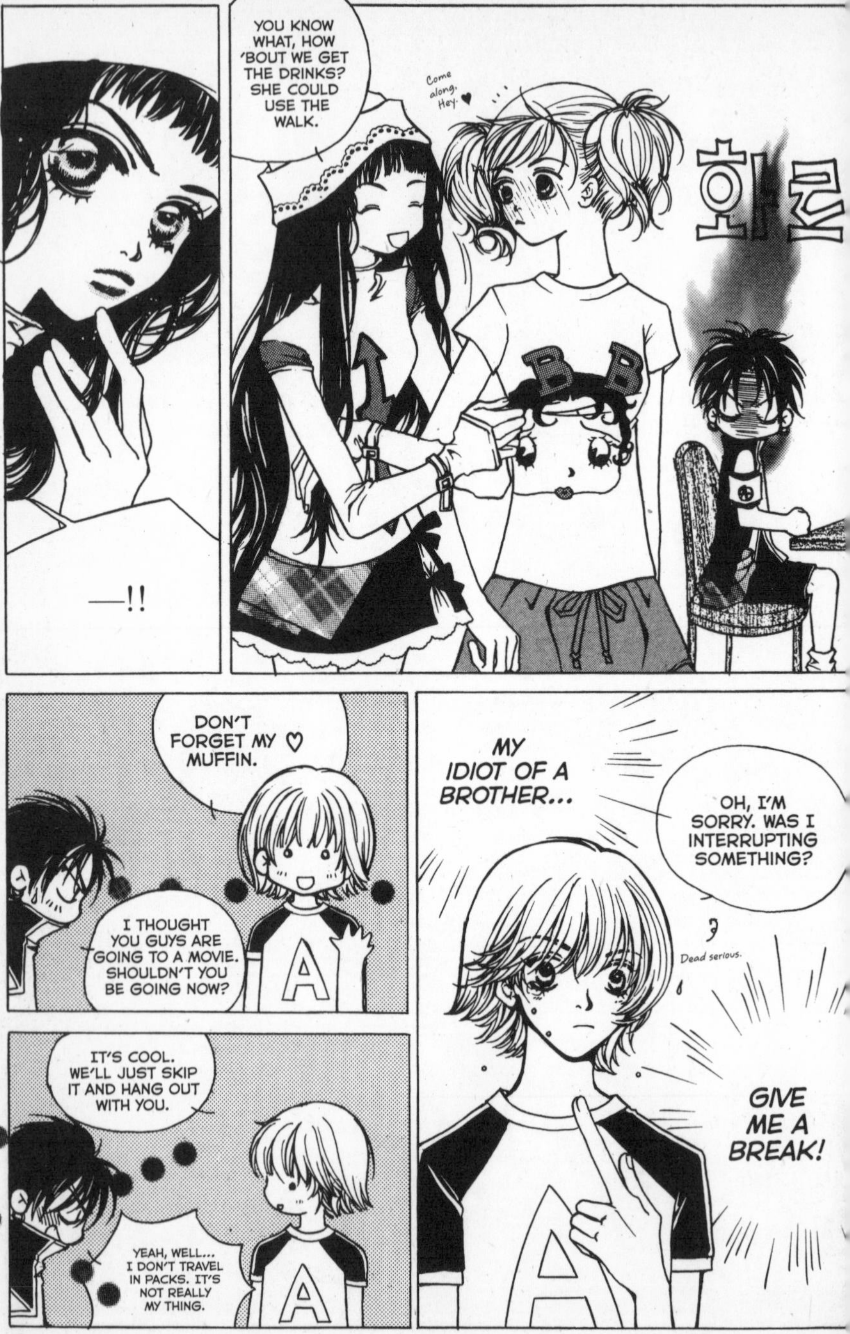
—!!
YOU KNOW WHAT, HOW 'BOUT WE GET THE DRINKS? SHE COULD USE THE WALK.
Come along. Hey. ♥
DON'T FORGET MY ♡ MUFFIN.
I THOUGHT YOU GUYS ARE GOING TO A MOVIE. SHOULDN'T YOU BE GOING NOW?
IT'S COOL. WE'LL JUST SKIP IT AND HANG OUT WITH YOU.
YEAH, WELL... I DON'T TRAVEL IN PACKS. IT'S NOT REALLY MY THING.
MY IDIOT OF A BROTHER...
OH, I'M SORRY. WAS I INTERRUPTING SOMETHING?
Dead serious.
GIVE ME A BREAK!

YEAH, ACTUALLY YOU KNOW WHAT? I AM A LITTLE PISSED OFF RIGHT NOW.

WHY DOES HEY BLUSH WHEN SHE LOOKS AT YOU?

HUH? WHAT ARE YOU TALKING ABOUT?

OH, NOW YOU'RE GIVING ME THE "I DON'T KNOW WHAT'S GOING ON" FACE?

SORRY, BRO. I WAS BORN WITH THIS FACE. IT'S MY CURSE.

CAN YOU BE SERIOUS ABOUT ANYTHING? IT'S ALL A BIG JOKE TO YOU, ISN'T IT?! JUST LIKE WITH GA-YOUNG!

DO YOU EXPECT ME TO WALK AROUND WITH A MASK?

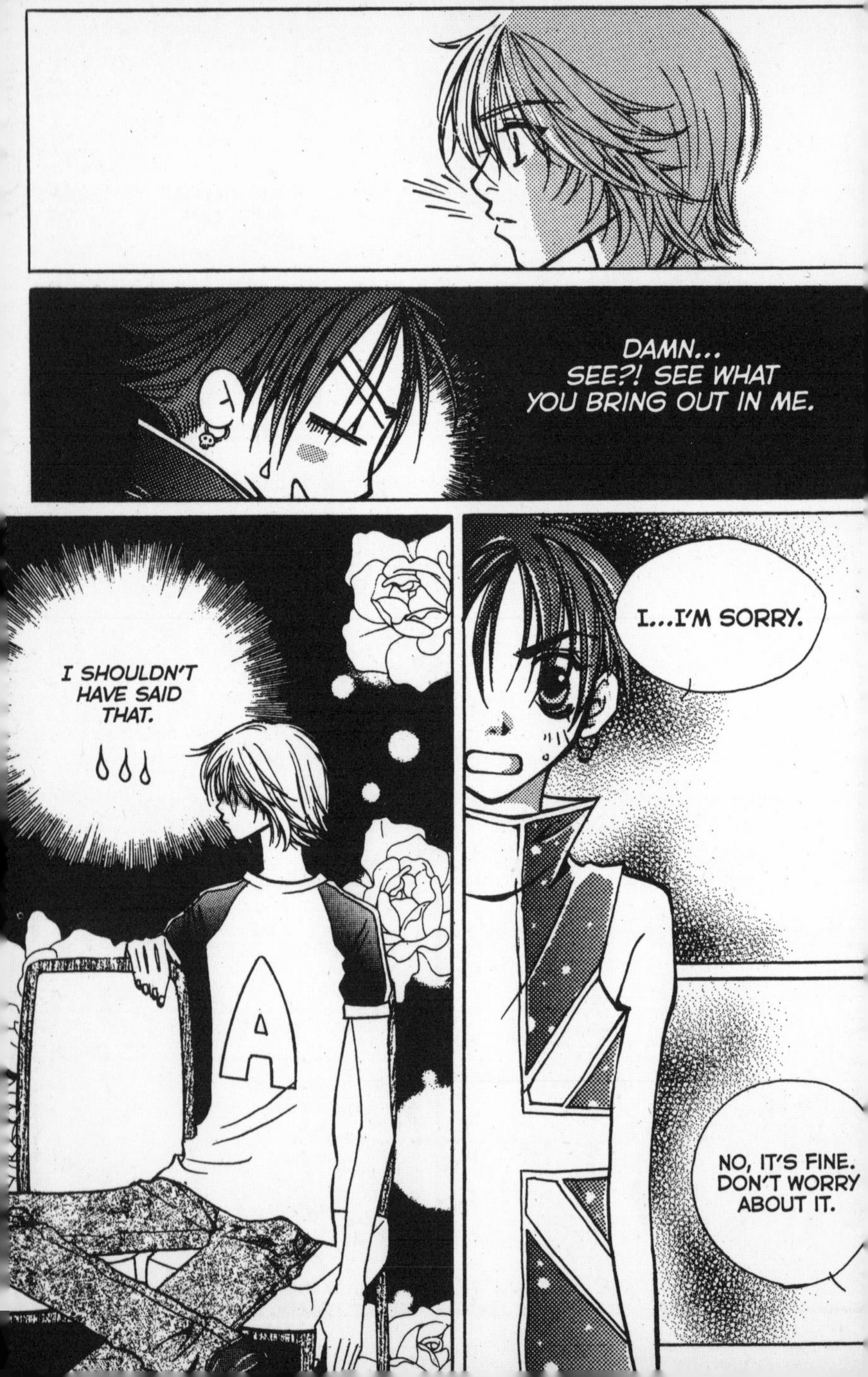
DAMN...
SEE?! SEE WHAT
YOU BRING OUT IN ME.
I SHOULDN'T
HAVE SAID
THAT.
I...I'M SORRY.
NO, IT'S FINE.
DON'T WORRY
ABOUT IT.

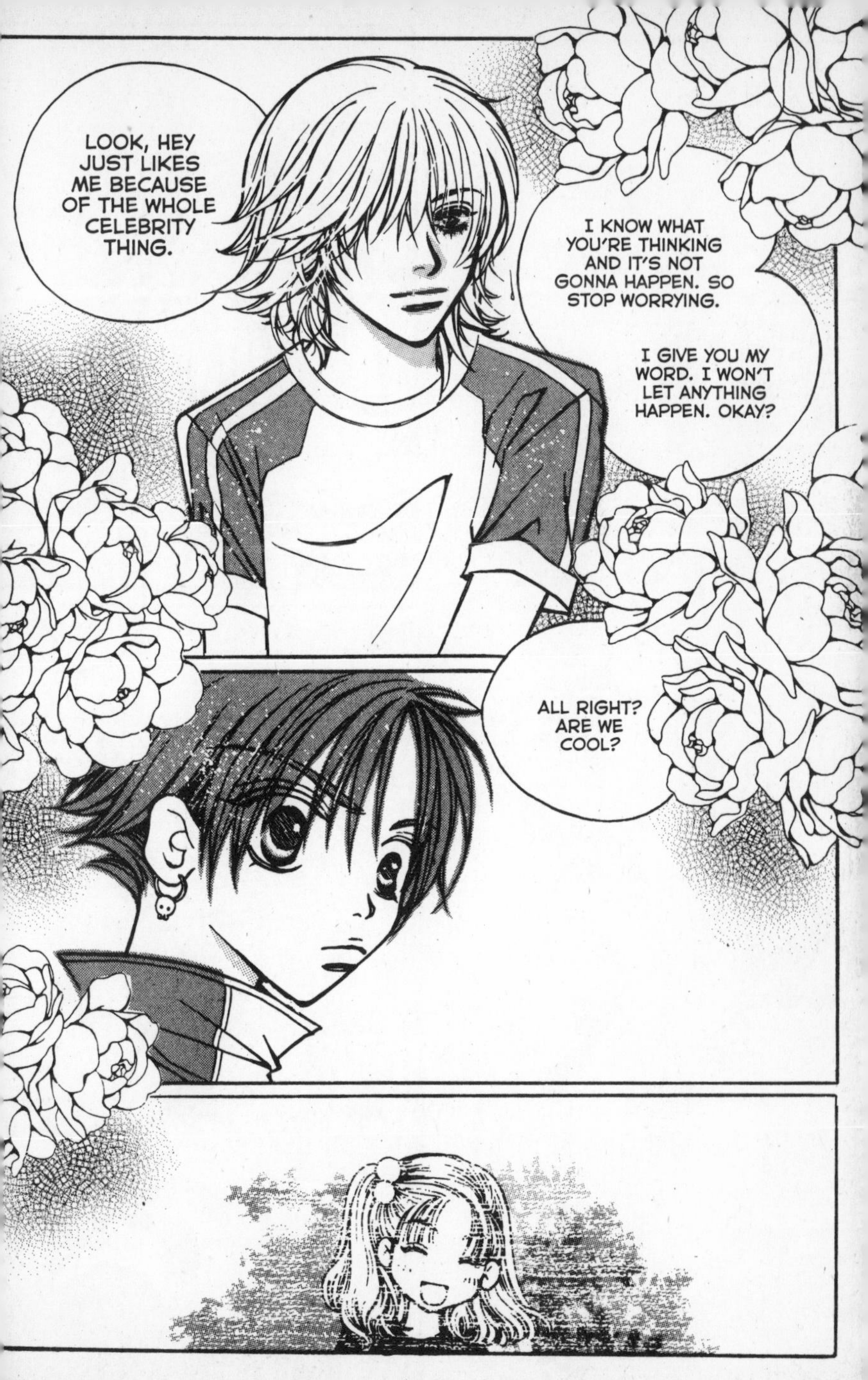
LOOK, HEY JUST LIKES ME BECAUSE OF THE WHOLE CELEBRITY THING.
I KNOW WHAT YOU'RE THINKING AND IT'S NOT GONNA HAPPEN. SO STOP WORRYING.
I GIVE YOU MY WORD. I WON'T LET ANYTHING HAPPEN. OKAY?
ALL RIGHT? ARE WE COOL?

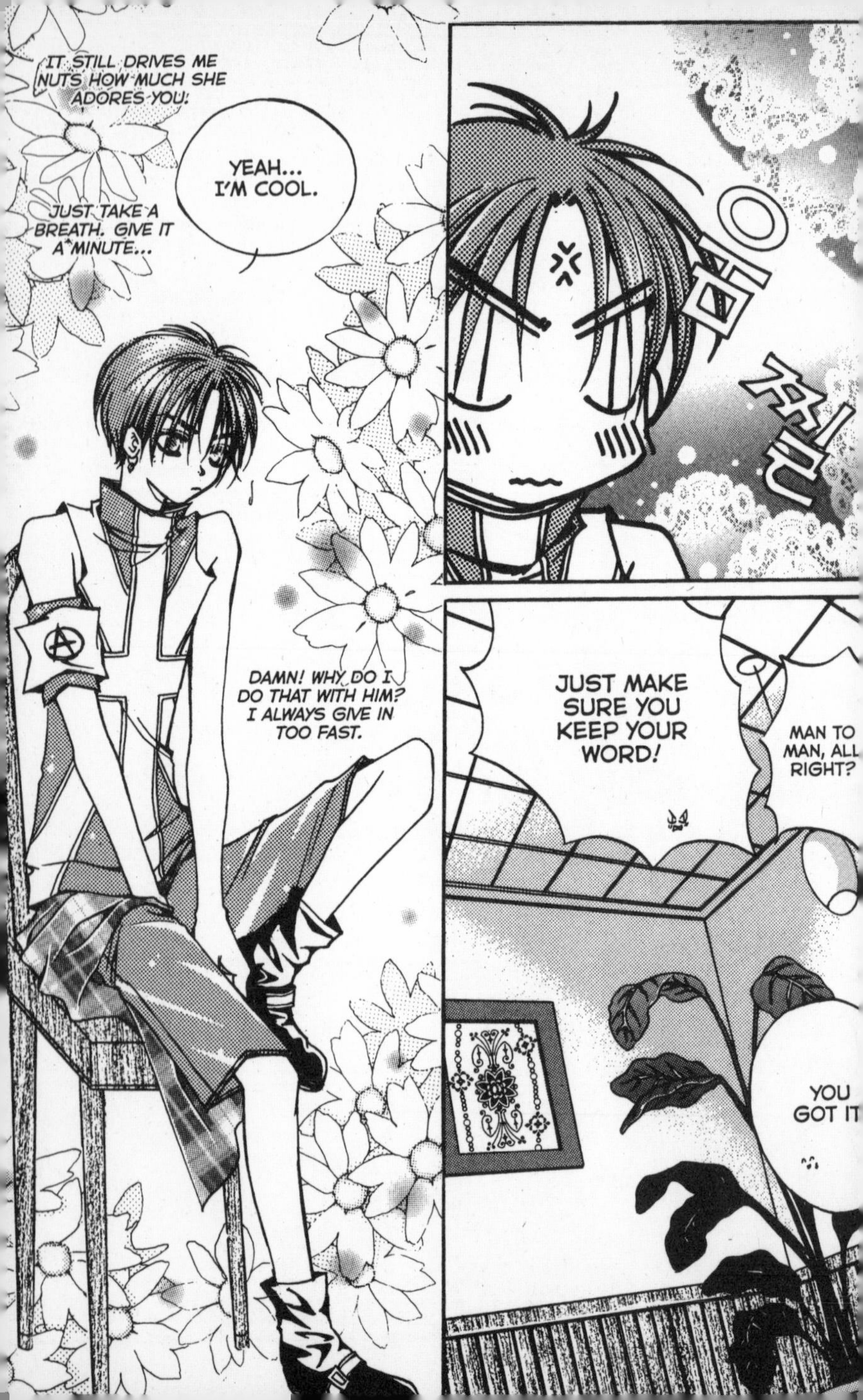
IT STILL DRIVES ME NUTS HOW MUCH SHE ADORES YOU.
YEAH... I'M COOL.
JUST TAKE A BREATH. GIVE IT A MINUTE...
DAMN! WHY DO I DO THAT WITH HIM? I ALWAYS GIVE IN TOO FAST.
JUST MAKE SURE YOU KEEP YOUR WORD!
MAN TO MAN, ALL RIGHT?
YOU GOT IT

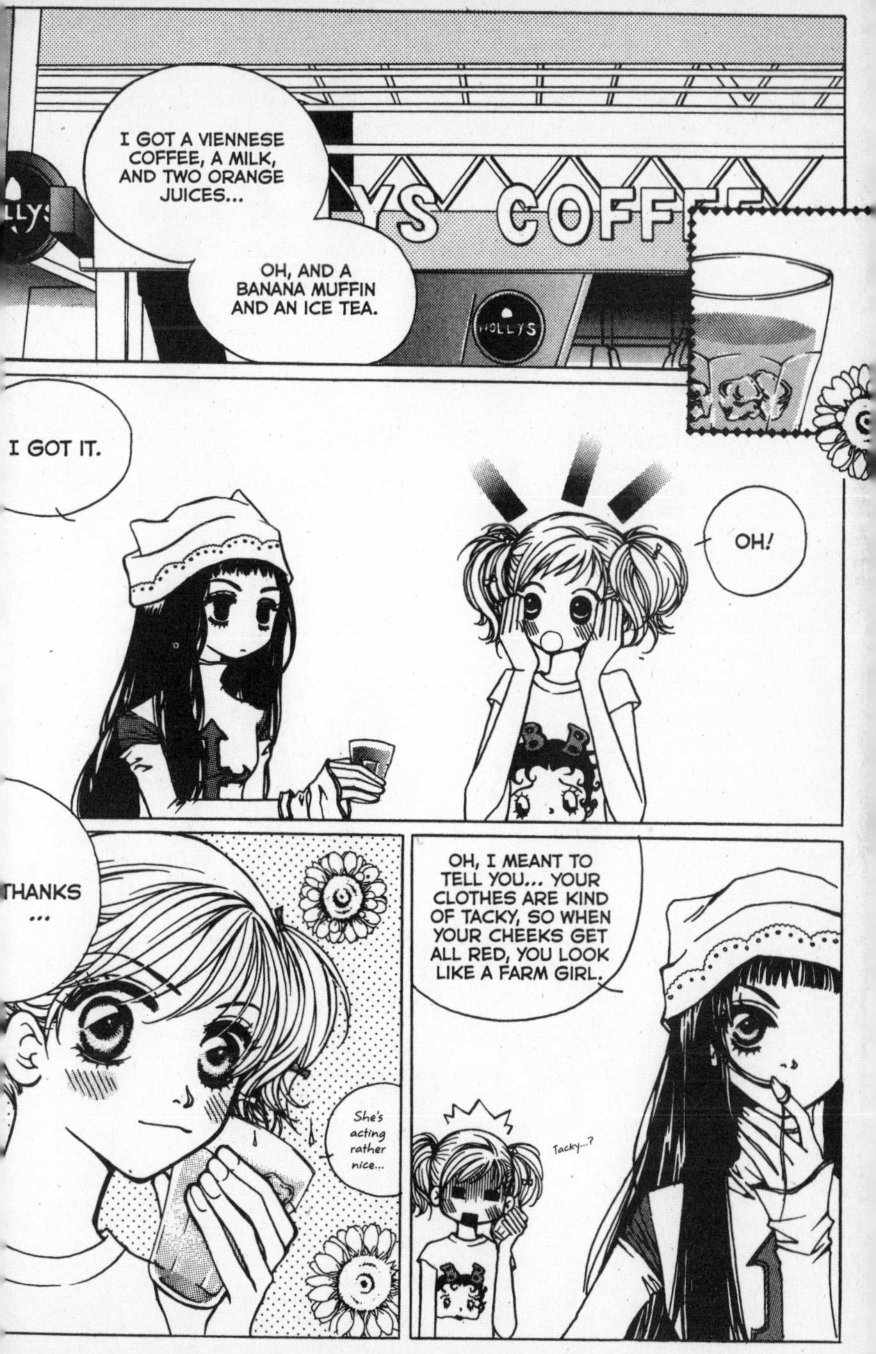
I GOT A VIENNESE COFFEE, A MILK, AND TWO ORANGE JUICES...
OH, AND A BANANA MUFFIN AND AN ICE TEA.
I GOT IT.
OH!
THANKS ...
She's acting rather nice...
OH, I MEANT TO TELL YOU... YOUR CLOTHES ARE KIND OF TACKY, SO WHEN YOUR CHEEKS GET ALL RED, YOU LOOK LIKE A FARM GIRL.
Tacky...?

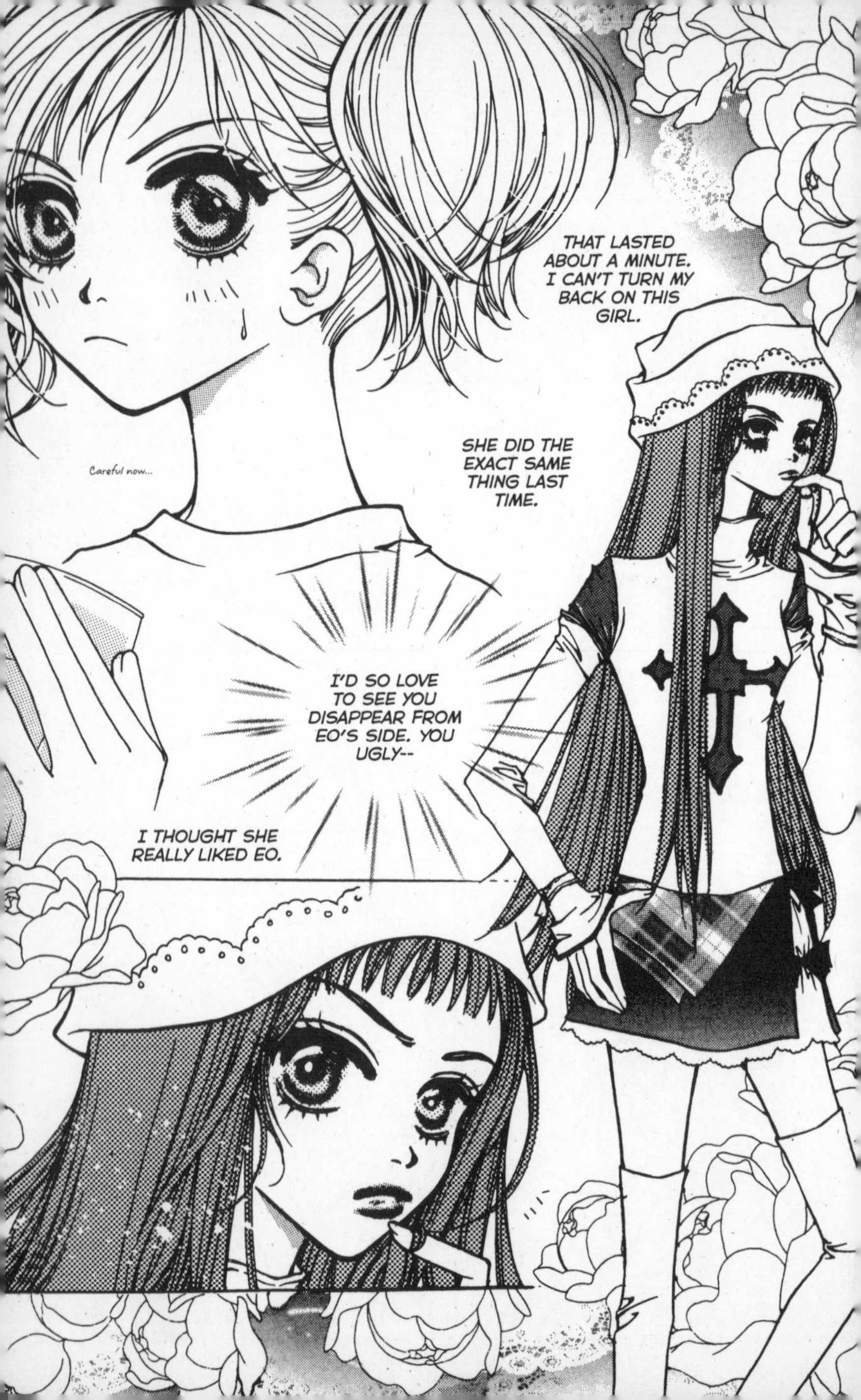
Careful now...
I'D SO LOVE TO SEE YOU DISAPPEAR FROM EO'S SIDE. YOU UGLY--
I THOUGHT SHE REALLY LIKED EO.
THAT LASTED ABOUT A MINUTE. I CAN'T TURN MY BACK ON THIS GIRL.
SHE DID THE EXACT SAME THING LAST TIME.

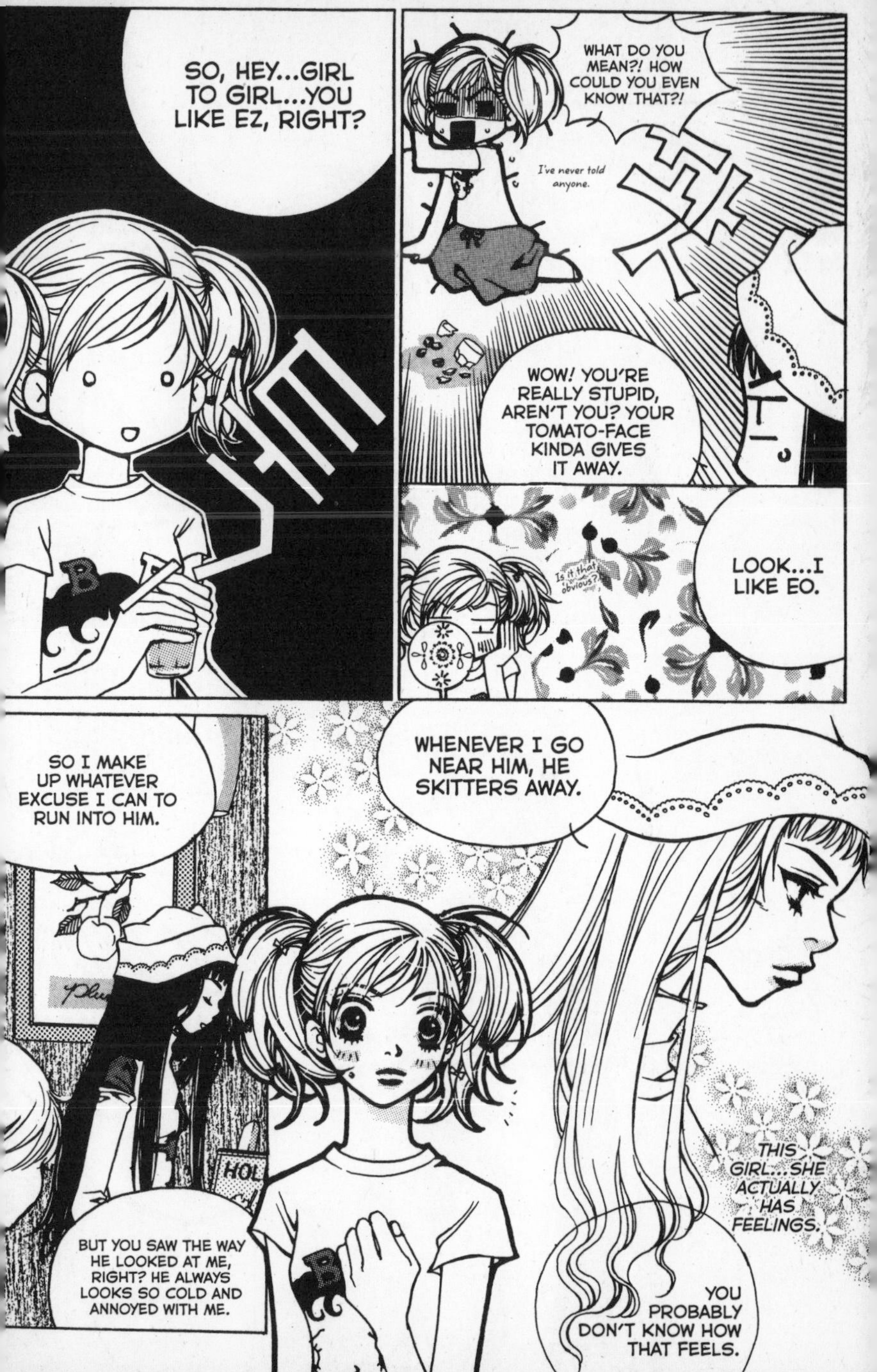
SO, HEY...GIRL TO GIRL...YOU LIKE EZ, RIGHT?
WHAT DO YOU MEAN?! HOW COULD YOU EVEN KNOW THAT?!
I've never told anyone.
WOW! YOU'RE REALLY STUPID, AREN'T YOU? YOUR TOMATO-FACE KINDA GIVES IT AWAY.
Is it that obvious?
LOOK...I LIKE EO.
WHENEVER I GO NEAR HIM, HE SKITTERS AWAY.
SO I MAKE UP WHATEVER EXCUSE I CAN TO RUN INTO HIM.
BUT YOU SAW THE WAY HE LOOKED AT ME, RIGHT? HE ALWAYS LOOKS SO COLD AND ANNOYED WITH ME.
THIS GIRL...SHE ACTUALLY HAS FEELINGS.
YOU PROBABLY DON'T KNOW HOW THAT FEELS.

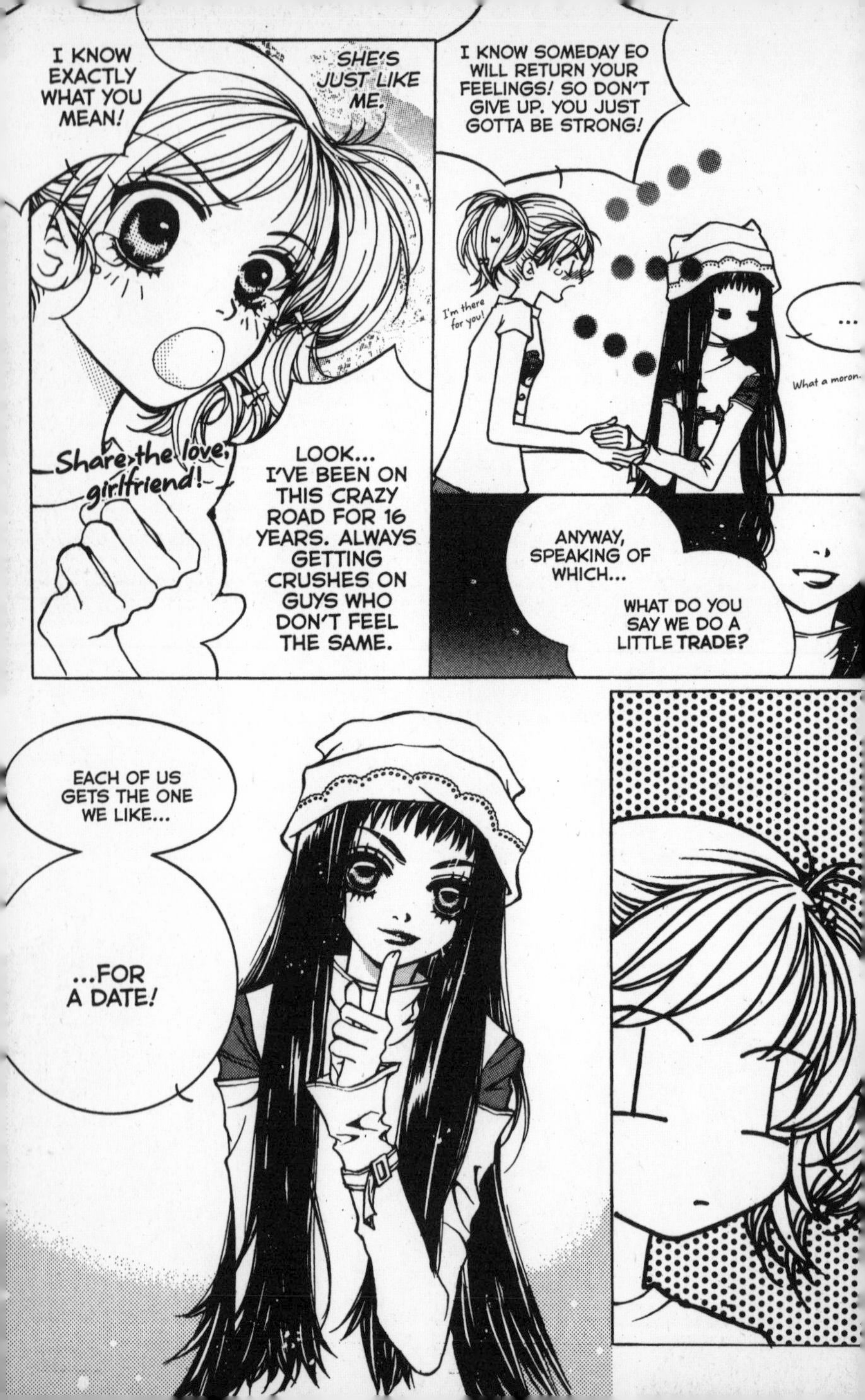
I KNOW EXACTLY WHAT YOU MEAN!
SHE'S JUST LIKE ME.
Share the love, girlfriend!
LOOK... I'VE BEEN ON THIS CRAZY ROAD FOR 16 YEARS. ALWAYS GETTING CRUSHES ON GUYS WHO DON'T FEEL THE SAME.
I KNOW SOMEDAY EO WILL RETURN YOUR FEELINGS! SO DON'T GIVE UP. YOU JUST GOTTA BE STRONG!
I'm there for you!
...
What a moron.
ANYWAY, SPEAKING OF WHICH...
WHAT DO YOU SAY WE DO A LITTLE TRADE?
EACH OF US GETS THE ONE WE LIKE...
...FOR A DATE!

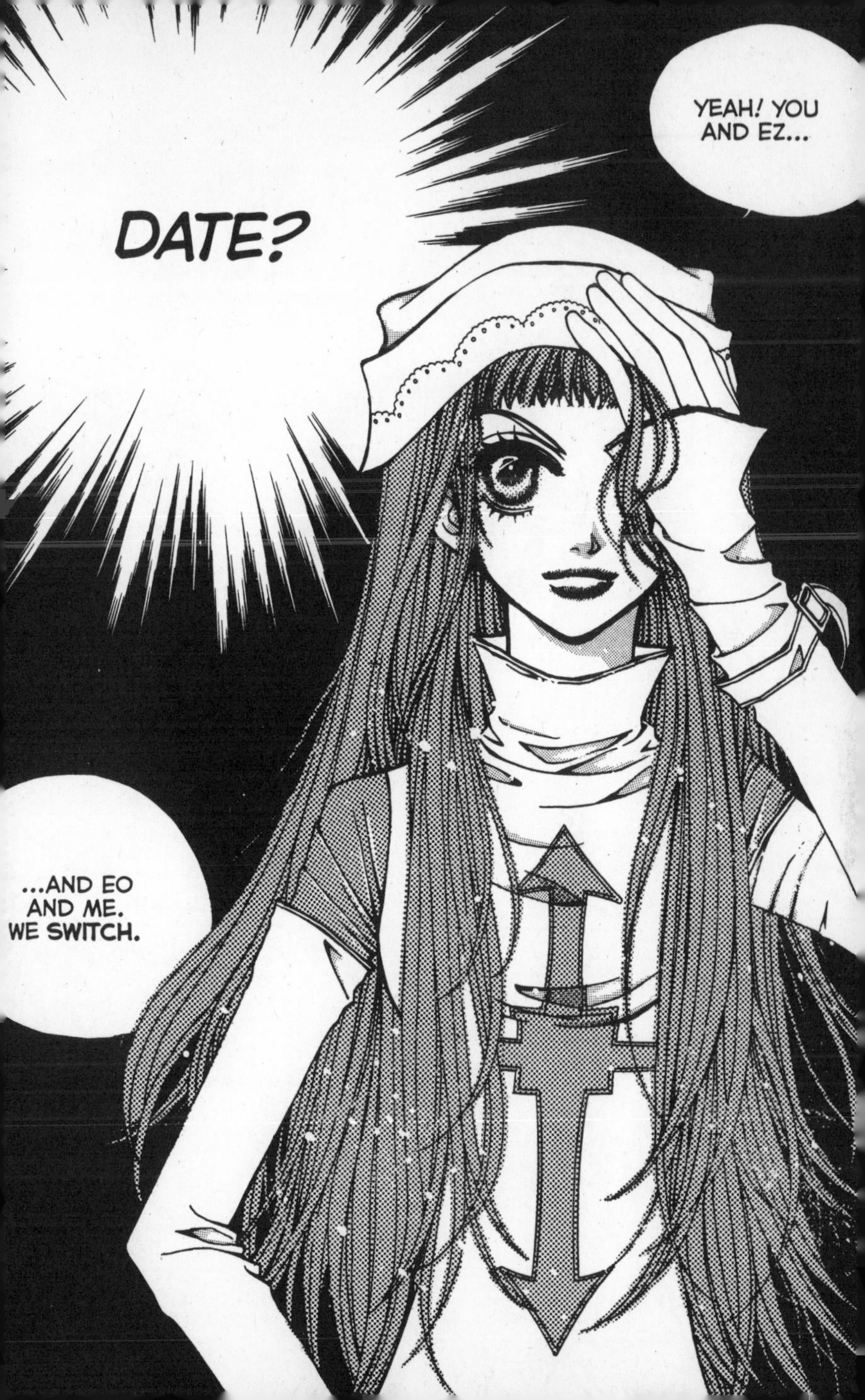
DATE?
YEAH! YOU AND EZ...
...AND EO AND ME. WE SWITCH.

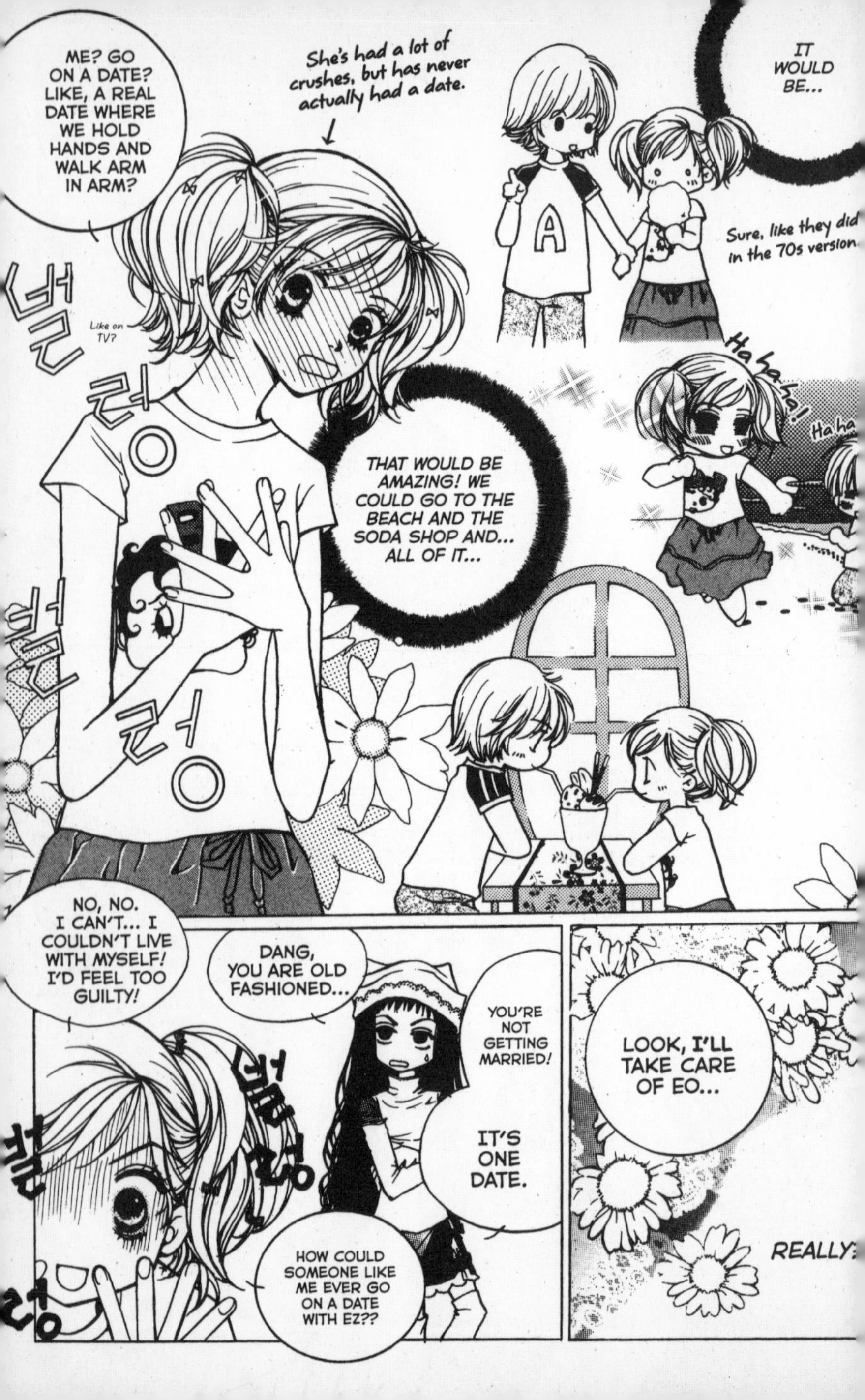
ME? GO ON A DATE? LIKE, A REAL DATE WHERE WE HOLD HANDS AND WALK ARM IN ARM?
She's had a lot of crushes, but has never actually had a date.
Like on TV?
IT WOULD BE...
Sure, like they did in the 70s version.
THAT WOULD BE AMAZING! WE COULD GO TO THE BEACH AND THE SODA SHOP AND... ALL OF IT...
Ha ha ha!
Ha ha
NO, NO. I CAN'T... I COULDN'T LIVE WITH MYSELF! I'D FEEL TOO GUILTY!
DANG, YOU ARE OLD FASHIONED...
YOU'RE NOT GETTING MARRIED!
IT'S ONE DATE.
HOW COULD SOMEONE LIKE ME EVER GO ON A DATE WITH EZ??
LOOK, I'LL TAKE CARE OF EO...
REALLY

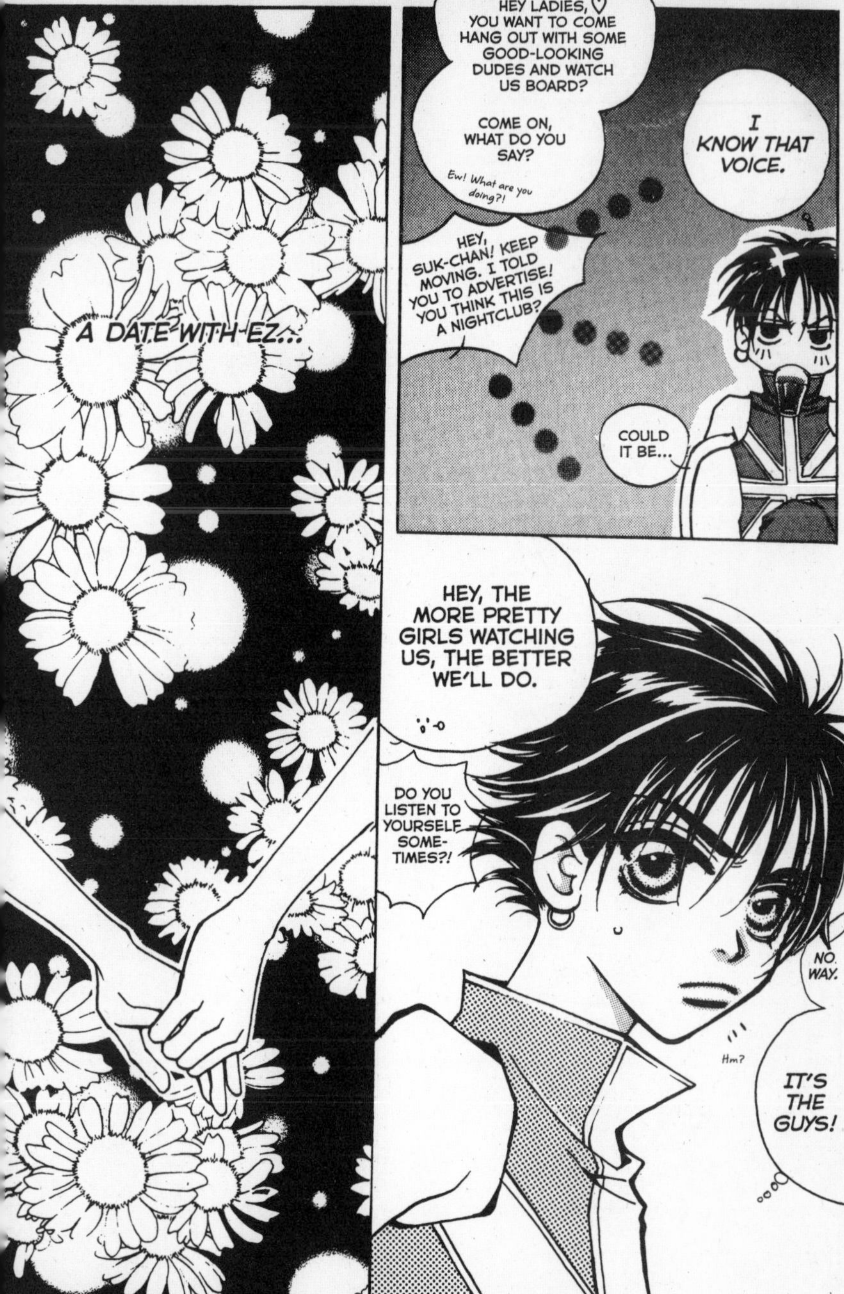
A DATE WITH EZ...
HEY LADIES, ♡ YOU WANT TO COME HANG OUT WITH SOME GOOD-LOOKING DUDES AND WATCH US BOARD?
COME ON, WHAT DO YOU SAY?
Ew! What are you doing?!
HEY, SUK-CHAN! KEEP MOVING. I TOLD YOU TO ADVERTISE! YOU THINK THIS IS A NIGHTCLUB?
I KNOW THAT VOICE.
COULD IT BE...
HEY, THE MORE PRETTY GIRLS WATCHING US, THE BETTER WE'LL DO.
DO YOU LISTEN TO YOURSELF SOME-TIMES?!
NO. WAY.
Hm?
IT'S THE GUYS!

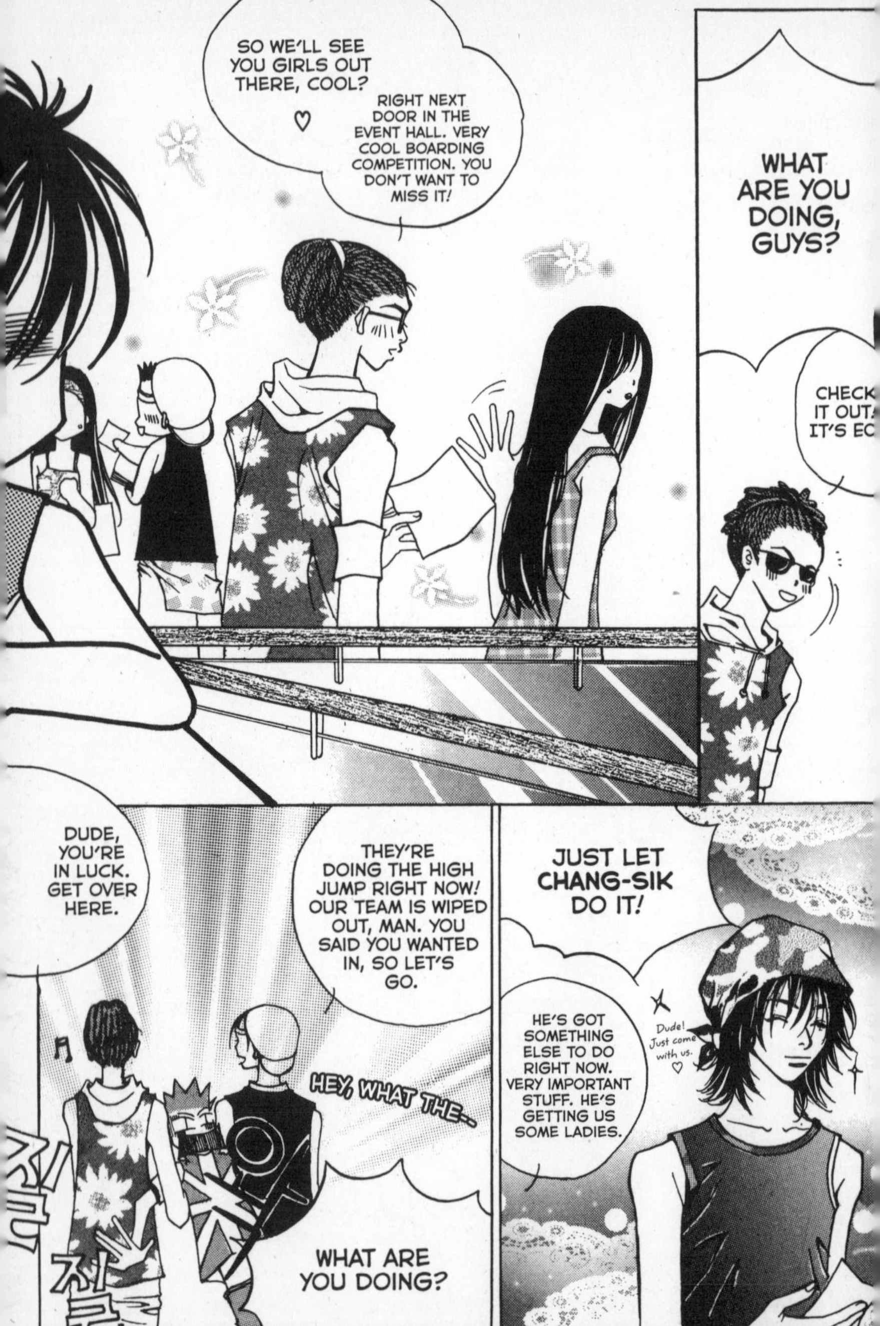

SO WE'LL SEE YOU GIRLS OUT THERE, COOL?
RIGHT NEXT DOOR IN THE EVENT HALL. VERY COOL BOARDING COMPETITION. YOU DON'T WANT TO MISS IT!
WHAT ARE YOU DOING, GUYS?
CHECK IT OUT! IT'S EC
DUDE, YOU'RE IN LUCK. GET OVER HERE.
THEY'RE DOING THE HIGH JUMP RIGHT NOW! OUR TEAM IS WIPED OUT, MAN. YOU SAID YOU WANTED IN, SO LET'S GO.
HEY, WHAT THE--
WHAT ARE YOU DOING?
JUST LET CHANG-SIK DO IT!
HE'S GOT SOMETHING ELSE TO DO RIGHT NOW. VERY IMPORTANT STUFF. HE'S GETTING US SOME LADIES.
Dude! Just come with us. ♡

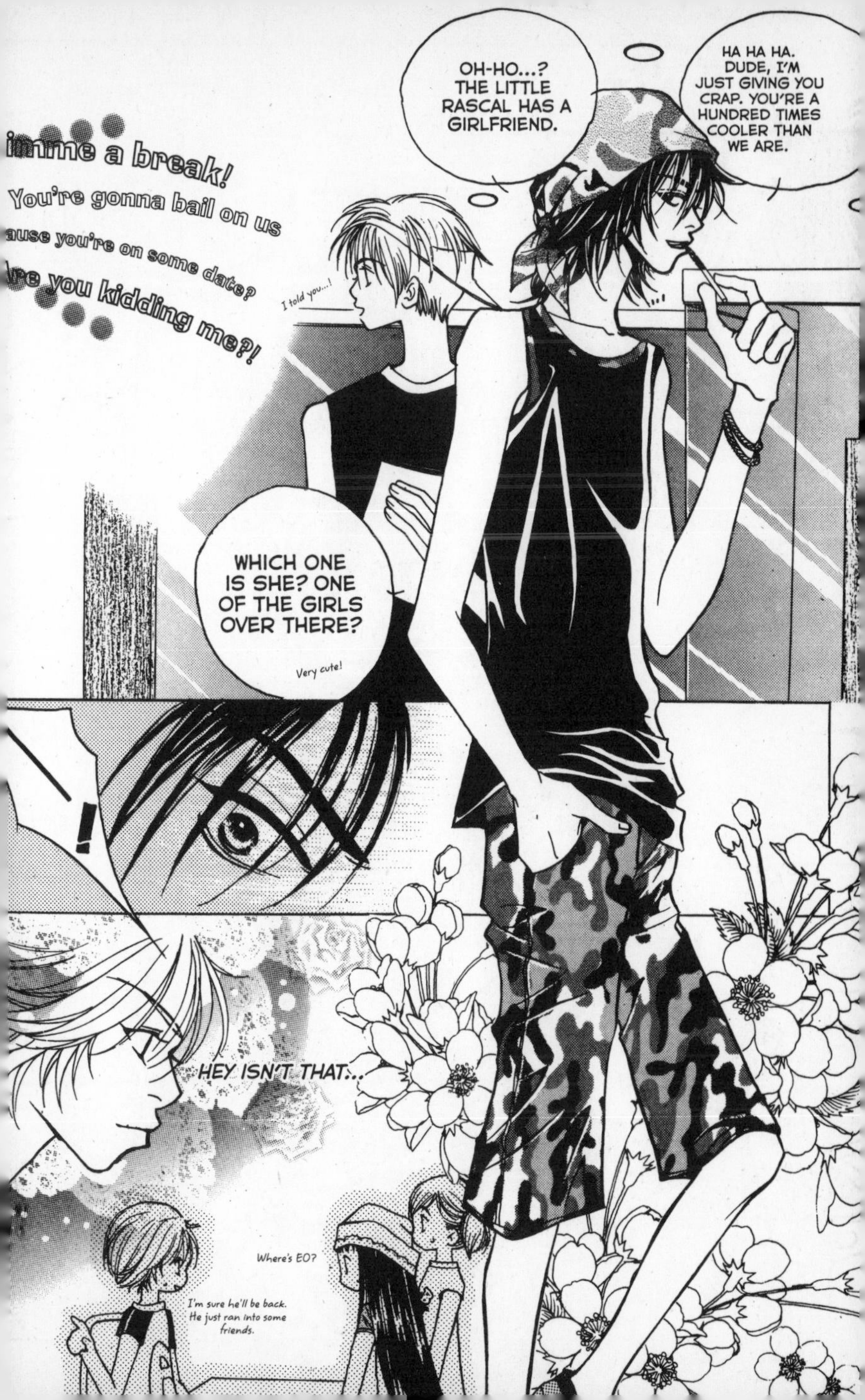
imme a break!
You're gonna bail on us
ause you're on some date?
re you kidding me?!
I told you...!
OH-HO...? THE LITTLE RASCAL HAS A GIRLFRIEND.
HA HA HA. DUDE, I'M JUST GIVING YOU CRAP. YOU'RE A HUNDRED TIMES COOLER THAN WE ARE.
WHICH ONE IS SHE? ONE OF THE GIRLS OVER THERE?
Very cute!
!
HEY ISN'T THAT...
Where's EO?
I'm sure he'll be back. He just ran into some friends.

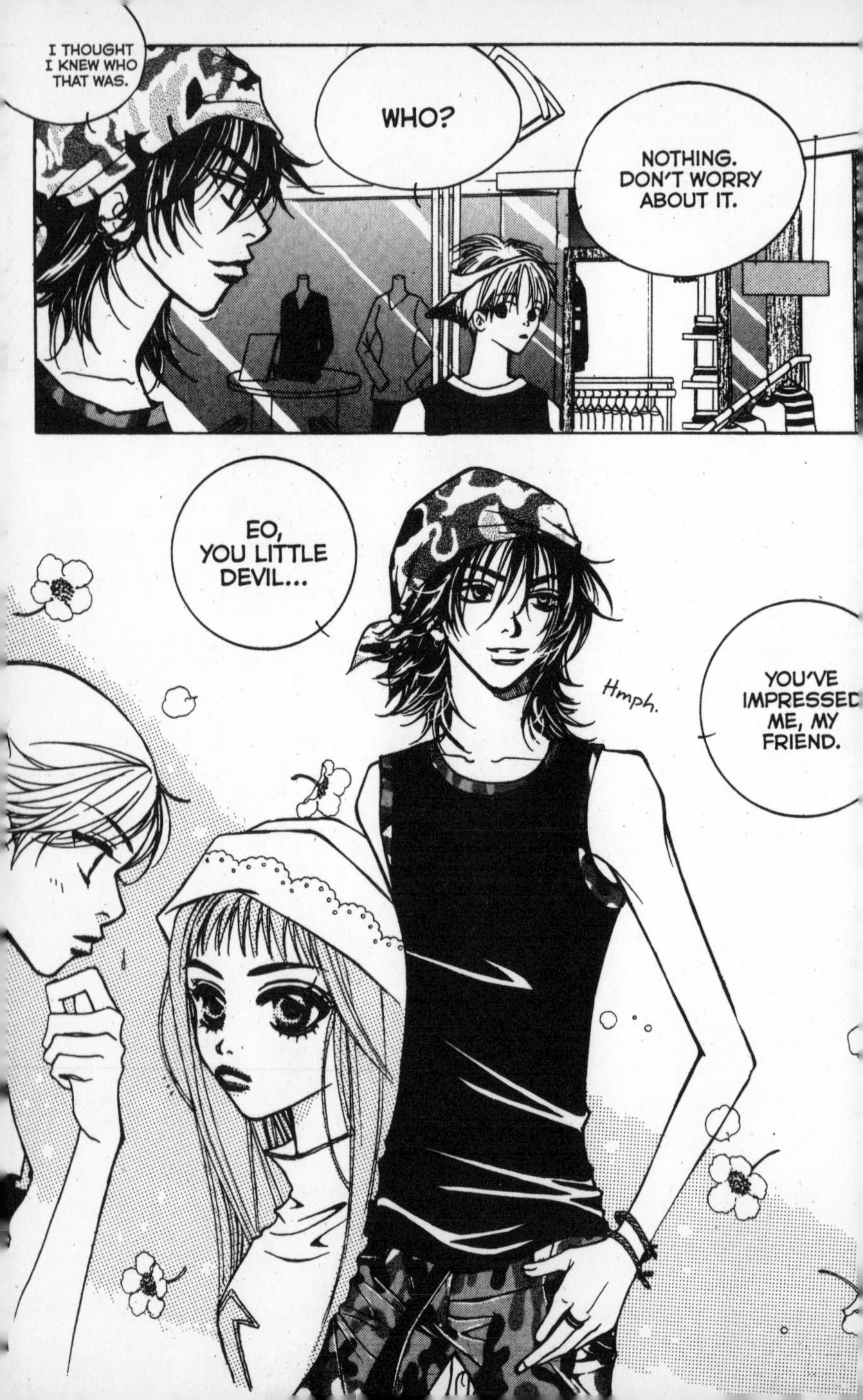
I THOUGHT I KNEW WHO THAT WAS.
WHO?
NOTHING. DON'T WORRY ABOUT IT.
EO, YOU LITTLE DEVIL...
Hmph.
YOU'VE IMPRESSED ME, MY FRIEND.

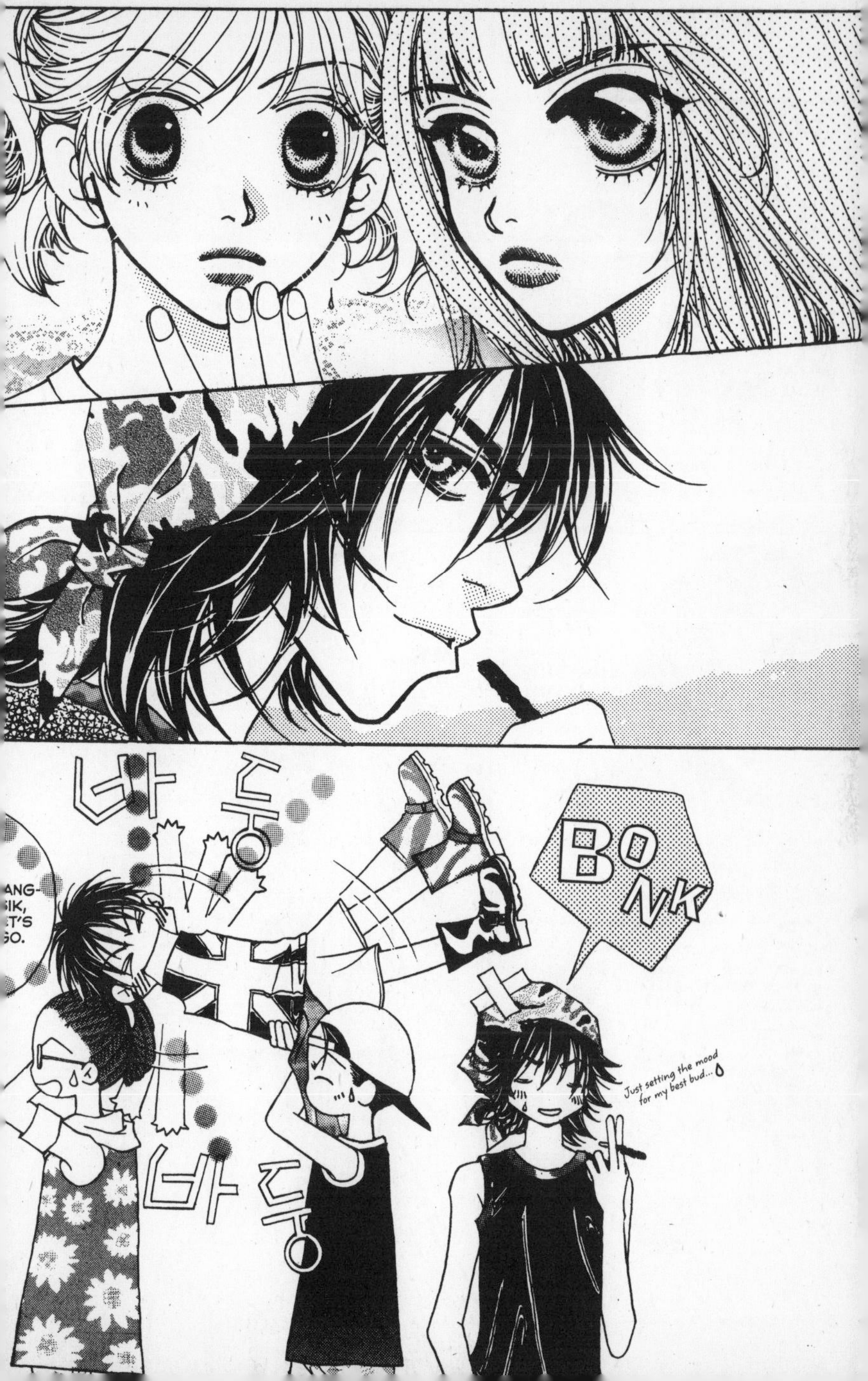
ANG- SIK, ET'S GO.
BONK
Just setting the mood for my best bud...

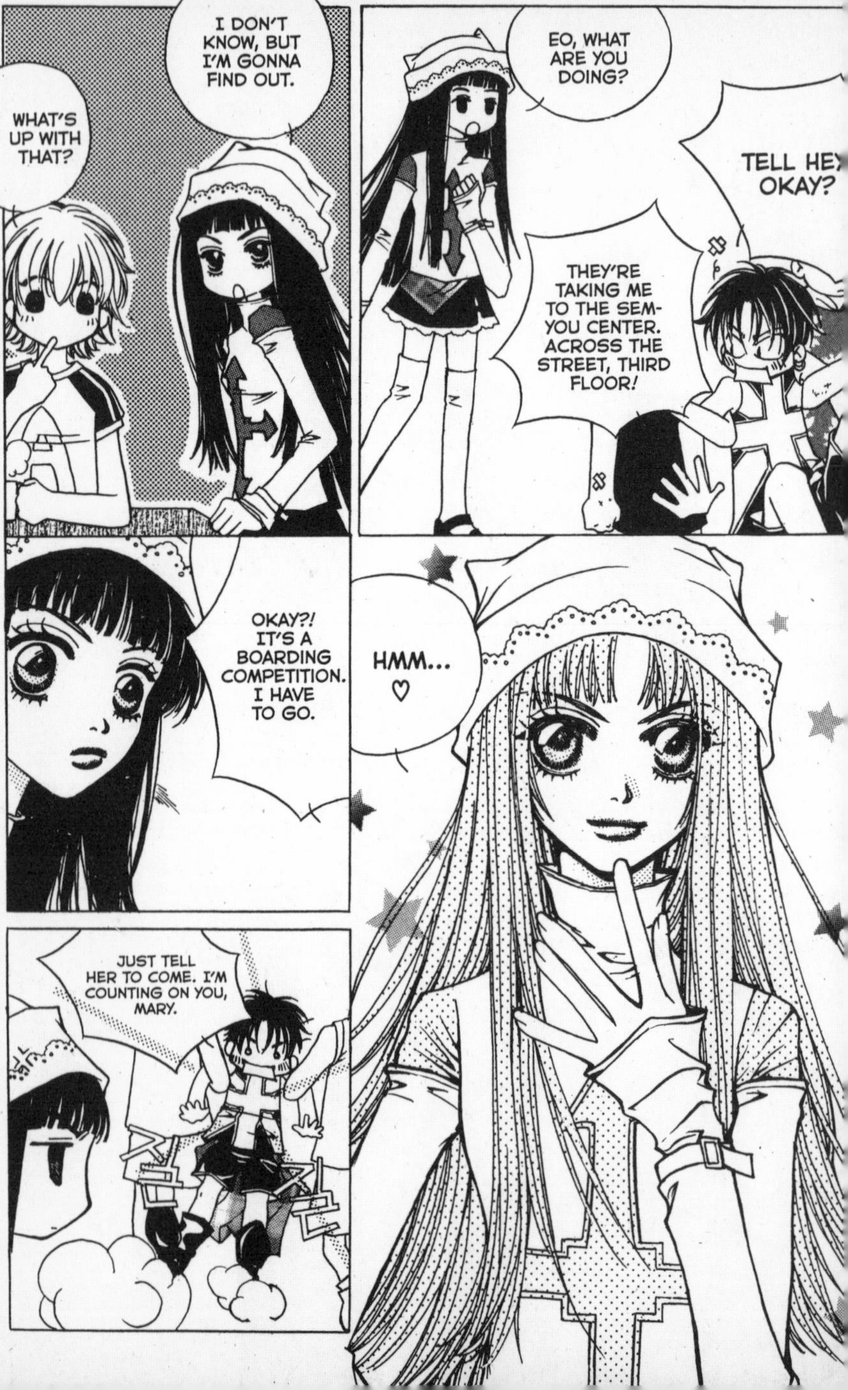
WHAT'S UP WITH THAT?
I DON'T KNOW, BUT I'M GONNA FIND OUT.
EO, WHAT ARE YOU DOING?
TELL HE
OKAY?
THEY'RE TAKING ME TO THE SEM-YOU CENTER. ACROSS THE STREET, THIRD FLOOR!
OKAY?! IT'S A BOARDING COMPETITION. I HAVE TO GO.
JUST TELL HER TO COME. I'M COUNTING ON YOU, MARY.
HMM... ♡

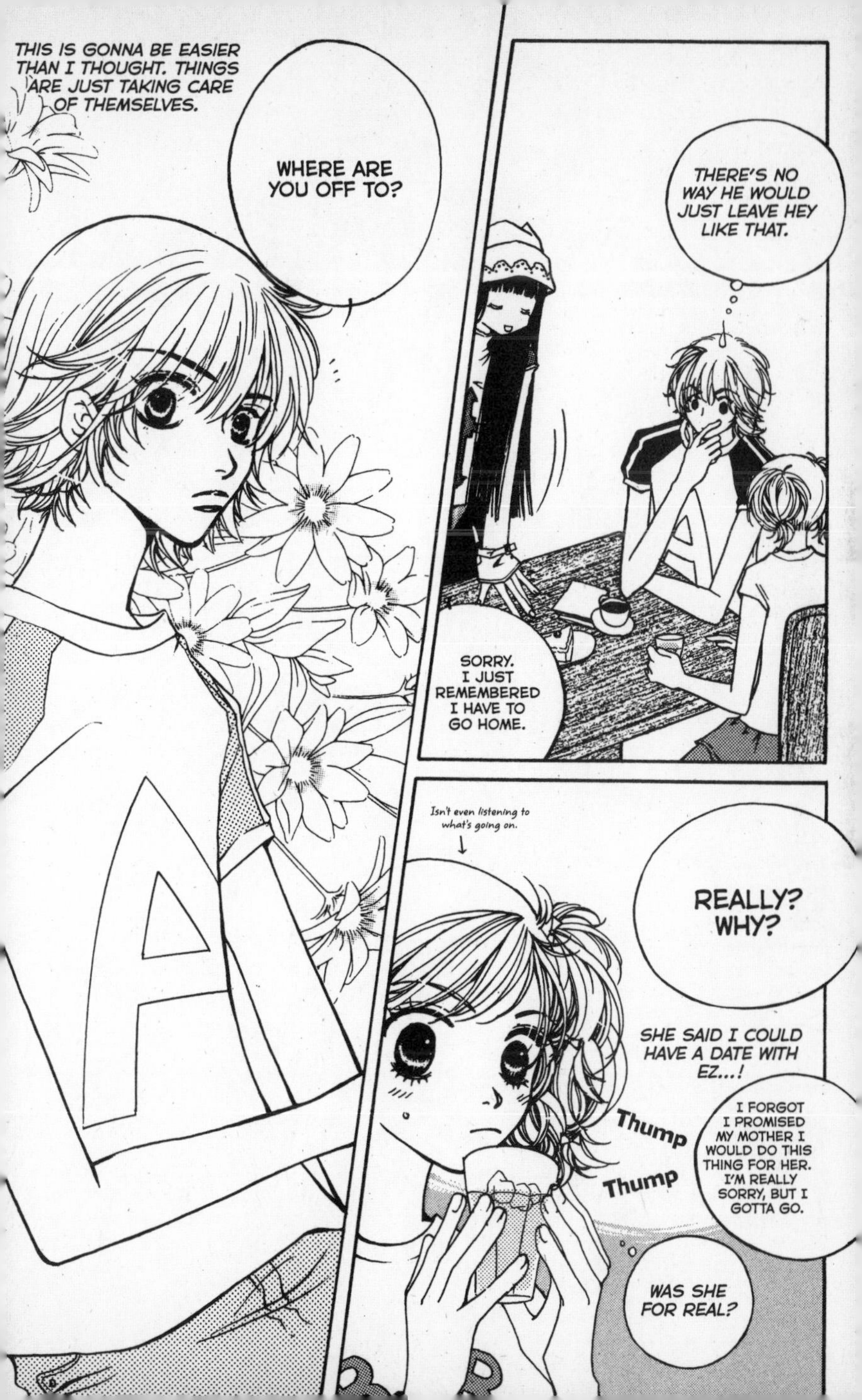
THIS IS GONNA BE EASIER THAN I THOUGHT. THINGS ARE JUST TAKING CARE OF THEMSELVES.
WHERE ARE YOU OFF TO?
THERE'S NO WAY HE WOULD JUST LEAVE HEY LIKE THAT.
SORRY. I JUST REMEMBERED I HAVE TO GO HOME.
Isn't even listening to what's going on.
REALLY? WHY?
SHE SAID I COULD HAVE A DATE WITH EZ...!
Thump
Thump
I FORGOT I PROMISED MY MOTHER I WOULD DO THIS THING FOR HER. I'M REALLY SORRY, BUT I GOTTA GO.
WAS SHE FOR REAL?

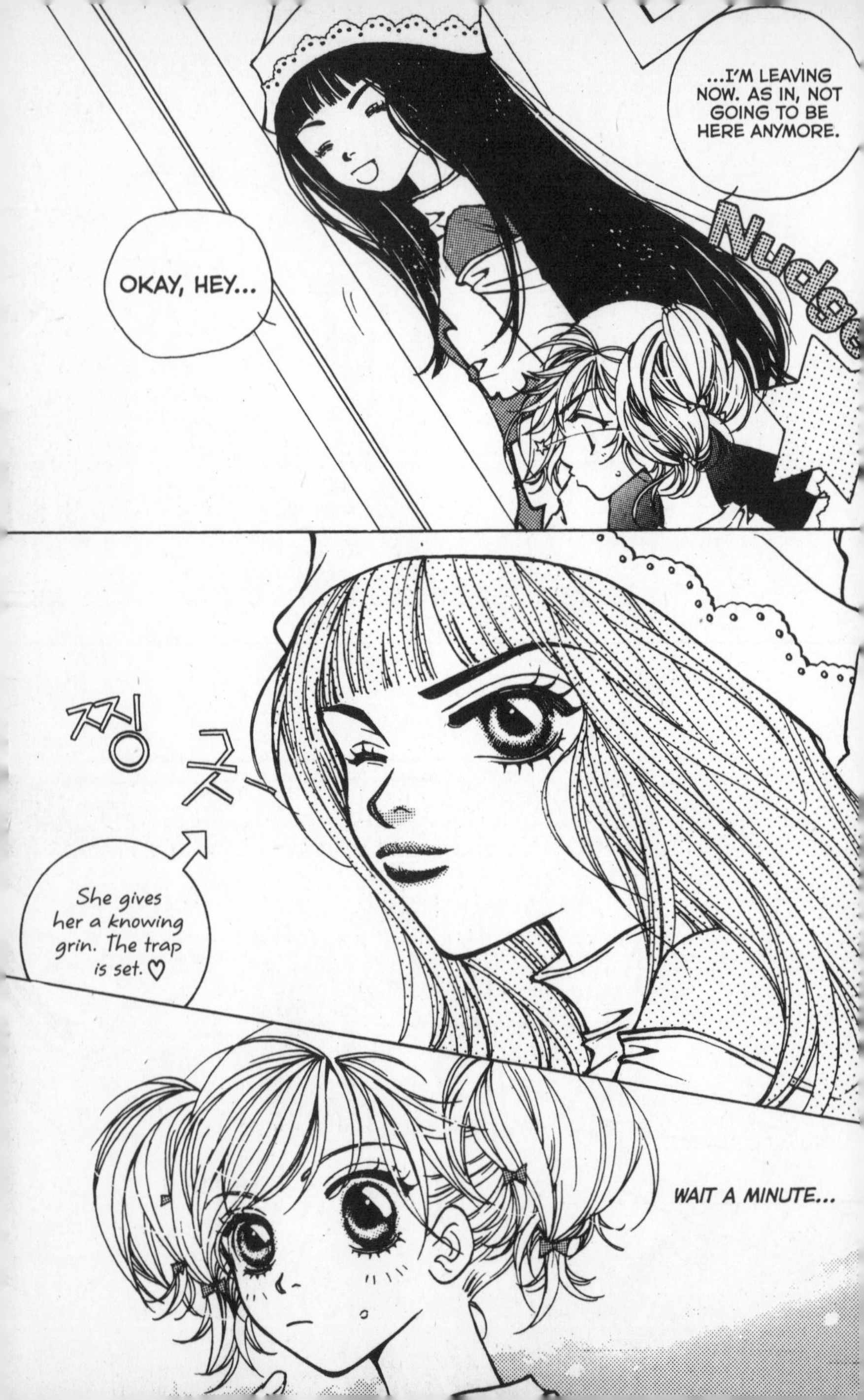
OKAY, HEY...
...I'M LEAVING NOW. AS IN, NOT GOING TO BE HERE ANYMORE.
Nudge
찡긋
She gives her a knowing grin. The trap is set. ♡
WAIT A MINUTE...

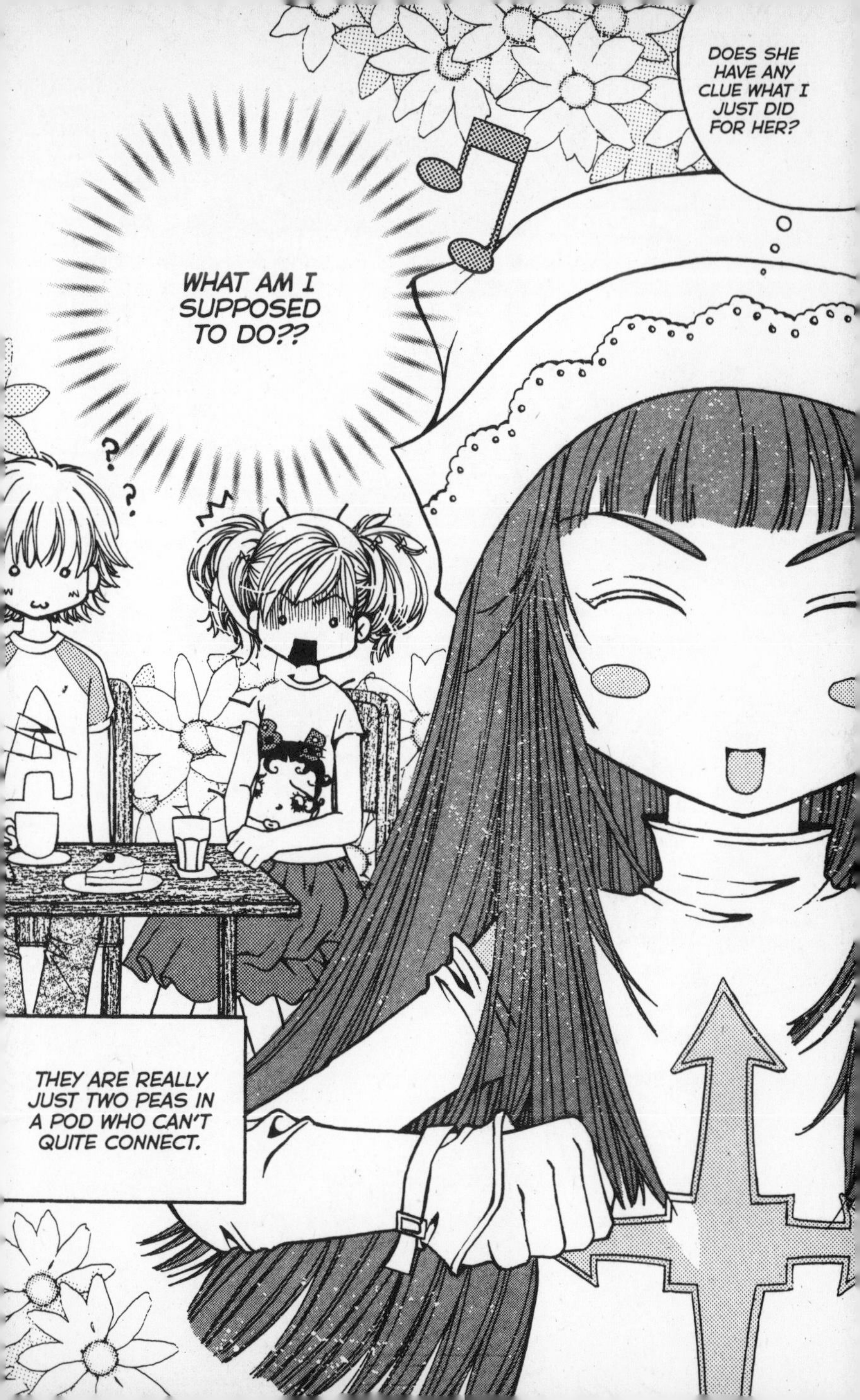
WHAT AM I SUPPOSED TO DO??
DOES SHE HAVE ANY CLUE WHAT I JUST DID FOR HER?
THEY ARE REALLY JUST TWO PEAS IN A POD WHO CAN'T QUITE CONNECT.

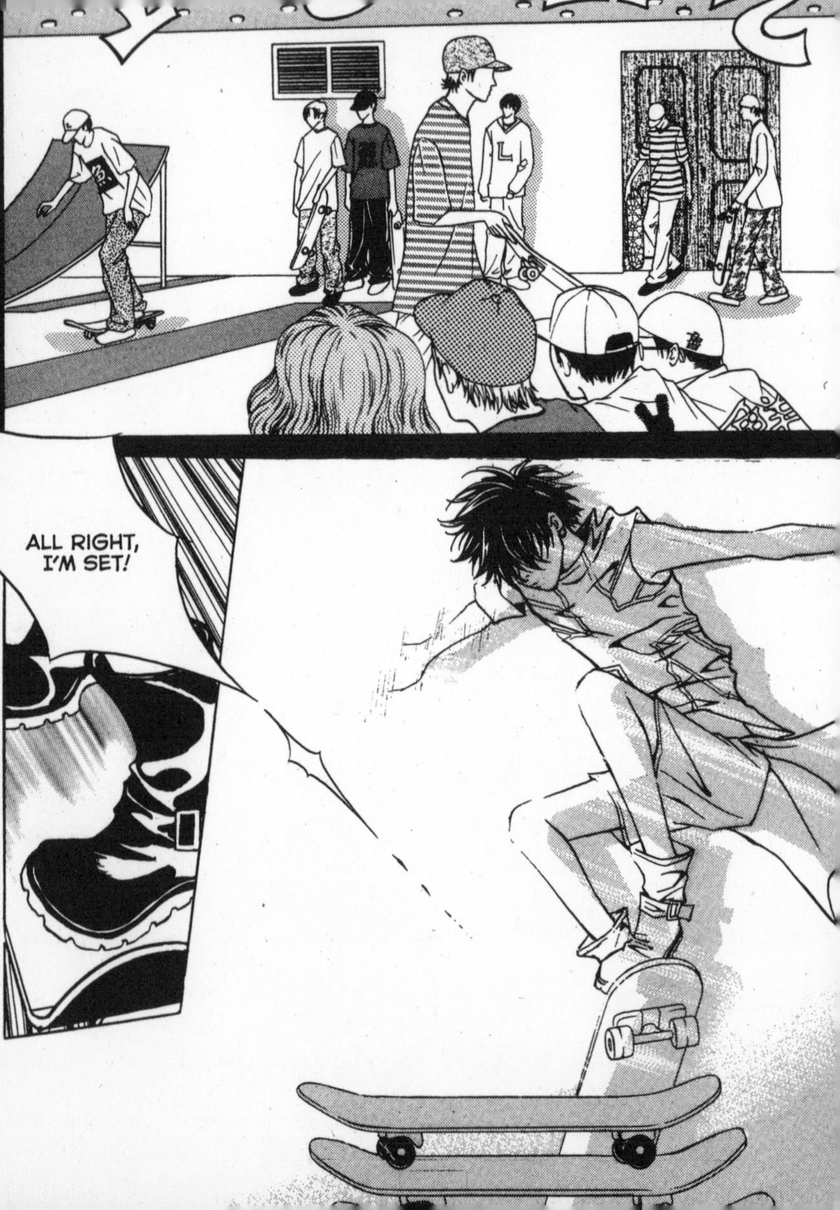
ALL RIGHT, I'M SET!

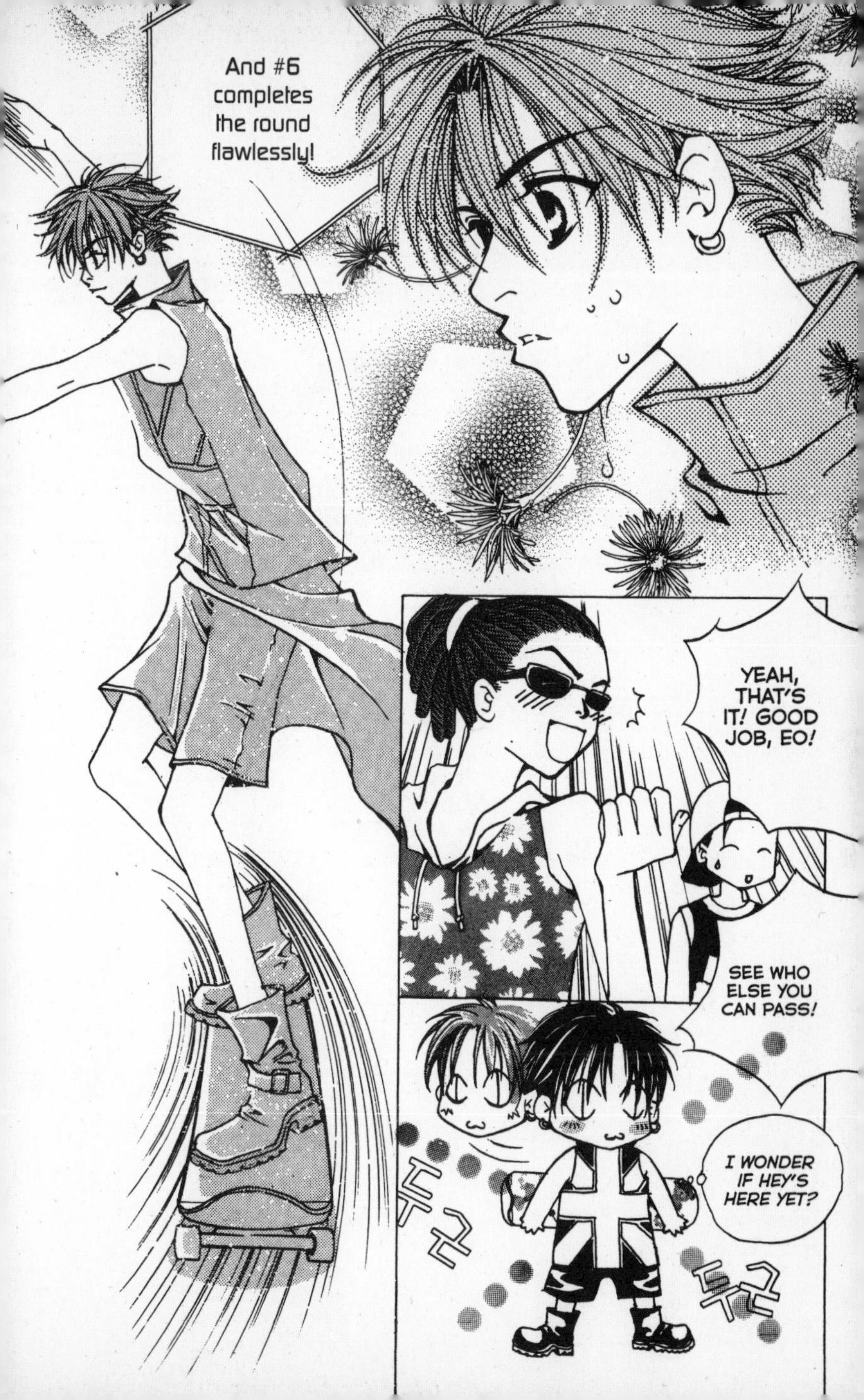
And #6 completes the round flawlessly!
YEAH, THAT'S IT! GOOD JOB, EO!
SEE WHO ELSE YOU CAN PASS!
I WONDER IF HEY'S HERE YET?

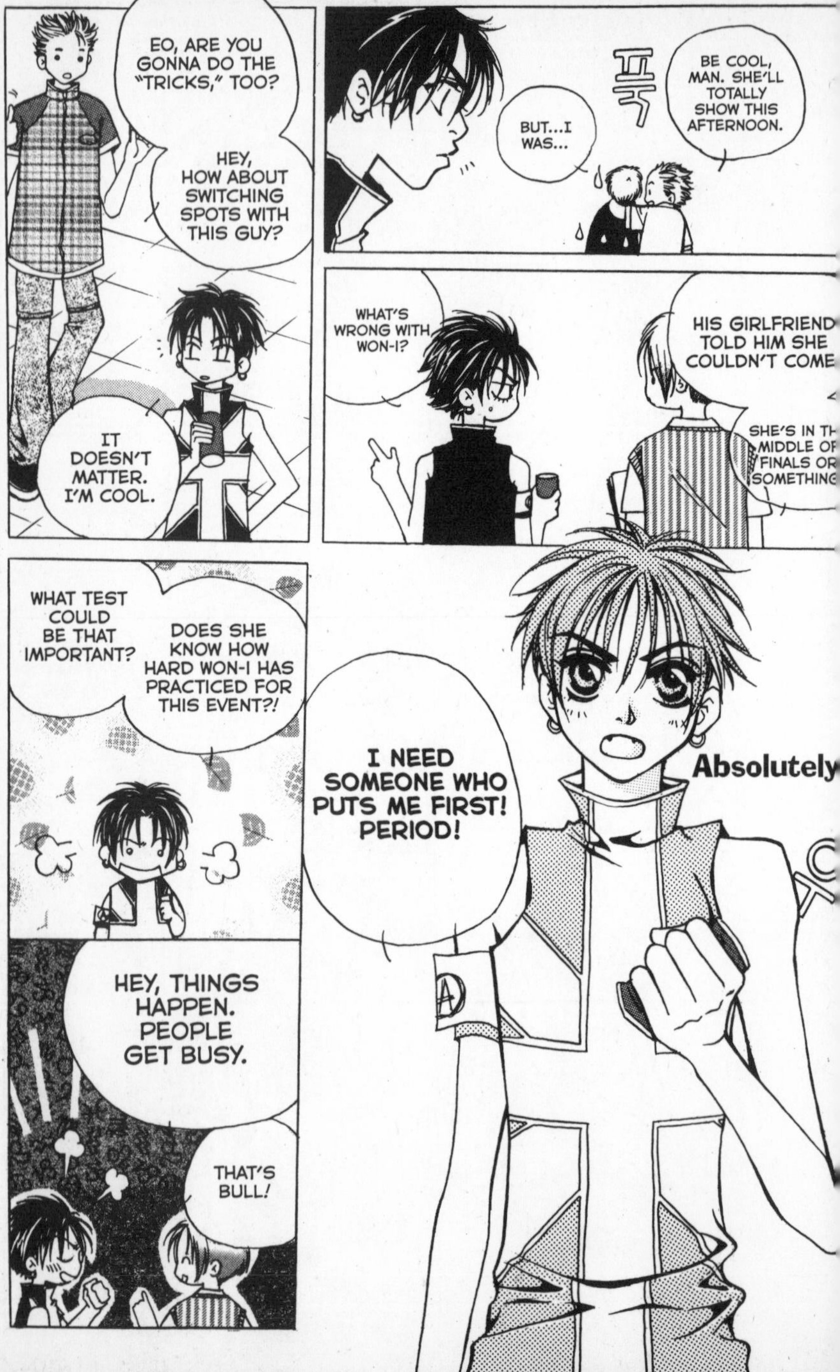
EO, ARE YOU GONNA DO THE "TRICKS," TOO?
HEY, HOW ABOUT SWITCHING SPOTS WITH THIS GUY?
IT DOESN'T MATTER. I'M COOL.
BUT...I WAS...
BE COOL, MAN. SHE'LL TOTALLY SHOW THIS AFTERNOON.
WHAT'S WRONG WITH WON-I?
HIS GIRLFRIEND TOLD HIM SHE COULDN'T COME
SHE'S IN THE MIDDLE OF FINALS OR SOMETHING
WHAT TEST COULD BE THAT IMPORTANT?
DOES SHE KNOW HOW HARD WON-I HAS PRACTICED FOR THIS EVENT?!
HEY, THINGS HAPPEN. PEOPLE GET BUSY.
THAT'S BULL!
I NEED SOMEONE WHO PUTS ME FIRST! PERIOD!
Absolutely

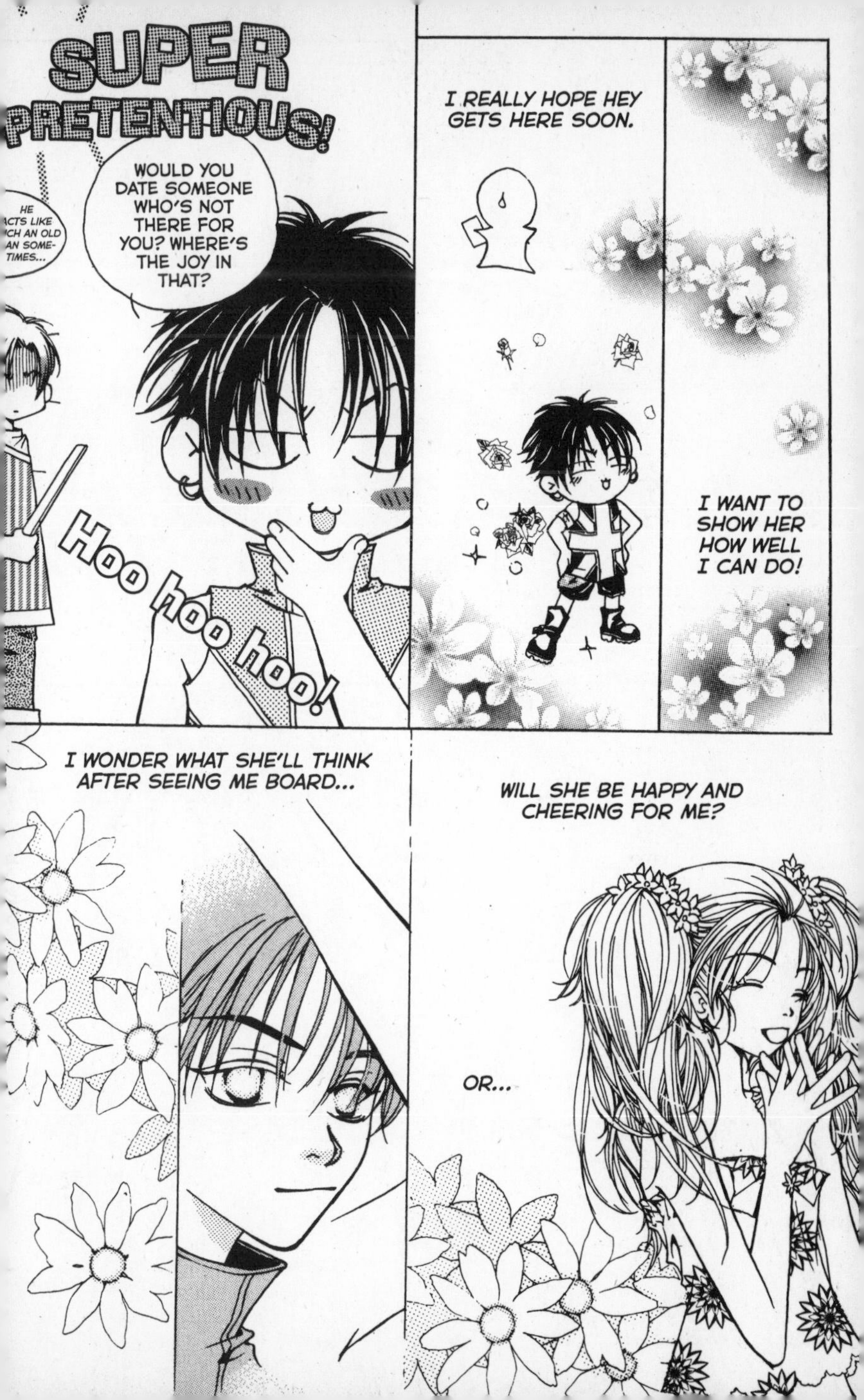
SUPER PRETENTIOUS!
HE ACTS LIKE CH AN OLD AN SOME- TIMES...
WOULD YOU DATE SOMEONE WHO'S NOT THERE FOR YOU? WHERE'S THE JOY IN THAT?
Hoo hoo hoo!
I REALLY HOPE HEY GETS HERE SOON.
I WANT TO SHOW HER HOW WELL I CAN DO!
I WONDER WHAT SHE'LL THINK AFTER SEEING ME BOARD...
WILL SHE BE HAPPY AND CHEERING FOR ME?
OR...

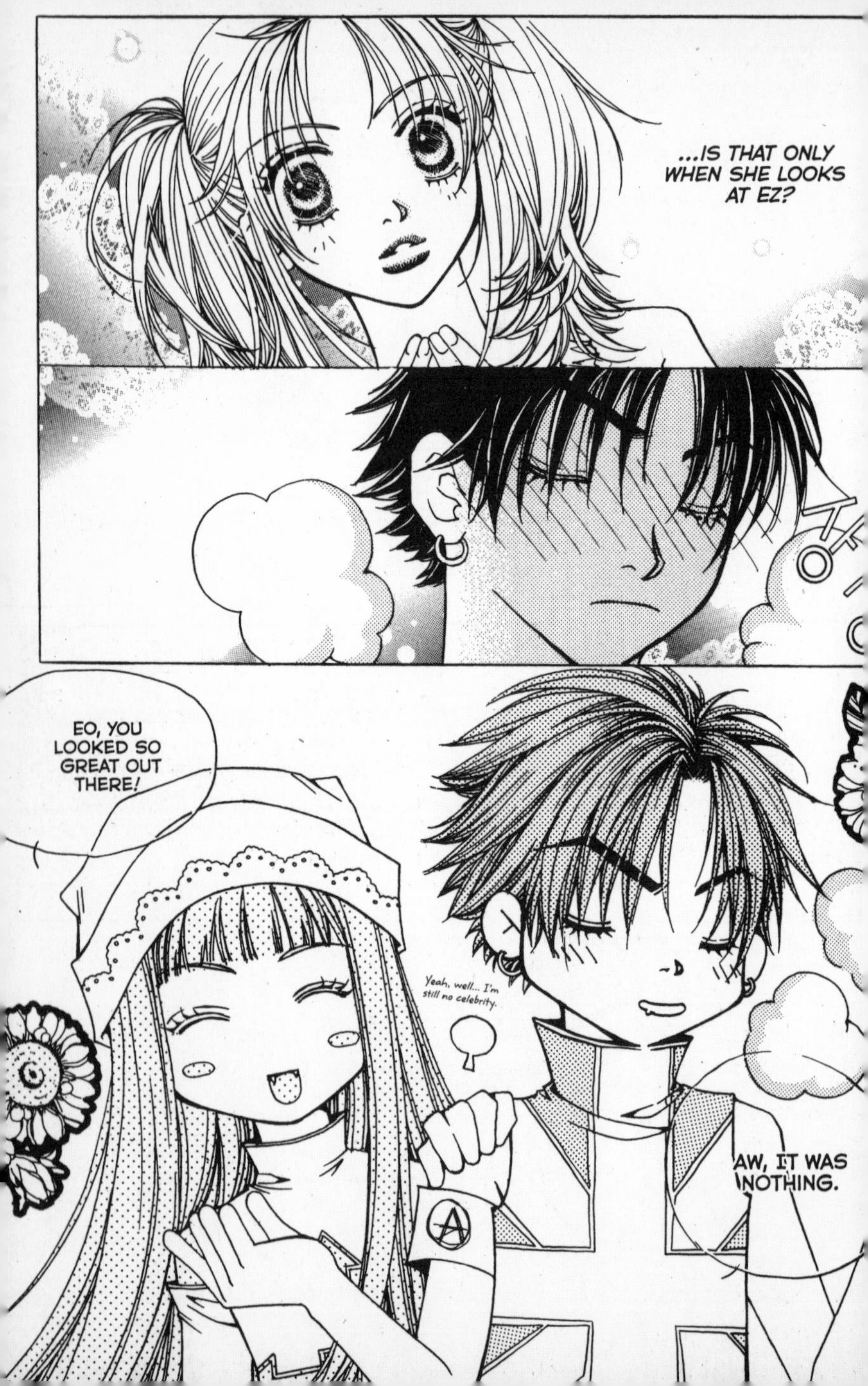
...IS THAT ONLY WHEN SHE LOOKS AT EZ?
EO, YOU LOOKED SO GREAT OUT THERE!
Yeah, well... I'm still no celebrity.
AW, IT WAS NOTHING.

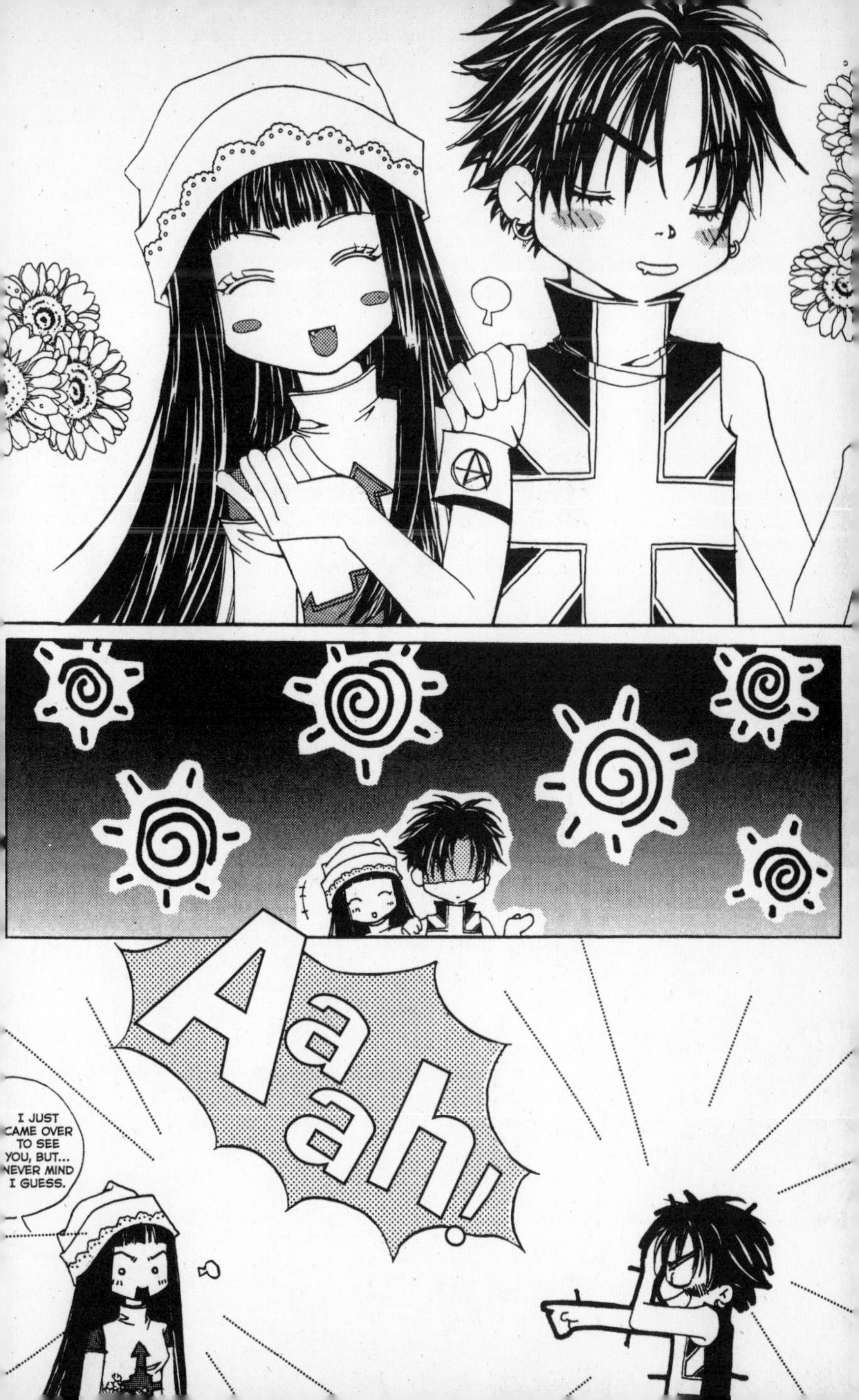
Aaah!!
I JUST CAME OVER TO SEE YOU, BUT... NEVER MIND I GUESS.

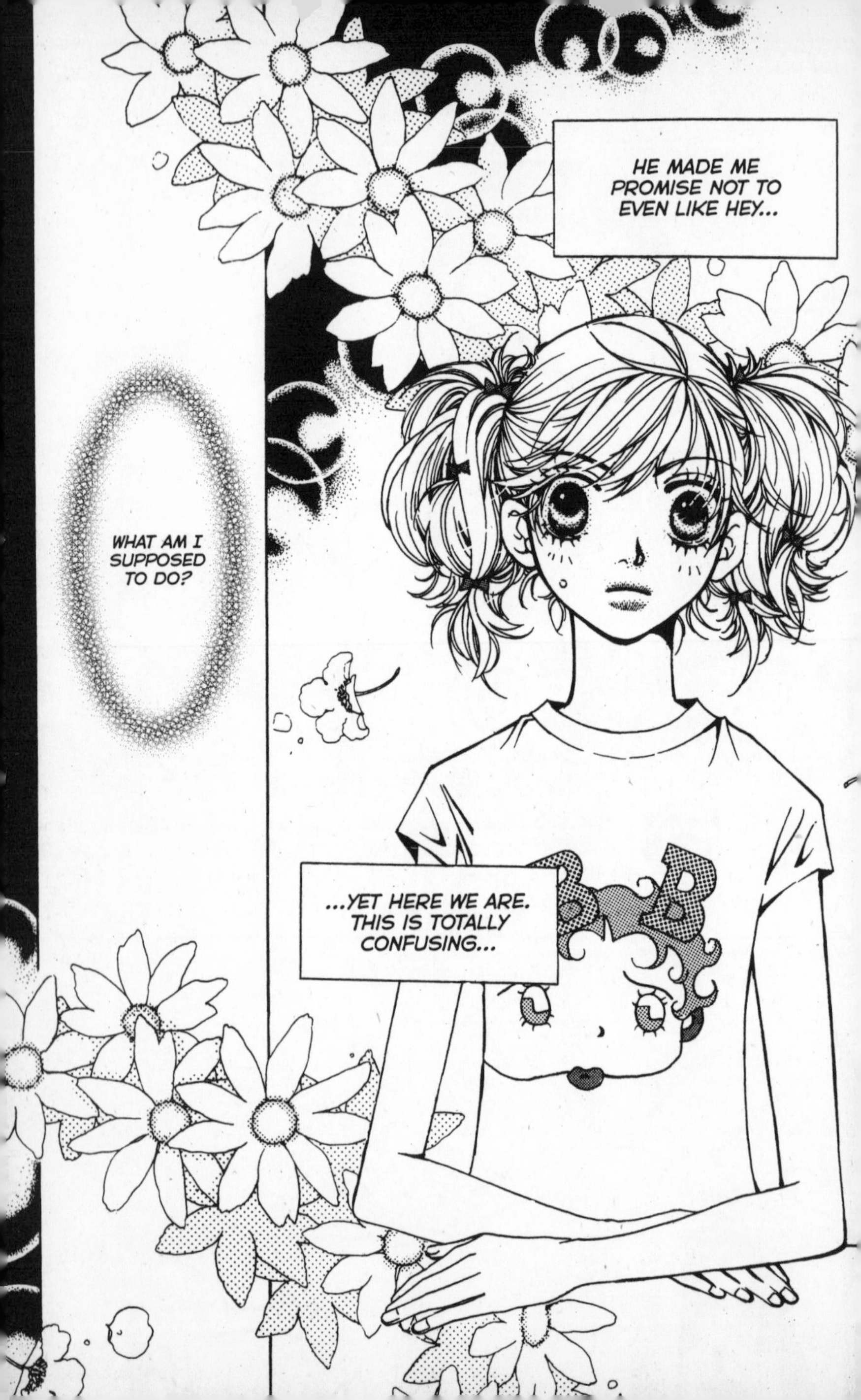
WHAT AM I SUPPOSED TO DO?
HE MADE ME PROMISE NOT TO EVEN LIKE HEY...
...YET HERE WE ARE. THIS IS TOTALLY CONFUSING...

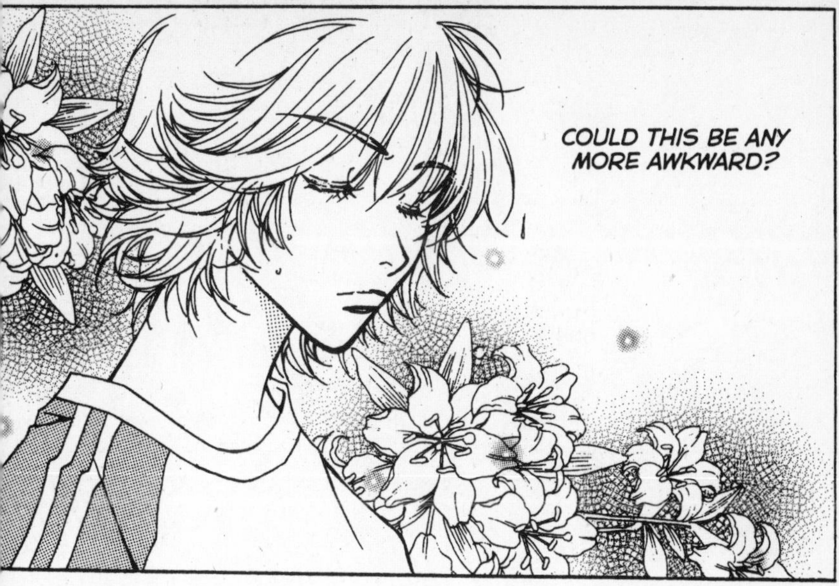
COULD THIS BE ANY MORE AWKWARD?

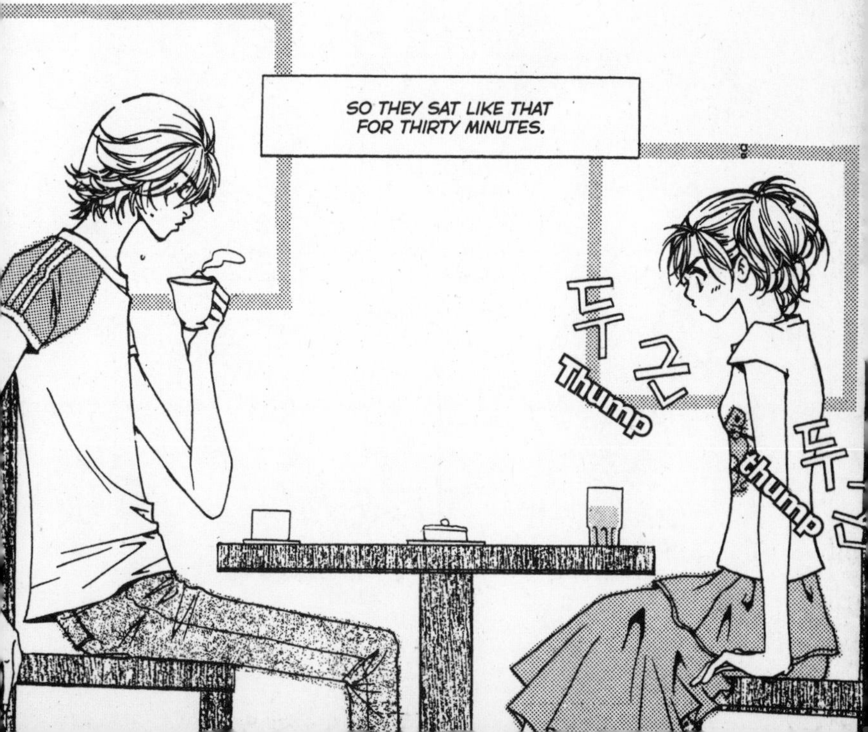
SO THEY SAT LIKE THAT FOR THIRTY MINUTES.
두근
Thump
두근
thump

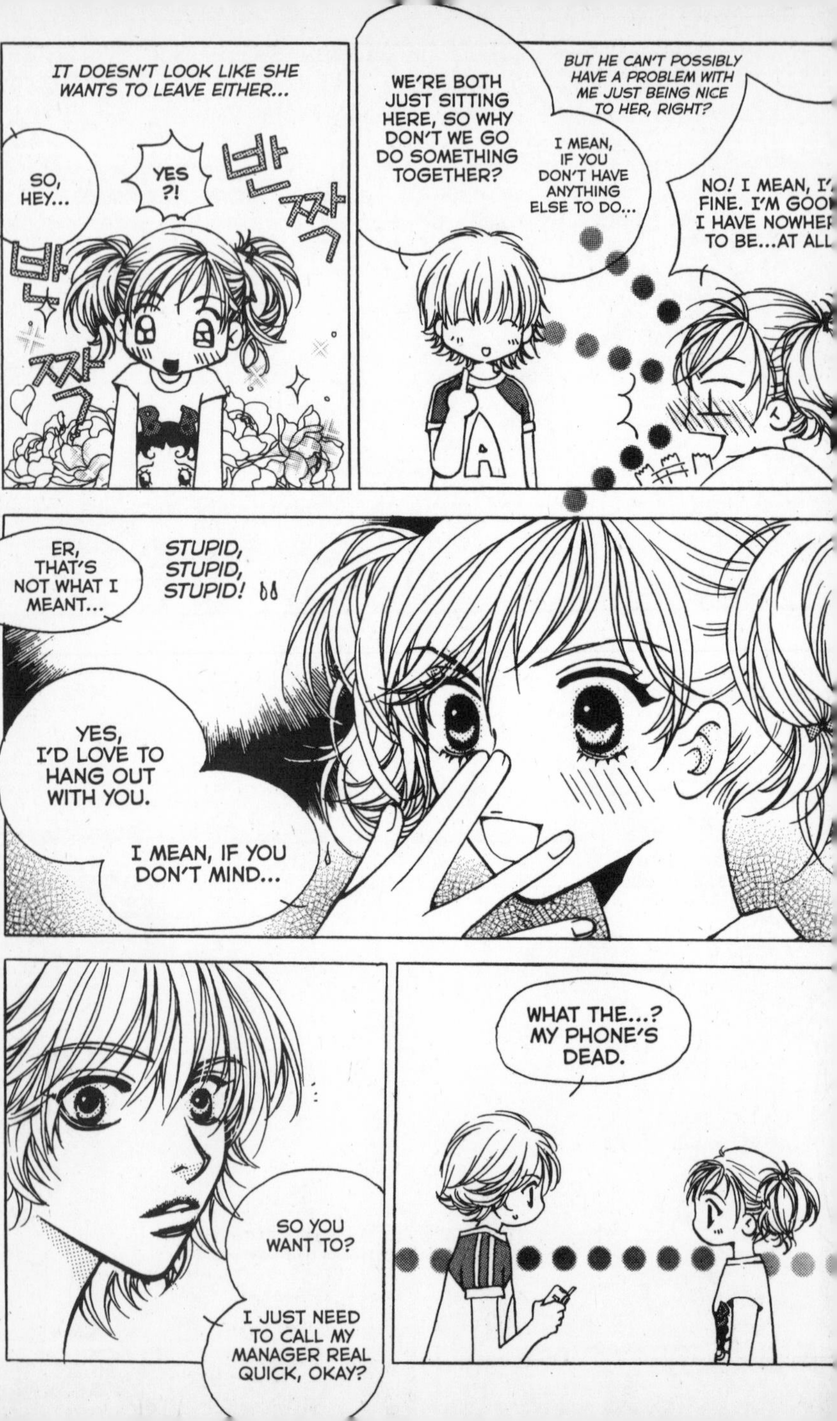
IT DOESN'T LOOK LIKE SHE WANTS TO LEAVE EITHER...
SO, HEY...
YES?!
반짝
반짝
WE'RE BOTH JUST SITTING HERE, SO WHY DON'T WE GO DO SOMETHING TOGETHER?
BUT HE CAN'T POSSIBLY HAVE A PROBLEM WITH ME JUST BEING NICE TO HER, RIGHT?
I MEAN, IF YOU DON'T HAVE ANYTHING ELSE TO DO...
NO! I MEAN, I' FINE. I'M GOO I HAVE NOWHER TO BE...AT ALL
ER, THAT'S NOT WHAT I MEANT...
STUPID, STUPID, STUPID!
YES, I'D LOVE TO HANG OUT WITH YOU.
I MEAN, IF YOU DON'T MIND...
SO YOU WANT TO?
I JUST NEED TO CALL MY MANAGER REAL QUICK, OKAY?
WHAT THE...? MY PHONE'S DEAD.

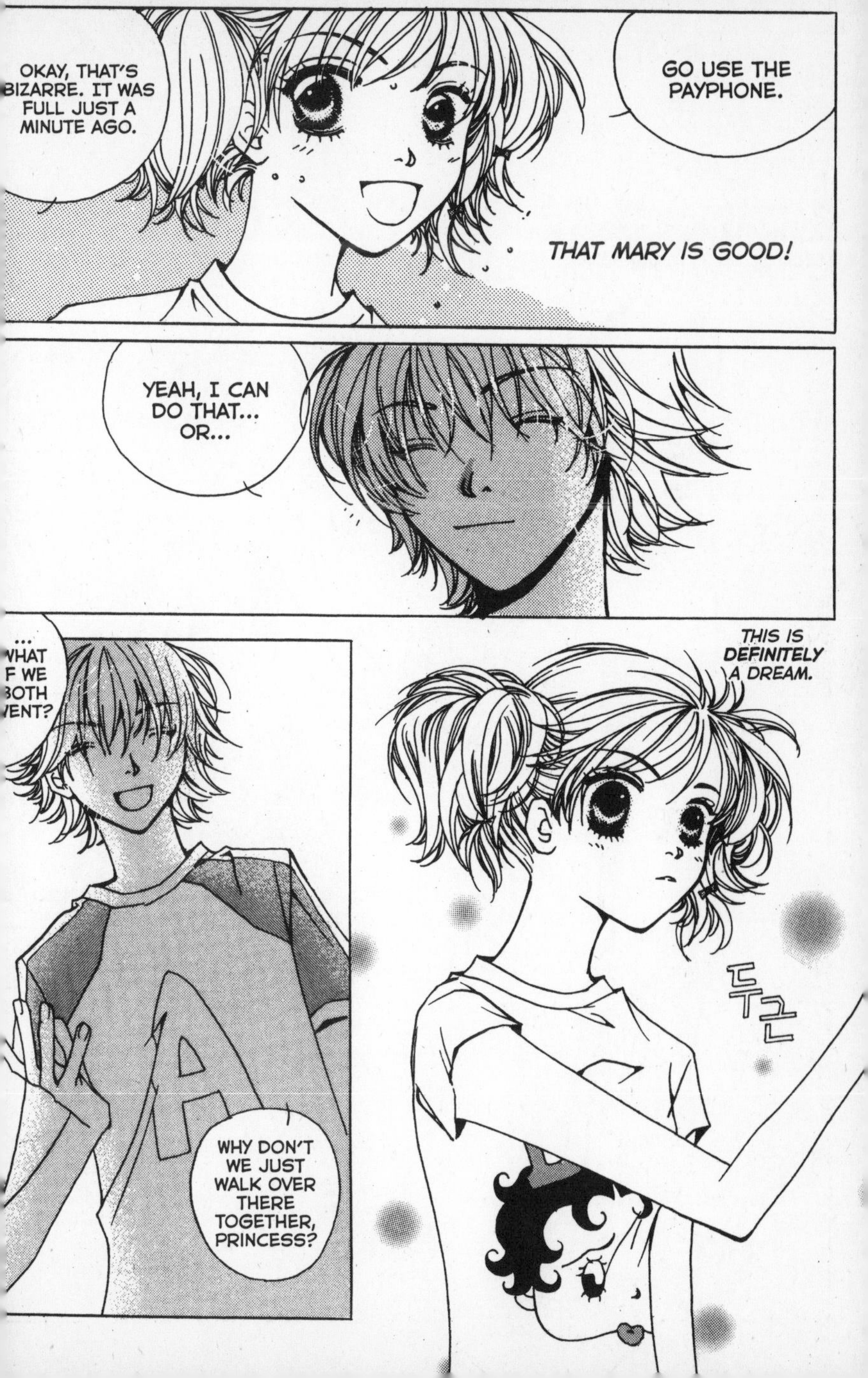
OKAY, THAT'S BIZARRE. IT WAS FULL JUST A MINUTE AGO.
GO USE THE PAYPHONE.
THAT MARY IS GOOD!
YEAH, I CAN DO THAT... OR...
... WHAT F WE BOTH WENT?
WHY DON'T WE JUST WALK OVER THERE TOGETHER, PRINCESS?
THIS IS DEFINITELY A DREAM.

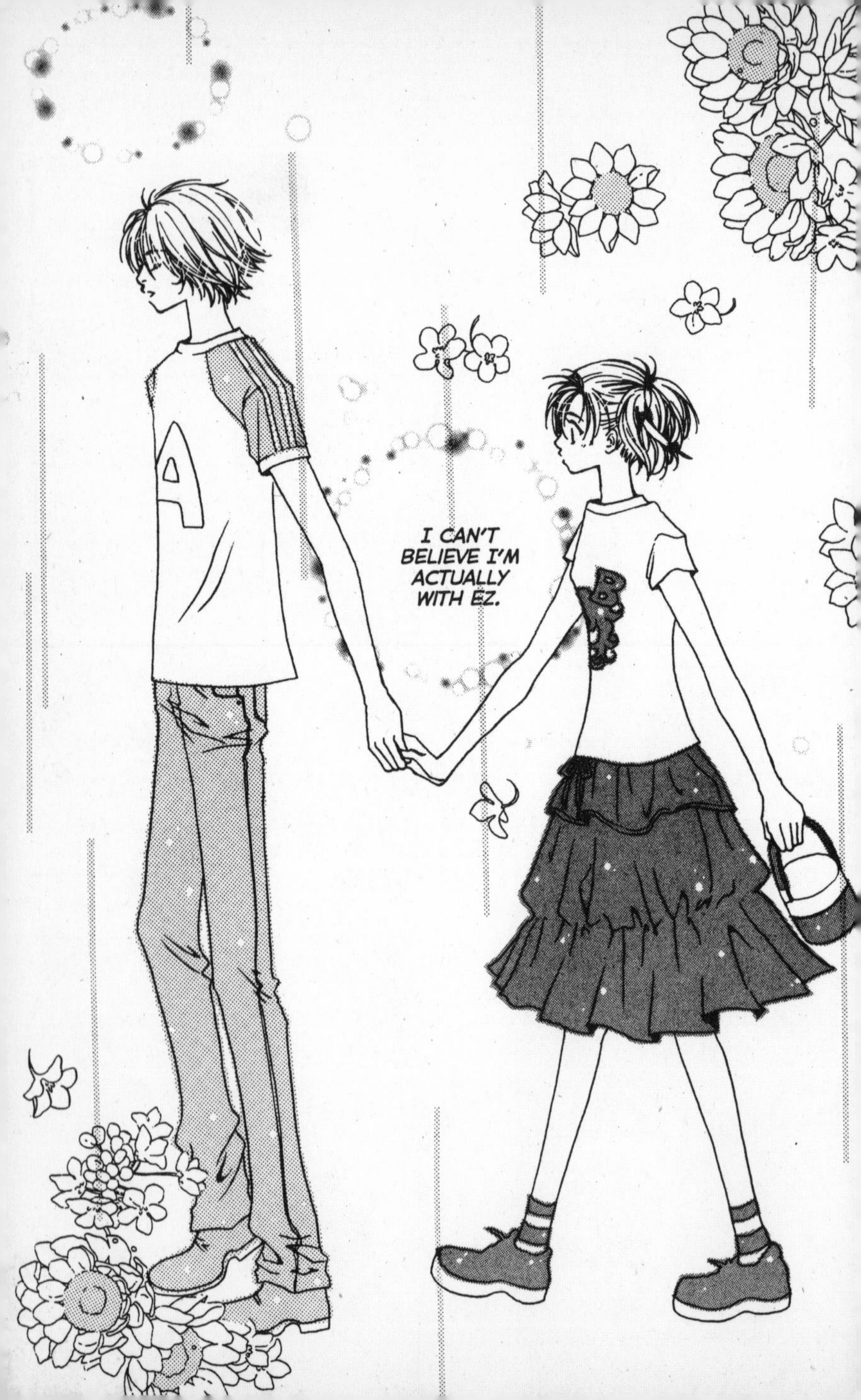
I CAN'T BELIEVE I'M ACTUALLY WITH EZ.

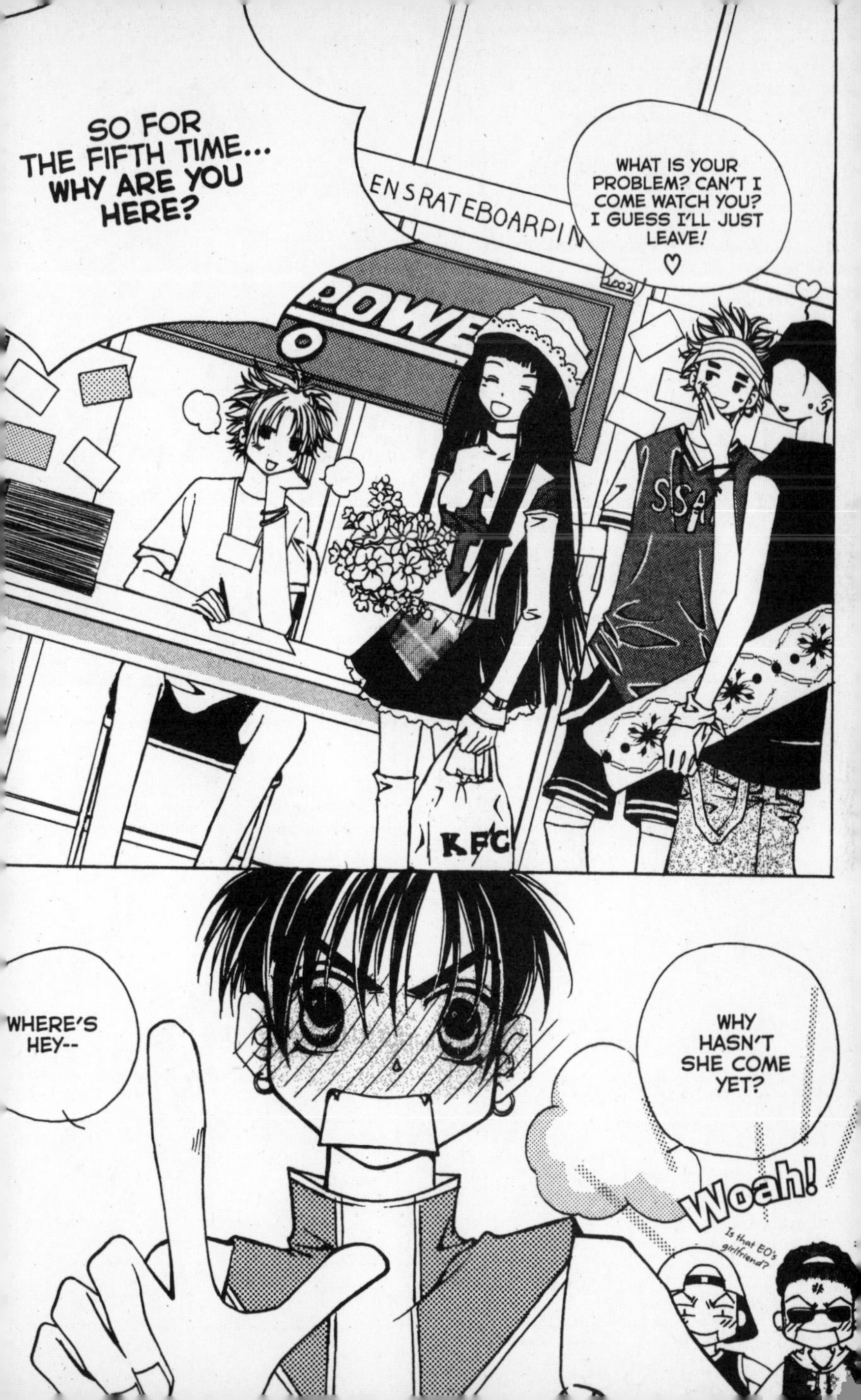
SO FOR THE FIFTH TIME... WHY ARE YOU HERE?
ENSRATEBOARPIN
POWE
WHAT IS YOUR PROBLEM? CAN'T I COME WATCH YOU? I GUESS I'LL JUST LEAVE! ♡
KFC
WHERE'S HEY--
WHY HASN'T SHE COME YET?
Woah!
Is that EO's girlfriend?

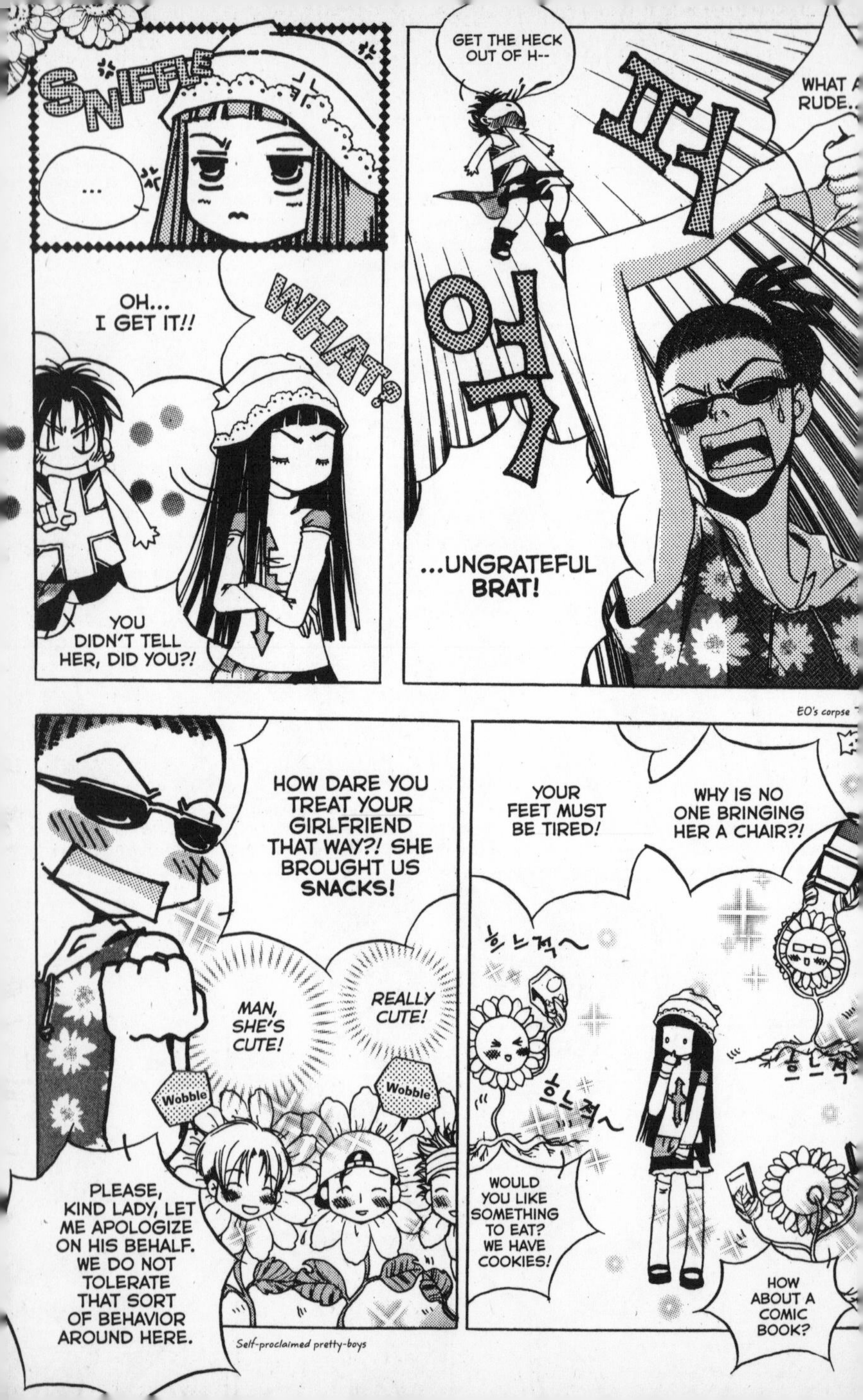
SNIFFLE
...
OH... I GET IT!!
WHAT?
YOU DIDN'T TELL HER, DID YOU?!
GET THE HECK OUT OF H--
퍽
WHAT A RUDE...
억
...UNGRATEFUL BRAT!
EO's corpse
HOW DARE YOU TREAT YOUR GIRLFRIEND THAT WAY?! SHE BROUGHT US SNACKS!
MAN, SHE'S CUTE!
REALLY CUTE!
Wobble
Wobble
PLEASE, KIND LADY, LET ME APOLOGIZE ON HIS BEHALF. WE DO NOT TOLERATE THAT SORT OF BEHAVIOR AROUND HERE.
Self-proclaimed pretty-boys
YOUR FEET MUST BE TIRED!
WHY IS NO ONE BRINGING HER A CHAIR?!
흐느적~
흐느적~
흐느적
WOULD YOU LIKE SOMETHING TO EAT? WE HAVE COOKIES!
HOW ABOUT A COMIC BOOK?

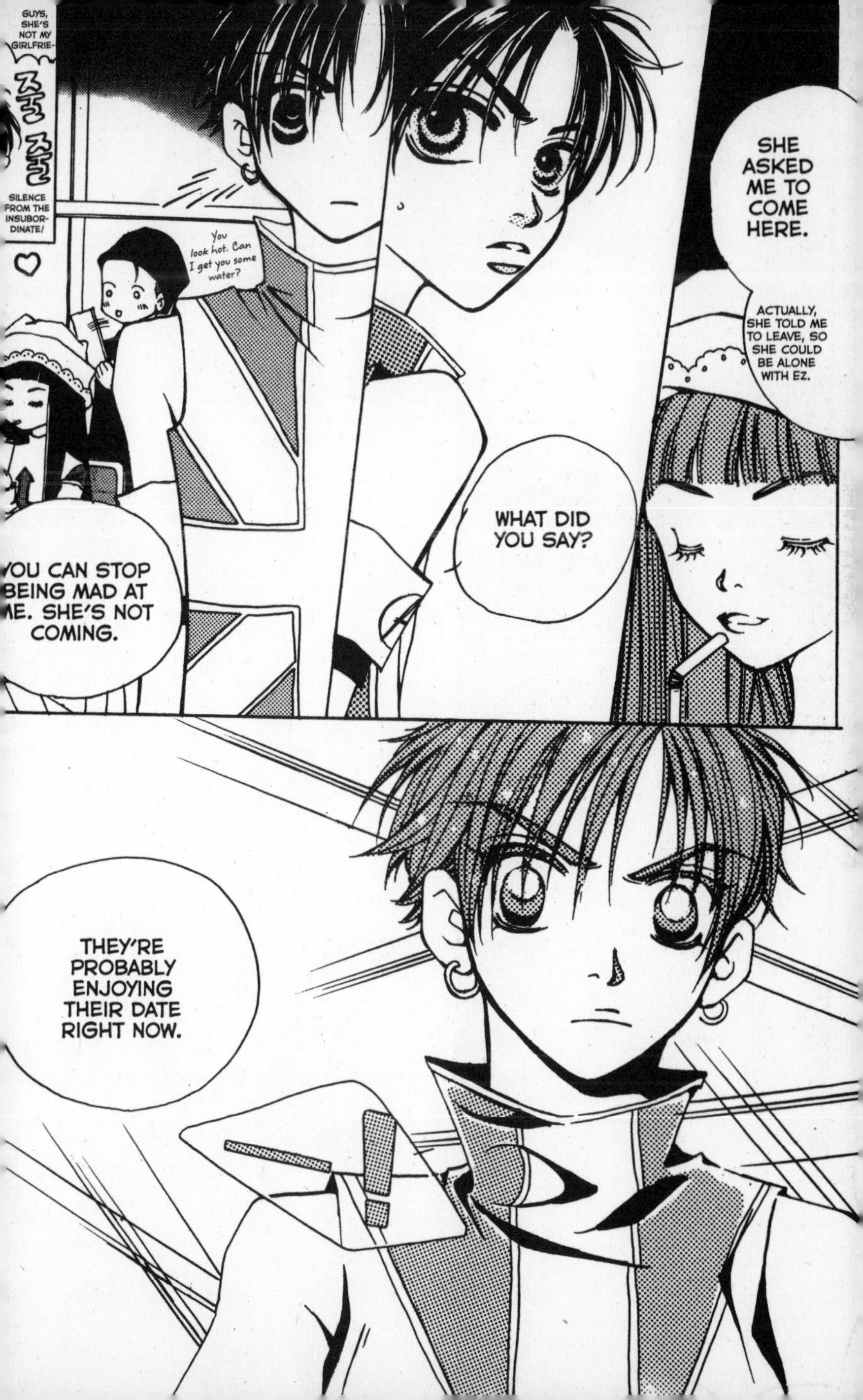
GUYS, SHE'S NOT MY GIRLFRIE-
SILENCE FROM THE INSUBORDINATE!
You look hot. Can I get you some water?
YOU CAN STOP BEING MAD AT ME. SHE'S NOT COMING.
WHAT DID YOU SAY?
SHE ASKED ME TO COME HERE.
ACTUALLY, SHE TOLD ME TO LEAVE, SO SHE COULD BE ALONE WITH EZ.
THEY'RE PROBABLY ENJOYING THEIR DATE RIGHT NOW.

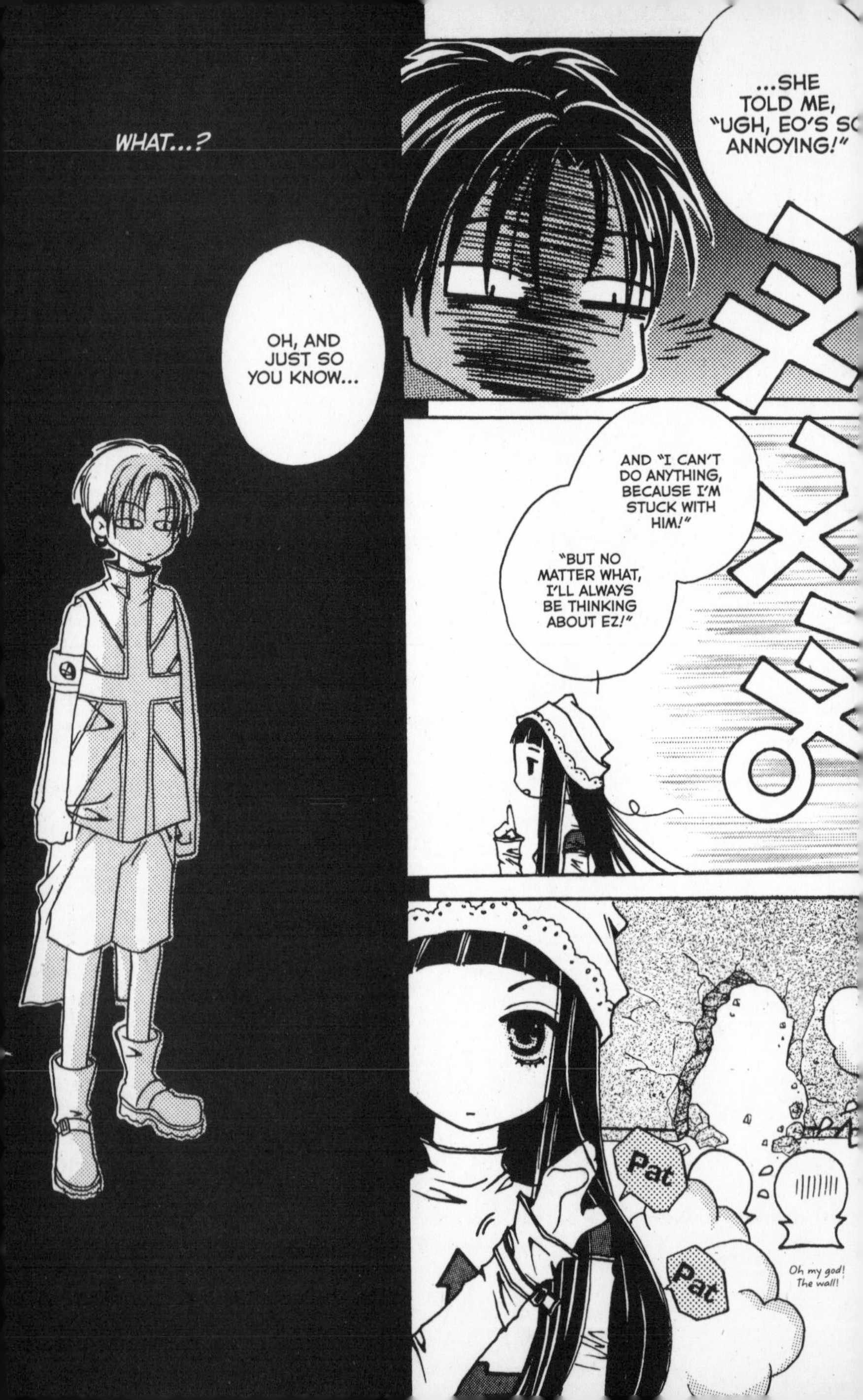
...SHE TOLD ME, "UGH, EO'S SO ANNOYING!"
AND "I CAN'T DO ANYTHING, BECAUSE I'M STUCK WITH HIM!"
"BUT NO MATTER WHAT, I'LL ALWAYS BE THINKING ABOUT EZ!"
Pat
Pat
Oh my god! The wall!
OH, AND JUST SO YOU KNOW...
WHAT...?

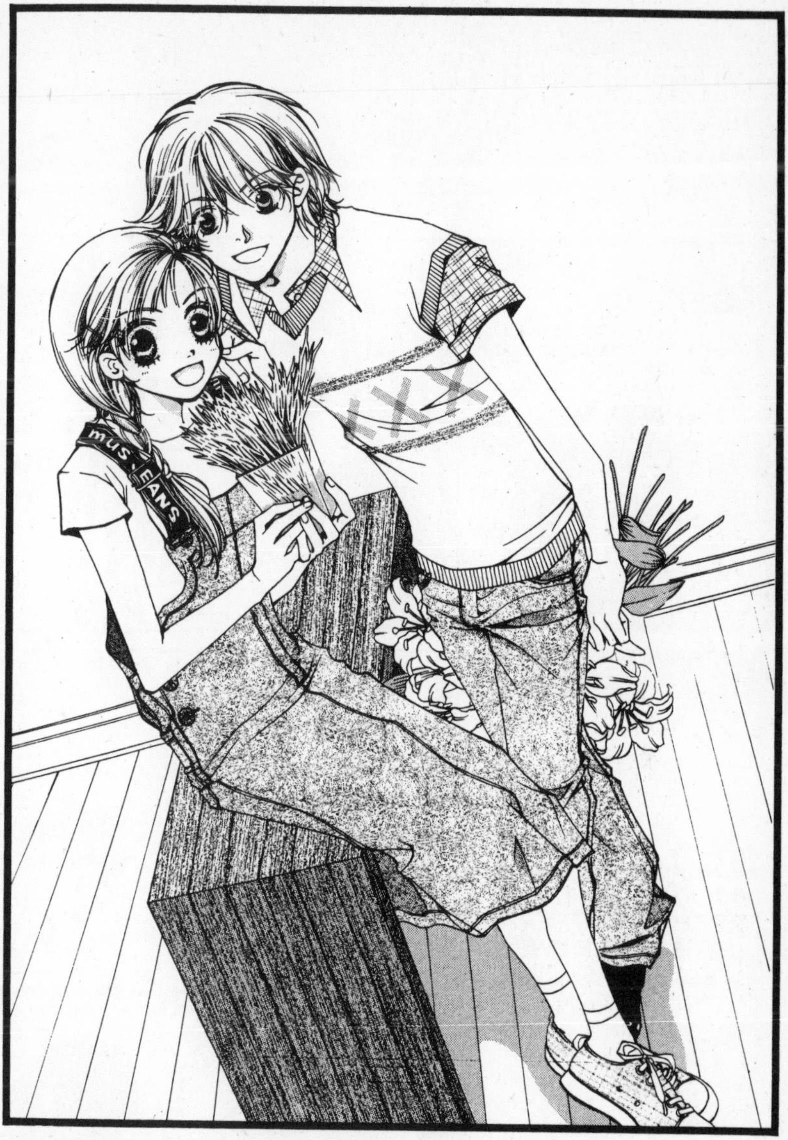
mus-JEANS

Chapter 2: Confession

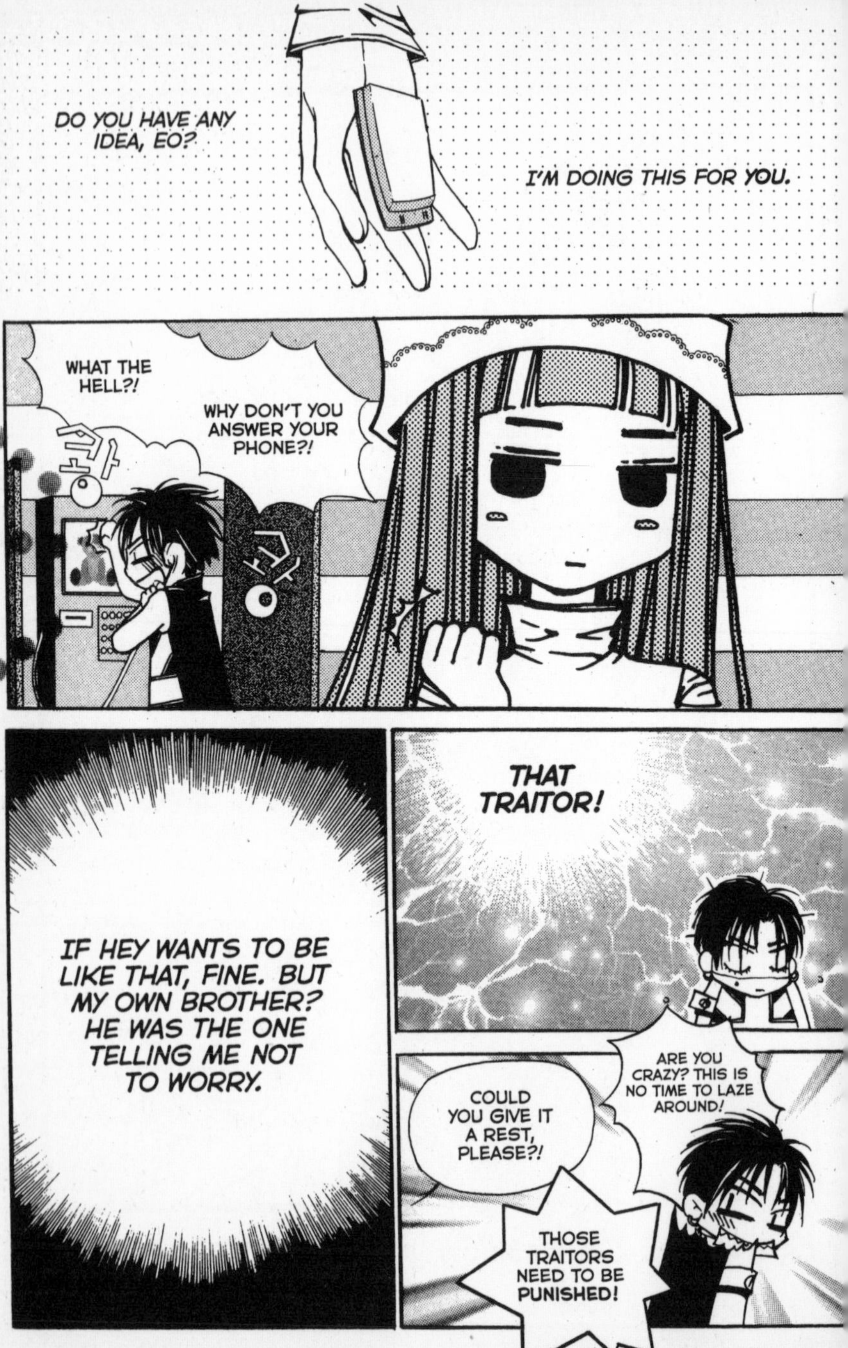
DO YOU HAVE ANY IDEA, EO?
I'M DOING THIS FOR YOU.
WHAT THE HELL?!
WHY DON'T YOU ANSWER YOUR PHONE?!
IF HEY WANTS TO BE LIKE THAT, FINE. BUT MY OWN BROTHER? HE WAS THE ONE TELLING ME NOT TO WORRY.
THAT TRAITOR!
COULD YOU GIVE IT A REST, PLEASE?!
ARE YOU CRAZY? THIS IS NO TIME TO LAZE AROUND!
THOSE TRAITORS NEED TO BE PUNISHED!

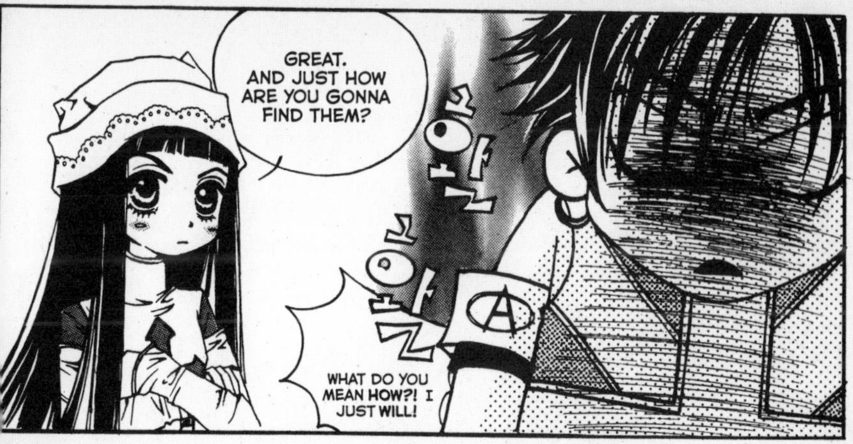
GREAT. AND JUST HOW ARE YOU GONNA FIND THEM?
WHAT DO YOU MEAN HOW?! I JUST WILL!

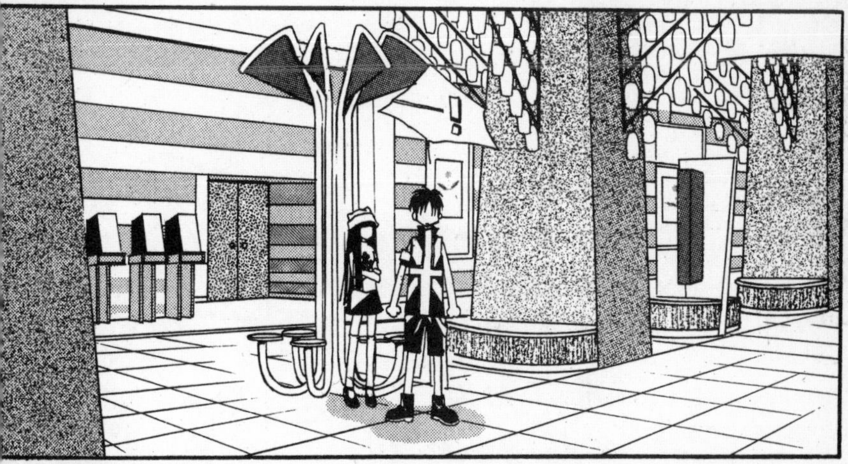
!

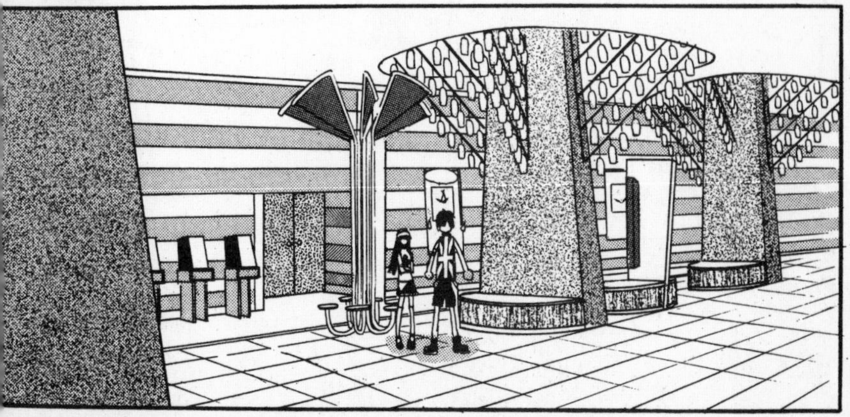

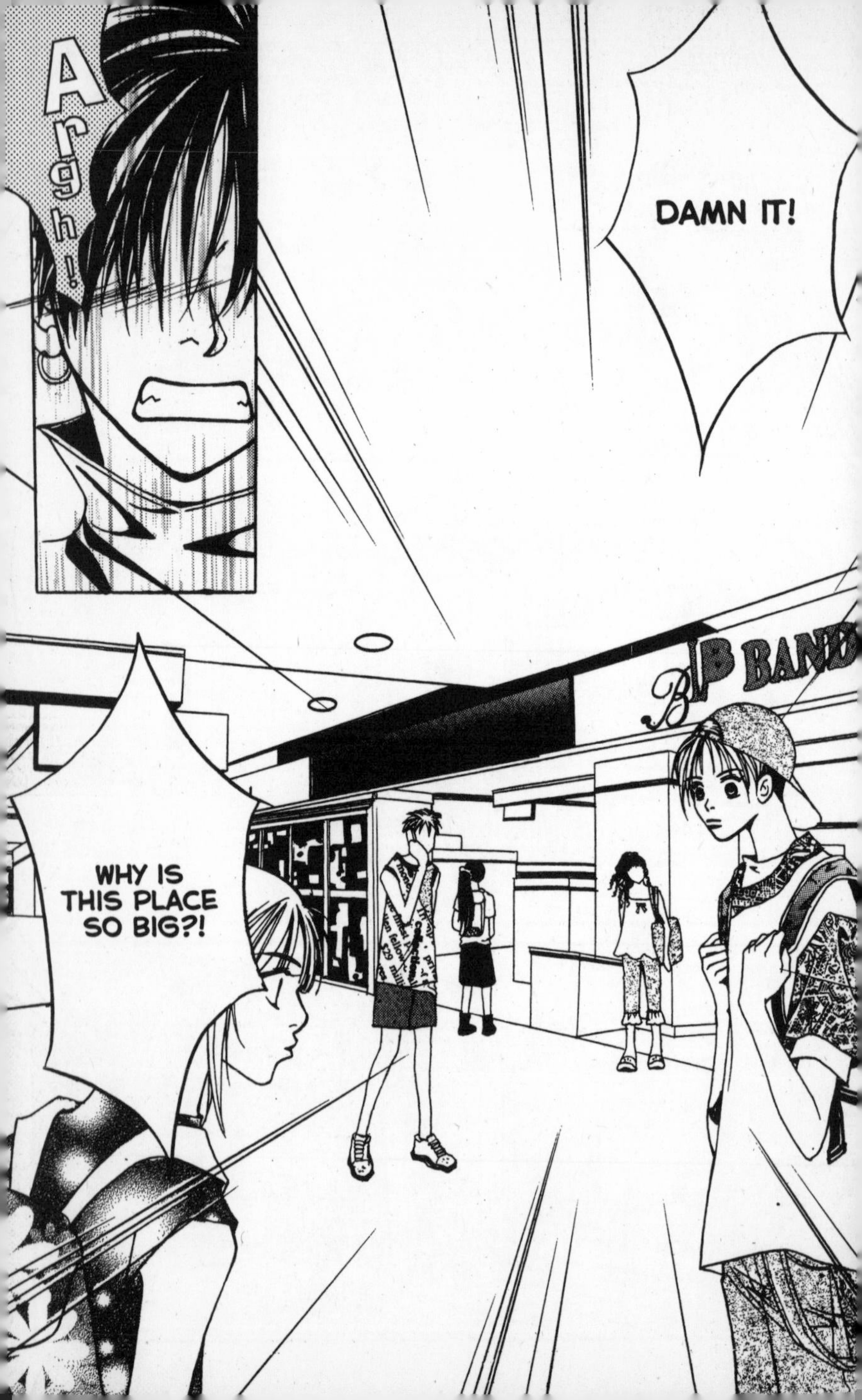
Argh!
DAMN IT!
BAND
WHY IS THIS PLACE SO BIG?!

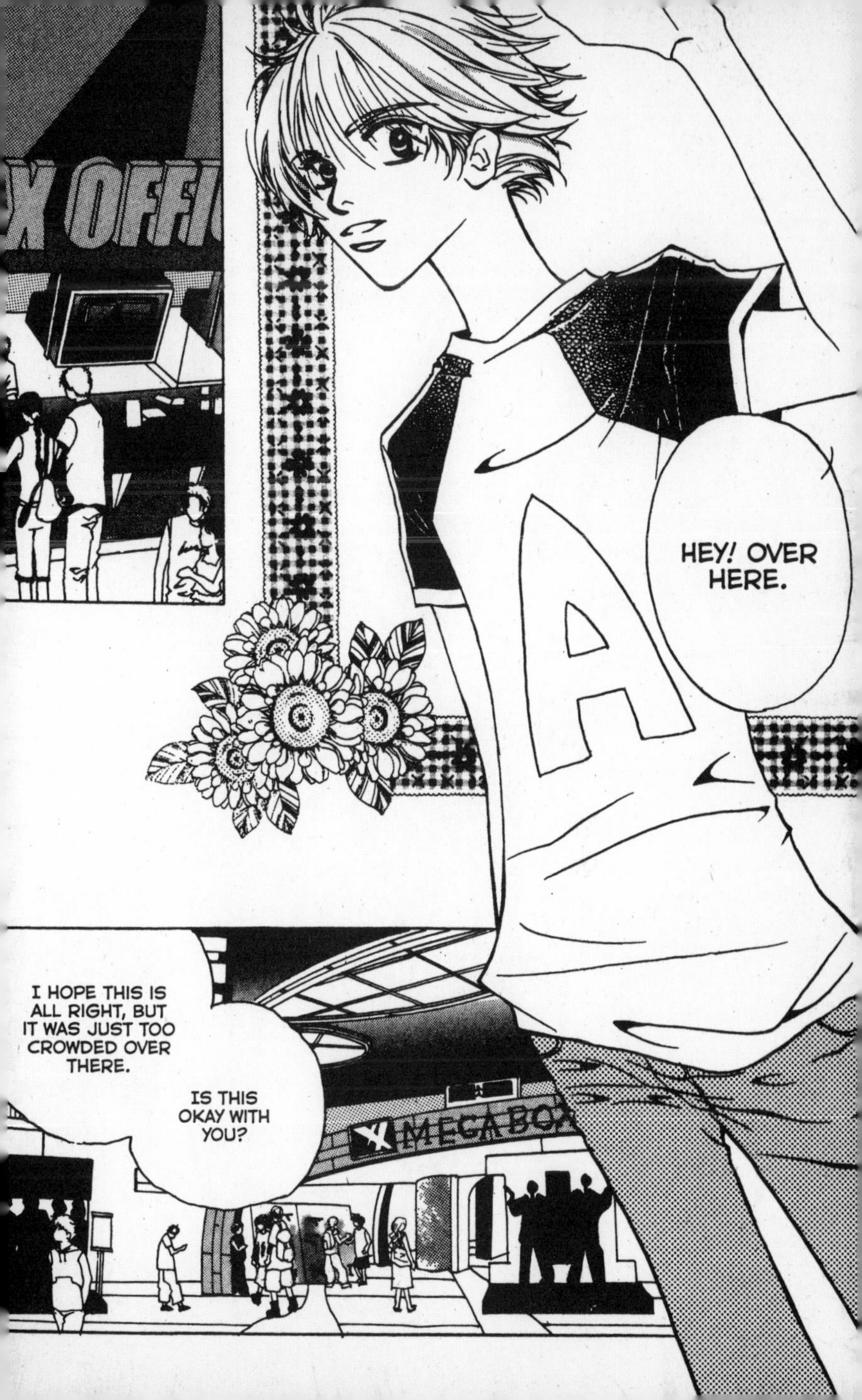
X OFFIC
HEY! OVER HERE.
I HOPE THIS IS ALL RIGHT, BUT IT WAS JUST TOO CROWDED OVER THERE.
IS THIS OKAY WITH YOU?
MEGA BOX

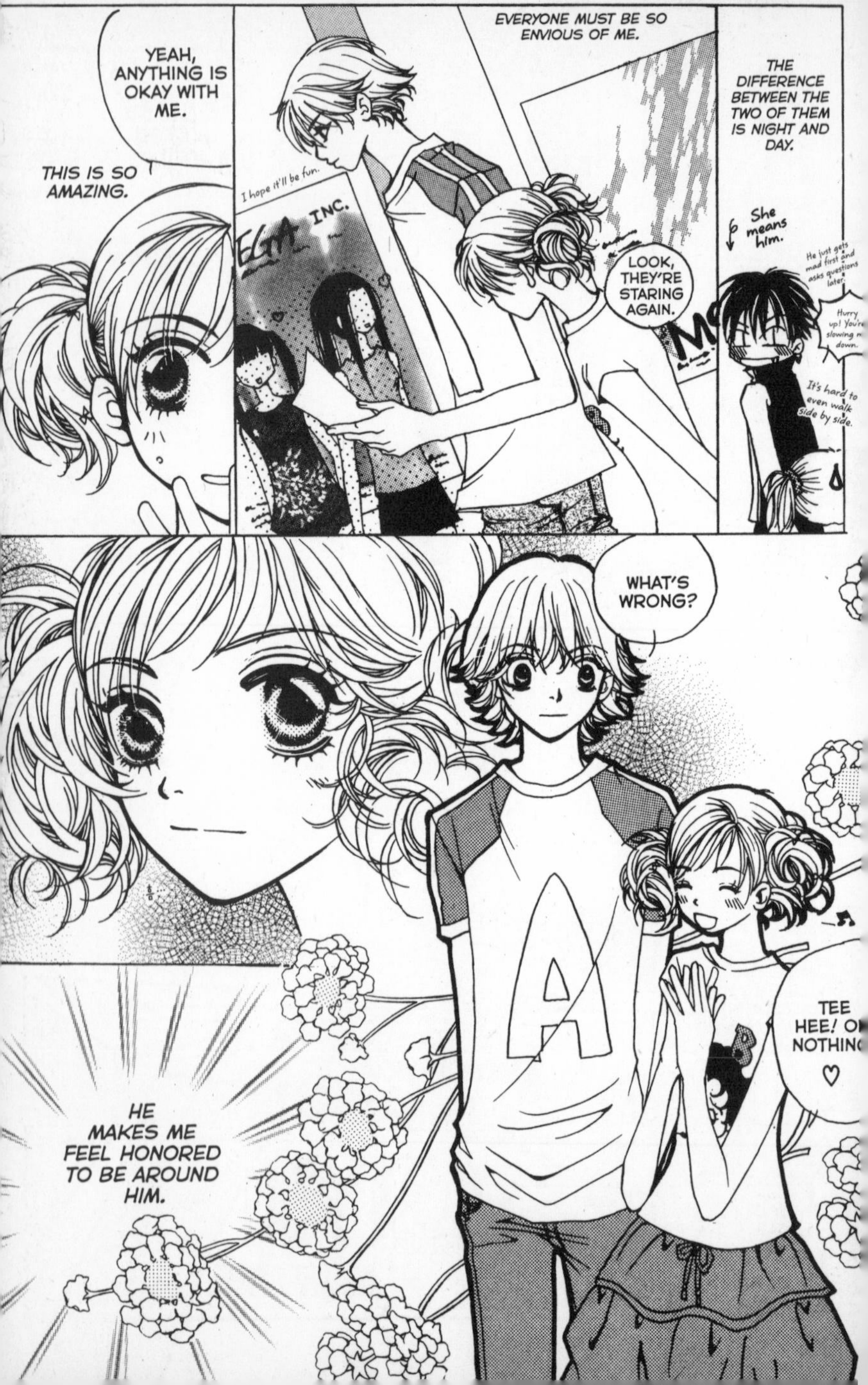

YEAH, ANYTHING IS OKAY WITH ME.
THIS IS SO AMAZING.
I hope it'll be fun.
EGTA INC.
EVERYONE MUST BE SO ENVIOUS OF ME.
LOOK, THEY'RE STARING AGAIN.
THE DIFFERENCE BETWEEN THE TWO OF THEM IS NIGHT AND DAY.
She means him.
He just gets mad first and asks questions later.
Hurry up! You're slowing m down.
It's hard to even walk side by side.
HE MAKES ME FEEL HONORED TO BE AROUND HIM.
WHAT'S WRONG?
TEE HEE! O NOTHIN ♡

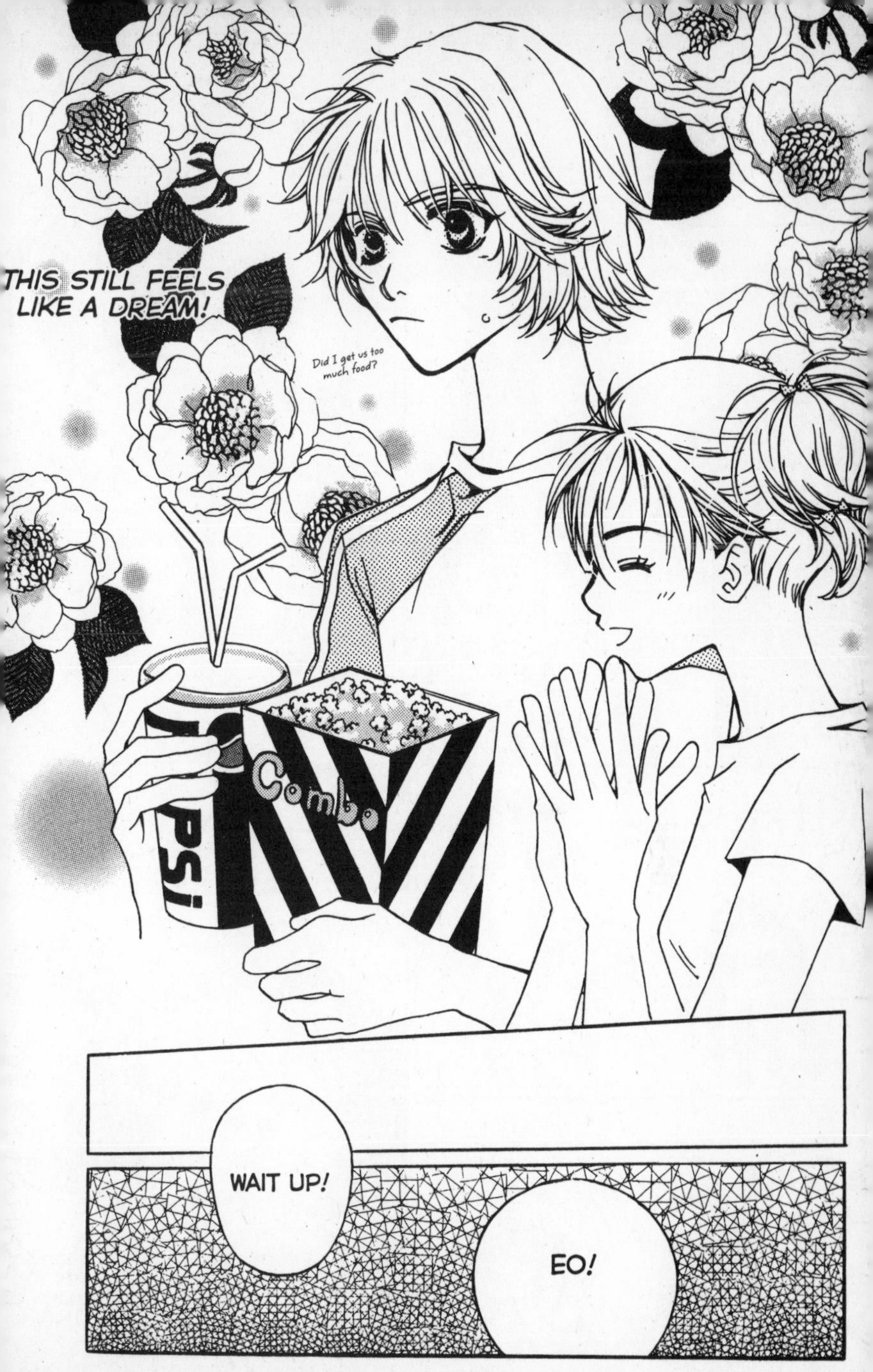
THIS STILL FEELS LIKE A DREAM!
Did I get us too much food?
WAIT UP!
EO!

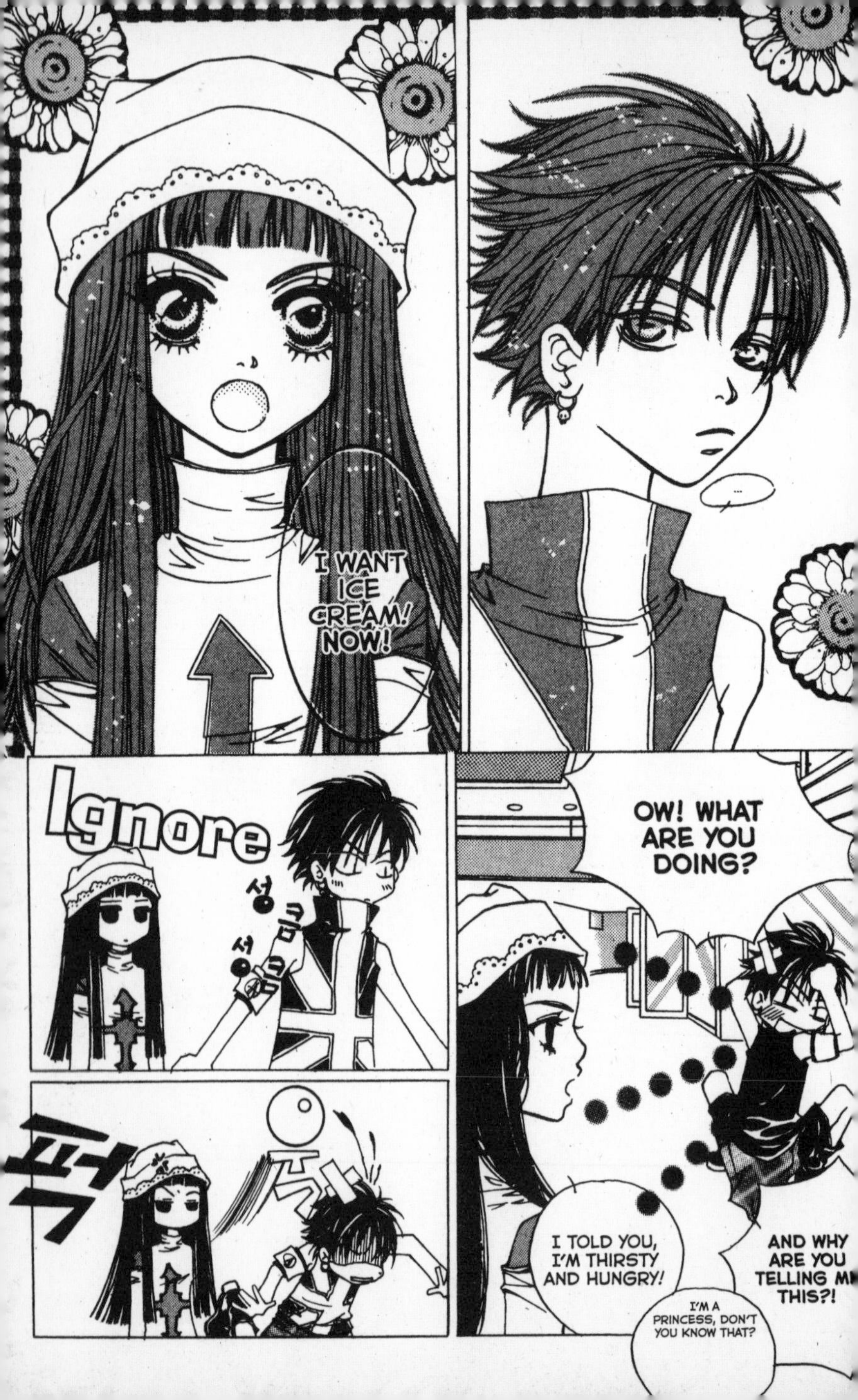
I WANT ICE CREAM! NOW!
...
Ignore
OW! WHAT ARE YOU DOING?
I TOLD YOU, I'M THIRSTY AND HUNGRY!
AND WHY ARE YOU TELLING M THIS?!
I'M A PRINCESS, DON'T YOU KNOW THAT?

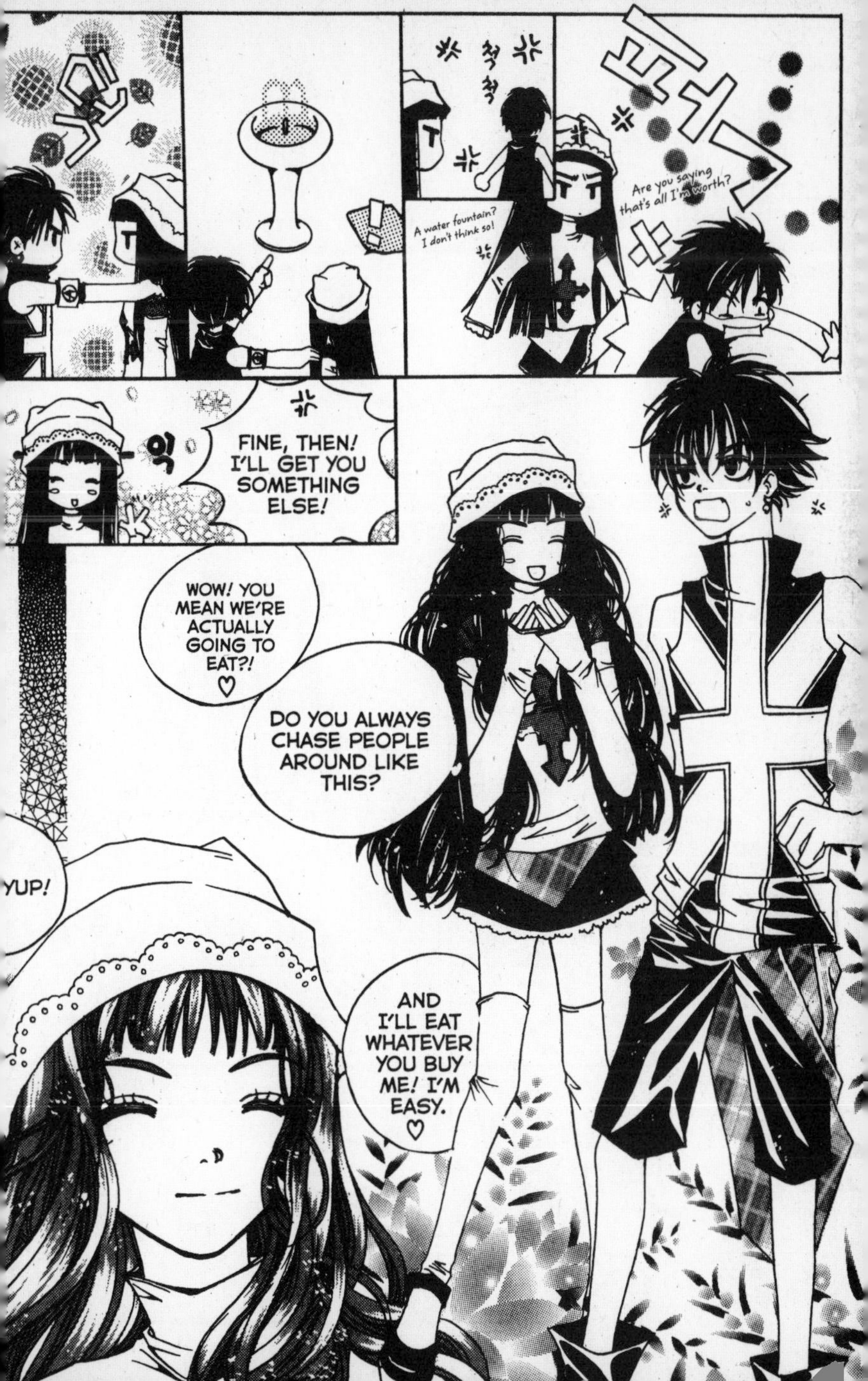
척
척
A water fountain? I don't think so!
Are you saying that's all I'm worth?
FINE, THEN! I'LL GET YOU SOMETHING ELSE!
WOW! YOU MEAN WE'RE ACTUALLY GOING TO EAT?! ♡
DO YOU ALWAYS CHASE PEOPLE AROUND LIKE THIS?
YUP!
AND I'LL EAT WHATEVER YOU BUY ME! I'M EASY. ♡

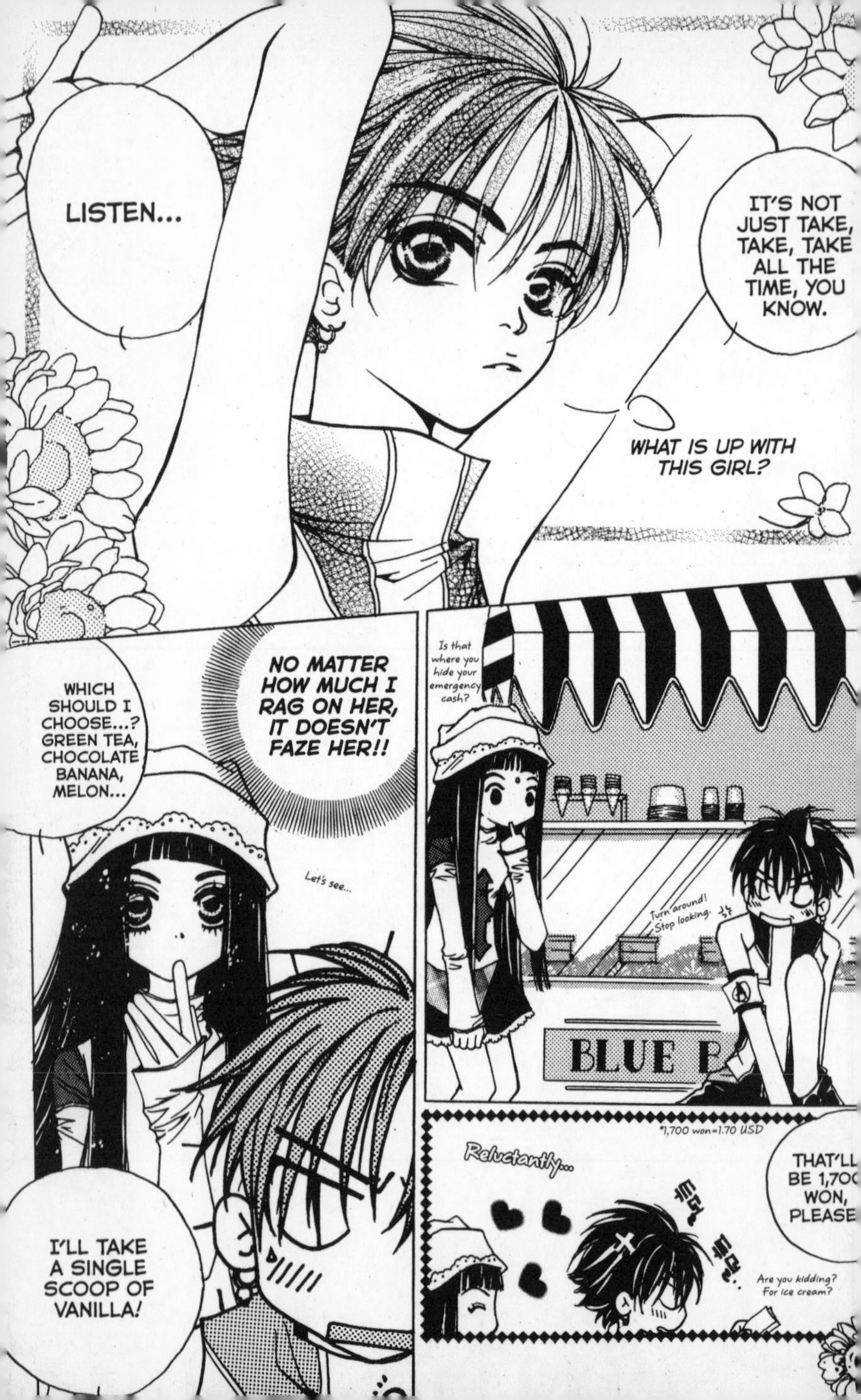
LISTEN...
IT'S NOT JUST TAKE, TAKE, TAKE ALL THE TIME, YOU KNOW.
WHAT IS UP WITH THIS GIRL?
WHICH SHOULD I CHOOSE...? GREEN TEA, CHOCOLATE BANANA, MELON...
NO MATTER HOW MUCH I RAG ON HER, IT DOESN'T FAZE HER!!
Let's see...
I'LL TAKE A SINGLE SCOOP OF VANILLA!
Is that where you hide your emergency cash?
Turn around! Stop looking.
BLUE B
*1,700 won=1.70 USD
Reluctantly...
THAT'LL BE 1,70 WON, PLEASE
Are you kidding? For ice cream?

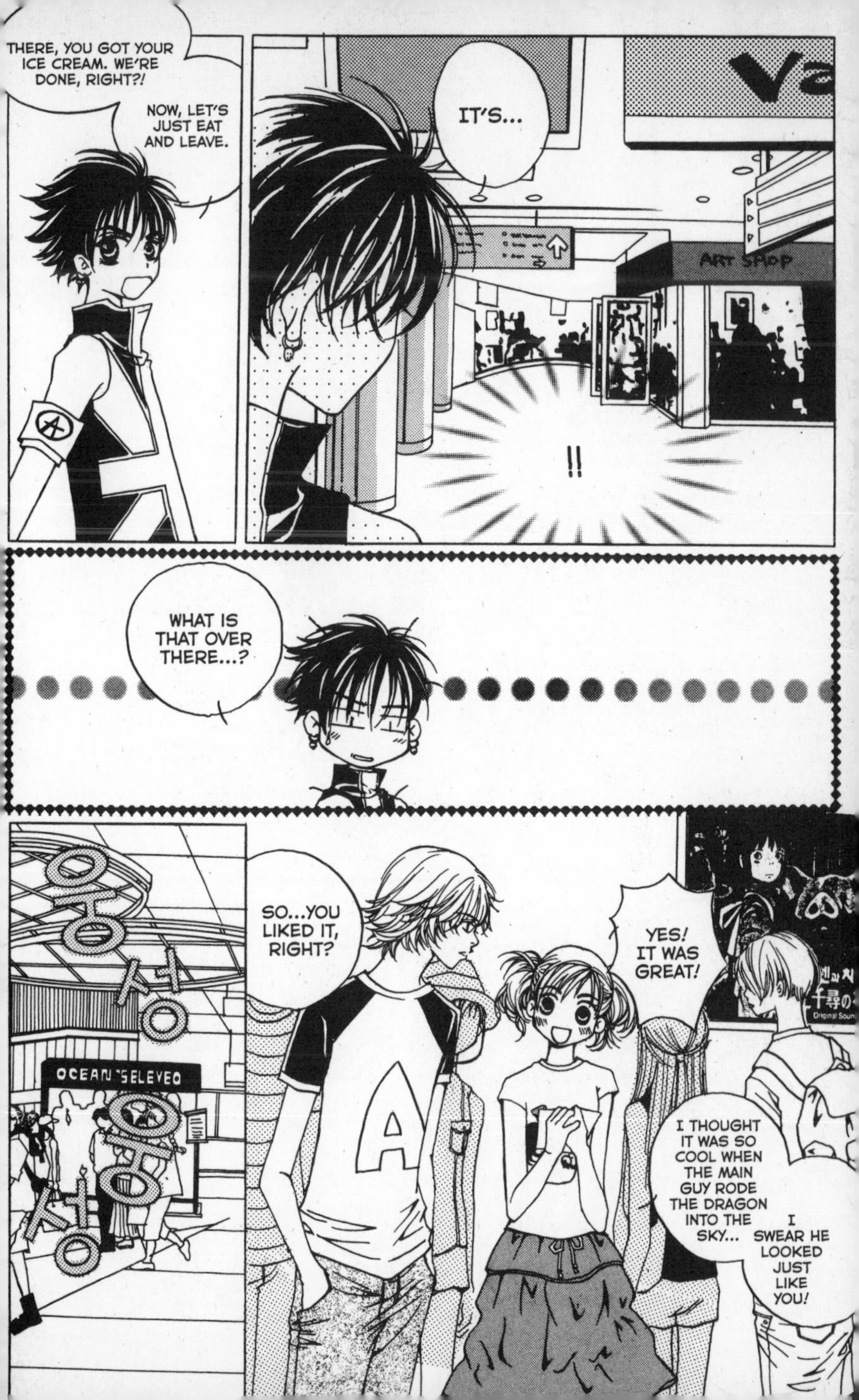
THERE, YOU GOT YOUR ICE CREAM. WE'RE DONE, RIGHT?!
NOW, LET'S JUST EAT AND LEAVE.
IT'S...
ART SHOP
!!
WHAT IS THAT OVER THERE...?
웅성
웅성
SO...YOU LIKED IT, RIGHT?
YES! IT WAS GREAT!
I THOUGHT IT WAS SO COOL WHEN THE MAIN GUY RODE THE DRAGON INTO THE SKY...
I SWEAR HE LOOKED JUST LIKE YOU!

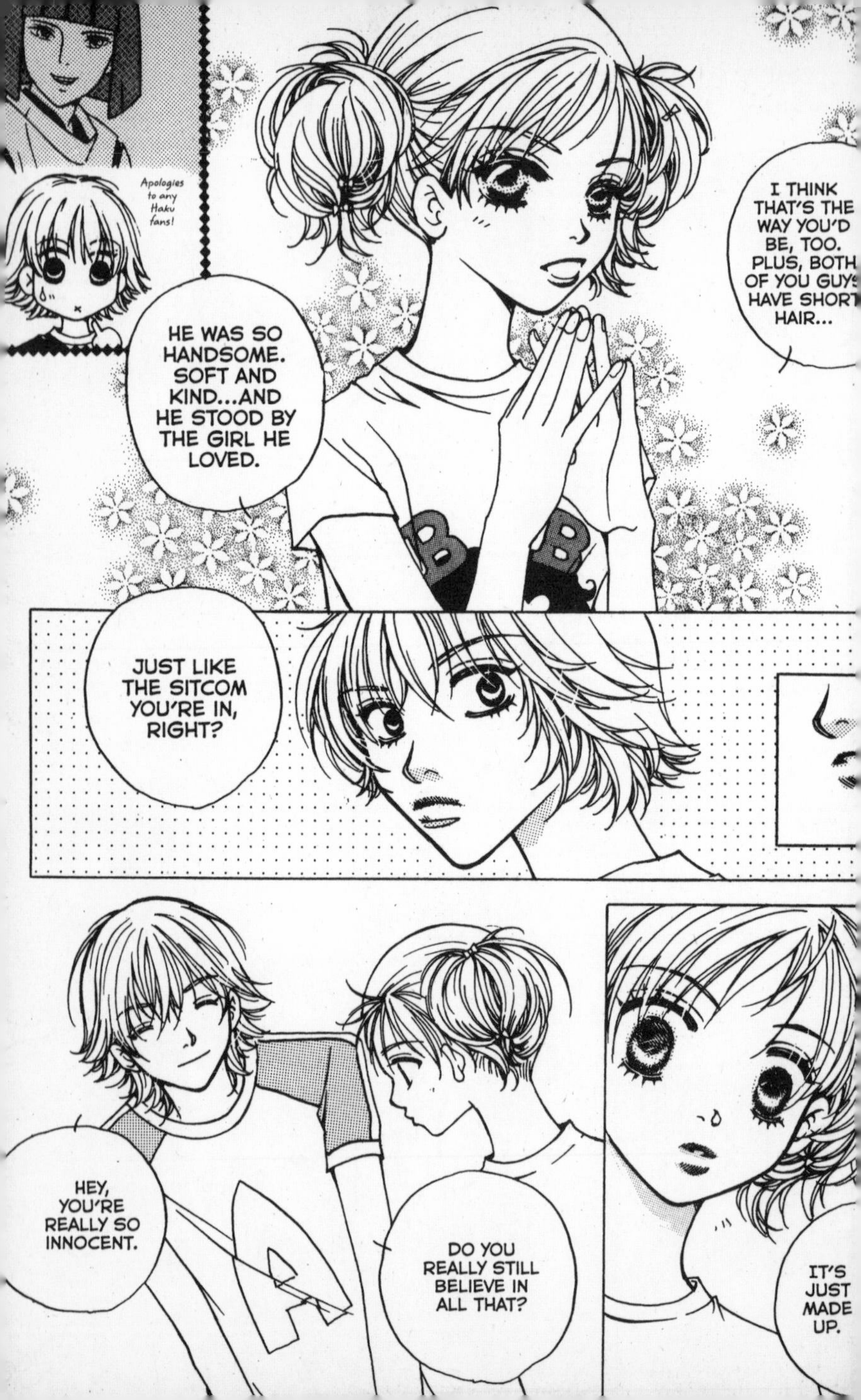

Apologies to any Haku fans!
HE WAS SO HANDSOME. SOFT AND KIND...AND HE STOOD BY THE GIRL HE LOVED.
I THINK THAT'S THE WAY YOU'D BE, TOO. PLUS, BOTH OF YOU GUYS HAVE SHORT HAIR...
JUST LIKE THE SITCOM YOU'RE IN, RIGHT?
HEY, YOU'RE REALLY SO INNOCENT.
DO YOU REALLY STILL BELIEVE IN ALL THAT?
IT'S JUST MADE UP.

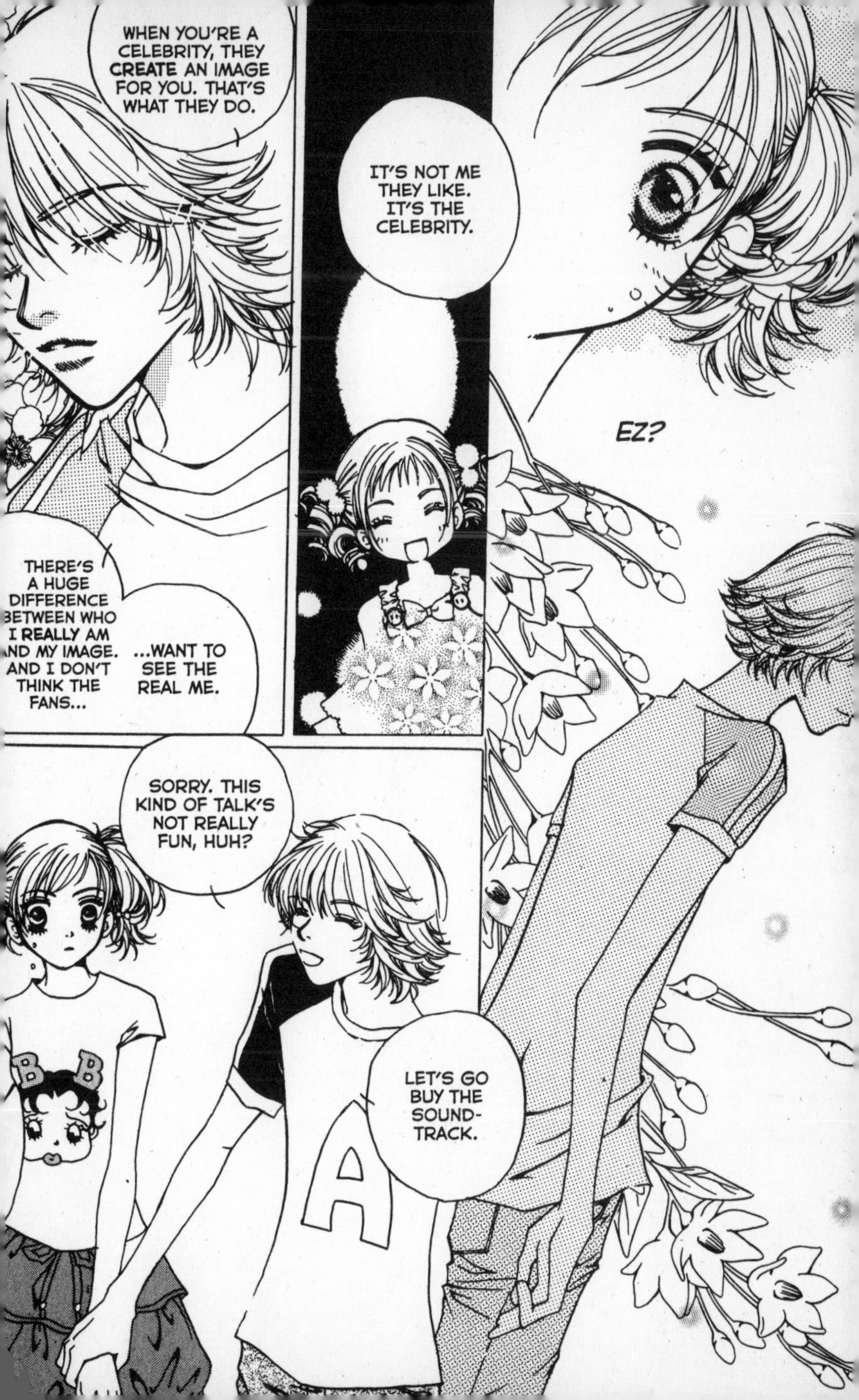
WHEN YOU'RE A CELEBRITY, THEY CREATE AN IMAGE FOR YOU. THAT'S WHAT THEY DO.
IT'S NOT ME THEY LIKE. IT'S THE CELEBRITY.
EZ?
THERE'S A HUGE DIFFERENCE BETWEEN WHO I REALLY AM AND MY IMAGE. AND I DON'T THINK THE FANS...
...WANT TO SEE THE REAL ME.
SORRY. THIS KIND OF TALK'S NOT REALLY FUN, HUH?
LET'S GO BUY THE SOUND-TRACK.

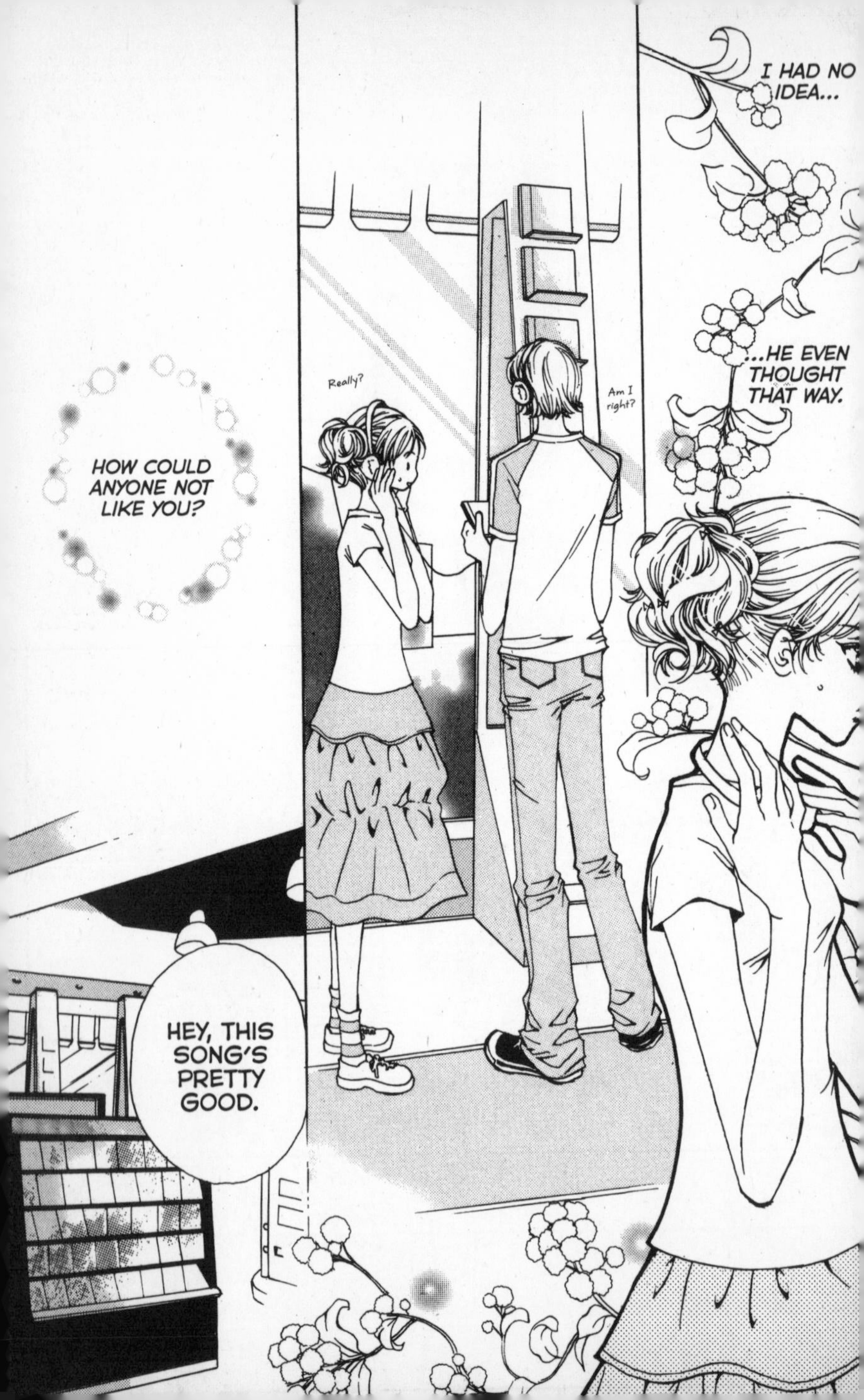

HOW COULD ANYONE NOT LIKE YOU?
HEY, THIS SONG'S PRETTY GOOD.
Really?
Am I right?
I HAD NO IDEA...
...HE EVEN THOUGHT THAT WAY.

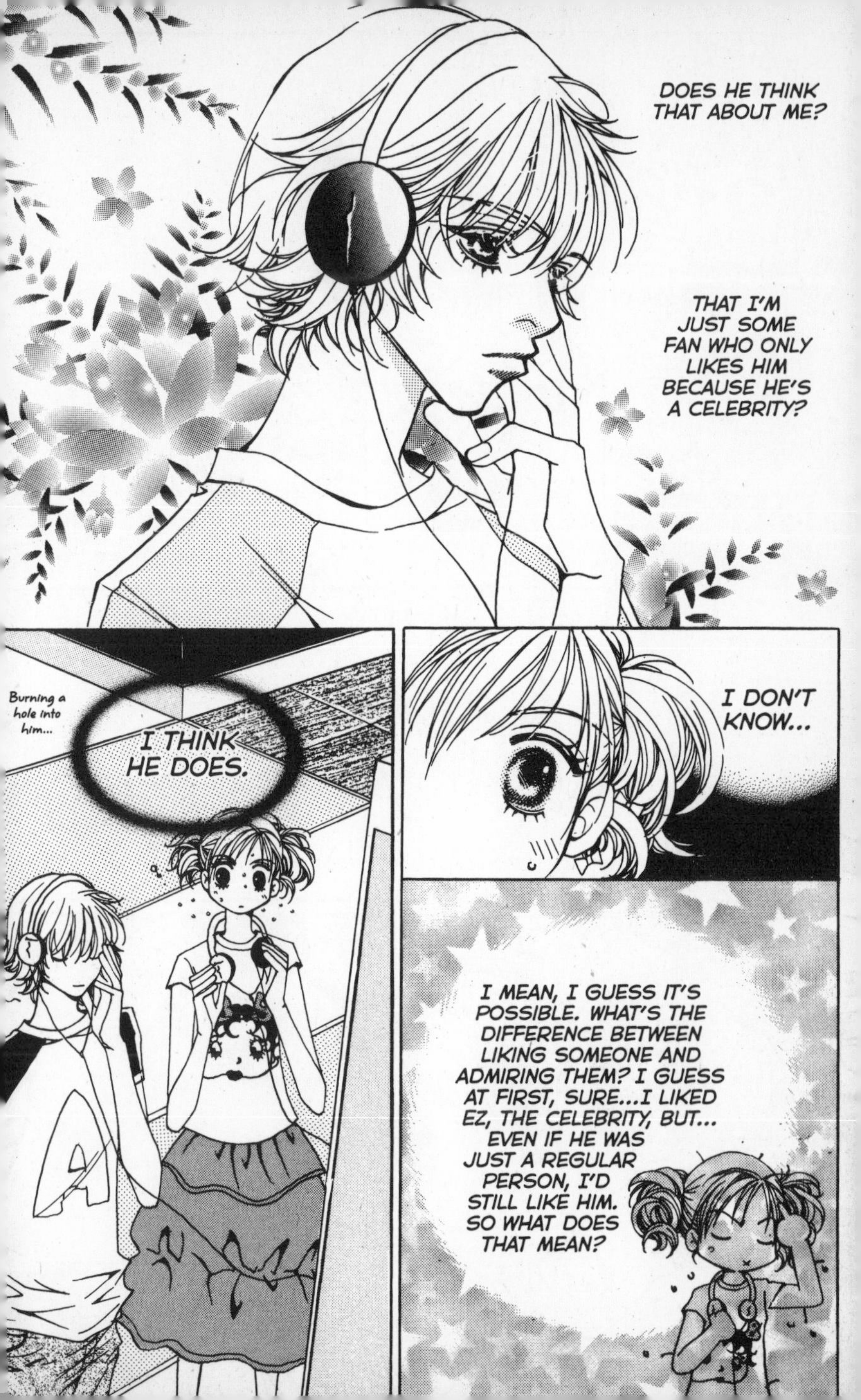
DOES HE THINK THAT ABOUT ME?
THAT I'M JUST SOME FAN WHO ONLY LIKES HIM BECAUSE HE'S A CELEBRITY?
Burning a hole into him...
I THINK HE DOES.
I DON'T KNOW...
I MEAN, I GUESS IT'S POSSIBLE. WHAT'S THE DIFFERENCE BETWEEN LIKING SOMEONE AND ADMIRING THEM? I GUESS AT FIRST, SURE...I LIKED EZ, THE CELEBRITY, BUT... EVEN IF HE WAS JUST A REGULAR PERSON, I'D STILL LIKE HIM. SO WHAT DOES THAT MEAN?

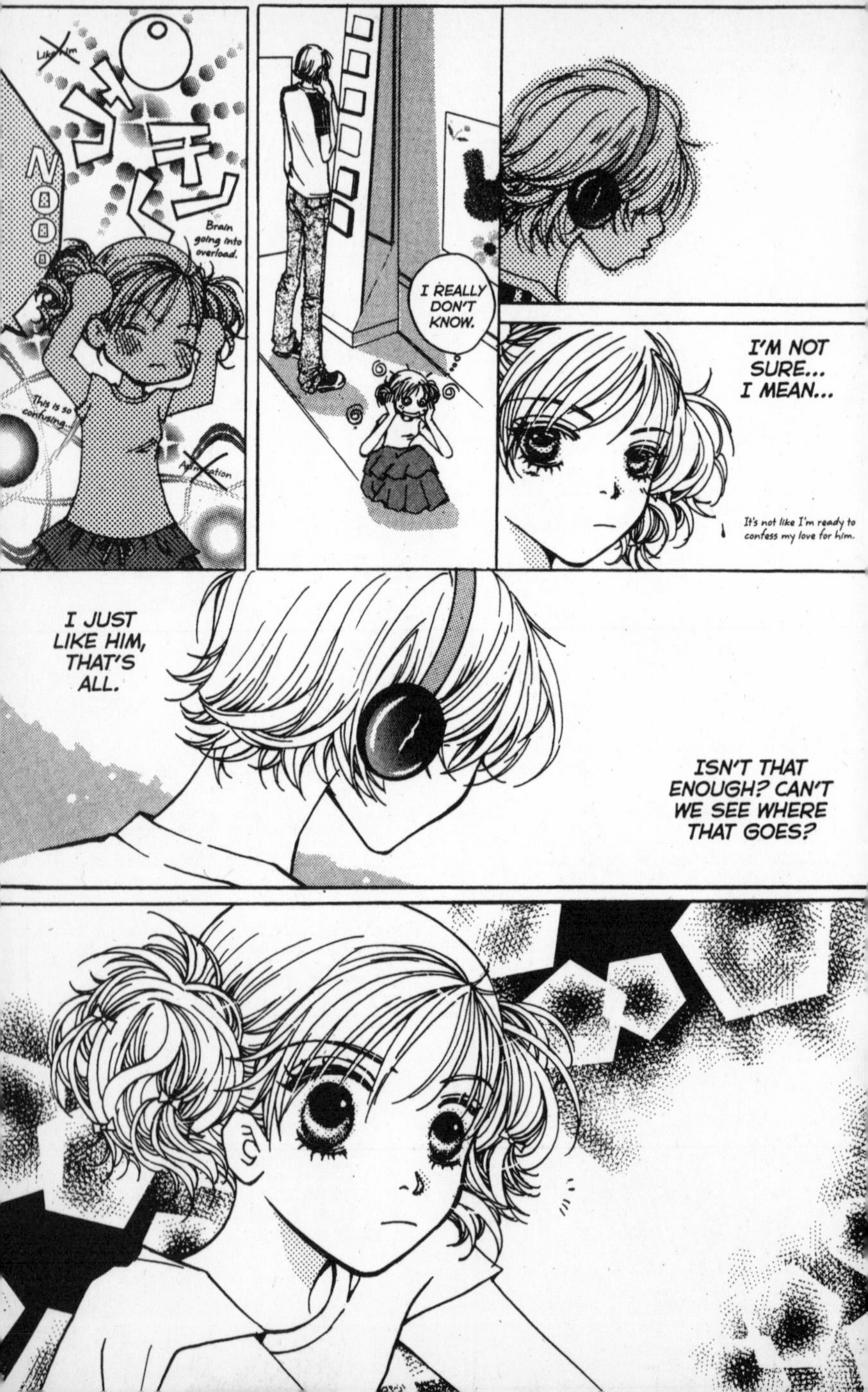

Like him
Brain going into overload.
This is so confusing...
Admiration
I REALLY DON'T KNOW.
I'M NOT SURE... I MEAN...
It's not like I'm ready to confess my love for him.
I JUST LIKE HIM, THAT'S ALL.
ISN'T THAT ENOUGH? CAN'T WE SEE WHERE THAT GOES?

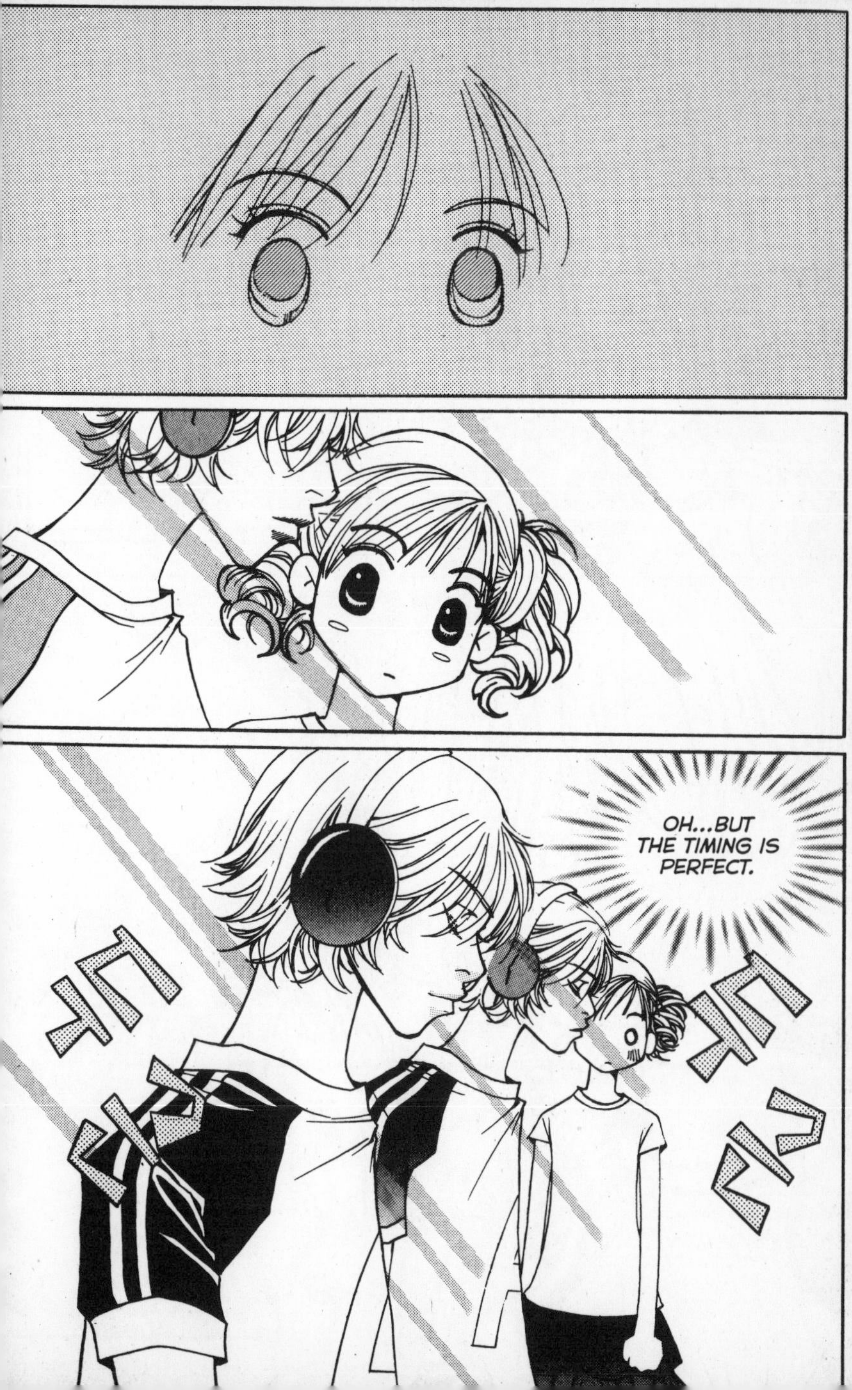
OH...BUT THE TIMING IS PERFECT.

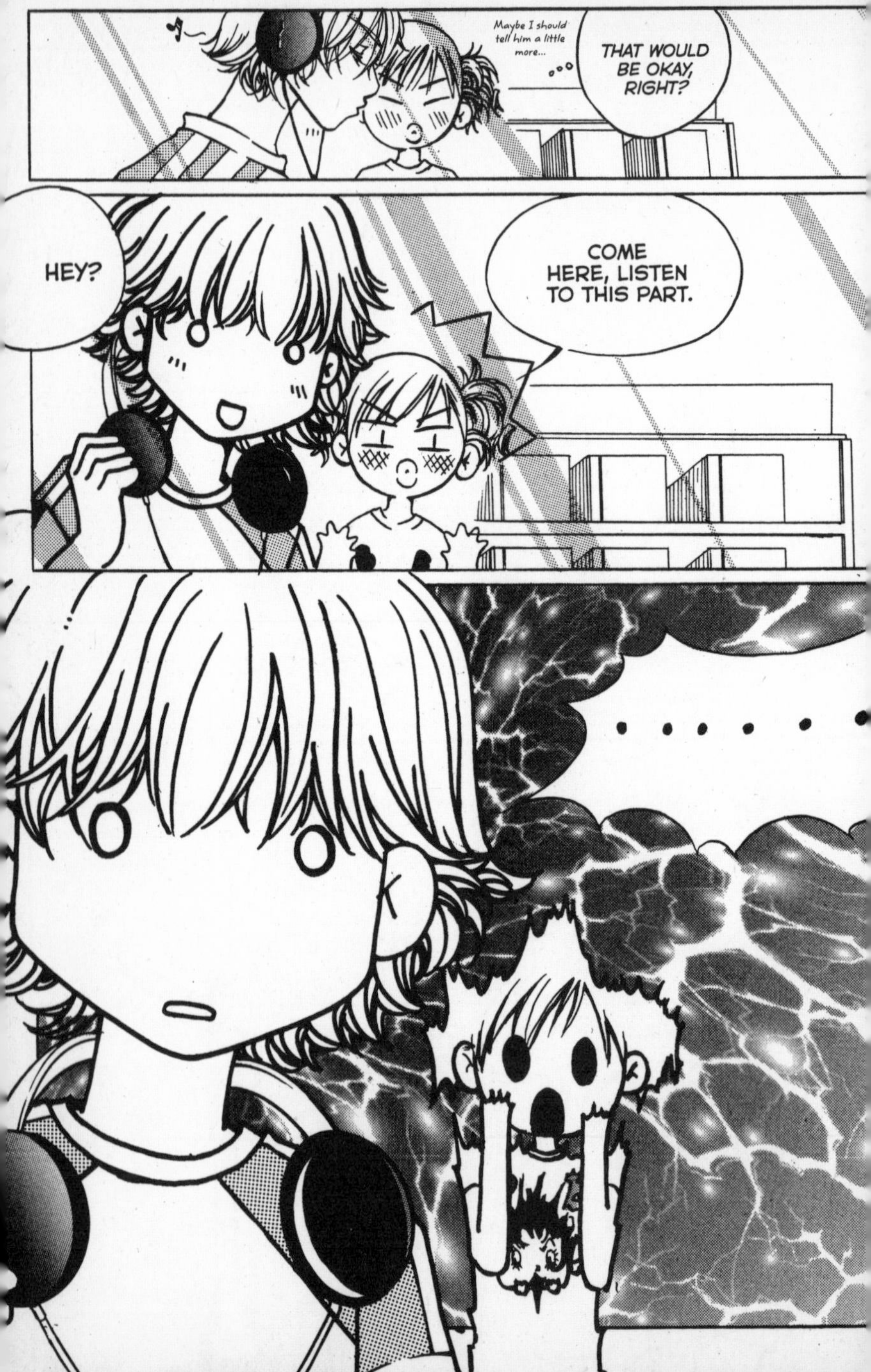
Maybe I should tell him a little more...
THAT WOULD BE OKAY, RIGHT?
HEY?
COME HERE, LISTEN TO THIS PART.
......

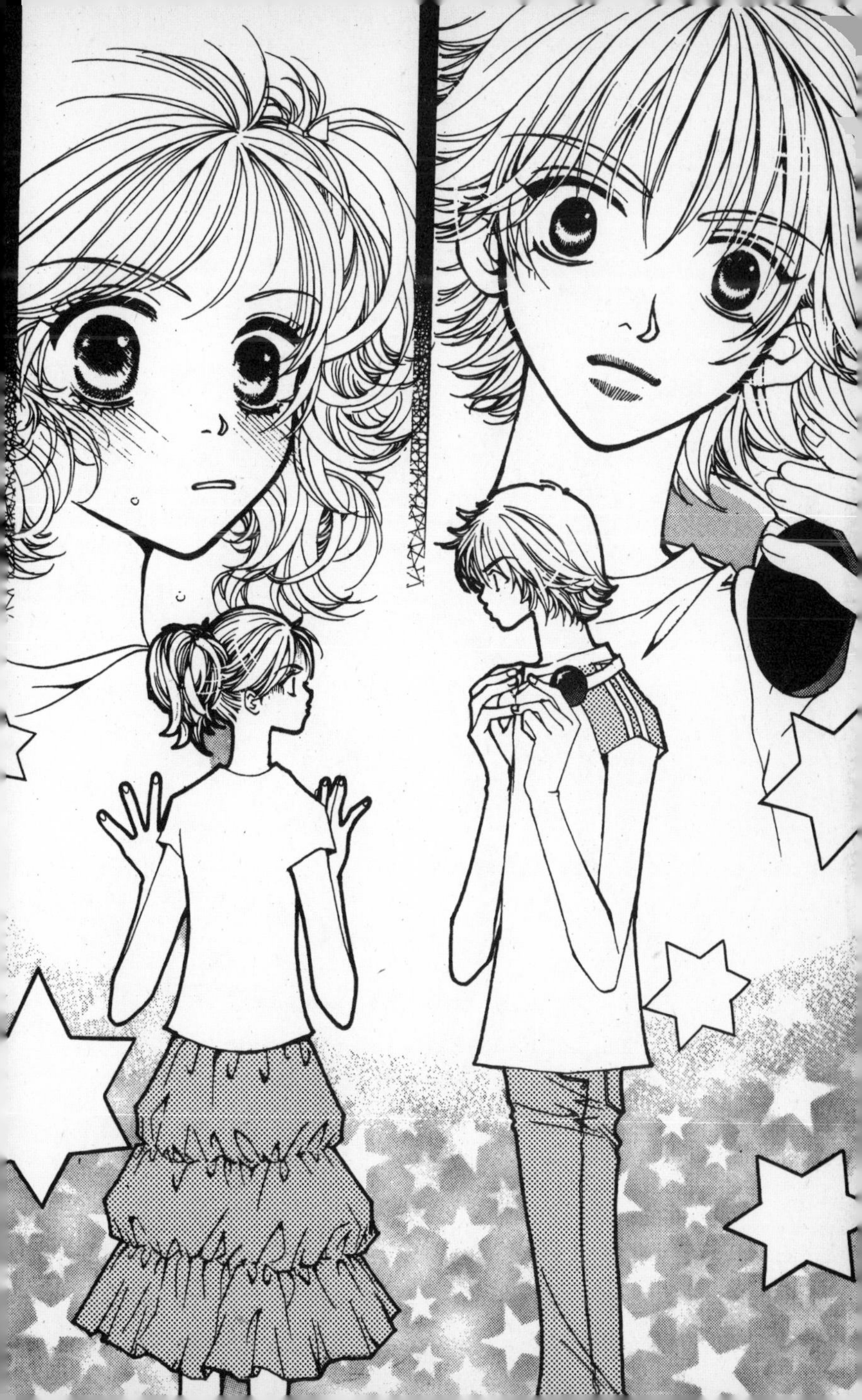

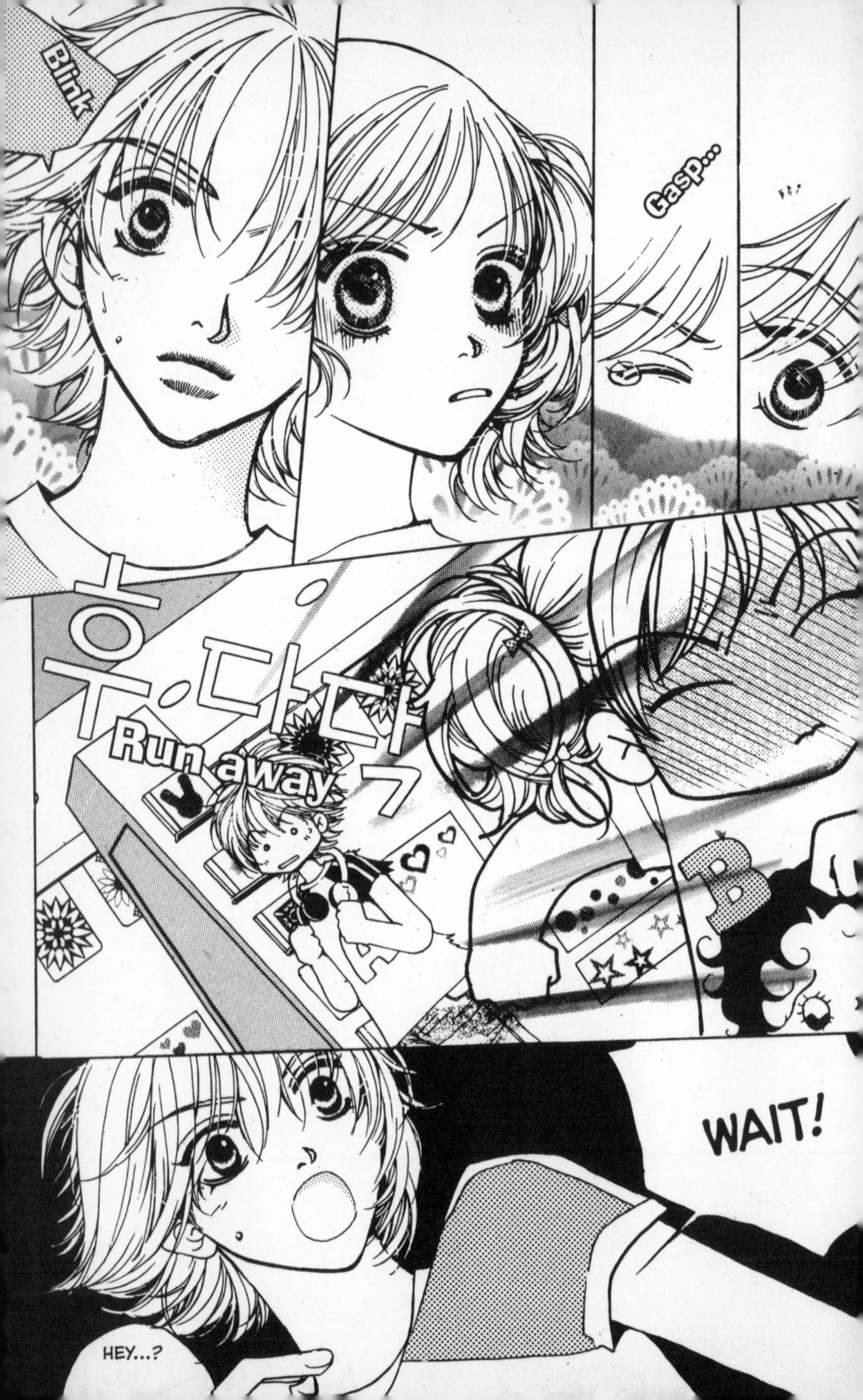

Blink
Gasp...
후다닥
Run away
WAIT!
HEY...?

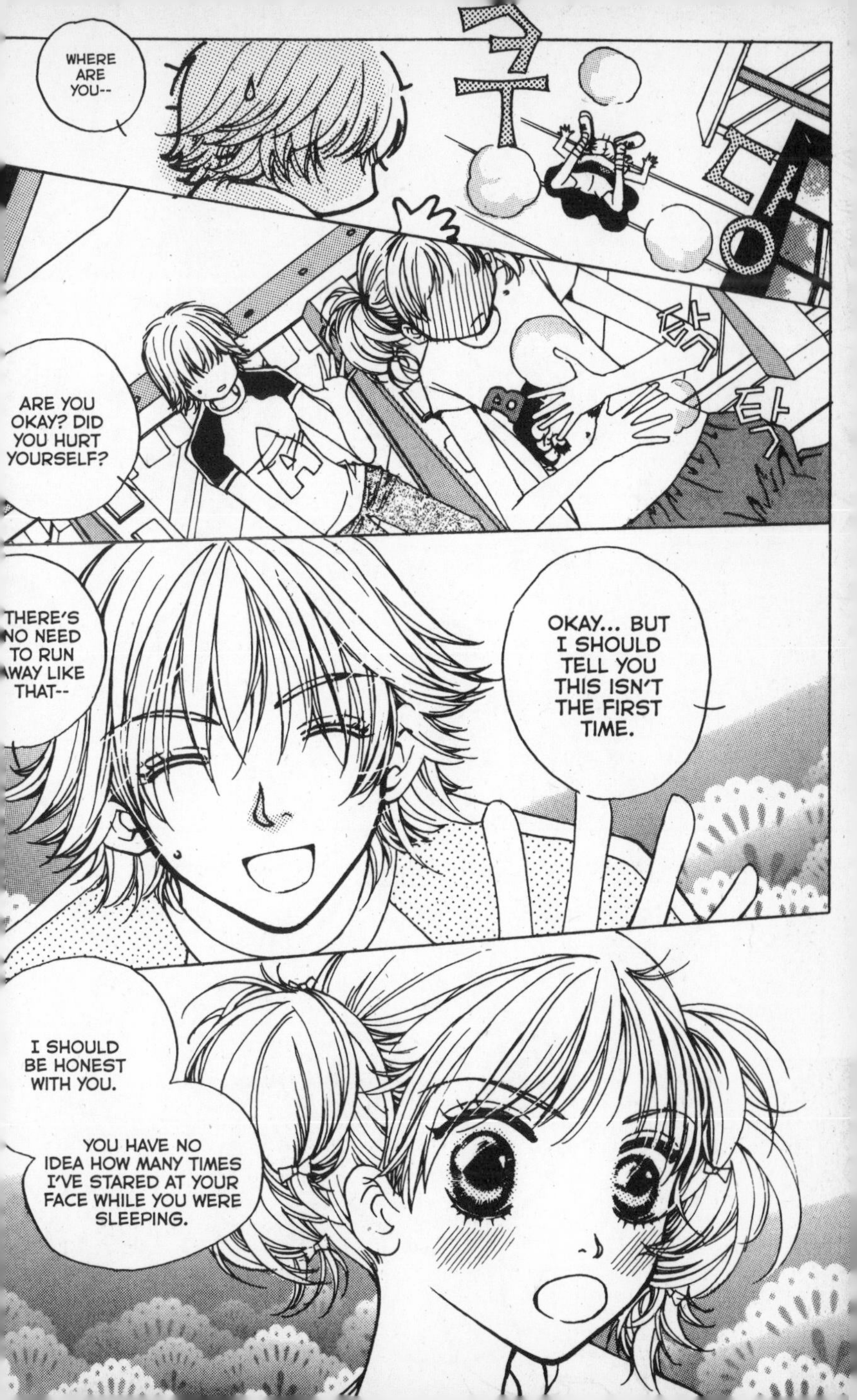
WHERE ARE YOU--
ARE YOU OKAY? DID YOU HURT YOURSELF?
THERE'S NO NEED TO RUN AWAY LIKE THAT--
OKAY... BUT I SHOULD TELL YOU THIS ISN'T THE FIRST TIME.
I SHOULD BE HONEST WITH YOU.
YOU HAVE NO IDEA HOW MANY TIMES I'VE STARED AT YOUR FACE WHILE YOU WERE SLEEPING.

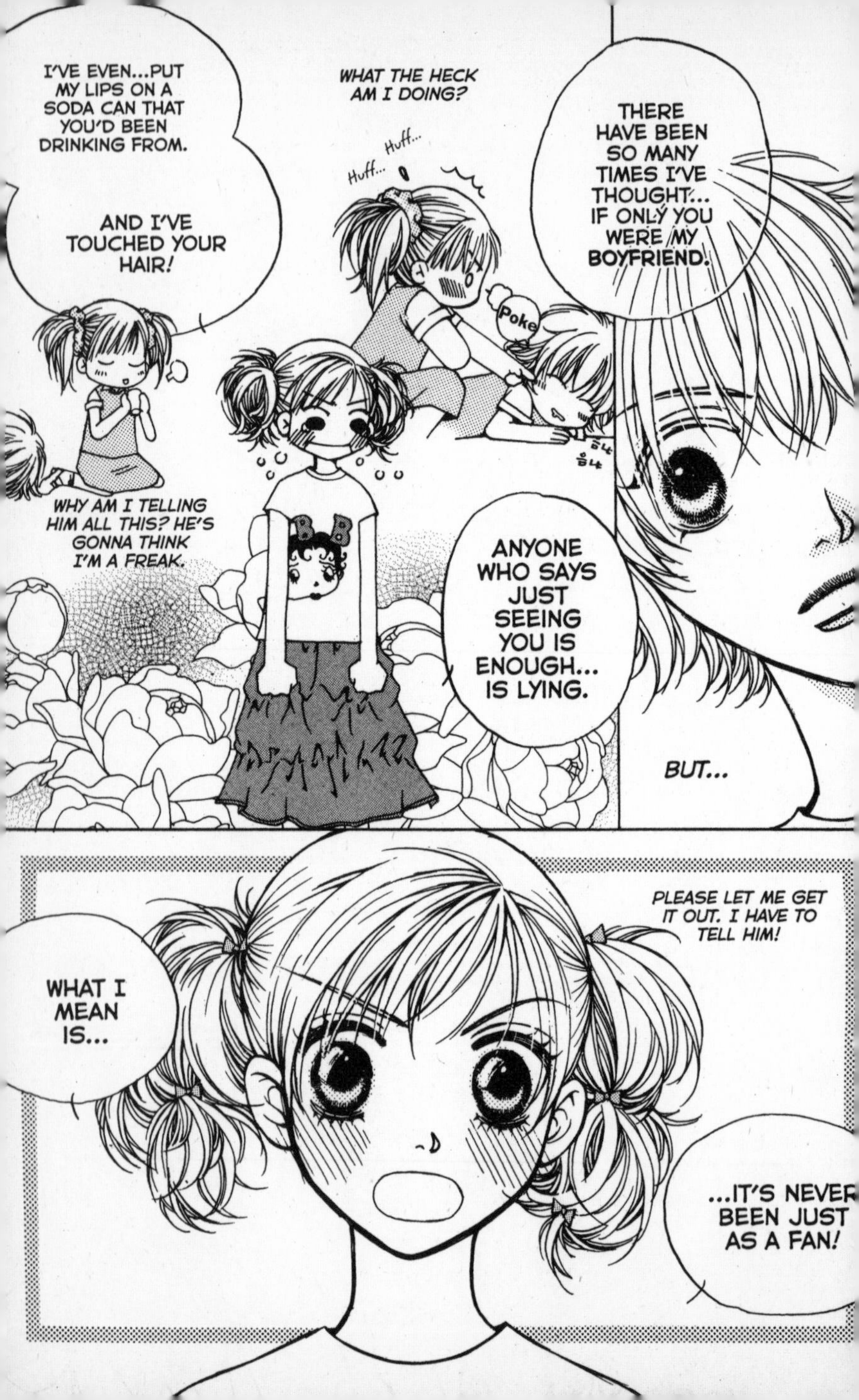
I'VE EVEN...PUT MY LIPS ON A SODA CAN THAT YOU'D BEEN DRINKING FROM.
AND I'VE TOUCHED YOUR HAIR!
WHAT THE HECK AM I DOING?
Huff... Huff...
Poke
WHY AM I TELLING HIM ALL THIS? HE'S GONNA THINK I'M A FREAK.
ANYONE WHO SAYS JUST SEEING YOU IS ENOUGH... IS LYING.
THERE HAVE BEEN SO MANY TIMES I'VE THOUGHT... IF ONLY YOU WERE MY BOYFRIEND.
BUT...
WHAT I MEAN IS...
PLEASE LET ME GET IT OUT. I HAVE TO TELL HIM!
...IT'S NEVER BEEN JUST AS A FAN!

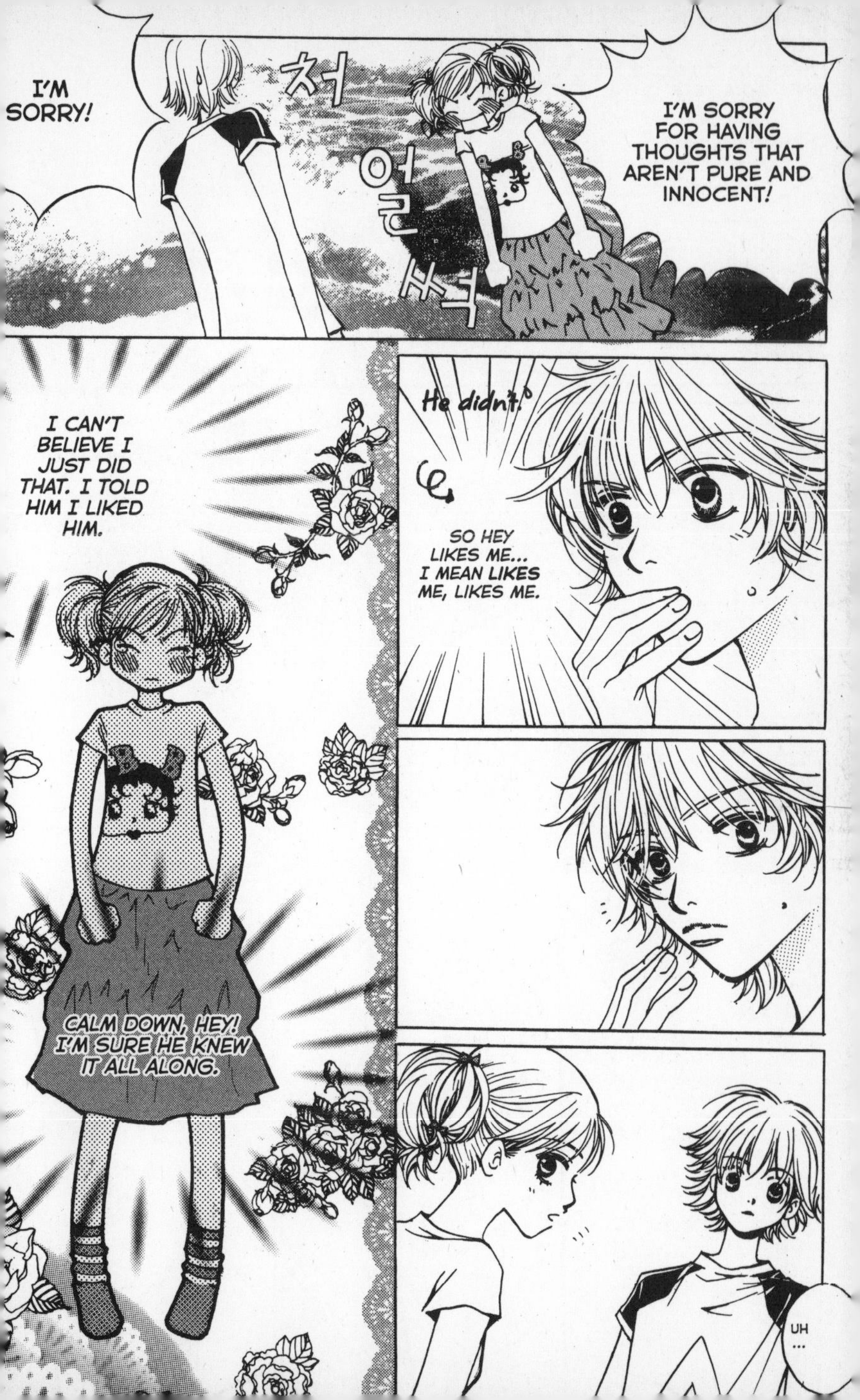
I'M SORRY!
처얼썩
I'M SORRY FOR HAVING THOUGHTS THAT AREN'T PURE AND INNOCENT!
I CAN'T BELIEVE I JUST DID THAT. I TOLD HIM I LIKED HIM.
CALM DOWN, HEY! I'M SURE HE KNEW IT ALL ALONG.
He didn't.
SO HEY LIKES ME... I MEAN LIKES ME, LIKES ME.
UH ...

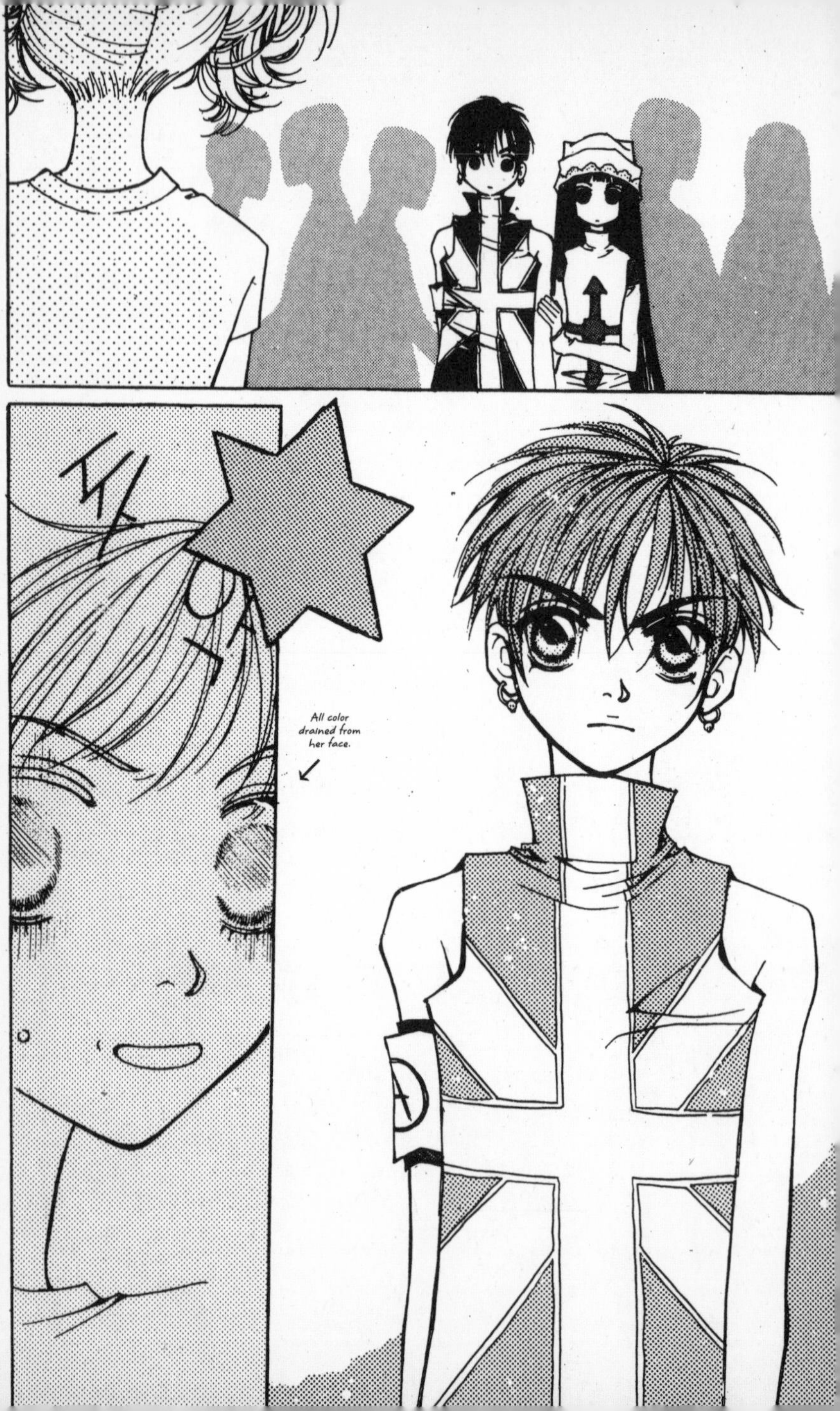
All color
drained from
her face.

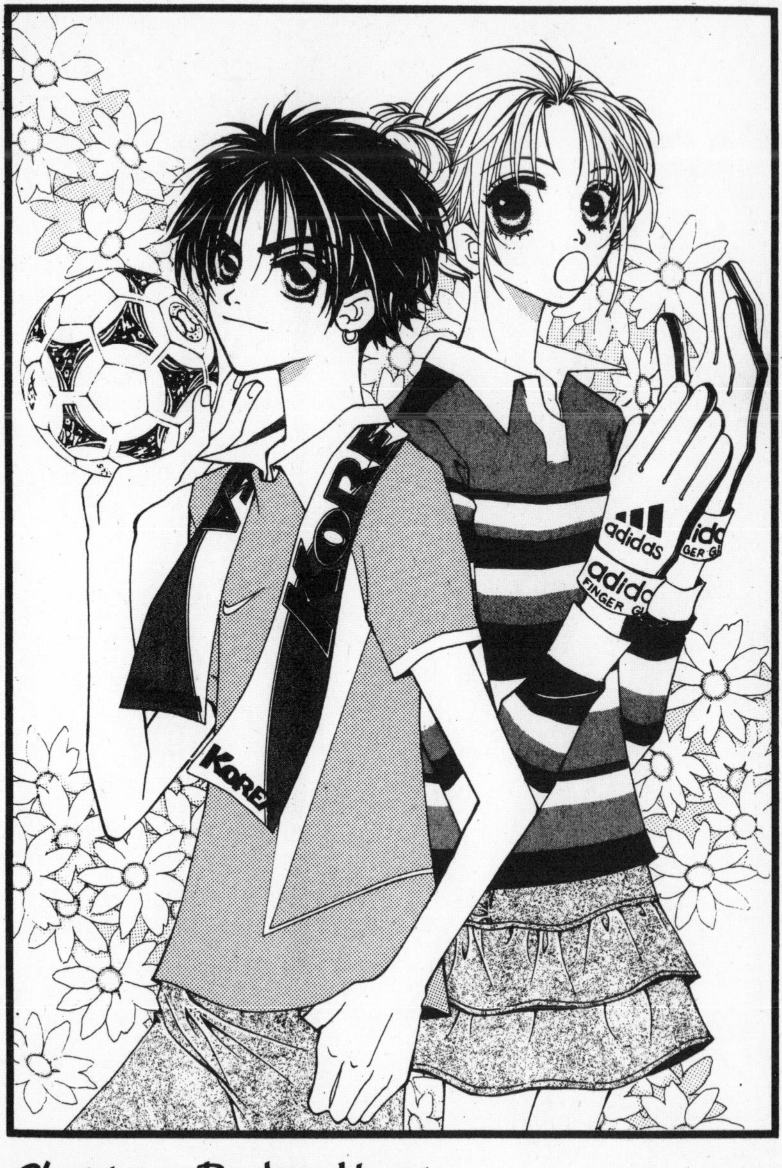
KOREA
adidas
FINGER GI
adidas
GER GI

Chapter 3: Broken Heart

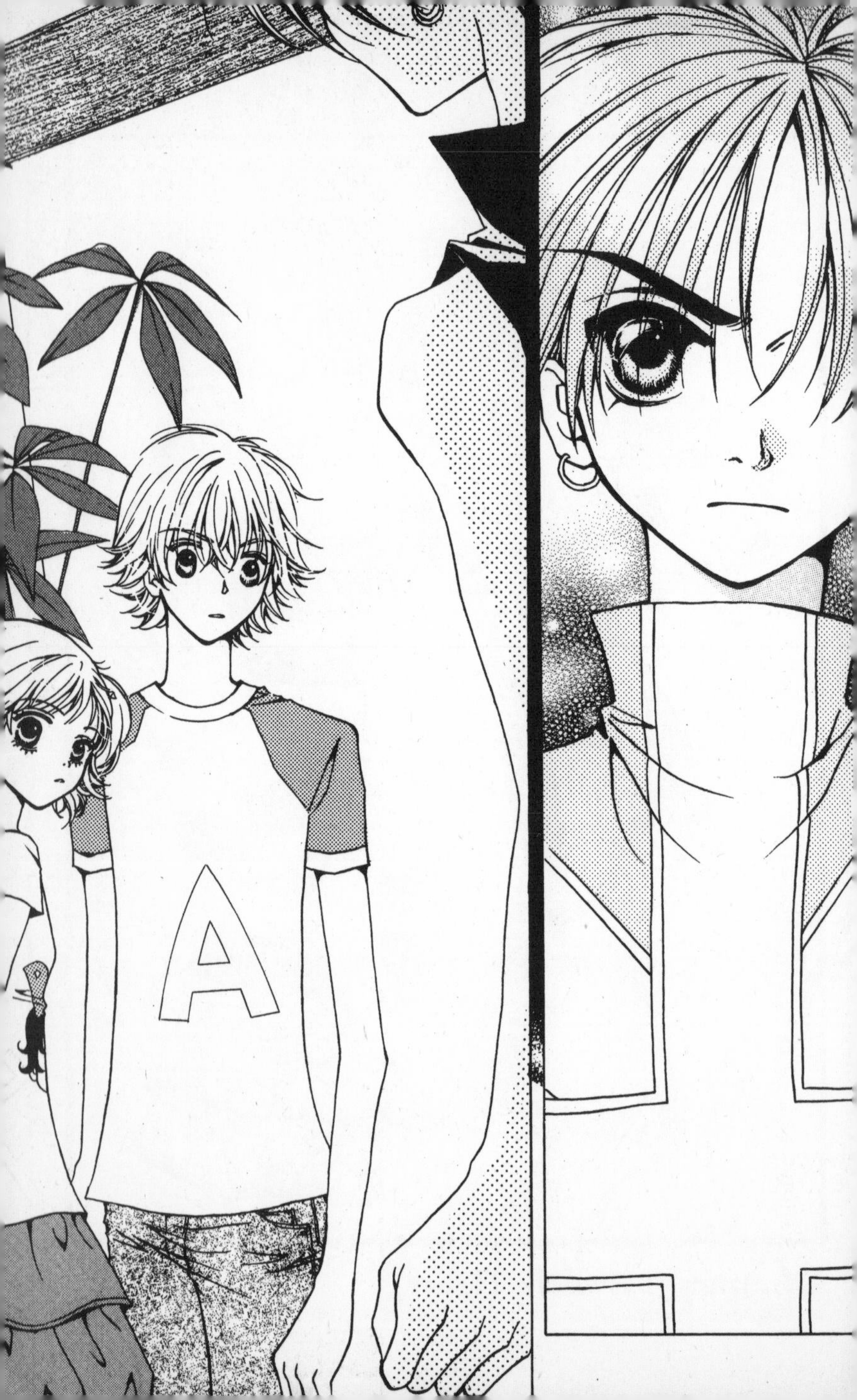

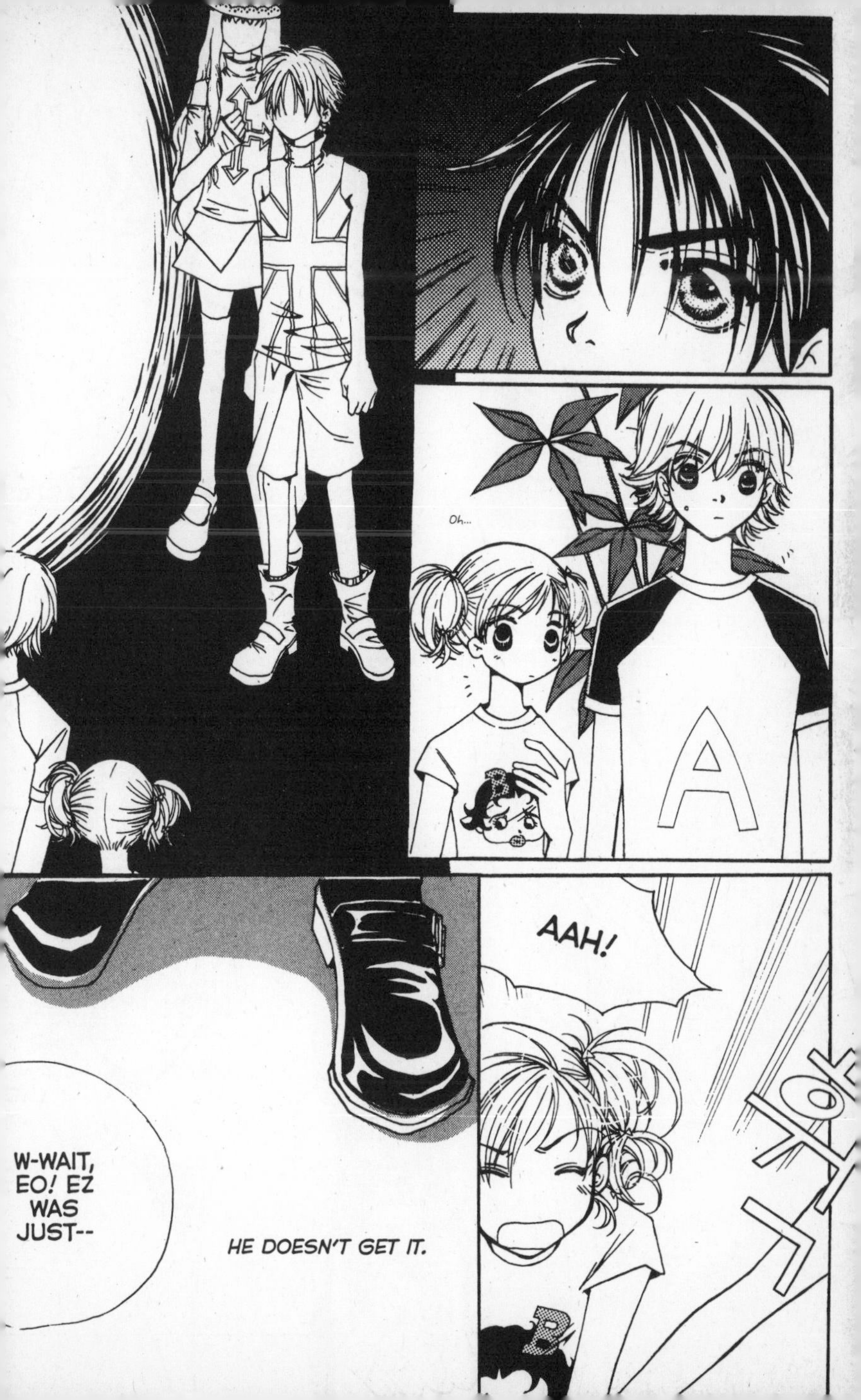
Oh...
W-WAIT, EO! EZ WAS JUST--
HE DOESN'T GET IT.
AAH!

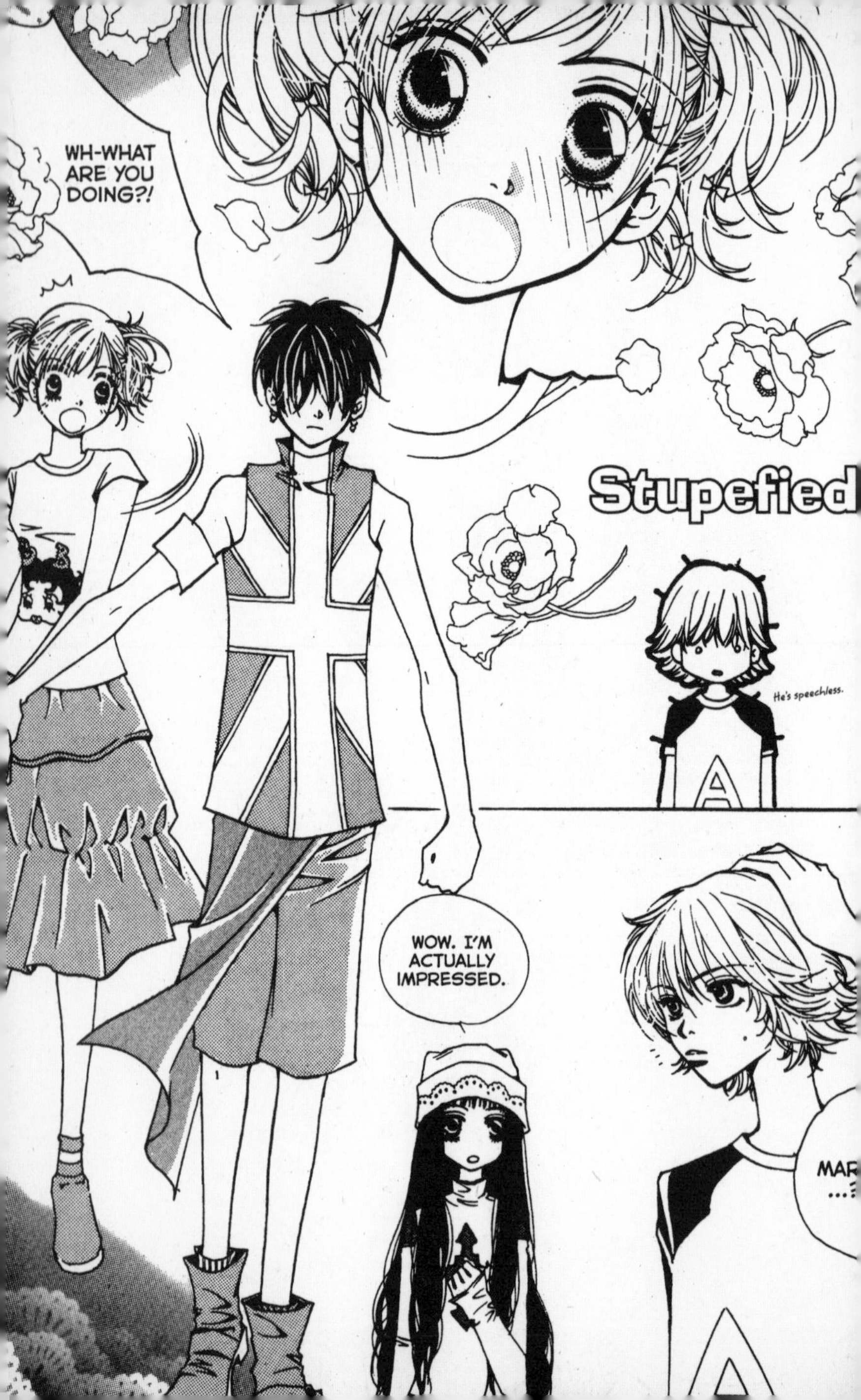
WH-WHAT ARE YOU DOING?!
Stupefied
He's speechless.
WOW. I'M ACTUALLY IMPRESSED.
MAR ...?

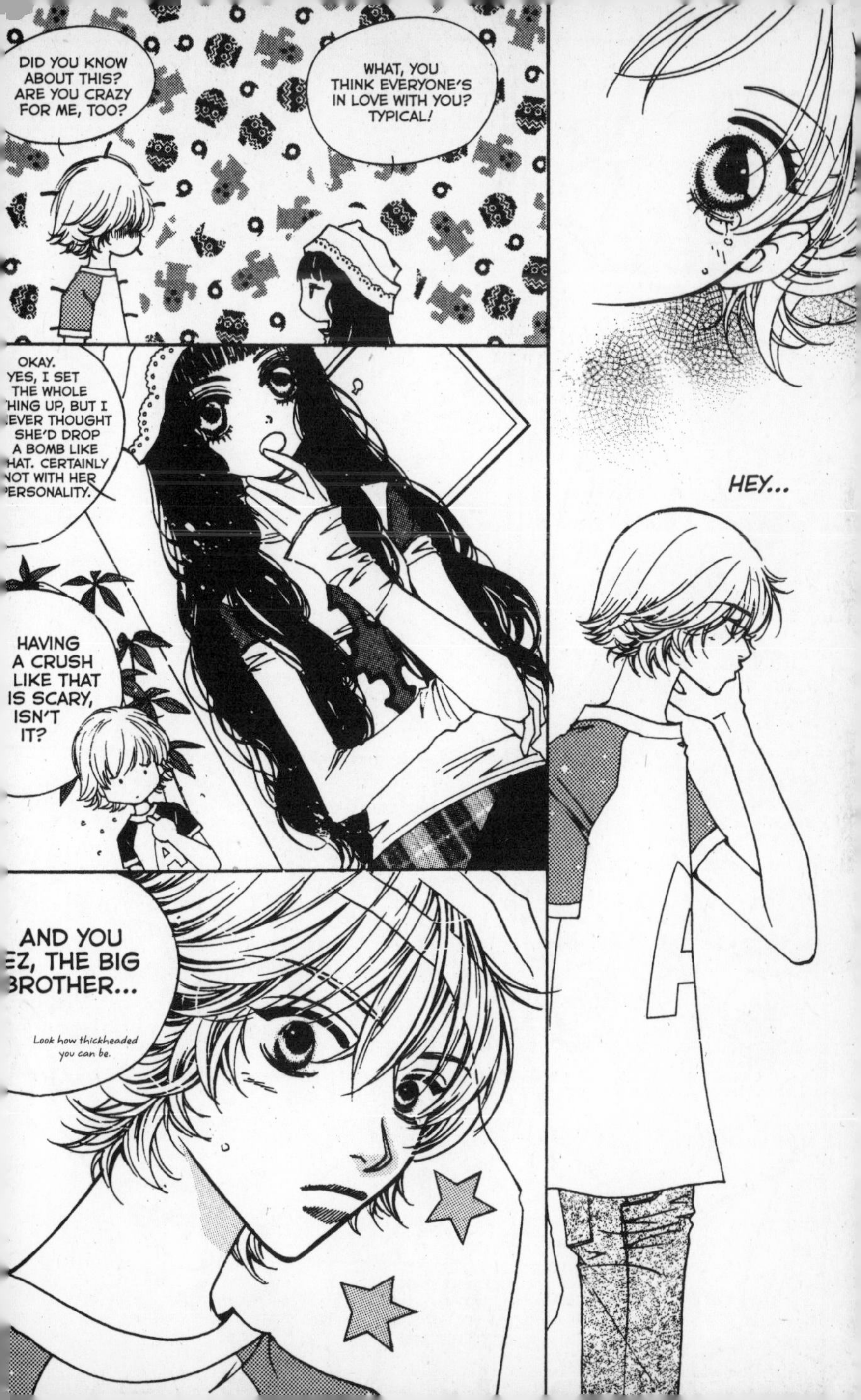
DID YOU KNOW ABOUT THIS? ARE YOU CRAZY FOR ME, TOO?
WHAT, YOU THINK EVERYONE'S IN LOVE WITH YOU? TYPICAL!
OKAY. YES, I SET THE WHOLE THING UP, BUT I NEVER THOUGHT SHE'D DROP A BOMB LIKE THAT. CERTAINLY NOT WITH HER PERSONALITY.
HAVING A CRUSH LIKE THAT IS SCARY, ISN'T IT?
AND YOU EZ, THE BIG BROTHER...
Look how thickheaded you can be.
HEY...

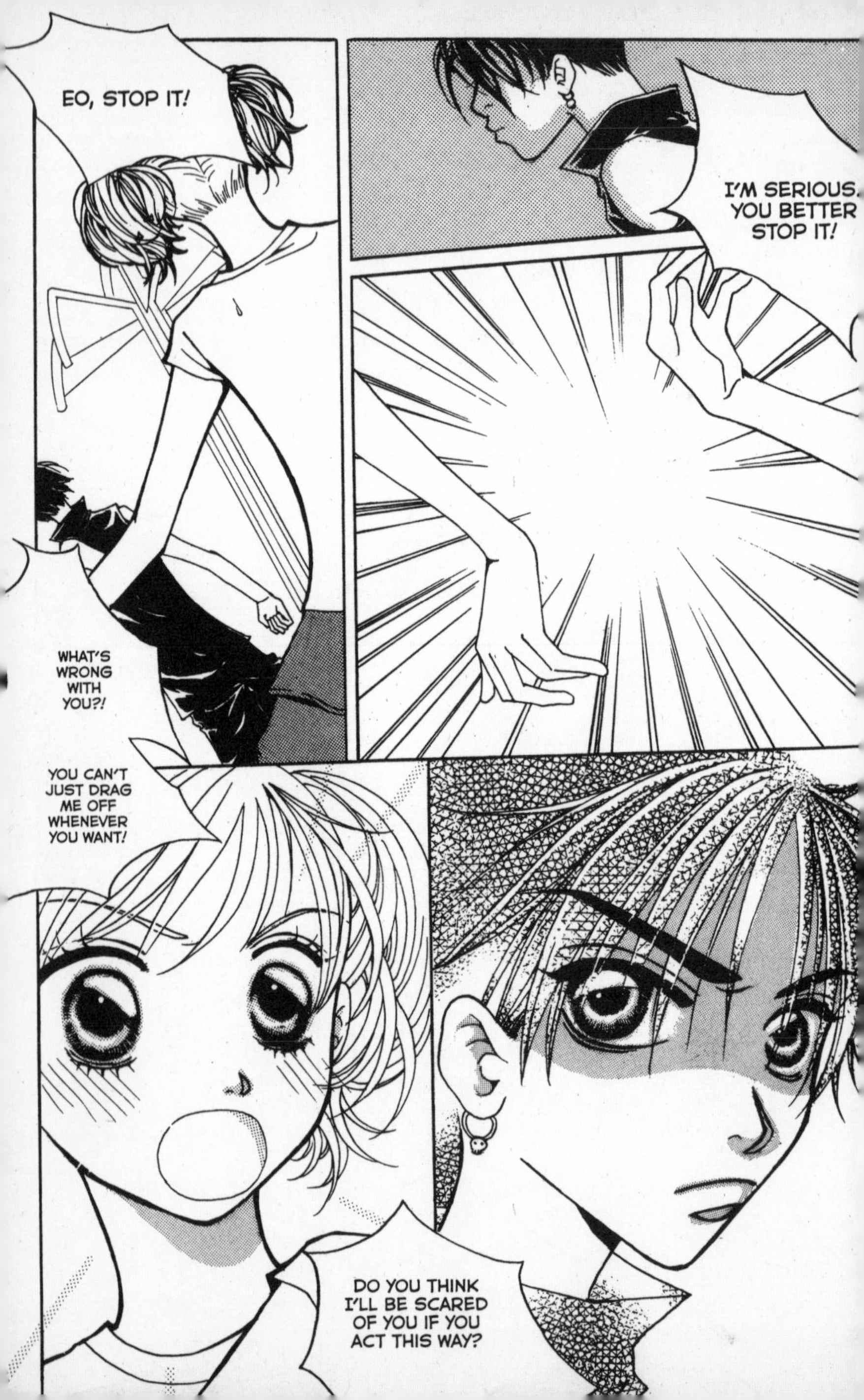
EO, STOP IT!
I'M SERIOUS. YOU BETTER STOP IT!
WHAT'S WRONG WITH YOU?!
YOU CAN'T JUST DRAG ME OFF WHENEVER YOU WANT!
DO YOU THINK I'LL BE SCARED OF YOU IF YOU ACT THIS WAY?

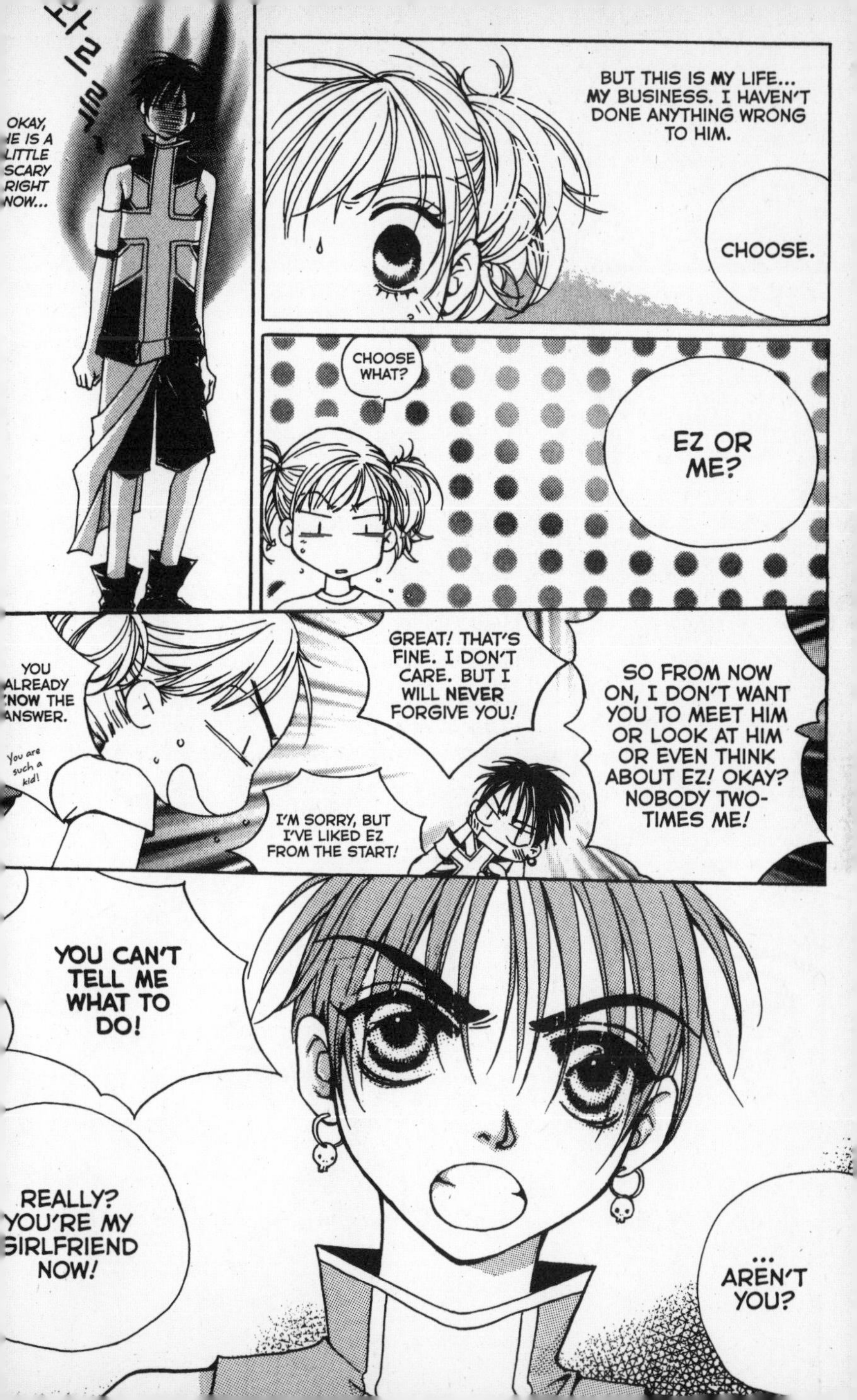

OKAY, HE IS A LITTLE SCARY RIGHT NOW...
BUT THIS IS MY LIFE... MY BUSINESS. I HAVEN'T DONE ANYTHING WRONG TO HIM.
CHOOSE.
CHOOSE WHAT?
EZ OR ME?
YOU ALREADY KNOW THE ANSWER.
You are such a kid!
I'M SORRY, BUT I'VE LIKED EZ FROM THE START!
GREAT! THAT'S FINE. I DON'T CARE. BUT I WILL NEVER FORGIVE YOU!
SO FROM NOW ON, I DON'T WANT YOU TO MEET HIM OR LOOK AT HIM OR EVEN THINK ABOUT EZ! OKAY? NOBODY TWO-TIMES ME!
YOU CAN'T TELL ME WHAT TO DO!
REALLY? YOU'RE MY GIRLFRIEND NOW!
...AREN'T YOU?

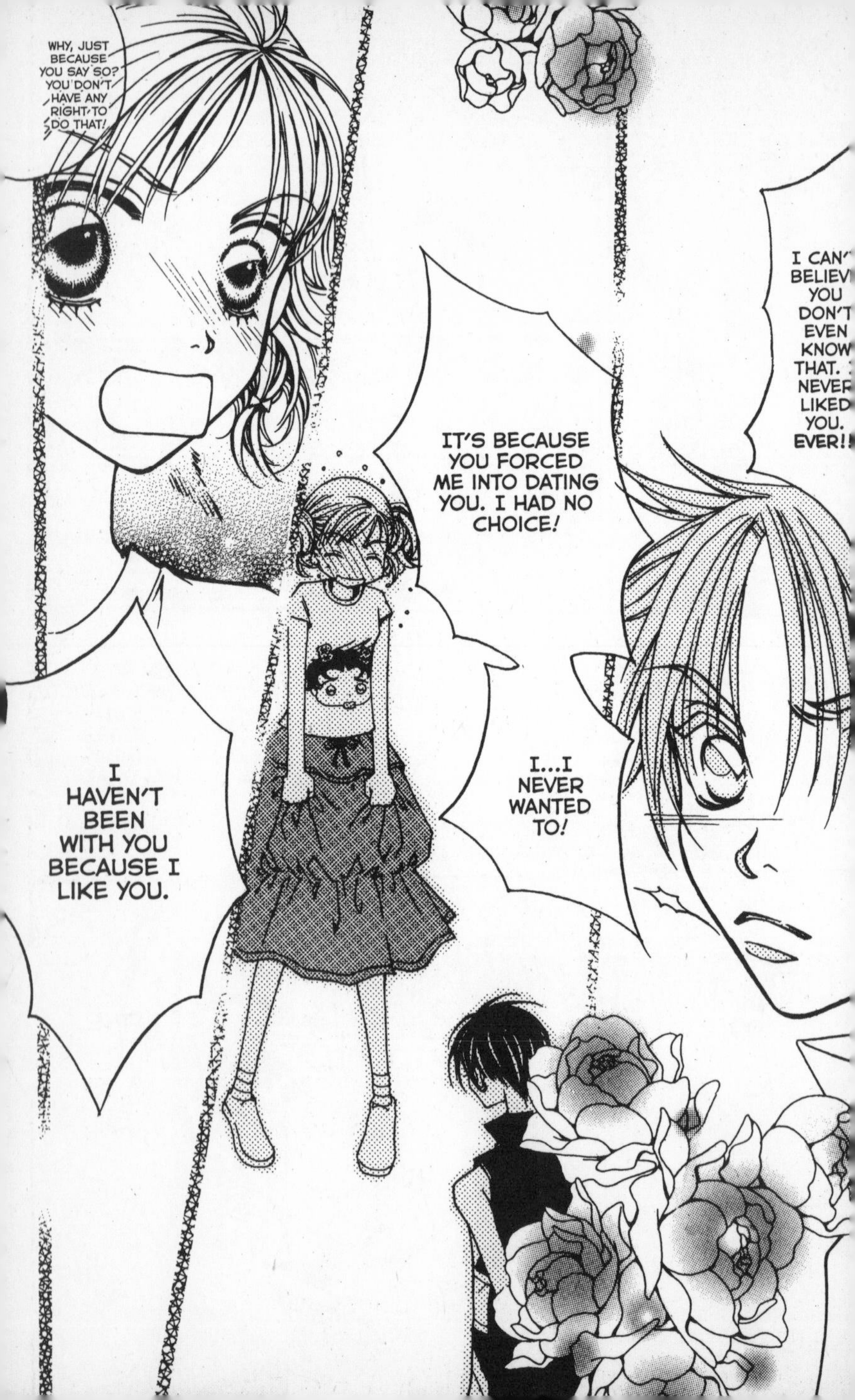
WHY, JUST BECAUSE YOU SAY SO? YOU DON'T HAVE ANY RIGHT TO DO THAT!
I HAVEN'T BEEN WITH YOU BECAUSE I LIKE YOU.
IT'S BECAUSE YOU FORCED ME INTO DATING YOU. I HAD NO CHOICE!
I...I NEVER WANTED TO!
I CAN' BELIEV YOU DON'T EVEN KNOW THAT. NEVER LIKED YOU. EVER!!

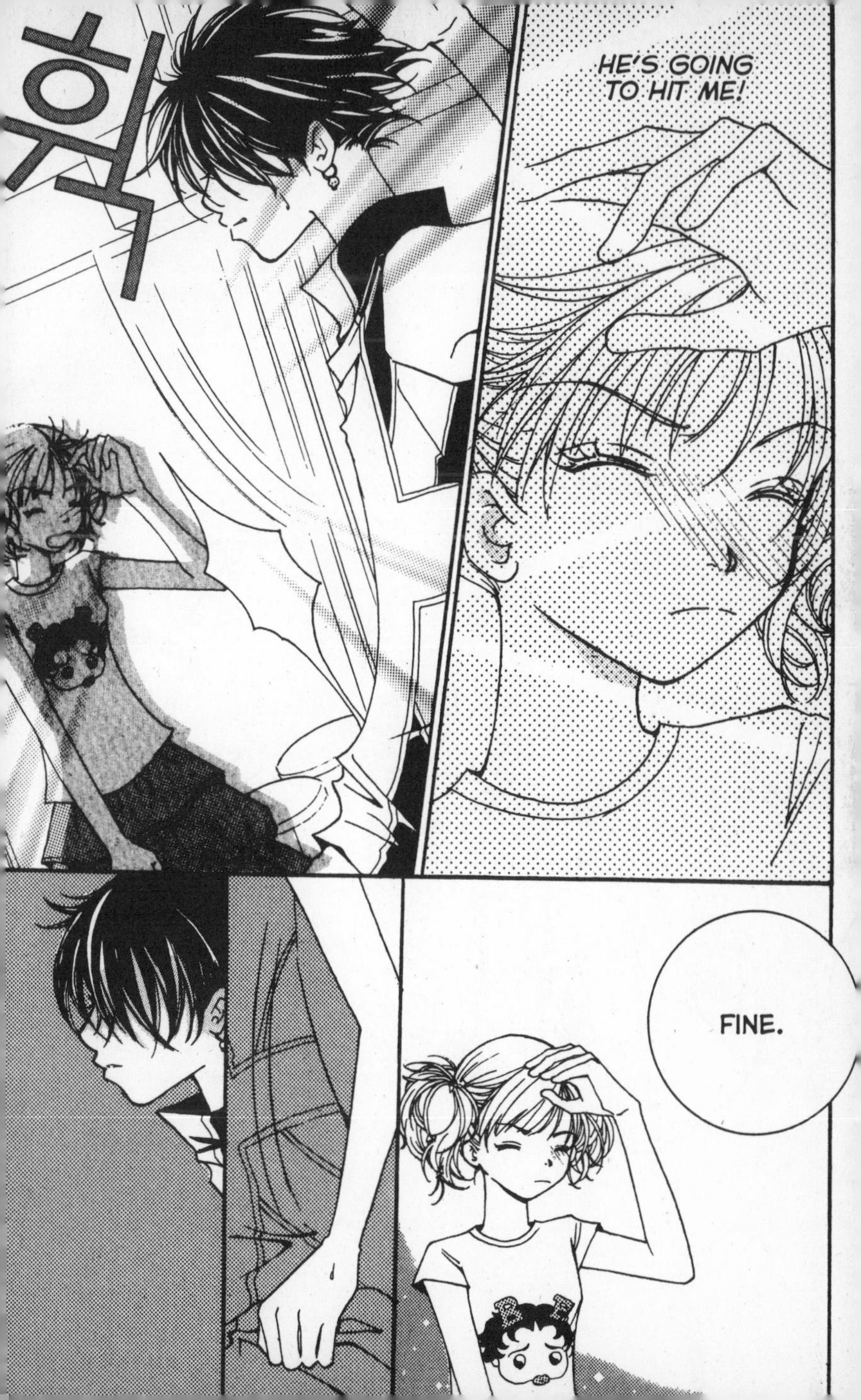
훅
HE'S GOING TO HIT ME!
FINE.

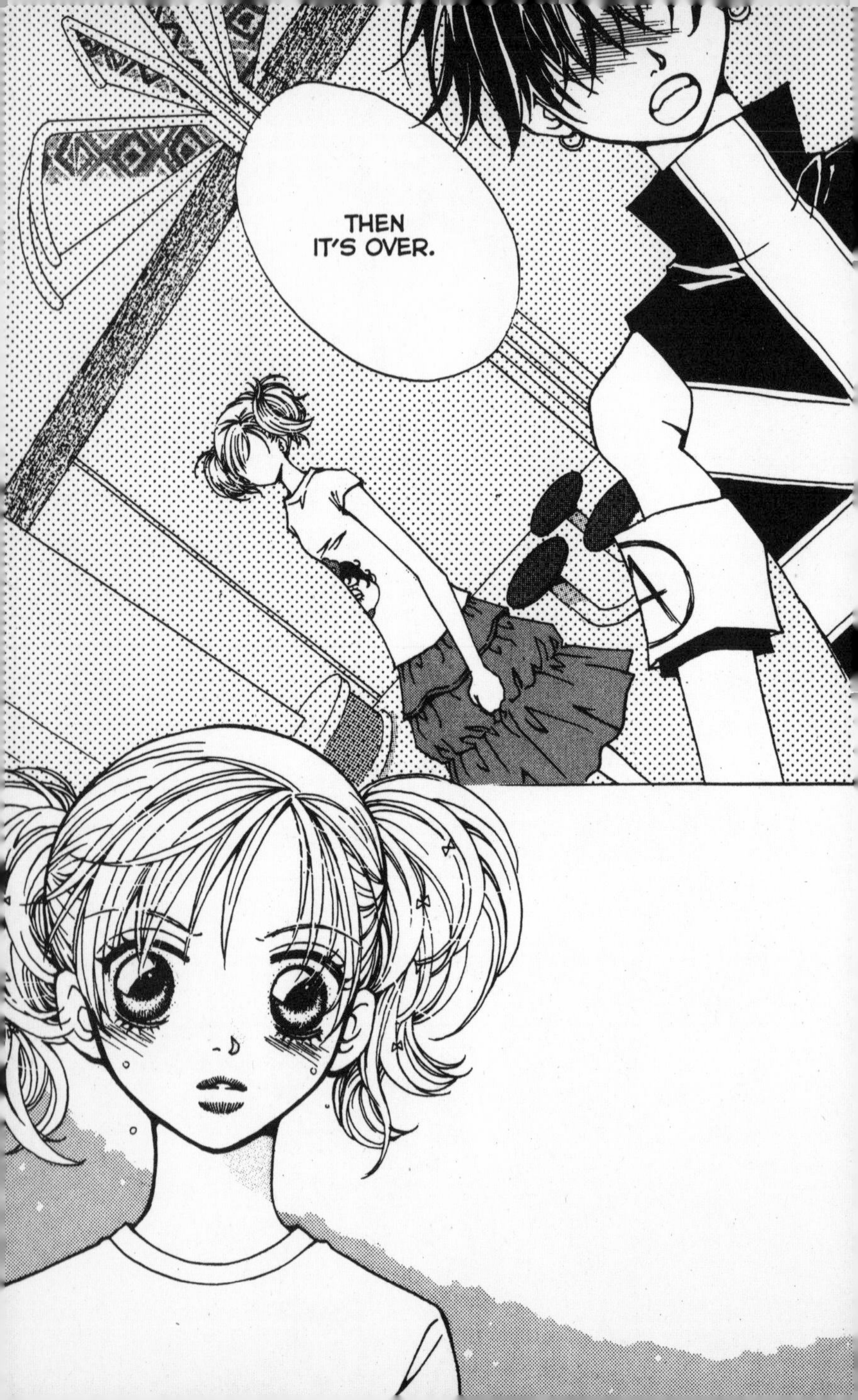
THEN IT'S OVER.

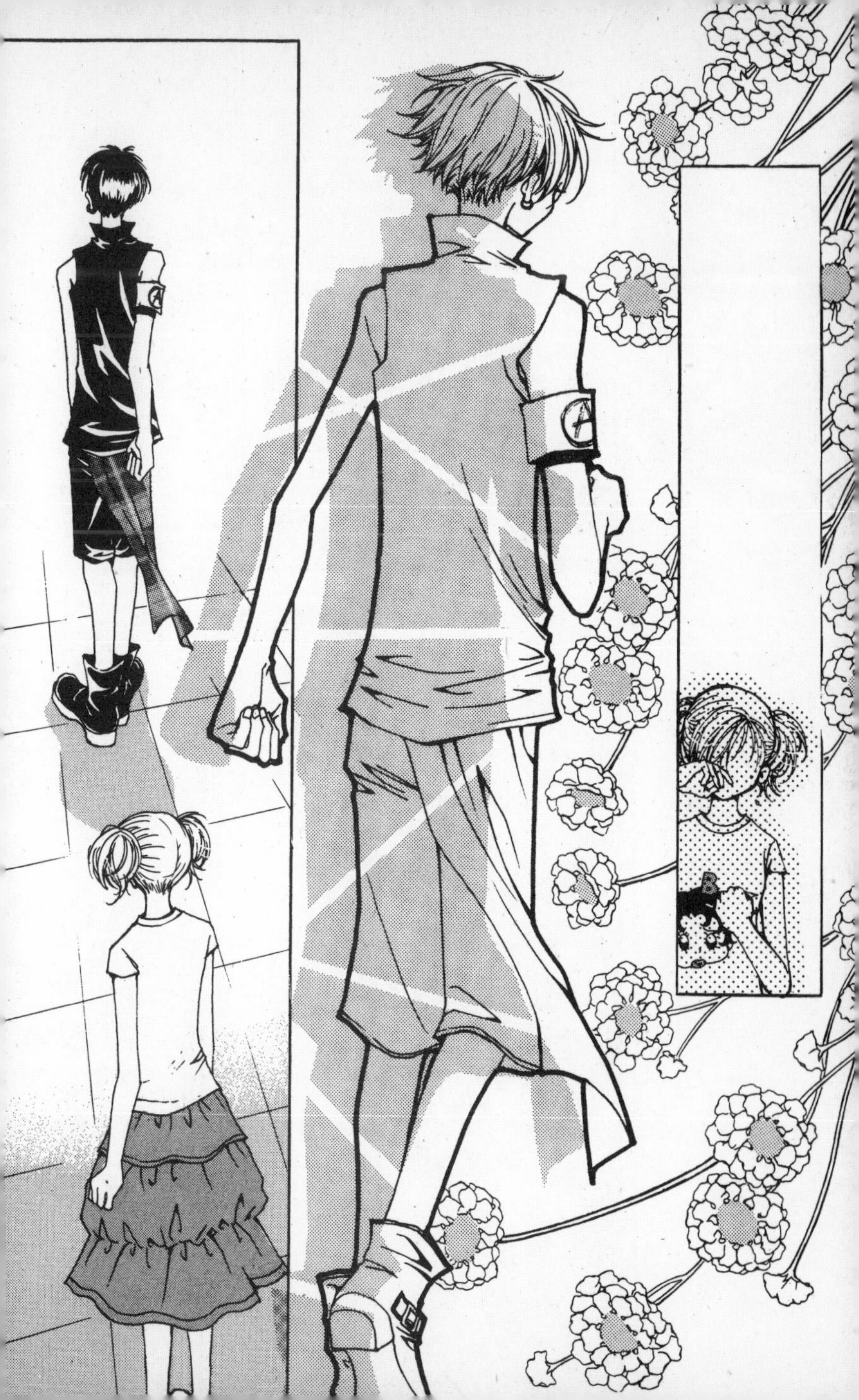

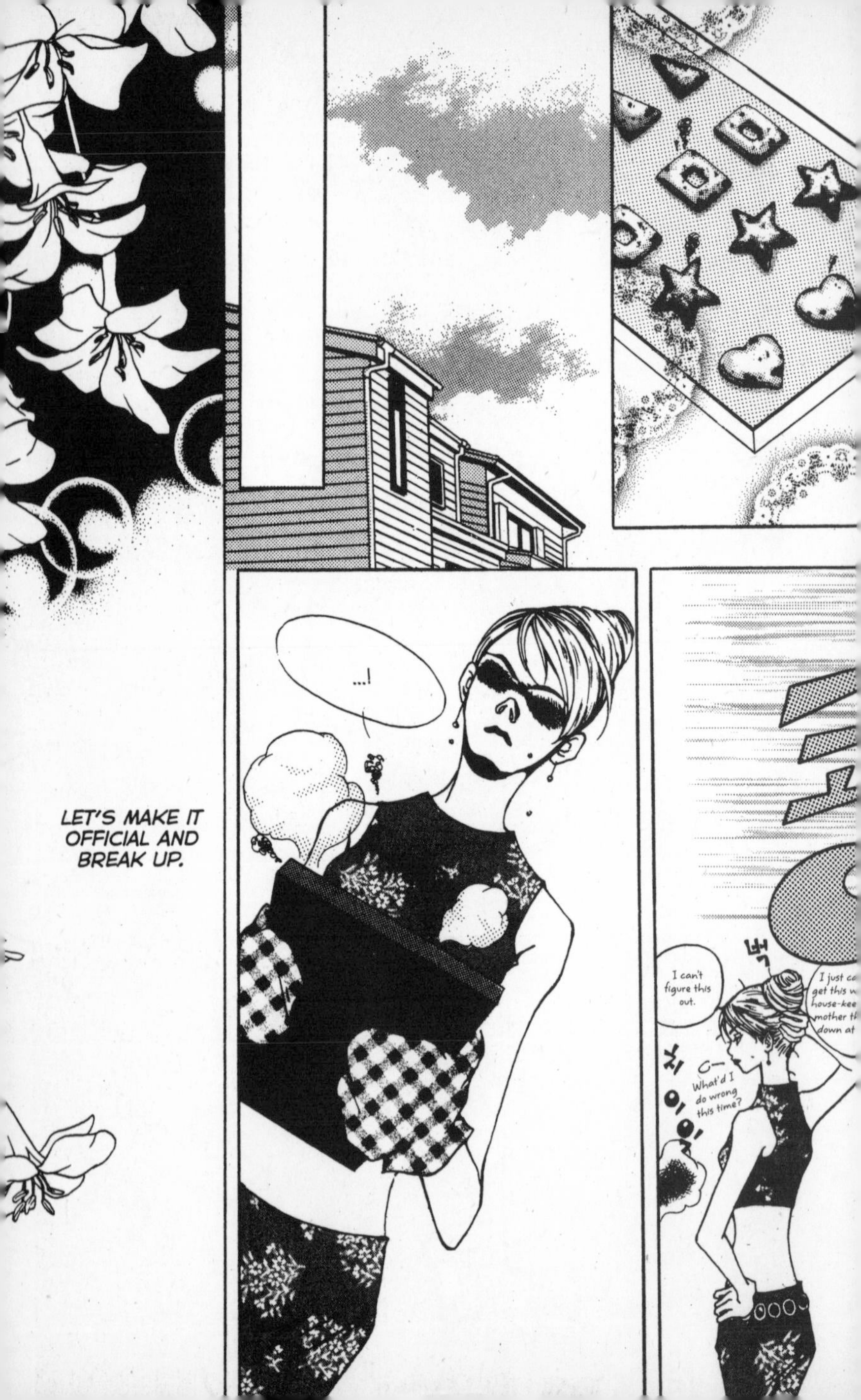
LET'S MAKE IT OFFICIAL AND BREAK UP.
...!
I can't figure this out.
C— What'd I do wrong this time?

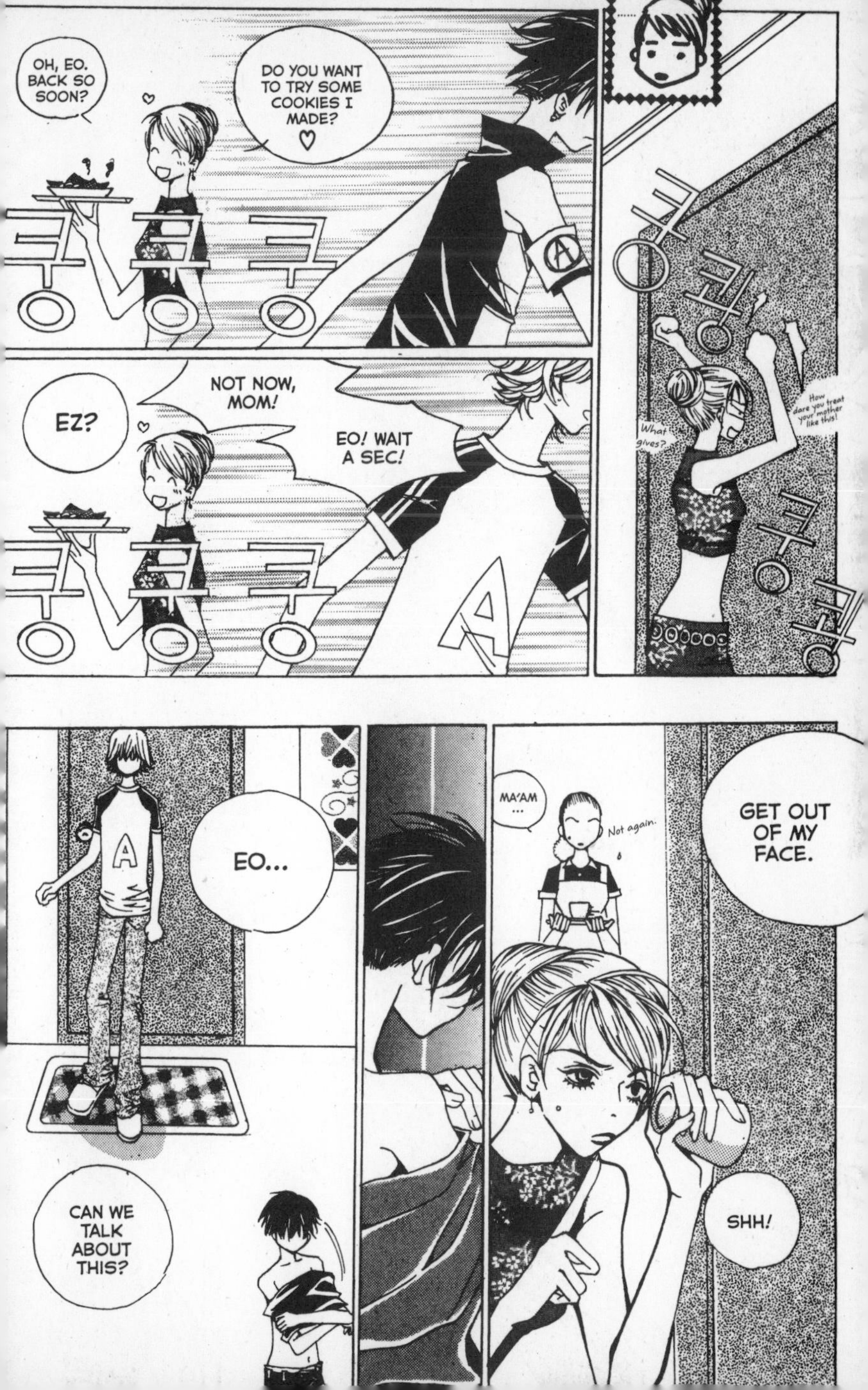
OH, EO. BACK SO SOON?
DO YOU WANT TO TRY SOME COOKIES I MADE? ♡
쿵 쿵 쿵
EZ?
NOT NOW, MOM!
EO! WAIT A SEC!
쿵 쿵 쿵
쾅 쾅
What gives?
How dare you treat your mother like this!
쾅 쾅
EO...
CAN WE TALK ABOUT THIS?
MA'AM ...
Not again.
GET OUT OF MY FACE.
SHH!

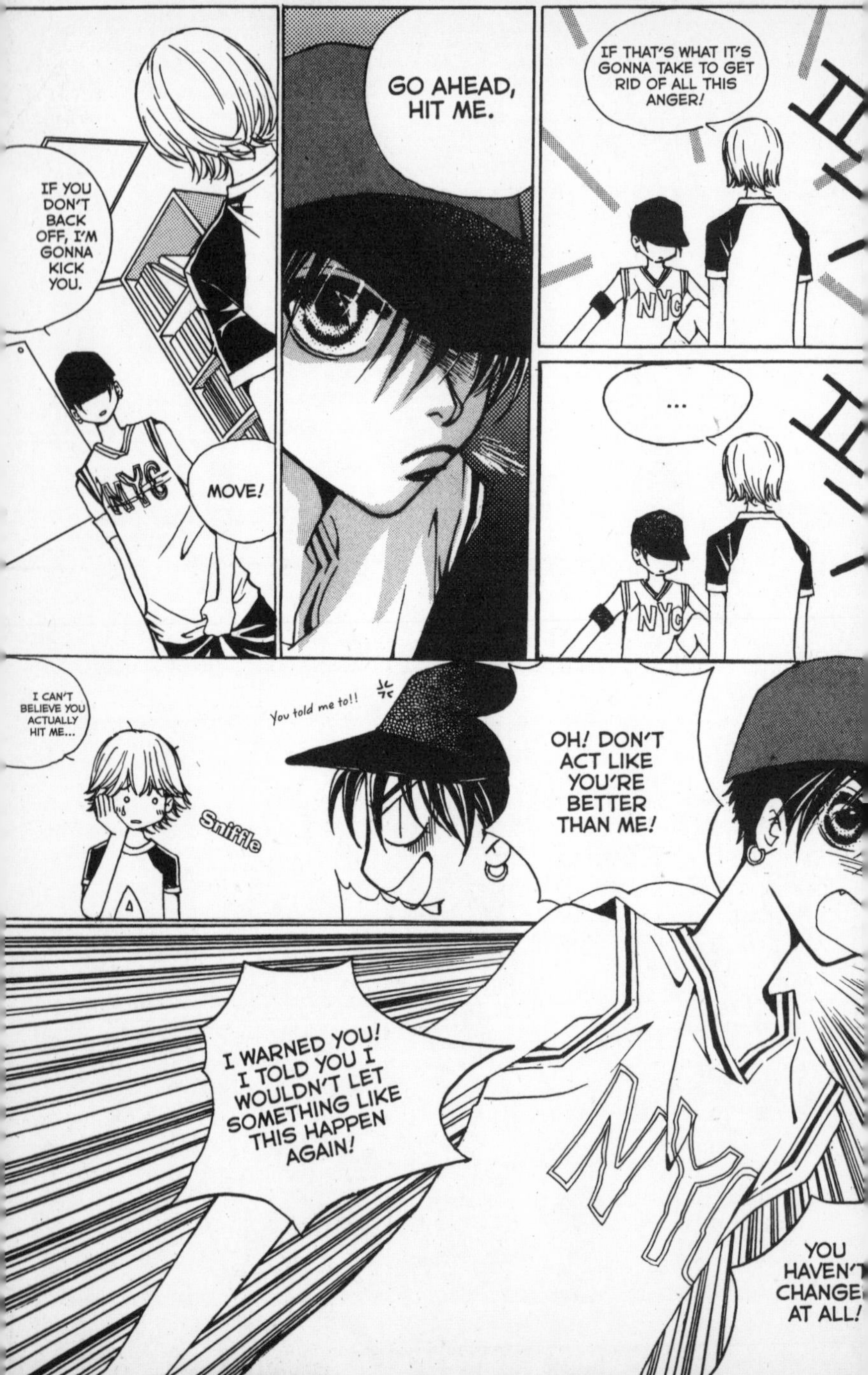
IF YOU DON'T BACK OFF, I'M GONNA KICK YOU.
MOVE!
GO AHEAD, HIT ME.
IF THAT'S WHAT IT'S GONNA TAKE TO GET RID OF ALL THIS ANGER!
...
I CAN'T BELIEVE YOU ACTUALLY HIT ME...
Sniffle
You told me to!!
OH! DON'T ACT LIKE YOU'RE BETTER THAN ME!
I WARNED YOU! I TOLD YOU I WOULDN'T LET SOMETHING LIKE THIS HAPPEN AGAIN!
YOU HAVEN'T CHANGE AT ALL!

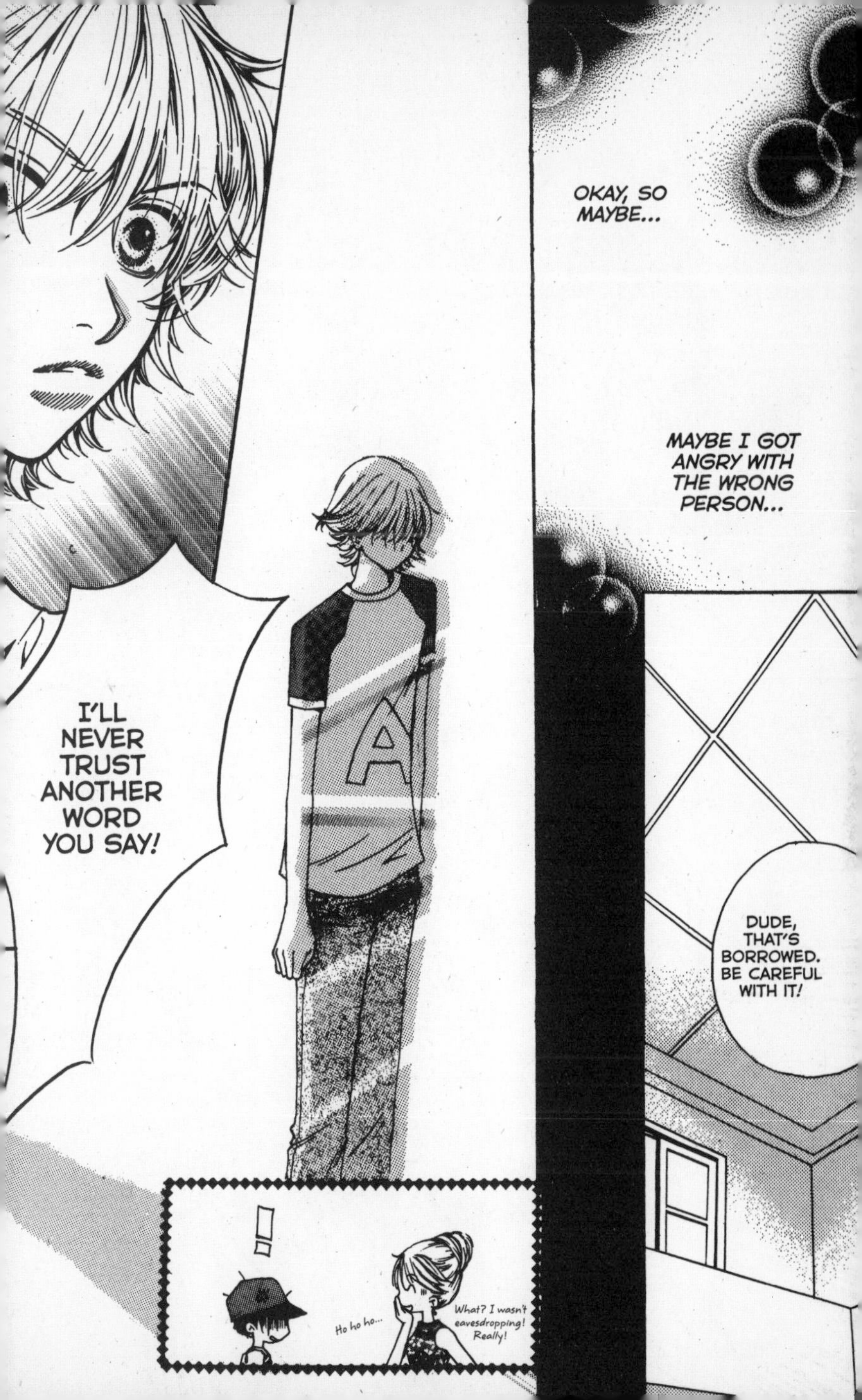

I'LL NEVER TRUST ANOTHER WORD YOU SAY!
!
Ho ho ho...
What? I wasn't eavesdropping! Really!
OKAY, SO MAYBE...
MAYBE I GOT ANGRY WITH THE WRONG PERSON...
DUDE, THAT'S BORROWED. BE CAREFUL WITH IT!

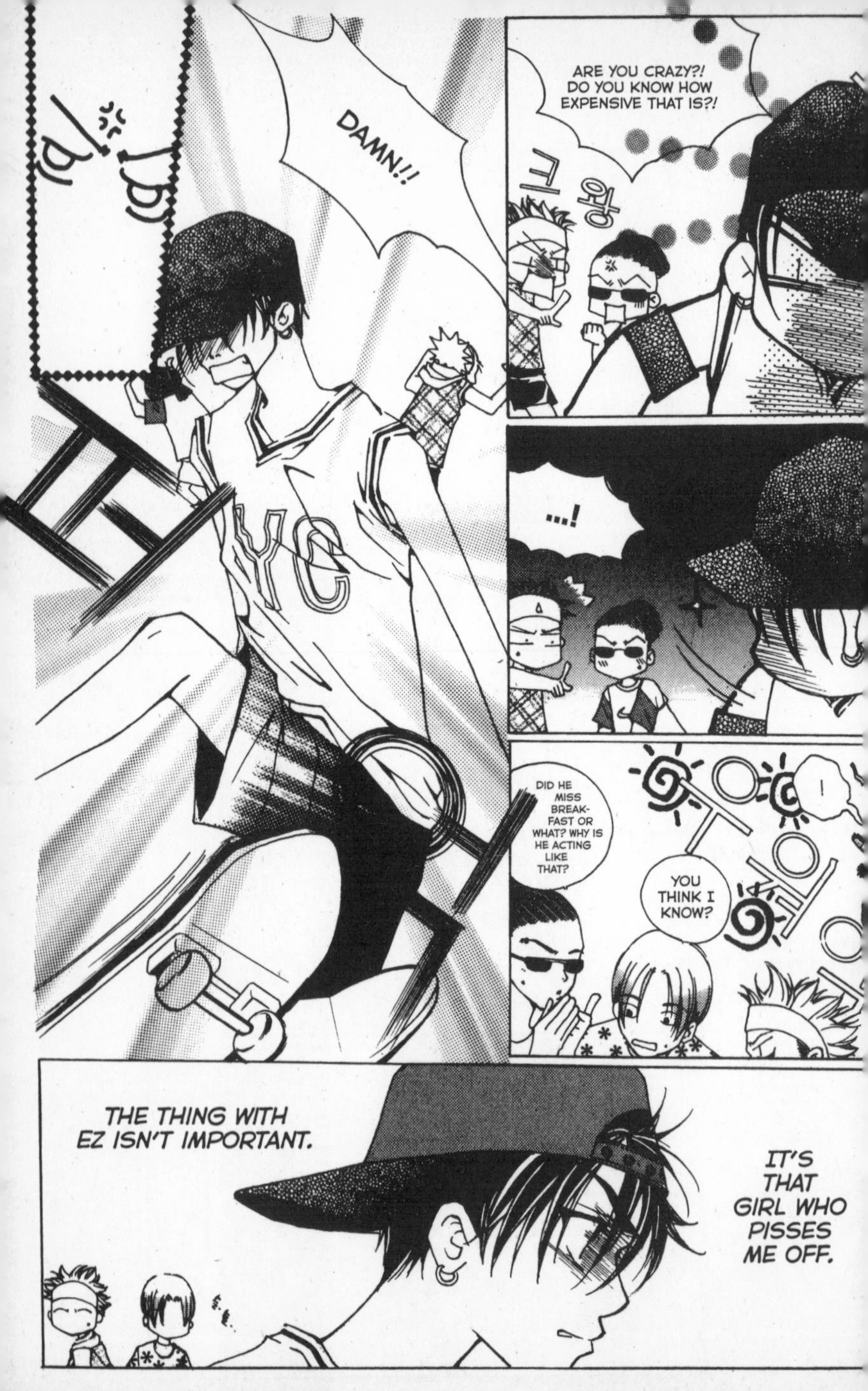
DAMN!!
ARE YOU CRAZY?! DO YOU KNOW HOW EXPENSIVE THAT IS?!
...!
DID HE MISS BREAK-FAST OR WHAT? WHY IS HE ACTING LIKE THAT?
YOU THINK I KNOW?
!
THE THING WITH EZ ISN'T IMPORTANT.
IT'S THAT GIRL WHO PISSES ME OFF.

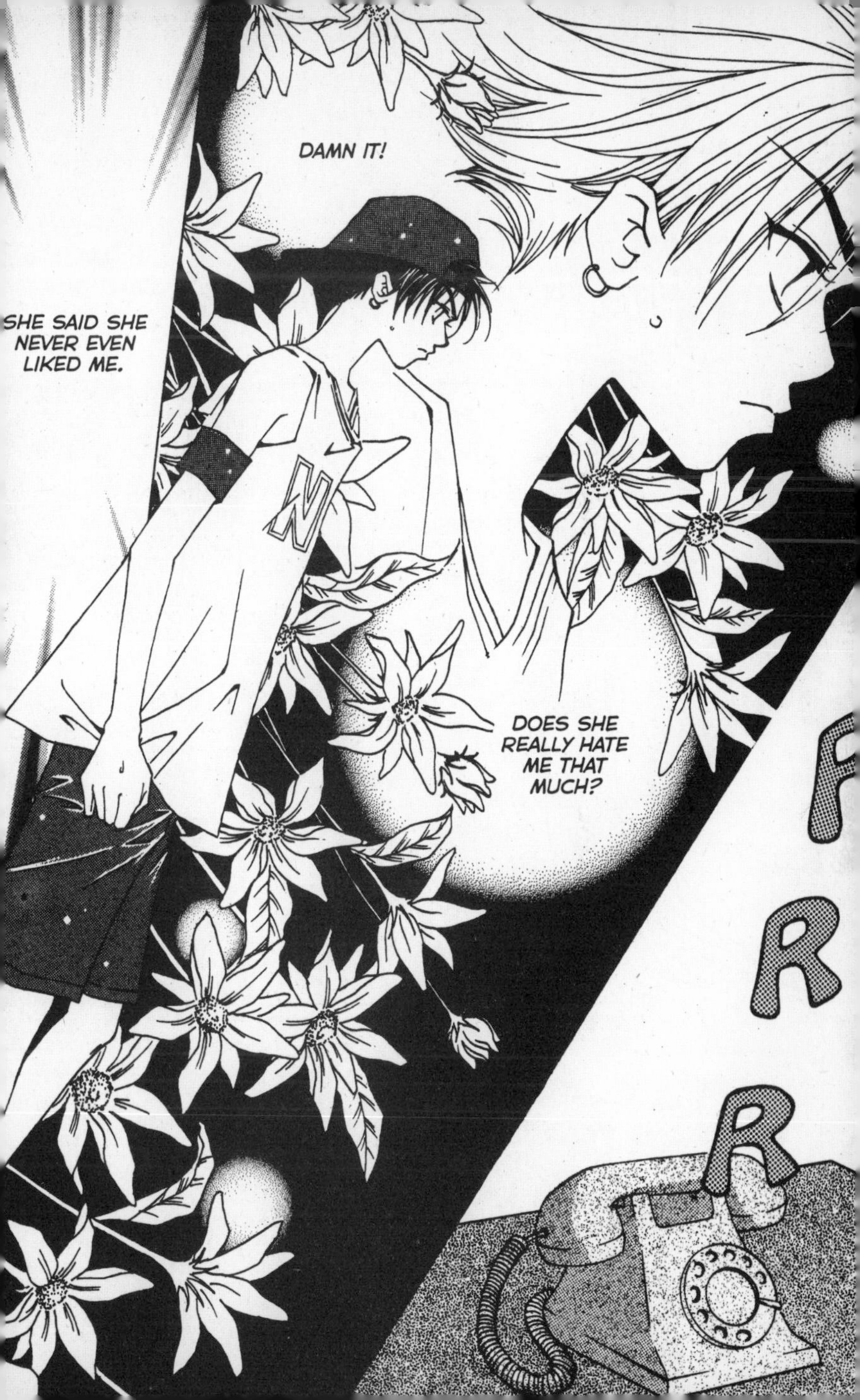
SHE SAID SHE NEVER EVEN LIKED ME.
DAMN IT!
DOES SHE REALLY HATE ME THAT MUCH?
RRR

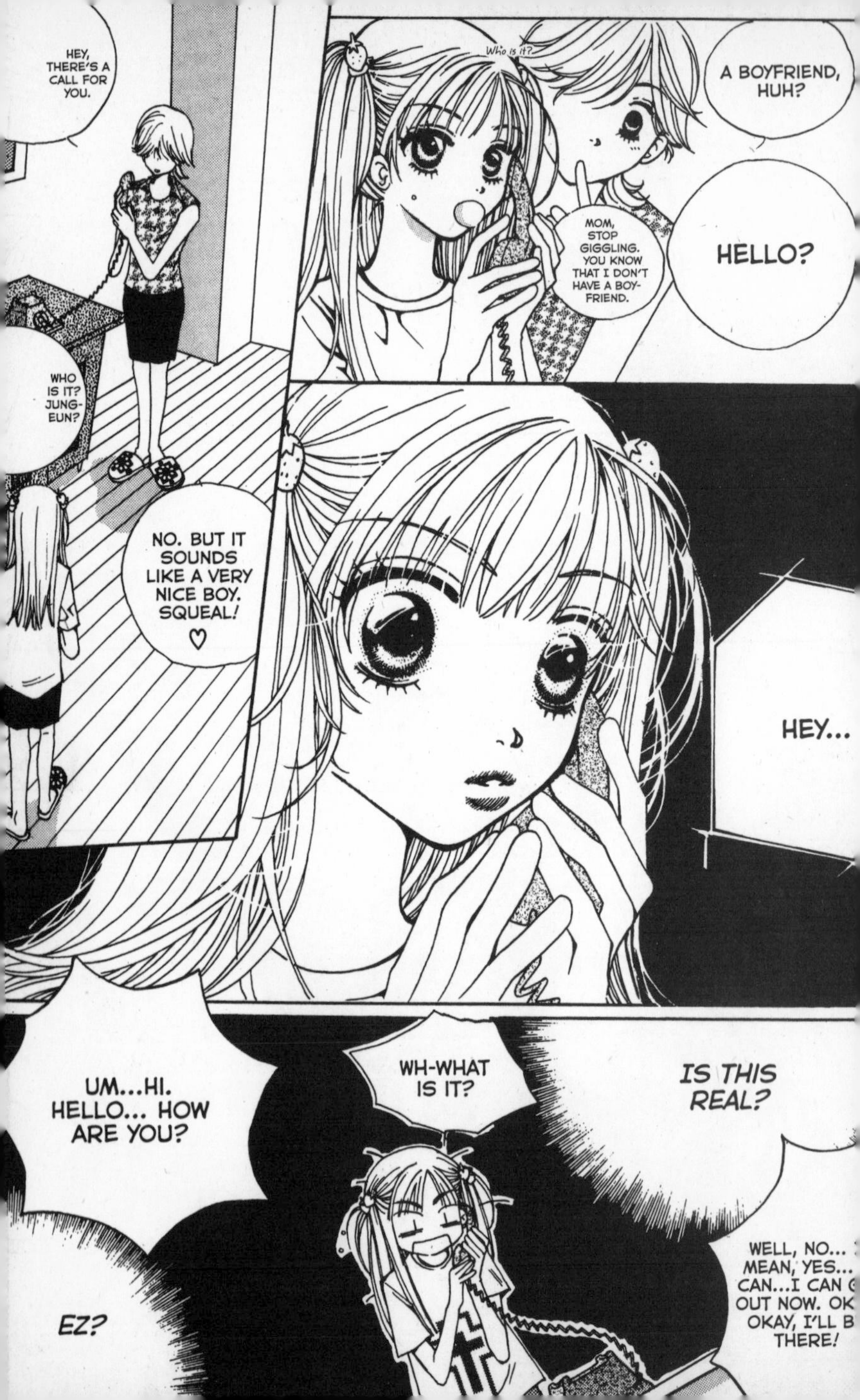
HEY, THERE'S A CALL FOR YOU.
WHO IS IT? JUNG-EUN?
NO. BUT IT SOUNDS LIKE A VERY NICE BOY. SQUEAL! ♡
Who is it?
A BOYFRIEND, HUH?
MOM, STOP GIGGLING. YOU KNOW THAT I DON'T HAVE A BOY-FRIEND.
HELLO?
HEY...
UM...HI. HELLO... HOW ARE YOU?
EZ?
WH-WHAT IS IT?
IS THIS REAL?
WELL, NO... MEAN, YES... CAN...I CAN OUT NOW. OKAY, I'LL THERE!

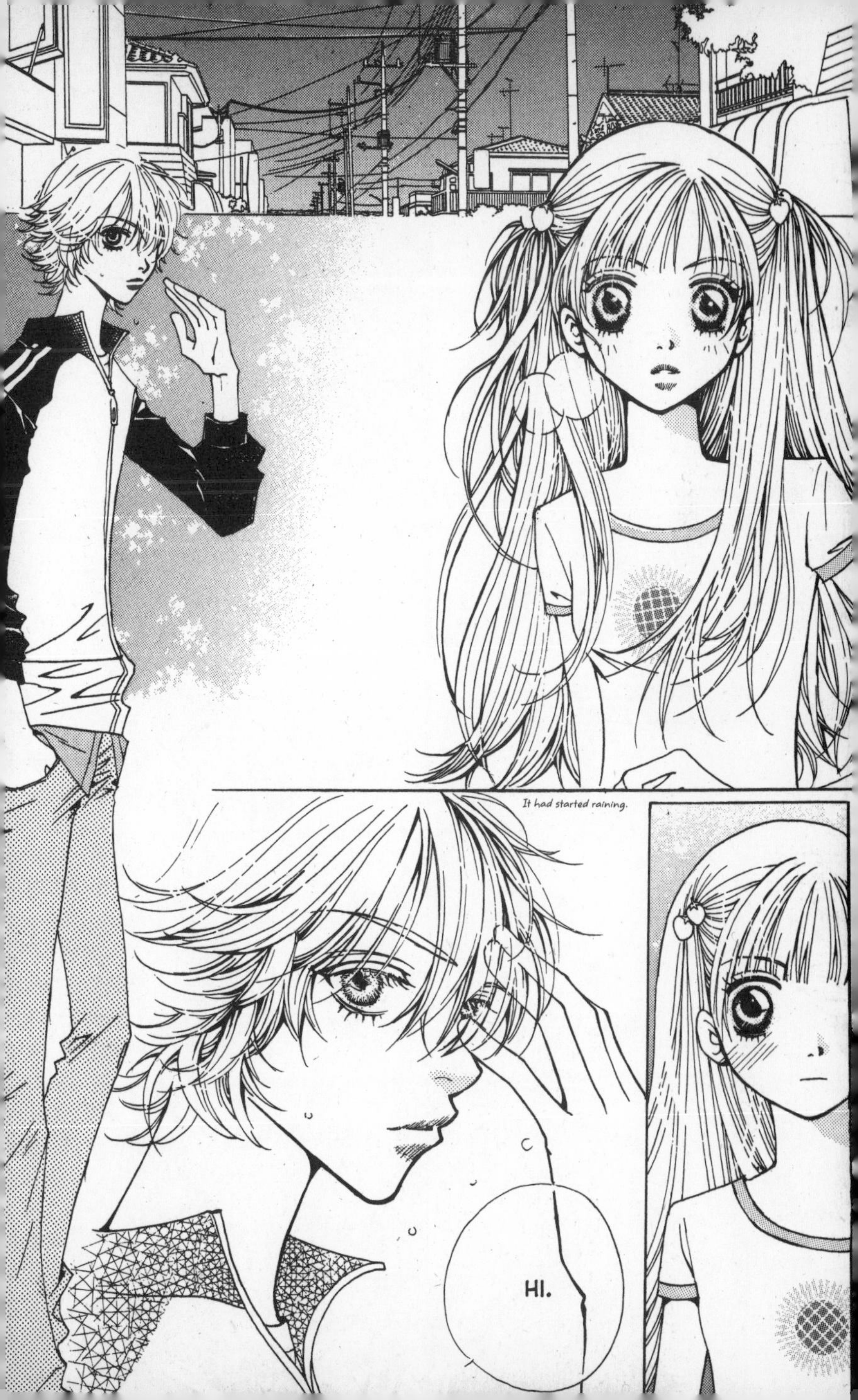
It had started raining.
HI.

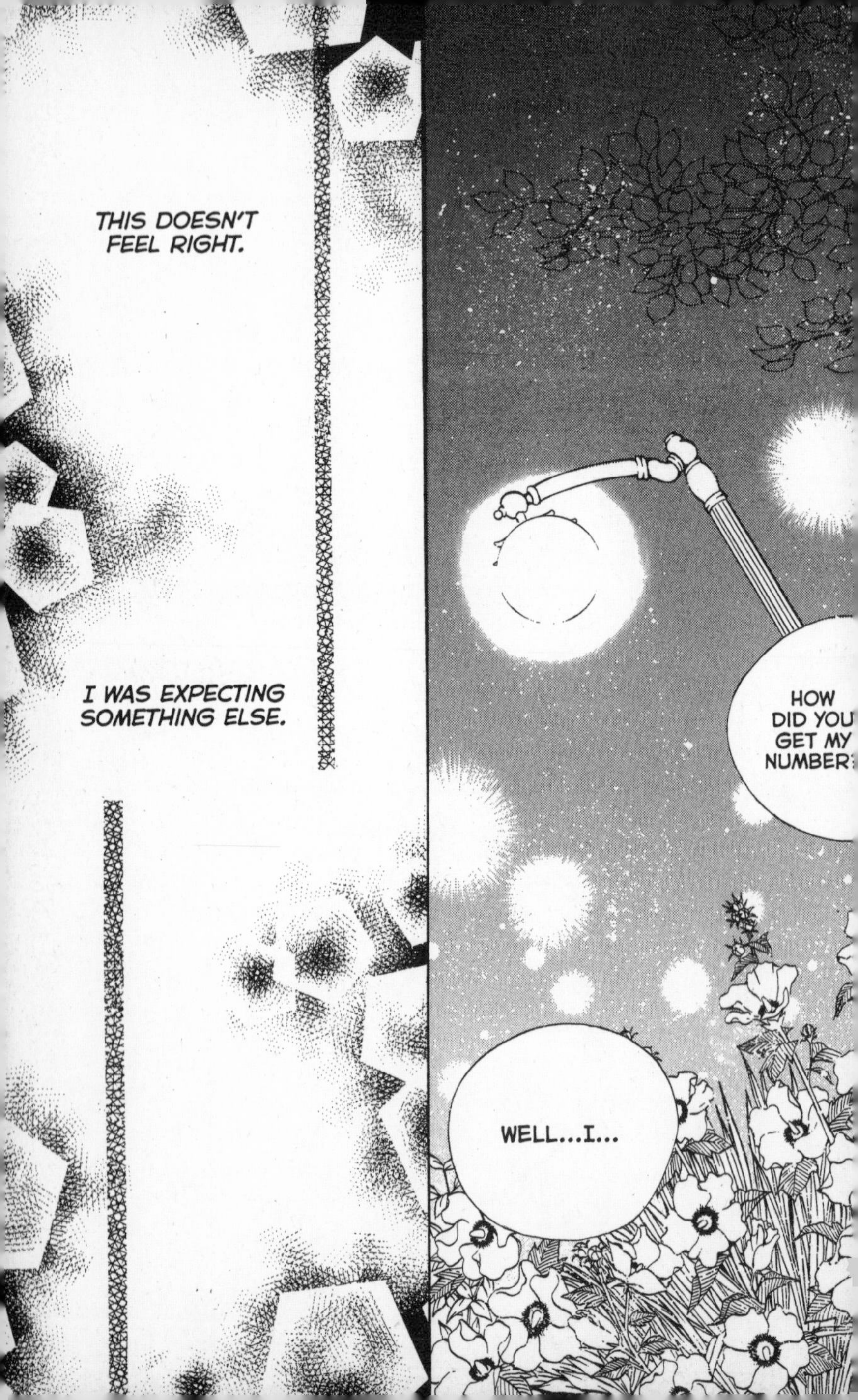
THIS DOESN'T FEEL RIGHT.
I WAS EXPECTING SOMETHING ELSE.
HOW DID YOU GET MY NUMBER
WELL...I...

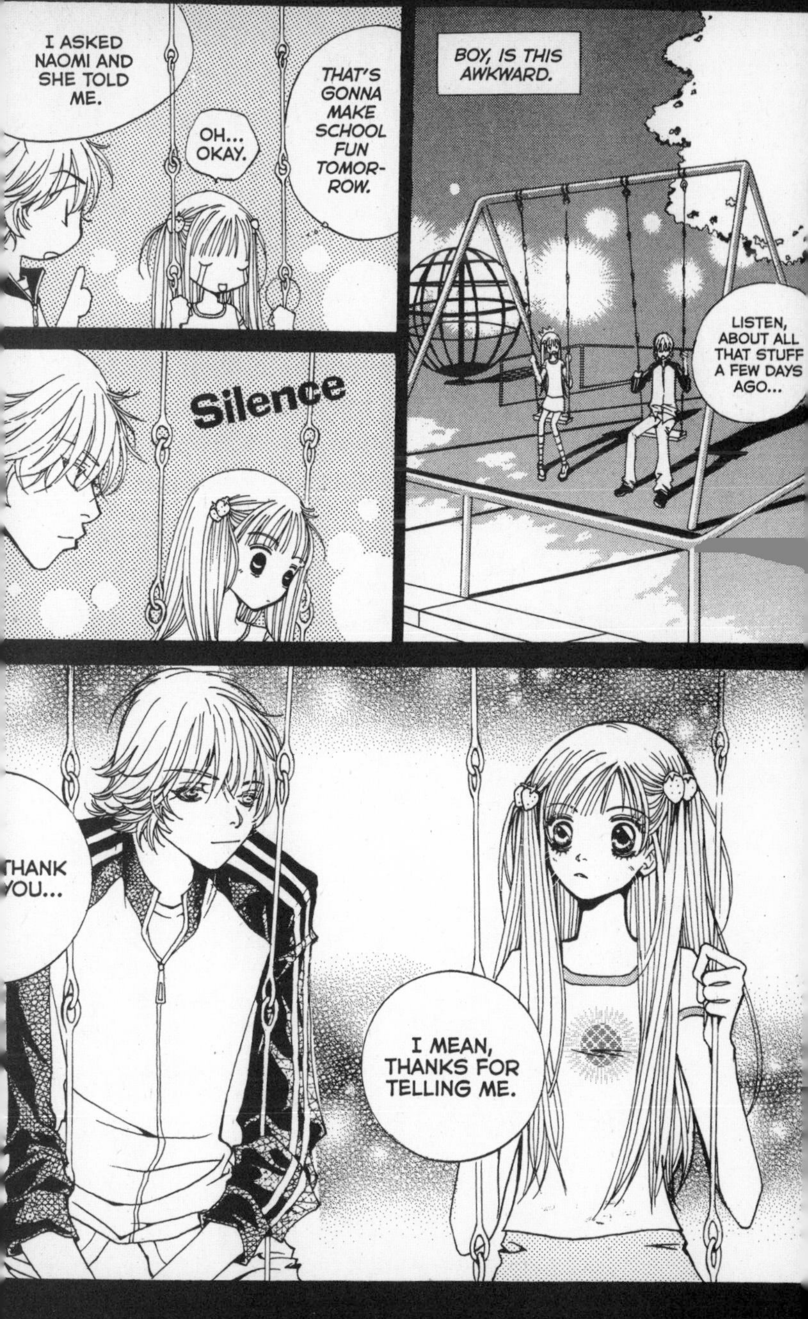
I ASKED NAOMI AND SHE TOLD ME.
OH... OKAY.
THAT'S GONNA MAKE SCHOOL FUN TOMORROW.
Silence
BOY, IS THIS AWKWARD.
LISTEN, ABOUT ALL THAT STUFF A FEW DAYS AGO...
THANK YOU...
I MEAN, THANKS FOR TELLING ME.

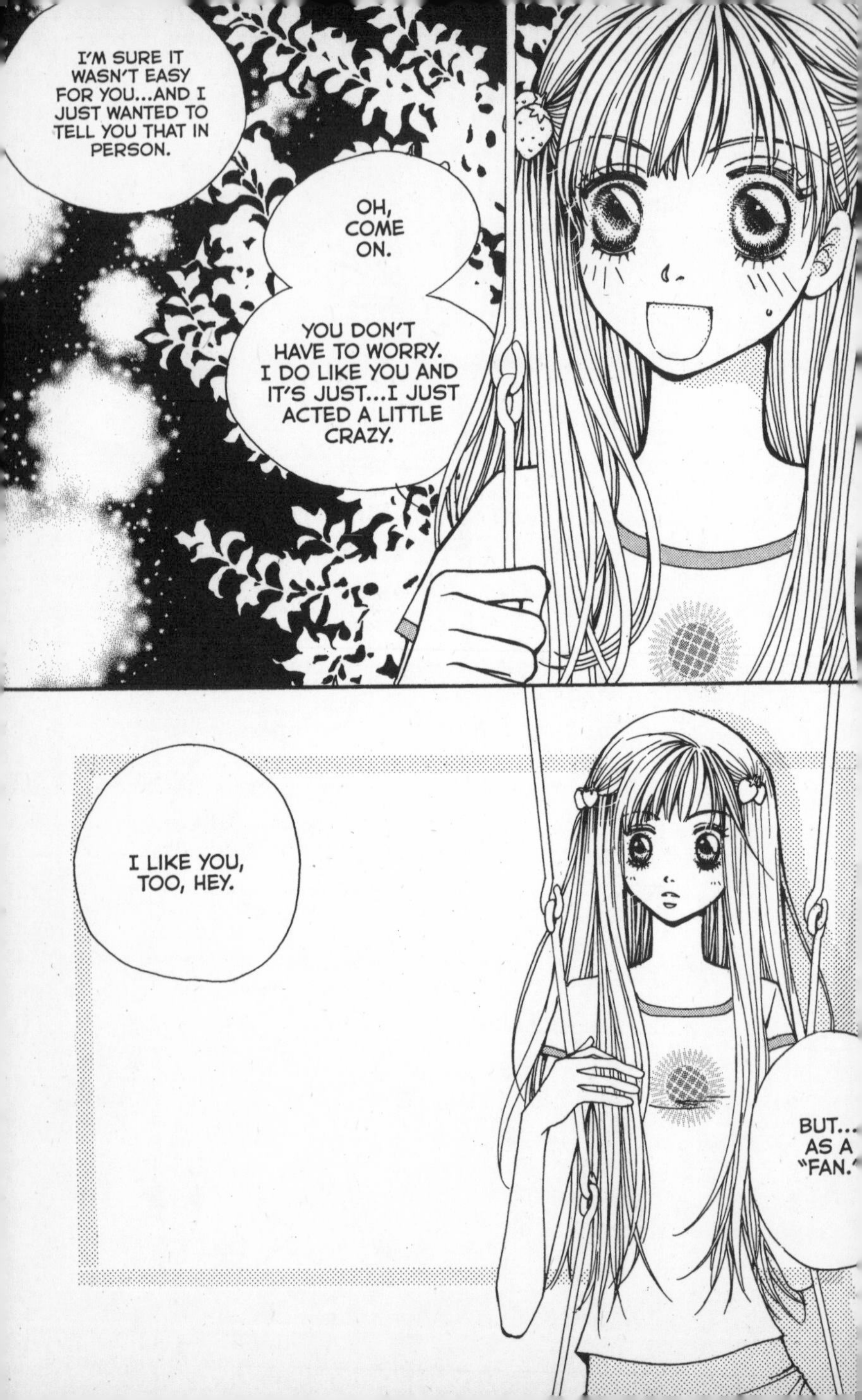
I'M SURE IT WASN'T EASY FOR YOU...AND I JUST WANTED TO TELL YOU THAT IN PERSON.
OH, COME ON.
YOU DON'T HAVE TO WORRY. I DO LIKE YOU AND IT'S JUST...I JUST ACTED A LITTLE CRAZY.
I LIKE YOU, TOO, HEY.
BUT... AS A "FAN."

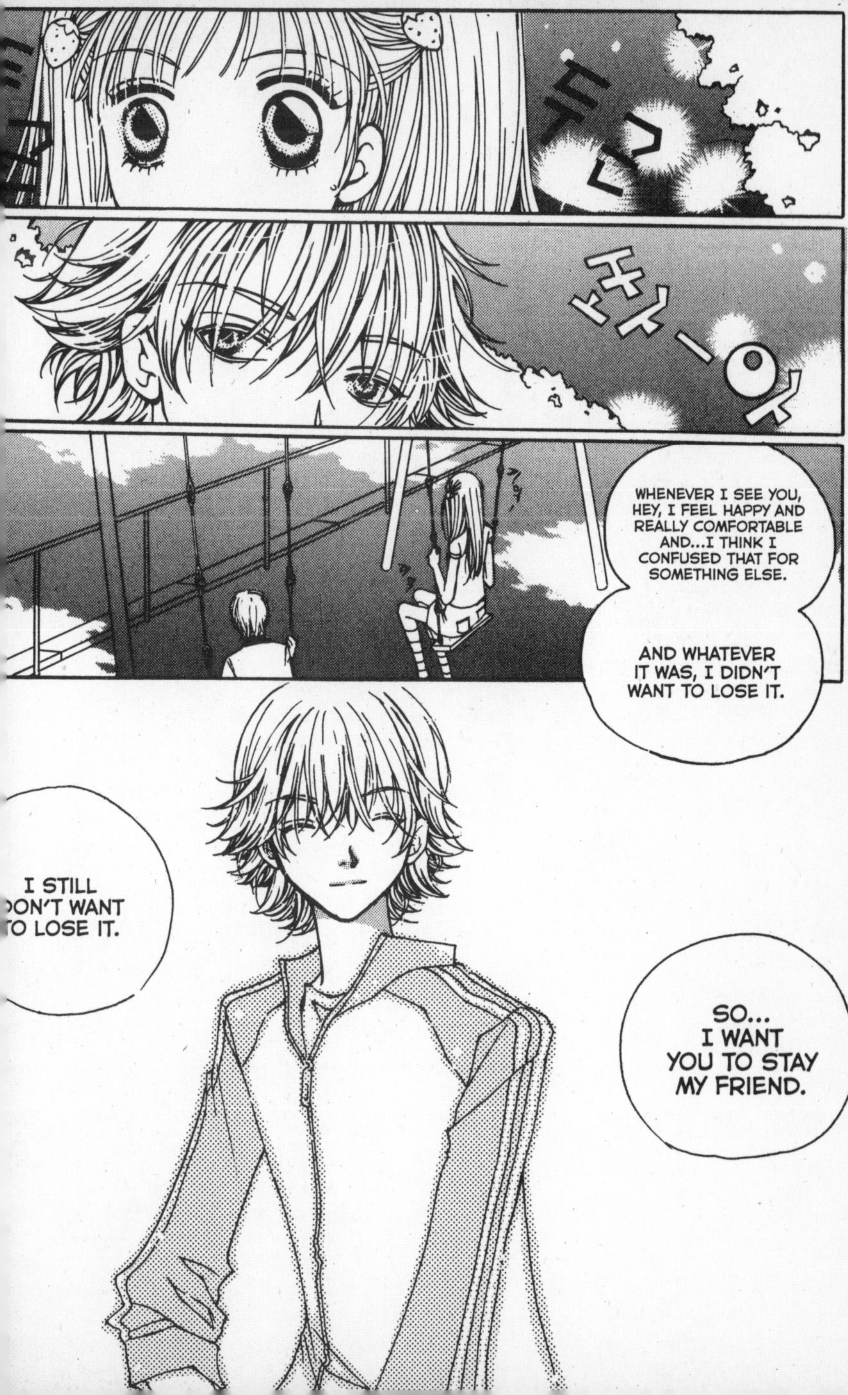
WHENEVER I SEE YOU, HEY, I FEEL HAPPY AND REALLY COMFORTABLE AND...I THINK I CONFUSED THAT FOR SOMETHING ELSE.
AND WHATEVER IT WAS, I DIDN'T WANT TO LOSE IT.
I STILL DON'T WANT TO LOSE IT.
SO... I WANT YOU TO STAY MY FRIEND.

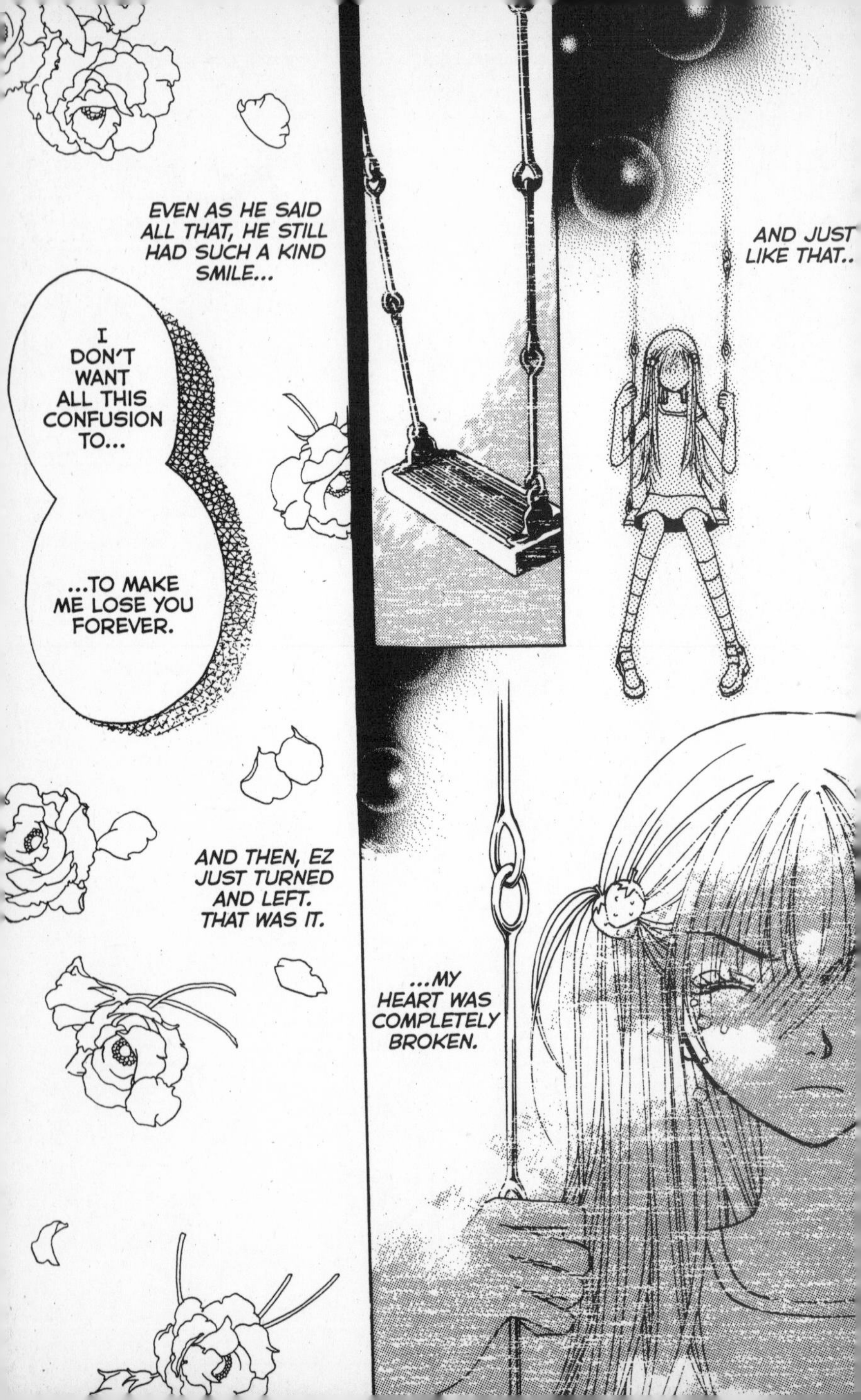
EVEN AS HE SAID ALL THAT, HE STILL HAD SUCH A KIND SMILE...
I DON'T WANT ALL THIS CONFUSION TO...
...TO MAKE ME LOSE YOU FOREVER.
AND THEN, EZ JUST TURNED AND LEFT. THAT WAS IT.
AND JUST LIKE THAT..
...MY HEART WAS COMPLETELY BROKEN.

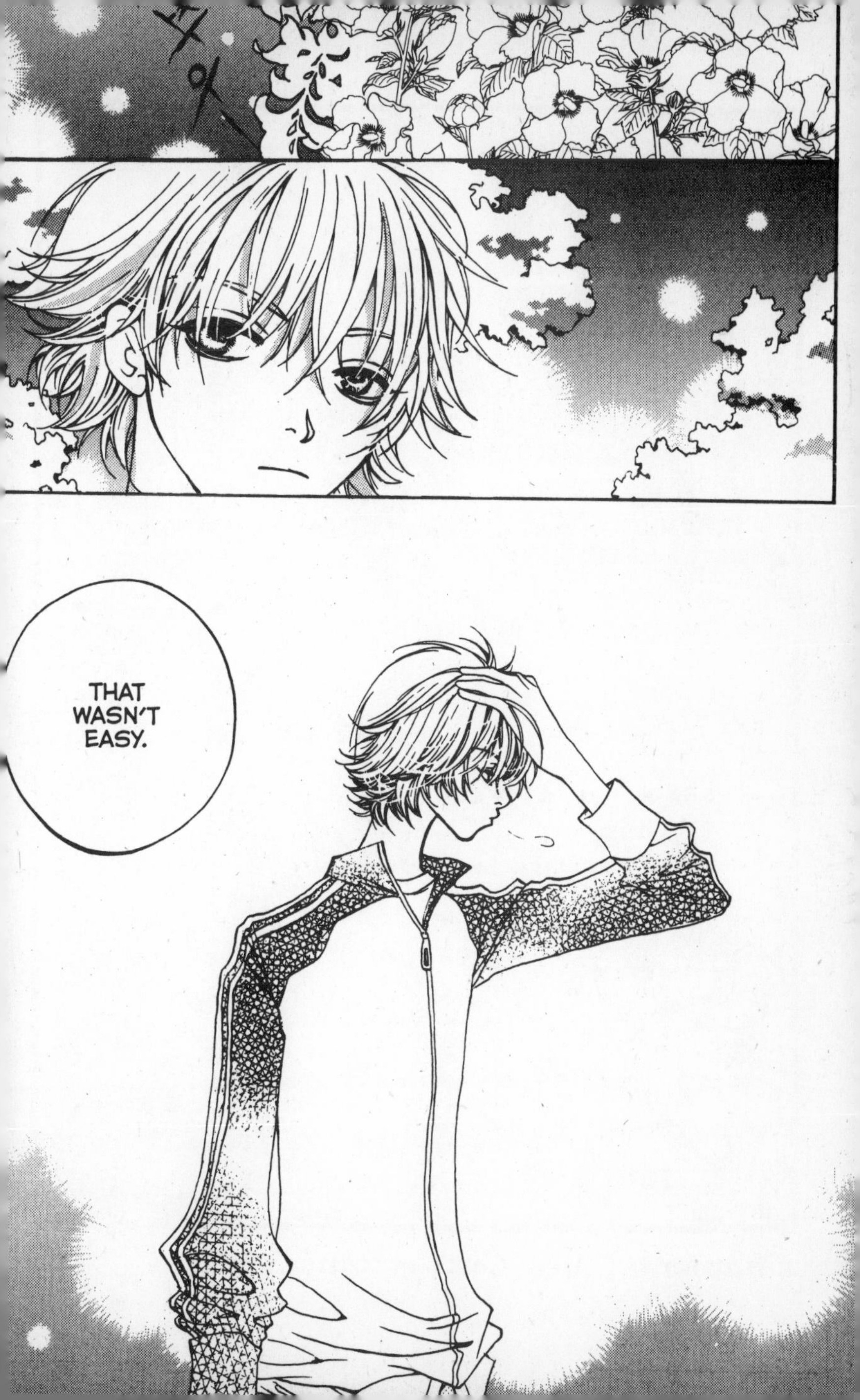
THAT WASN'T EASY.

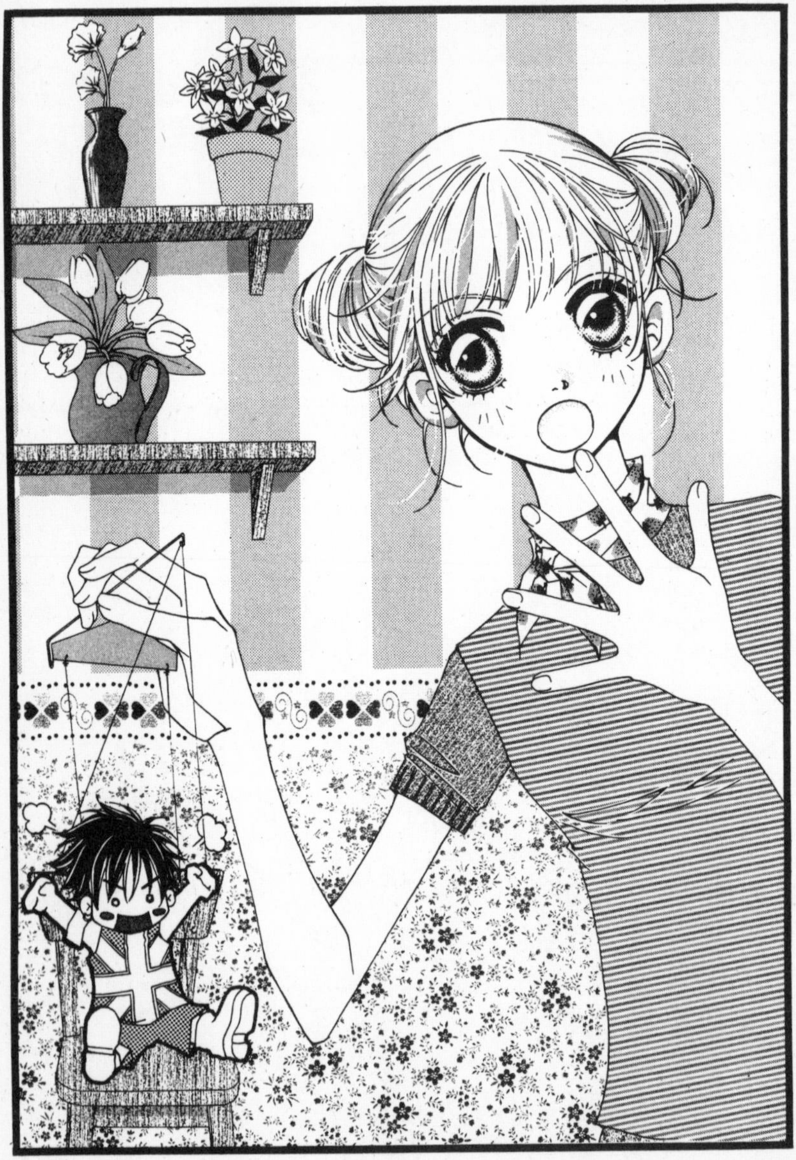

Chapter 4: Their Circumstances 1

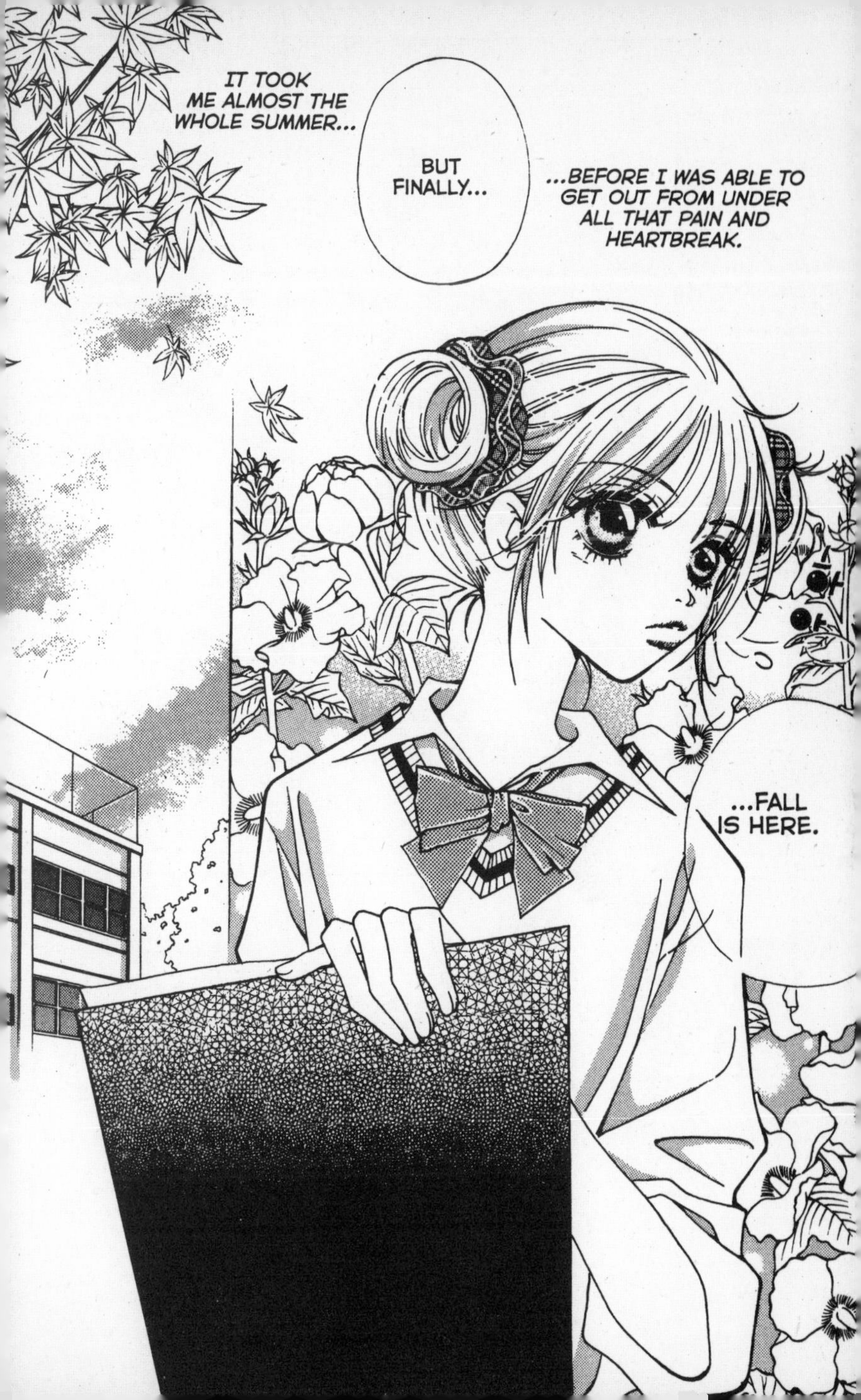
IT TOOK ME ALMOST THE WHOLE SUMMER...
BUT FINALLY...
...BEFORE I WAS ABLE TO GET OUT FROM UNDER ALL THAT PAIN AND HEARTBREAK.
...FALL IS HERE.

THE WEATHER'S PERFECT NOW, HUH? AND AFTER TWO YEARS WE CAN FINALLY CHANGE OUR UNIFORMS. ♡

NOTHING'S PERFECT WHEN YOU'RE TRYING TO FORGET A LOVE.

COME ON, YOU'VE BEEN CRYING FOR DAYS.

REMEMBER WHAT THEY SAY... "TIME HEALS ALL WOUNDS."

AND EITHER WAY, IT ENDED UP OKAY.

I MEAN YOU GOT TO CONFESS AND GET EVERYTHING OFF YOUR CHEST.

I ADMIRE YOU FOR THAT. IT TOOK GUTS.

THANKS, JUNG-EUN.

BUT, THE WAY YOU HANDLED THE WHOLE EO THING... THAT WAS KIND OF A BUMMER, HUH? I MEAN HE WAS PRETTY DECENT, RIGHT?

AND YOU REALLY CRUSHED HIM JUST AS HE WAS BLOSSOMING. THAT'S GONNA COME BACK AND GET YOU, HEY.

I was pretty surprised myself. Tee hee!

WHY ARE YO SAYIN THAT

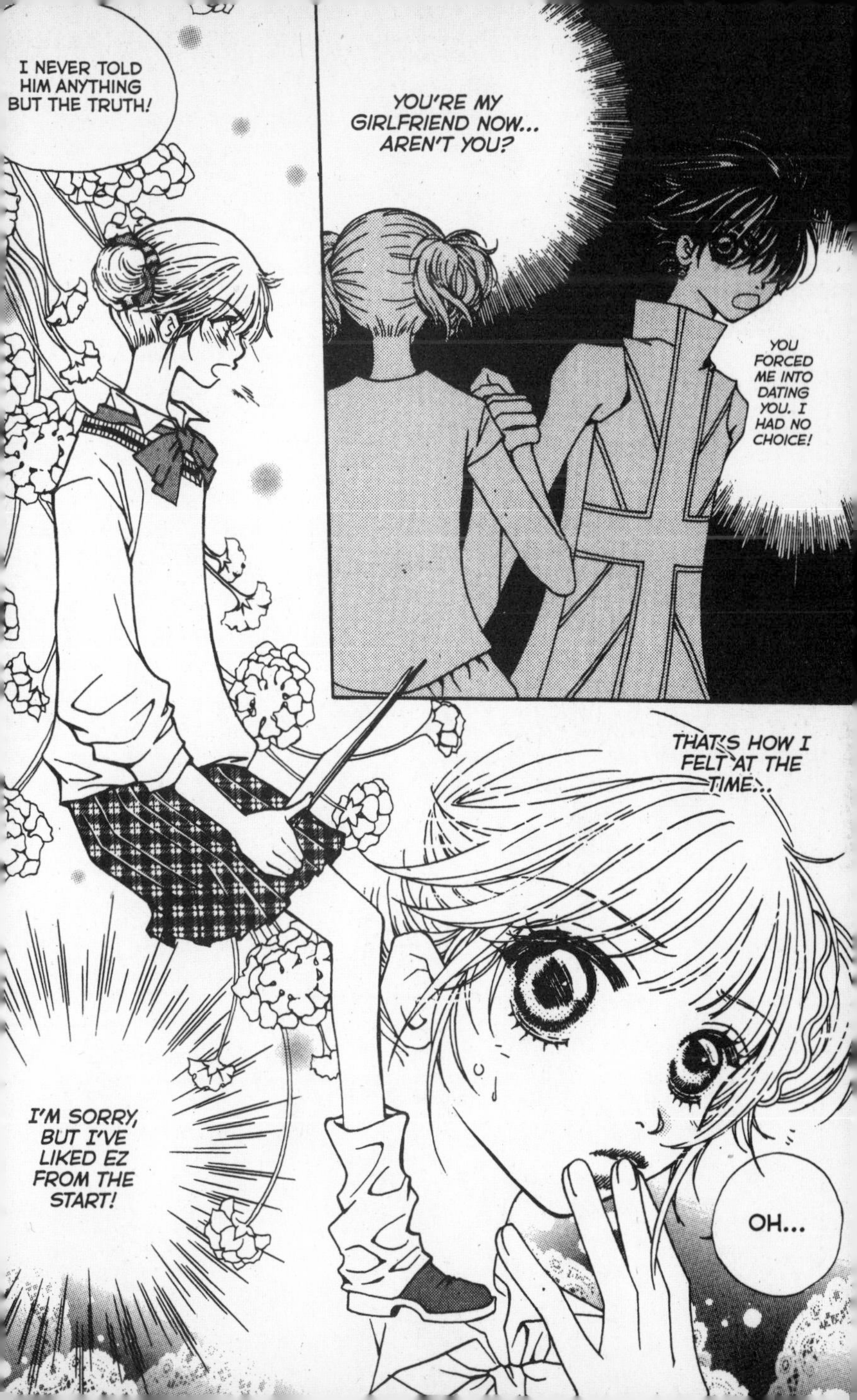
I NEVER TOLD HIM ANYTHING BUT THE TRUTH!
YOU'RE MY GIRLFRIEND NOW... AREN'T YOU?
YOU FORCED ME INTO DATING YOU. I HAD NO CHOICE!
THAT'S HOW I FELT AT THE TIME...
I'M SORRY, BUT I'VE LIKED EZ FROM THE START!
OH...

FINE. THEN IT'S OVER. LET'S MAKE IT OFFICIAL AND BREAK UP.

Ding Dang Dong!

MAYBE IT'S TRUE...

MAYBE HE REALLY DID FEEL THAT STRONGLY ABOUT ME.

YOU'RE RIGHT, I'M SORRY. LET'S JUST GO HOME.

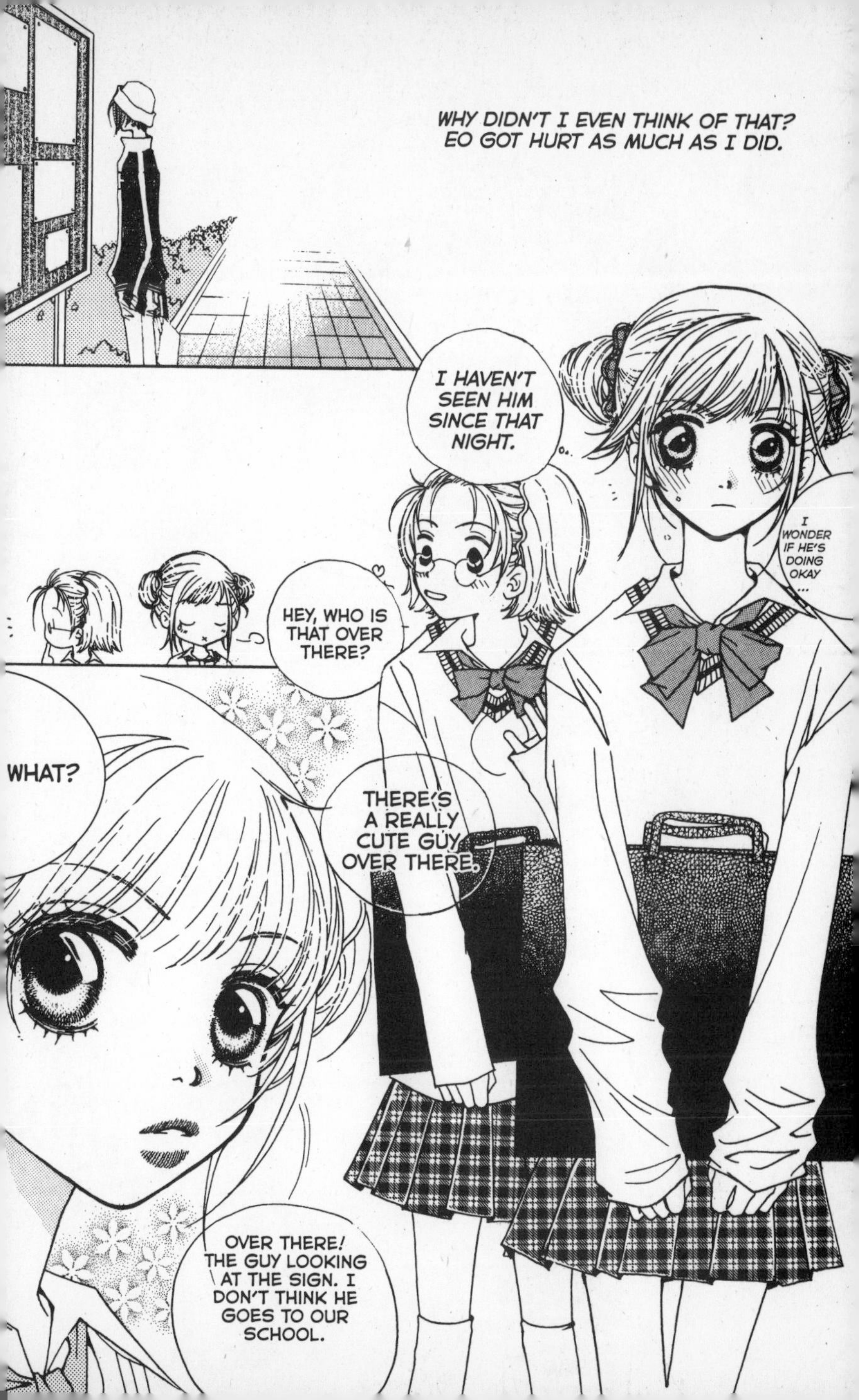
WHY DIDN'T I EVEN THINK OF THAT? EO GOT HURT AS MUCH AS I DID.
I HAVEN'T SEEN HIM SINCE THAT NIGHT.
I WONDER IF HE'S DOING OKAY...
HEY, WHO IS THAT OVER THERE?
WHAT?
THERE'S A REALLY CUTE GUY OVER THERE.
OVER THERE! THE GUY LOOKING AT THE SIGN. I DON'T THINK HE GOES TO OUR SCHOOL.

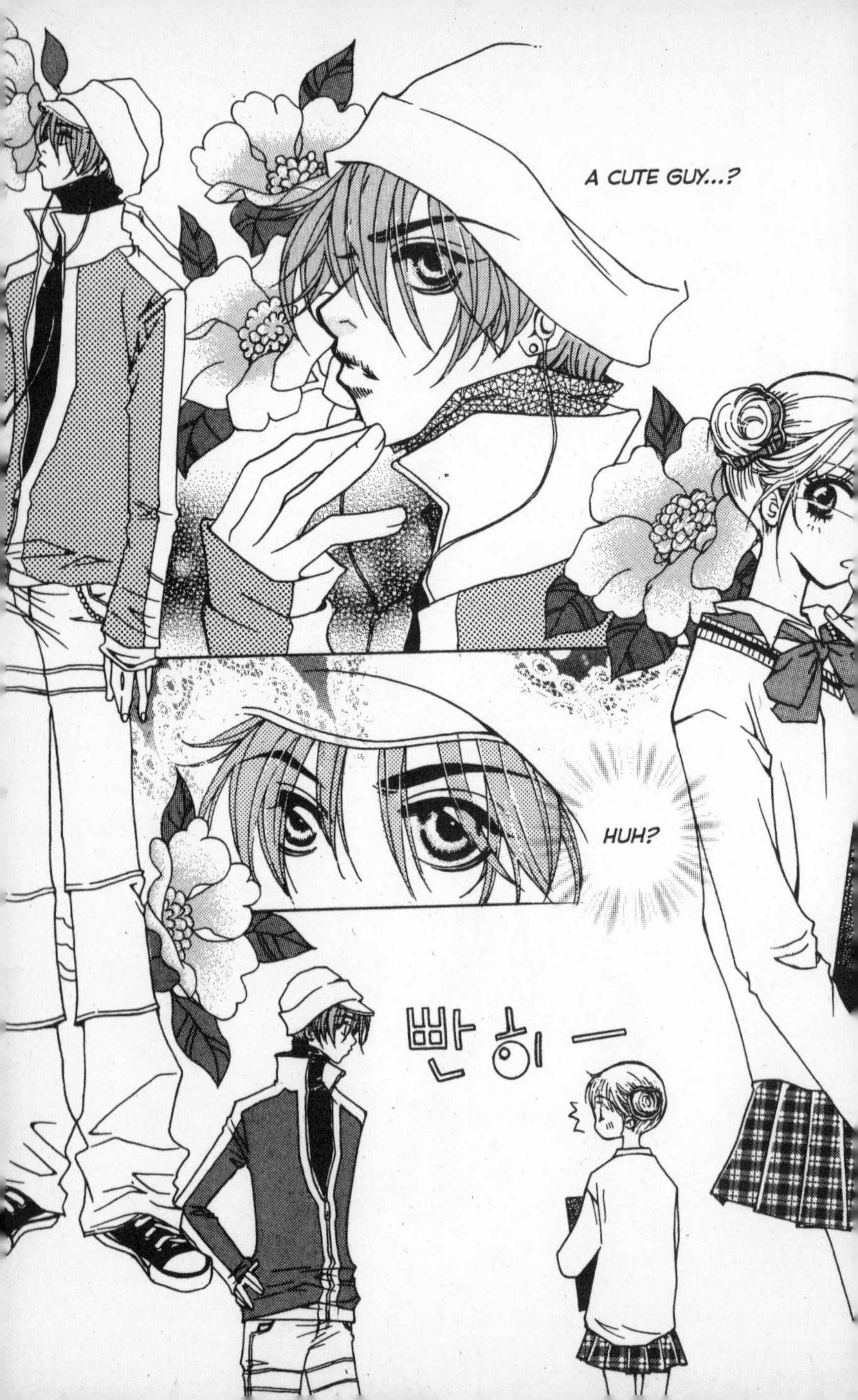
A CUTE GUY...?
HUH?
빤히 ㅡ

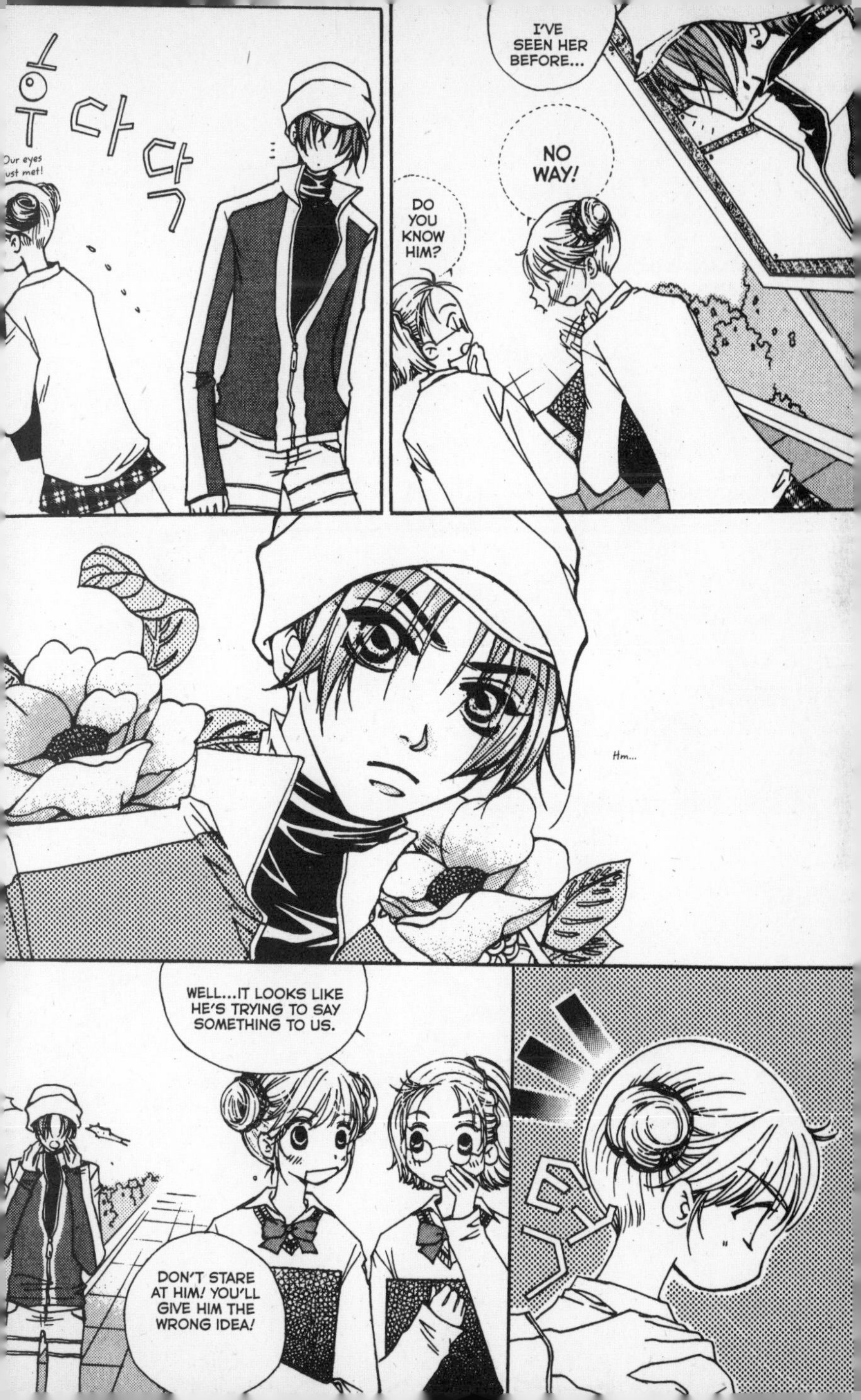

Our eyes ust met!
I'VE SEEN HER BEFORE...
DO YOU KNOW HIM?
NO WAY!
Hm...
WELL...IT LOOKS LIKE HE'S TRYING TO SAY SOMETHING TO US.
DON'T STARE AT HIM! YOU'LL GIVE HIM THE WRONG IDEA!

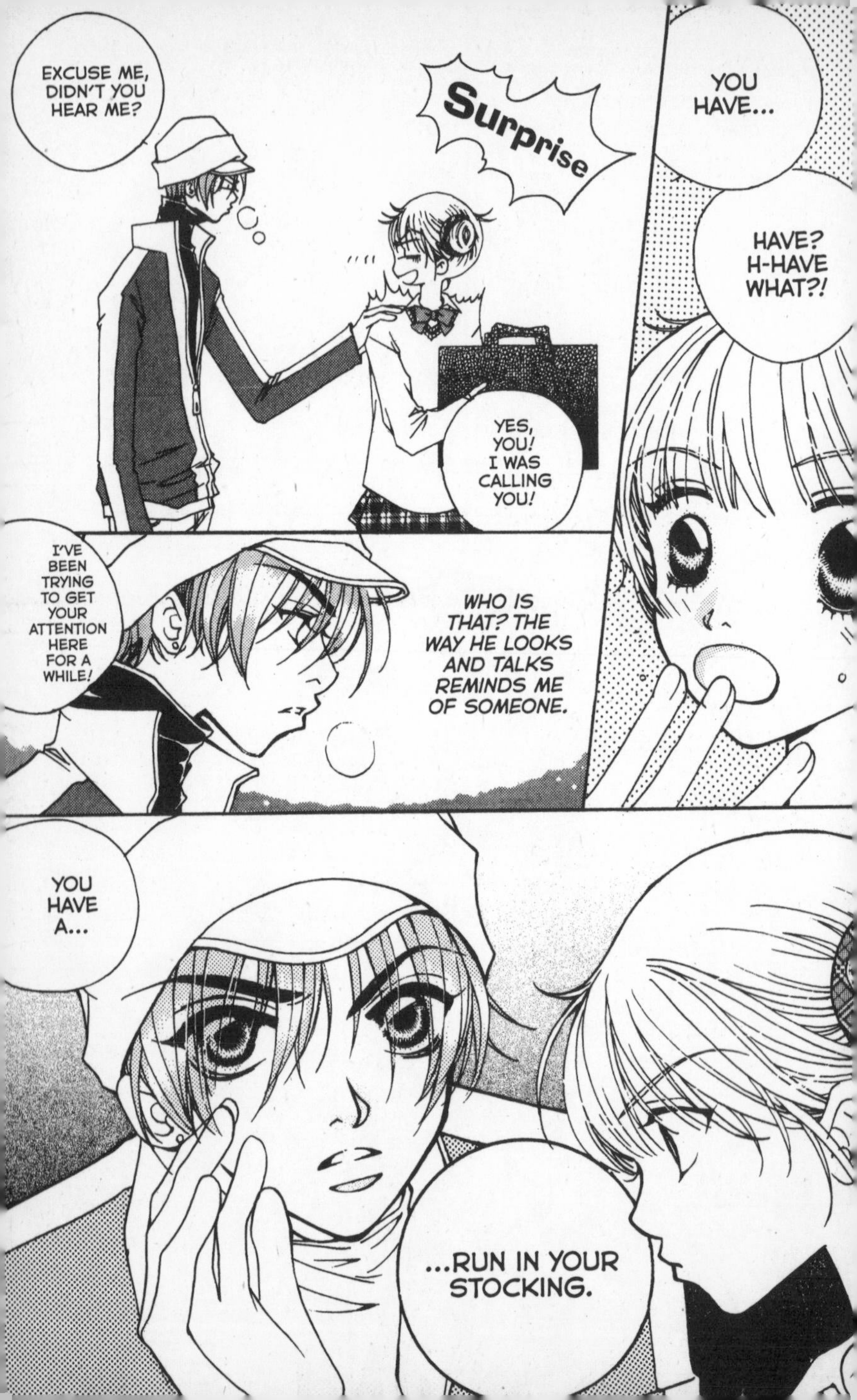
EXCUSE ME, DIDN'T YOU HEAR ME?
Surprise
YES, YOU! I WAS CALLING YOU!
I'VE BEEN TRYING TO GET YOUR ATTENTION HERE FOR A WHILE!
WHO IS THAT? THE WAY HE LOOKS AND TALKS REMINDS ME OF SOMEONE.
YOU HAVE...
HAVE? H-HAVE WHAT?!
YOU HAVE A...
...RUN IN YOUR STOCKING.

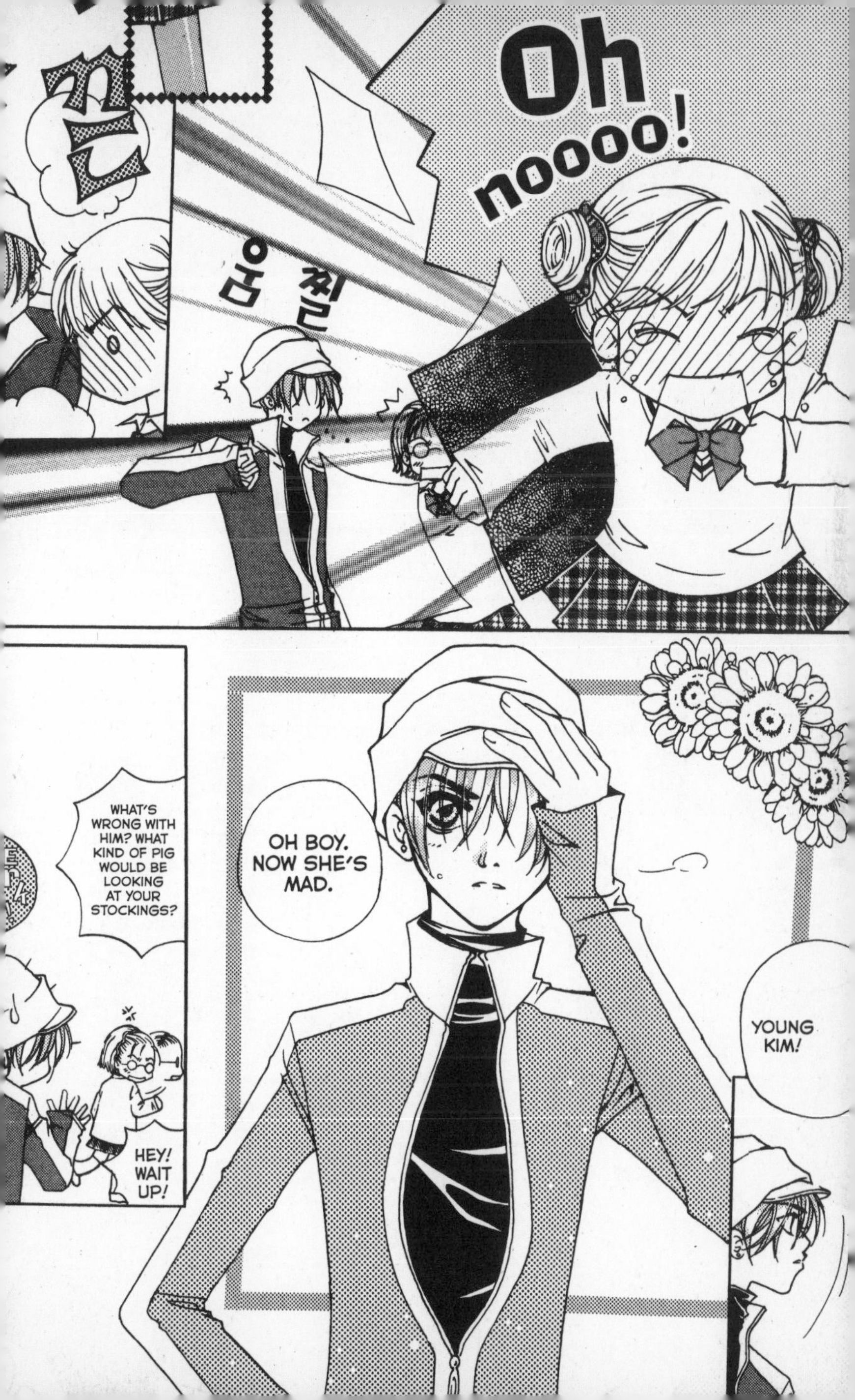
Oh noooo!
움찔
WHAT'S WRONG WITH HIM? WHAT KIND OF PIG WOULD BE LOOKING AT YOUR STOCKINGS?
HEY! WAIT UP!
OH BOY. NOW SHE'S MAD.
YOUNG KIM!

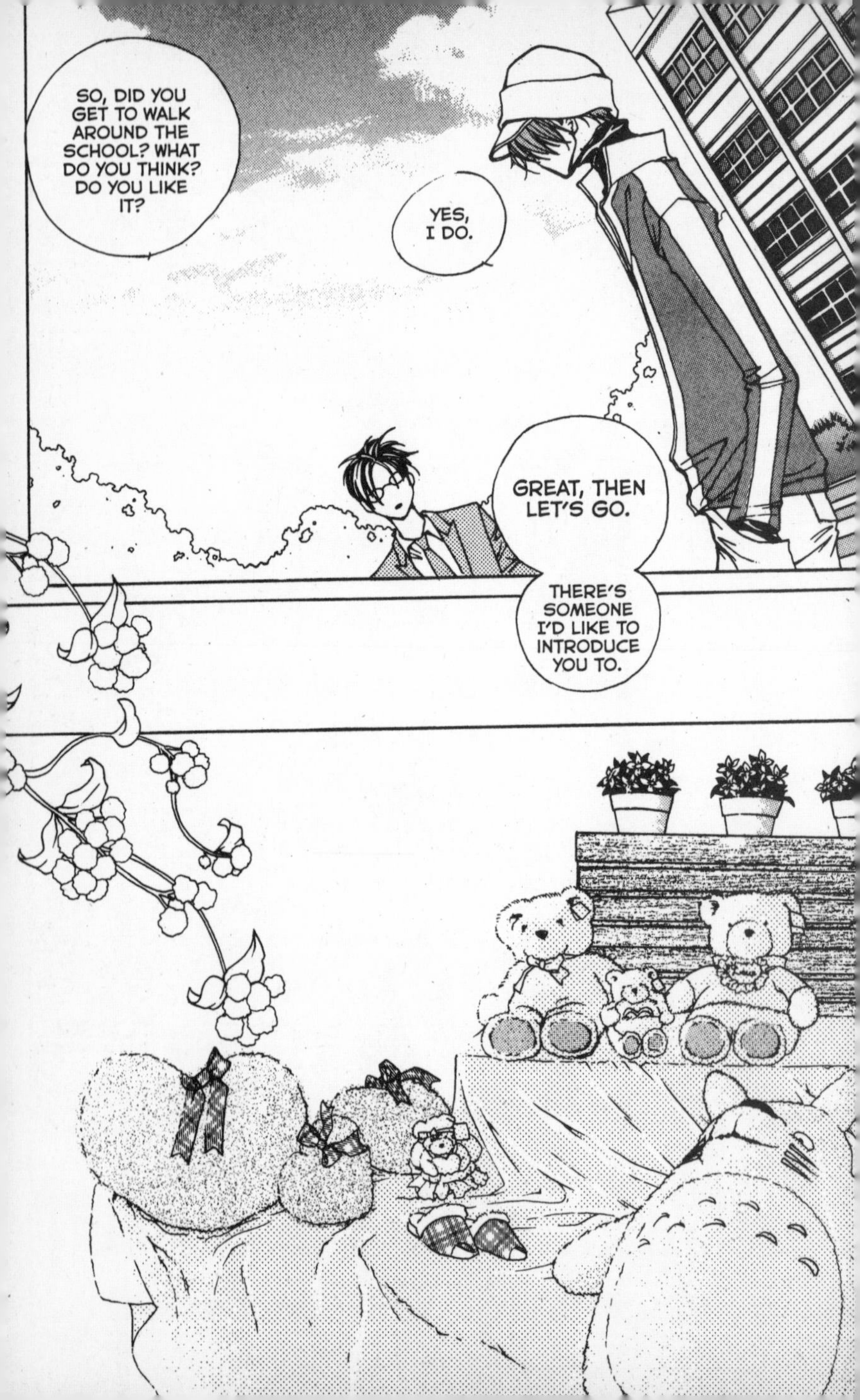
SO, DID YOU GET TO WALK AROUND THE SCHOOL? WHAT DO YOU THINK? DO YOU LIKE IT?
YES, I DO.
GREAT, THEN LET'S GO.
THERE'S SOMEONE I'D LIKE TO INTRODUCE YOU TO.

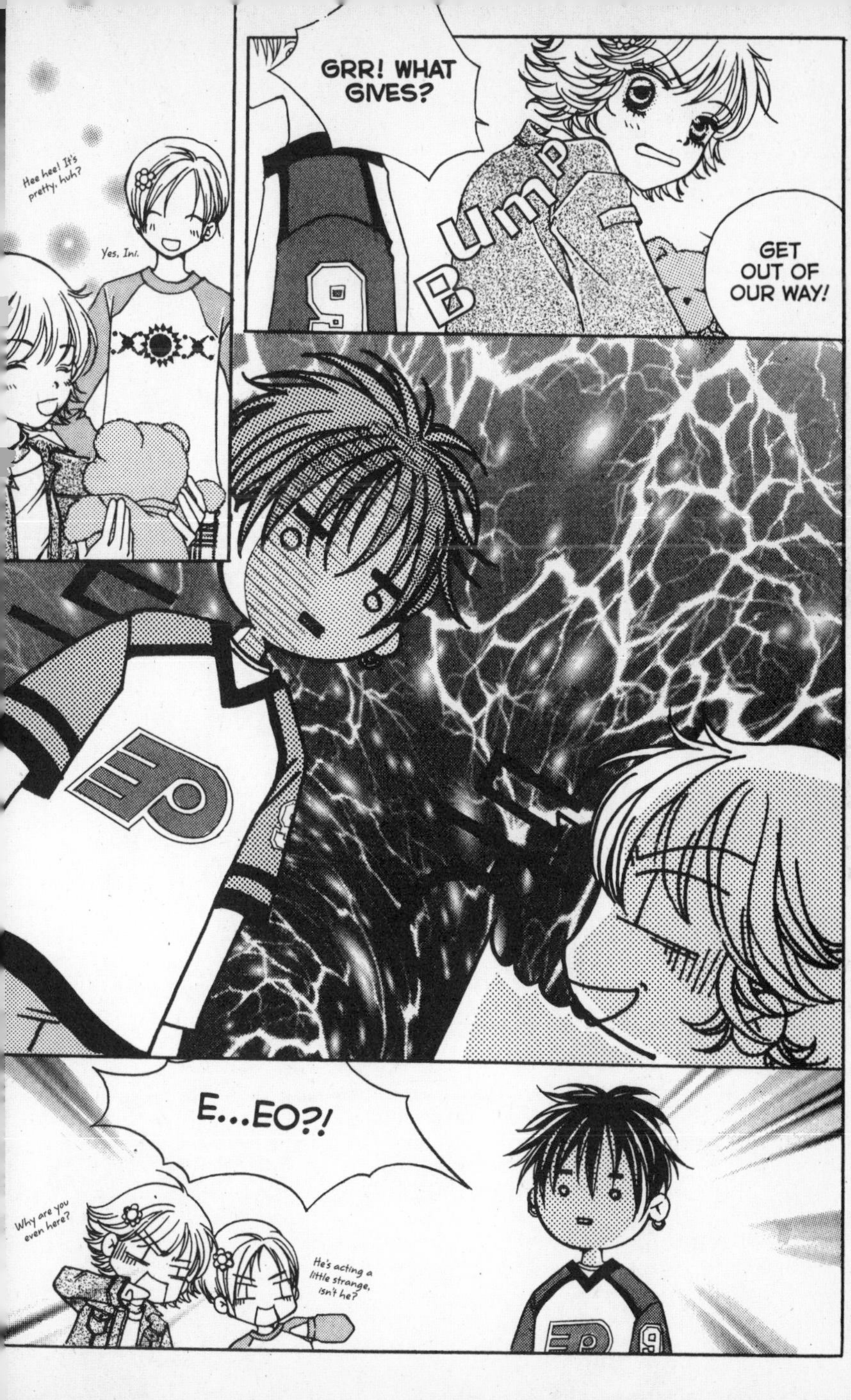
GET OUT OF OUR WAY!
BUMP
GRR! WHAT GIVES?
Yes, Ini.
Hee hee! It's pretty, huh?
E...EO?!
He's acting a little strange, isn't he?
Why are you even here?

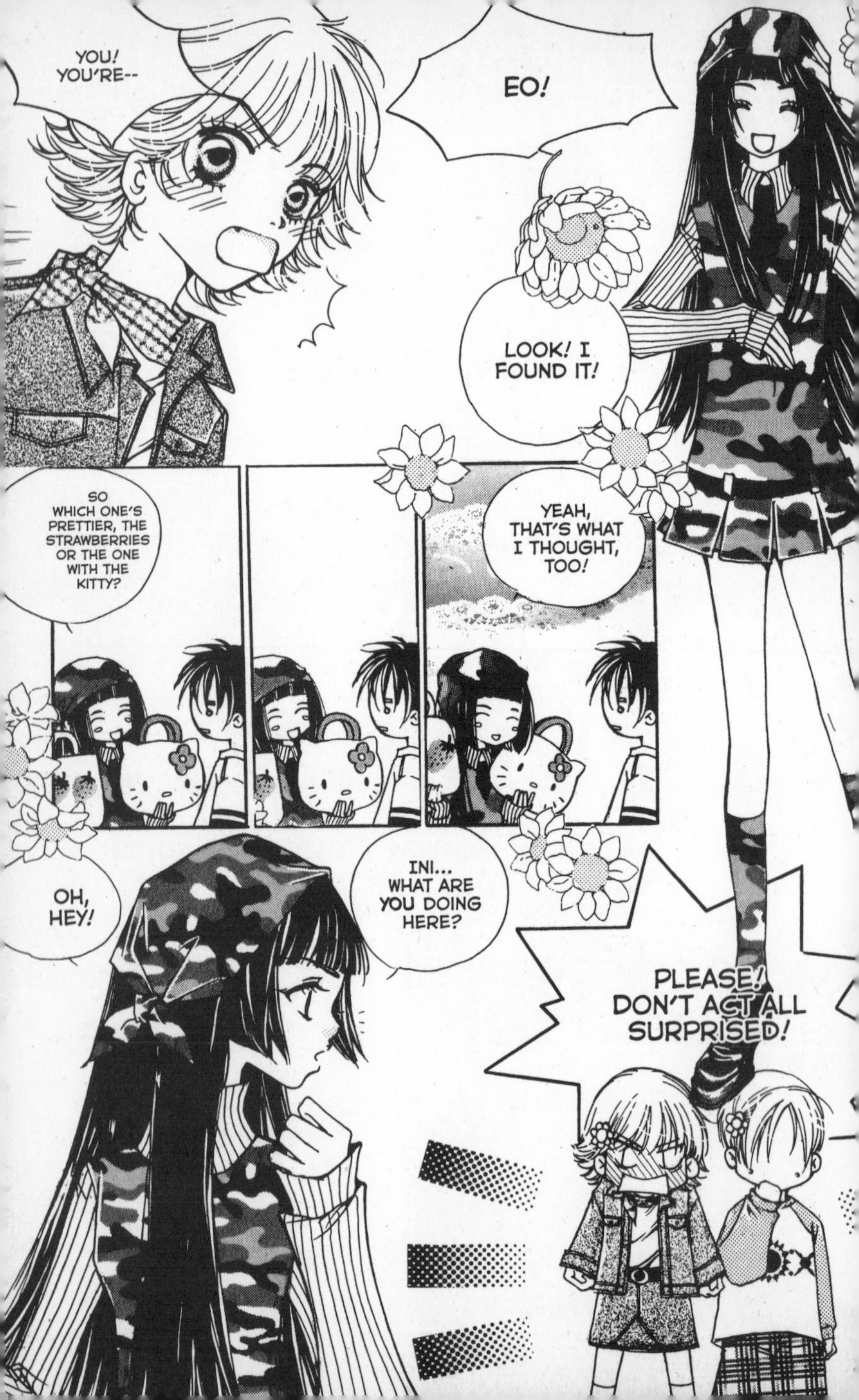
YOU! YOU'RE--
EO!
LOOK! I FOUND IT!
SO WHICH ONE'S PRETTIER, THE STRAWBERRIES OR THE ONE WITH THE KITTY?
YEAH, THAT'S WHAT I THOUGHT, TOO!
OH, HEY!
INI... WHAT ARE YOU DOING HERE?
PLEASE! DON'T ACT ALL SURPRISED!

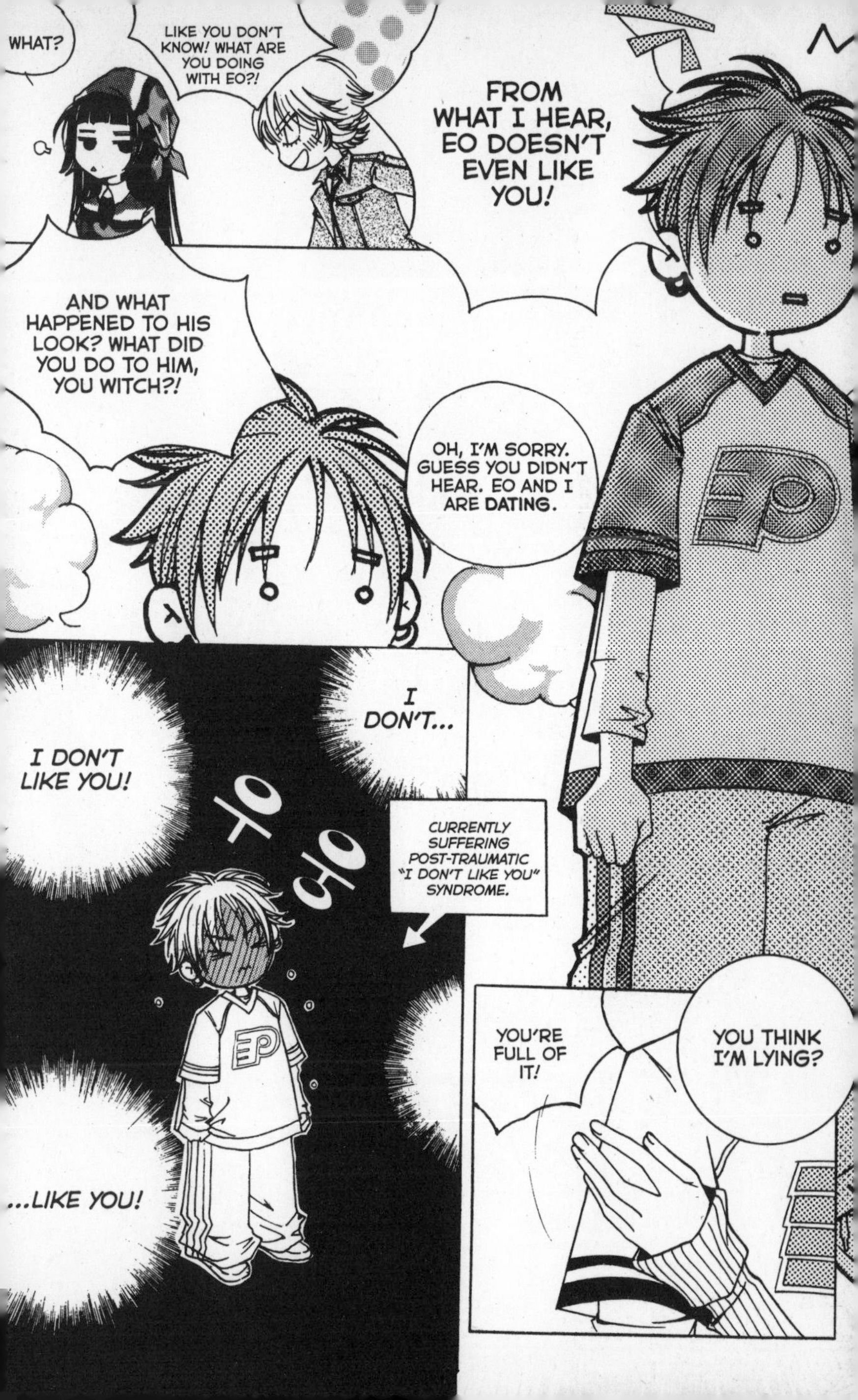
WHAT?
LIKE YOU DON'T KNOW! WHAT ARE YOU DOING WITH EO?!
FROM WHAT I HEAR, EO DOESN'T EVEN LIKE YOU!
AND WHAT HAPPENED TO HIS LOOK? WHAT DID YOU DO TO HIM, YOU WITCH?!
OH, I'M SORRY. GUESS YOU DIDN'T HEAR. EO AND I ARE DATING.
I DON'T...
I DON'T LIKE YOU!
...LIKE YOU!
CURRENTLY SUFFERING POST-TRAUMATIC "I DON'T LIKE YOU" SYNDROME.
YOU'RE FULL OF IT!
YOU THINK I'M LYING?

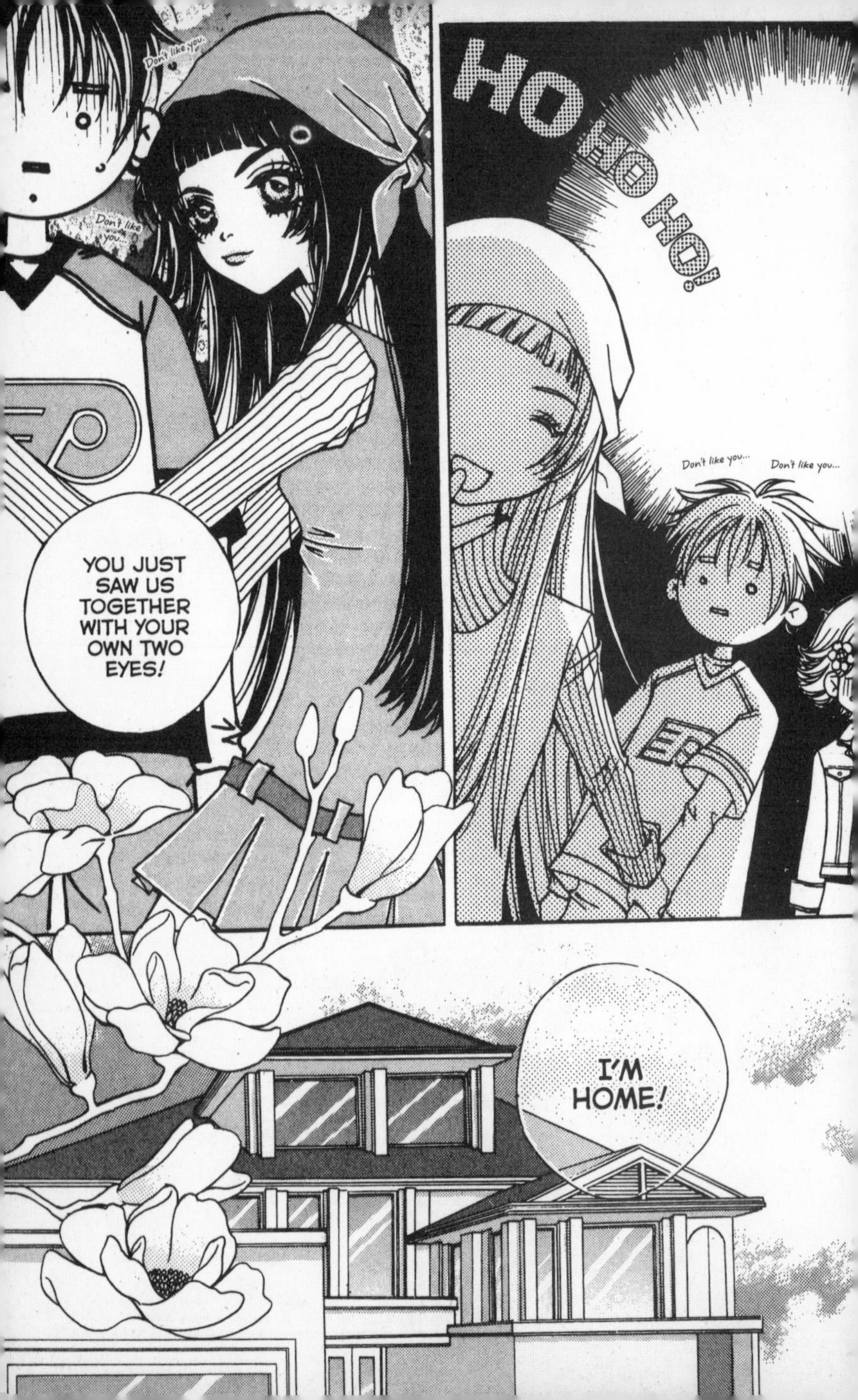
Don't like you.
Don't like you...
YOU JUST SAW US TOGETHER WITH YOUR OWN TWO EYES!
HO HO HO!
Don't like you...
Don't like you...
I'M HOME!

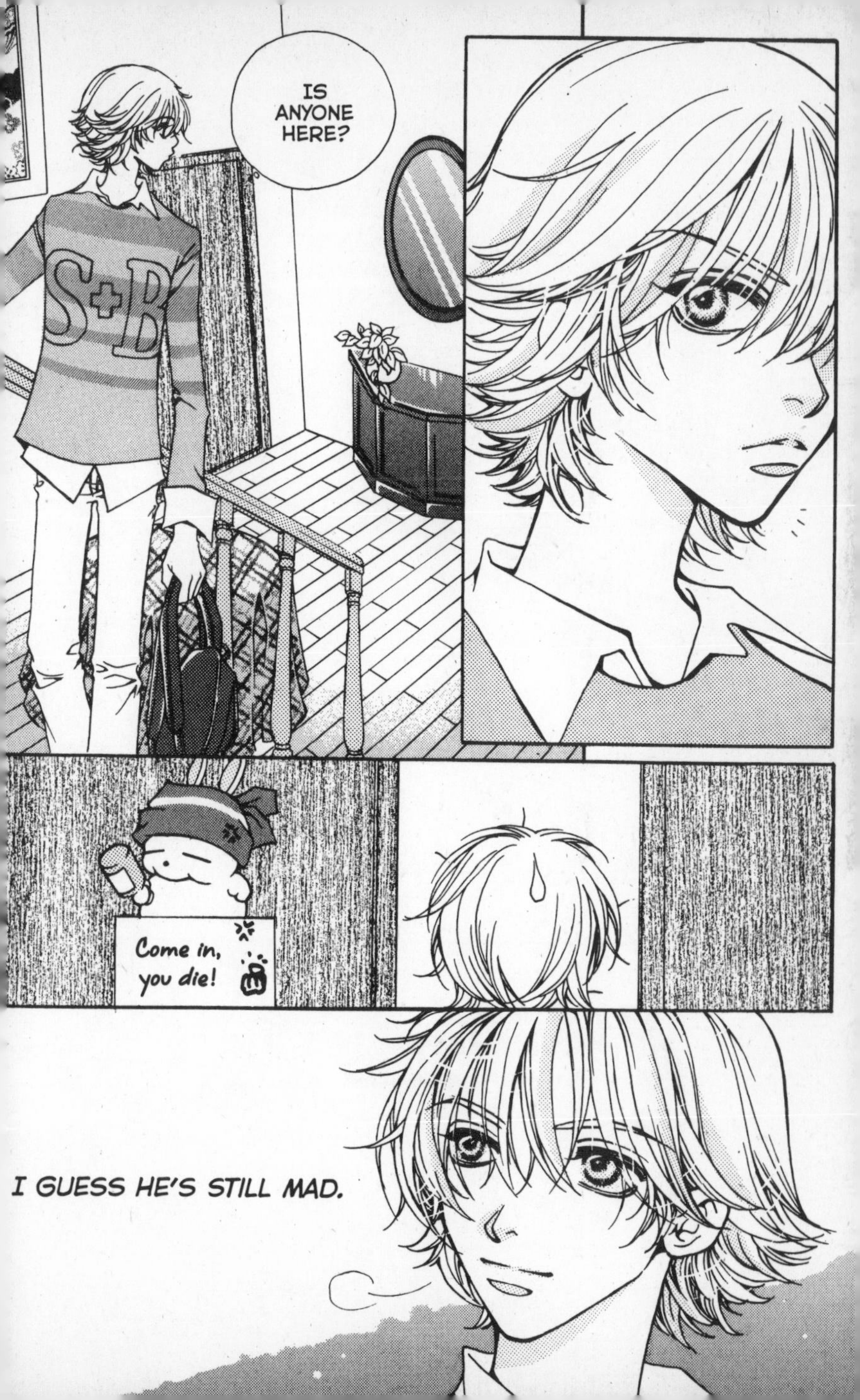
IS ANYONE HERE?
S+B
Come in, you die!
I GUESS HE'S STILL MAD.

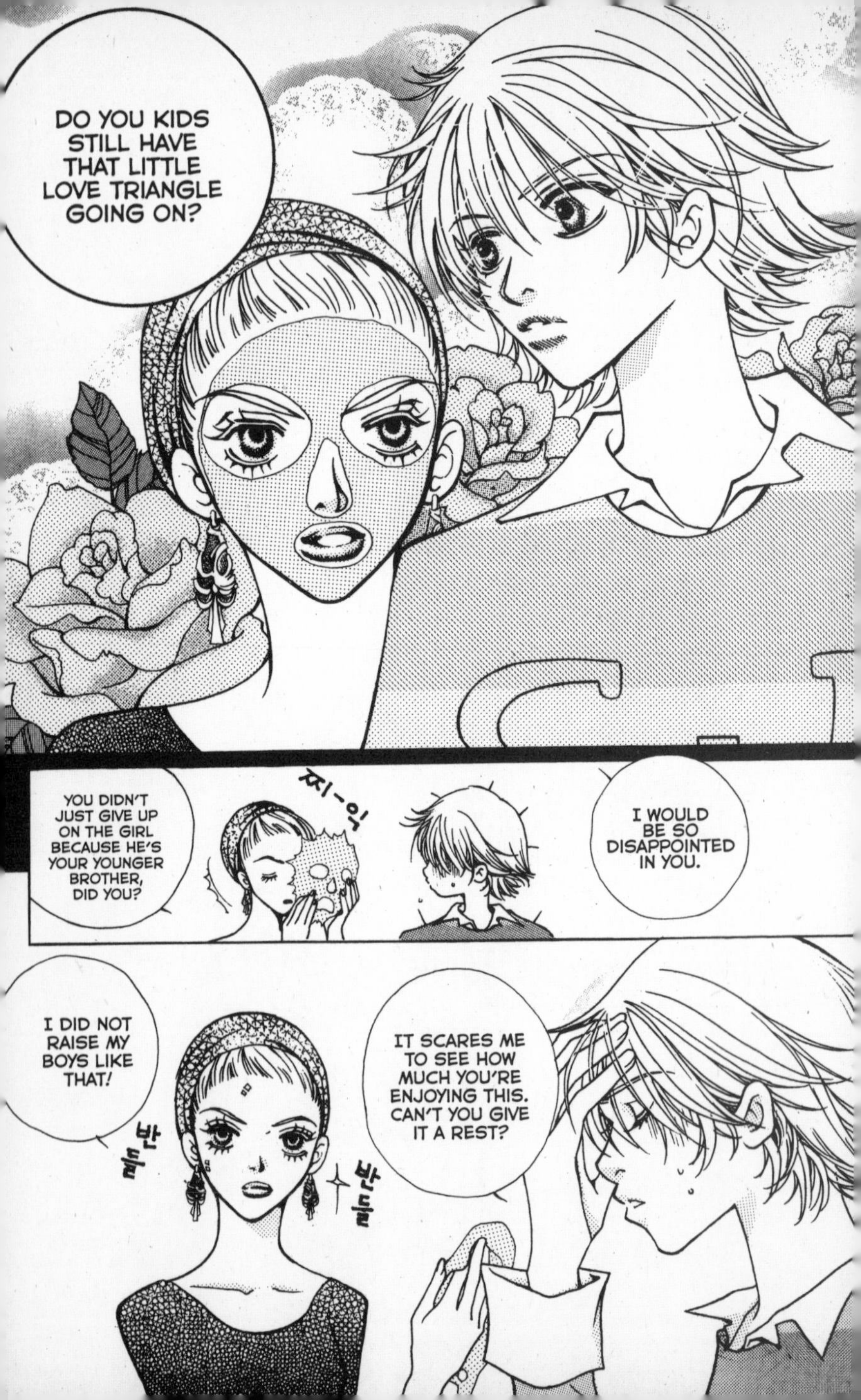
DO YOU KIDS STILL HAVE THAT LITTLE LOVE TRIANGLE GOING ON?
YOU DIDN'T JUST GIVE UP ON THE GIRL BECAUSE HE'S YOUR YOUNGER BROTHER, DID YOU?
찌~익
I WOULD BE SO DISAPPOINTED IN YOU.
I DID NOT RAISE MY BOYS LIKE THAT!
반들
반들
IT SCARES ME TO SEE HOW MUCH YOU'RE ENJOYING THIS. CAN'T YOU GIVE IT A REST?

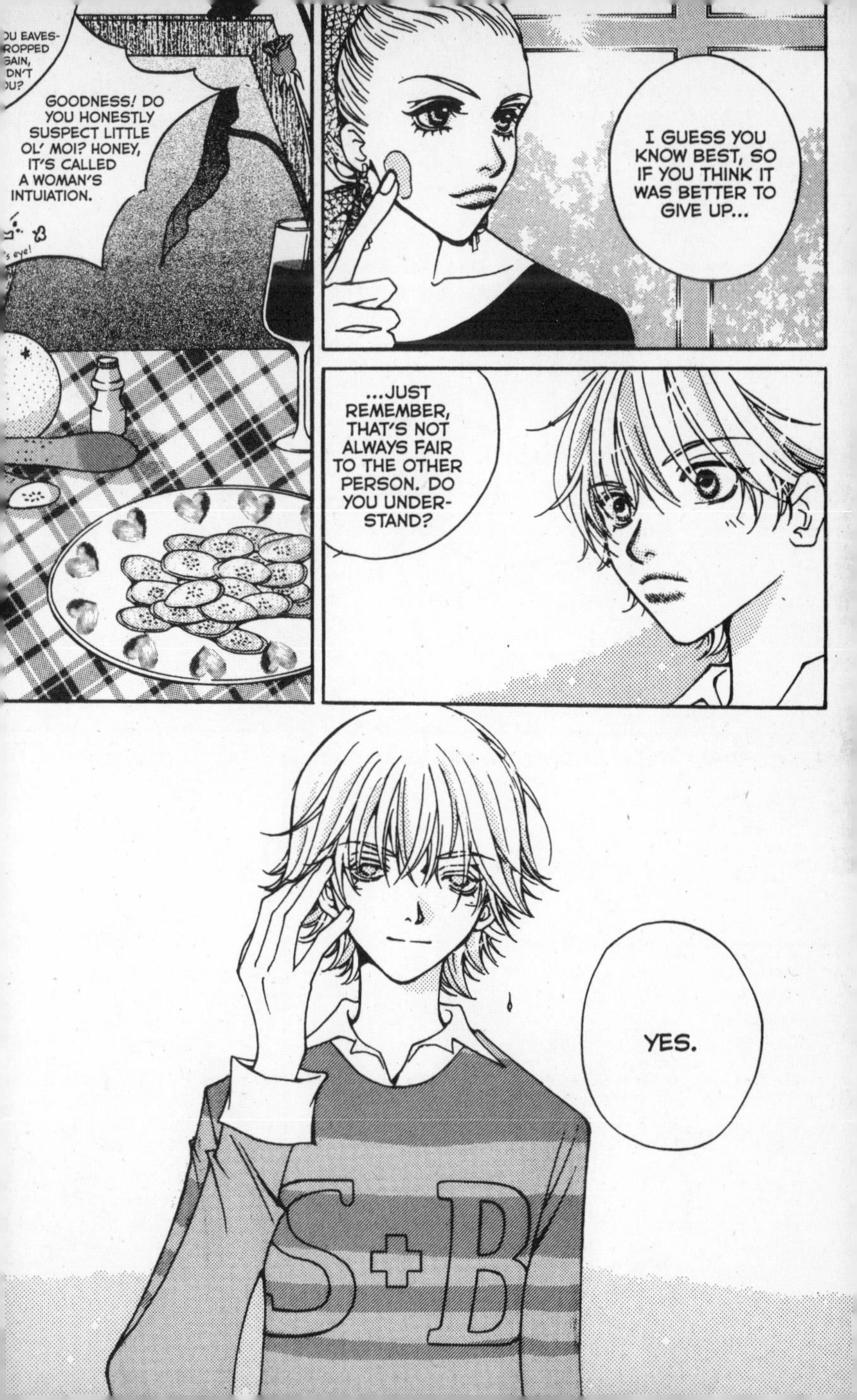
OU EAVES- ROPPED GAIN, DN'T OU?
GOODNESS! DO YOU HONESTLY SUSPECT LITTLE OL' MOI? HONEY, IT'S CALLED A WOMAN'S INTUIATION.
I GUESS YOU KNOW BEST, SO IF YOU THINK IT WAS BETTER TO GIVE UP...
...JUST REMEMBER, THAT'S NOT ALWAYS FAIR TO THE OTHER PERSON. DO YOU UNDER- STAND?
YES.

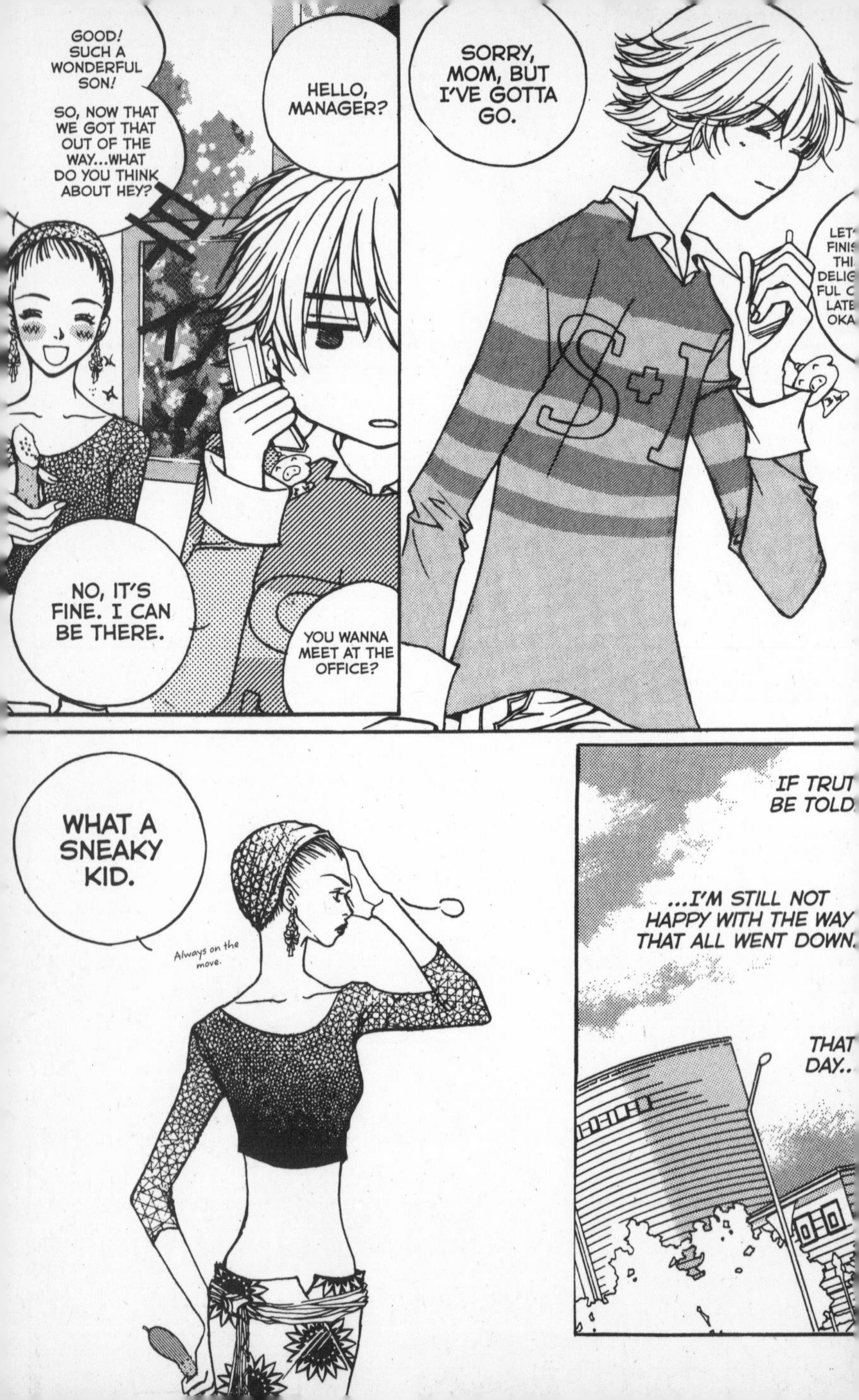
GOOD! SUCH A WONDERFUL SON!
SO, NOW THAT WE GOT THAT OUT OF THE WAY...WHAT DO YOU THINK ABOUT HEY?
HELLO, MANAGER?
NO, IT'S FINE. I CAN BE THERE.
YOU WANNA MEET AT THE OFFICE?
SORRY, MOM, BUT I'VE GOTTA GO.
WHAT A SNEAKY KID.
Always on the move.
IF TRUT BE TOLD
...I'M STILL NOT HAPPY WITH THE WAY THAT ALL WENT DOWN.
THAT DAY..

I WAS SO COLD TO HER...

"I'M FINE. DON'T WORRY ABOUT ME."

"AS LONG AS IT'S OKAY WITH YOU..."

"...I'M OKAY"."

AND IT WAS THE FIRST TIME...

...THAT I FELT I COULD ACTUALLY LOVE HEY.

AND THAT WAS IT. I ENDED IT.

AND NOW IT'S OVER.

Why did I do that?

WHERE IS THAT MUSIC COMING FROM?

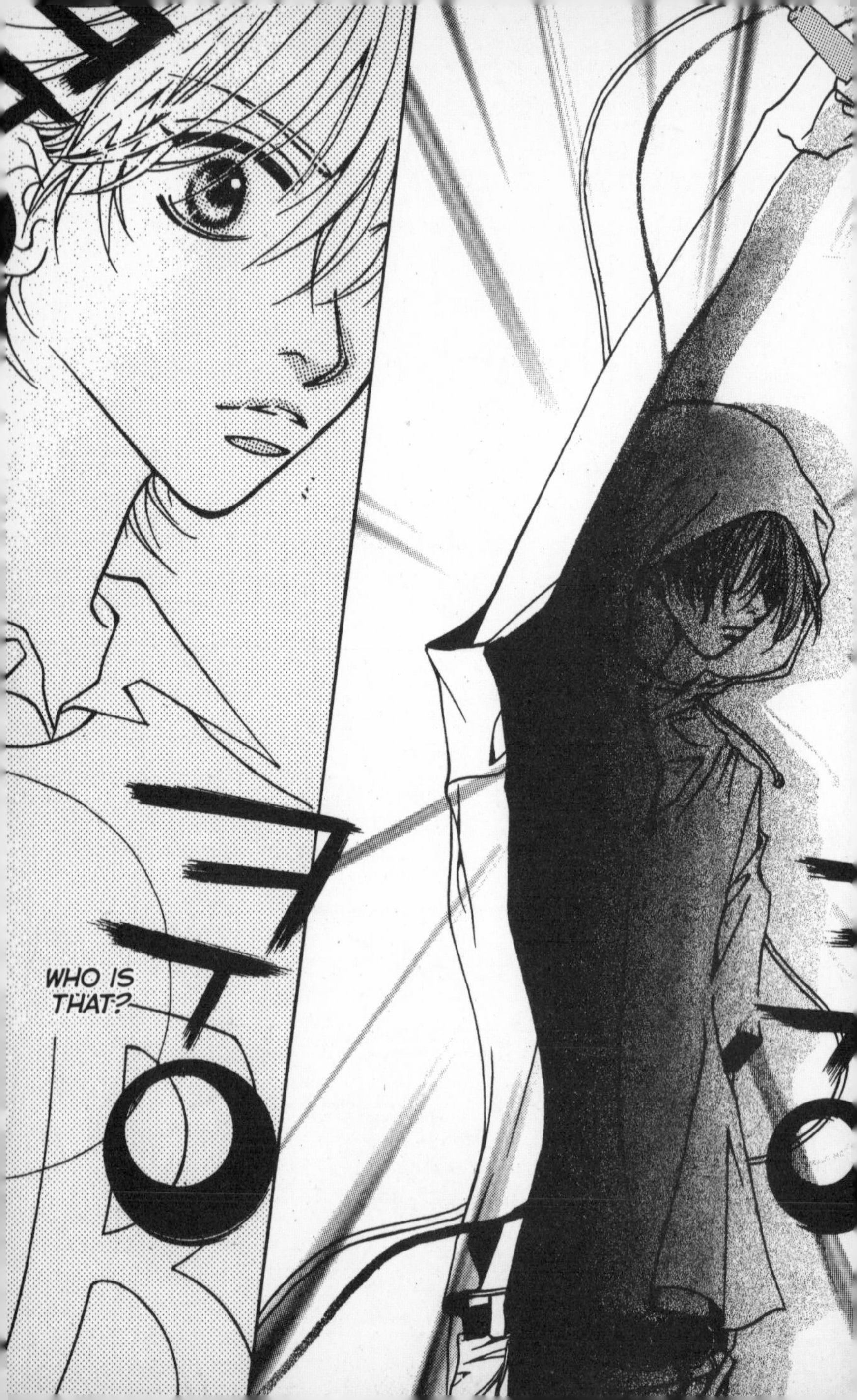
WHO IS THAT?

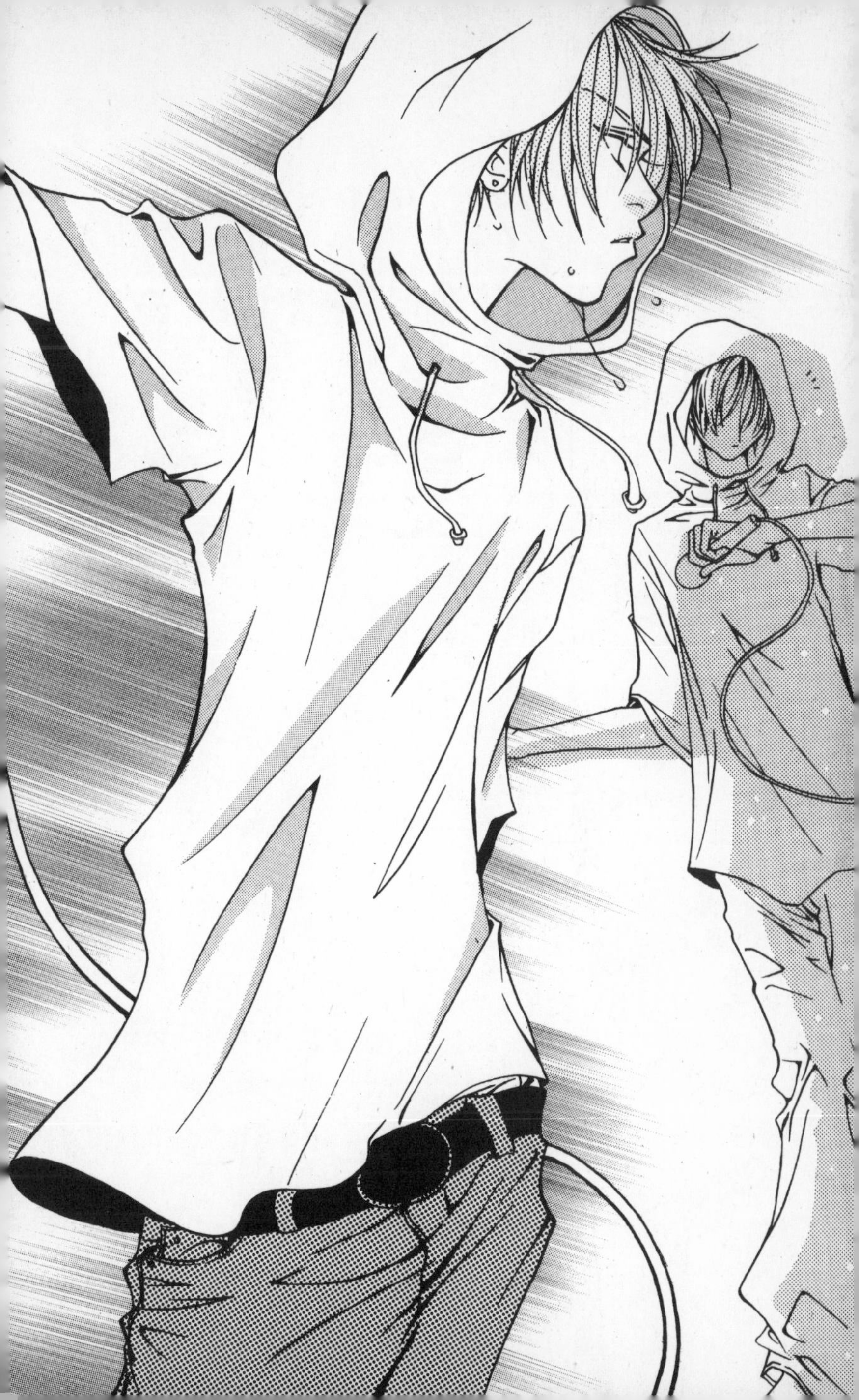

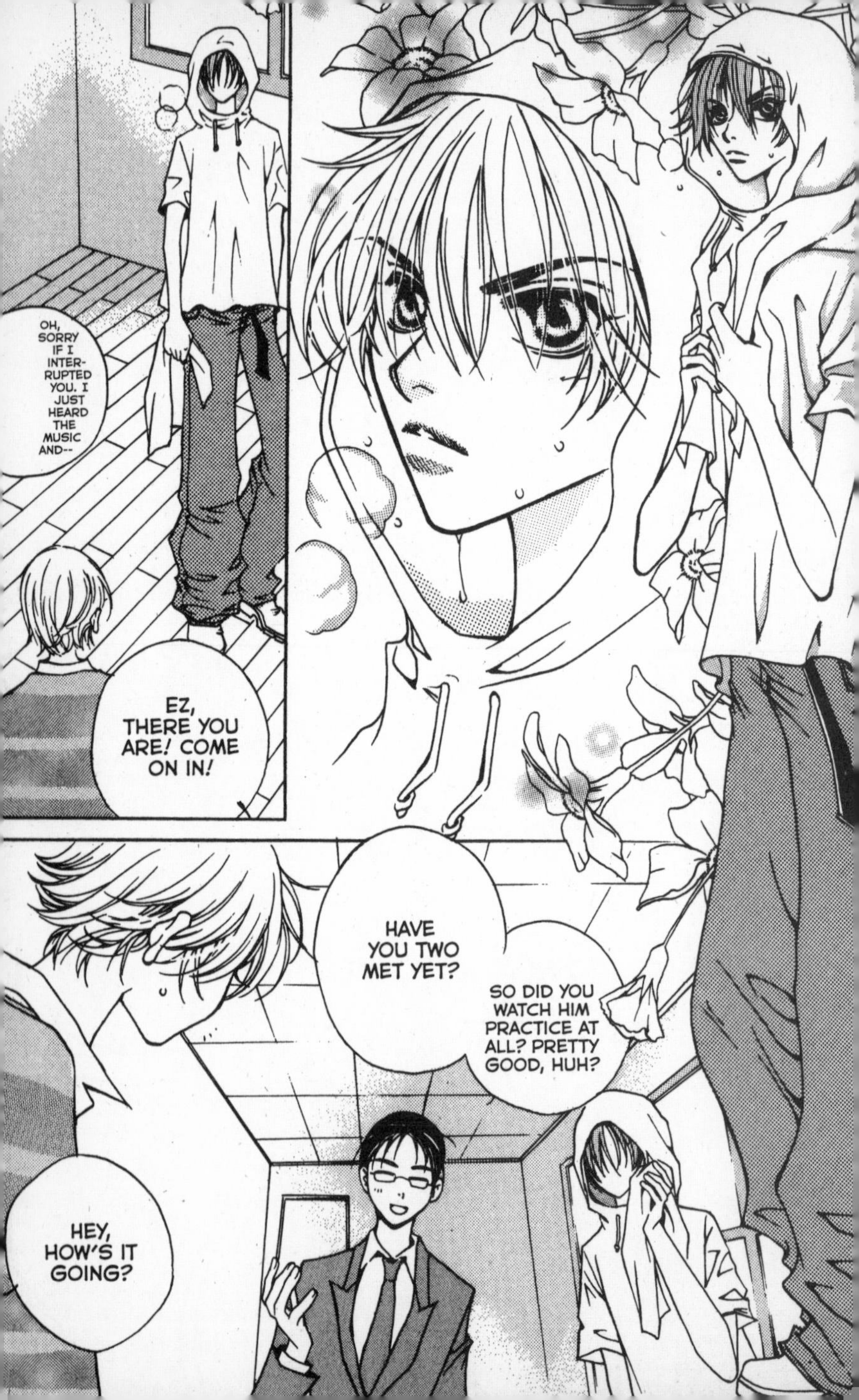
OH, SORRY IF I INTERRUPTED YOU. I JUST HEARD THE MUSIC AND--
EZ, THERE YOU ARE! COME ON IN!
HEY, HOW'S IT GOING?
HAVE YOU TWO MET YET?
SO DID YOU WATCH HIM PRACTICE AT ALL? PRETTY GOOD, HUH?

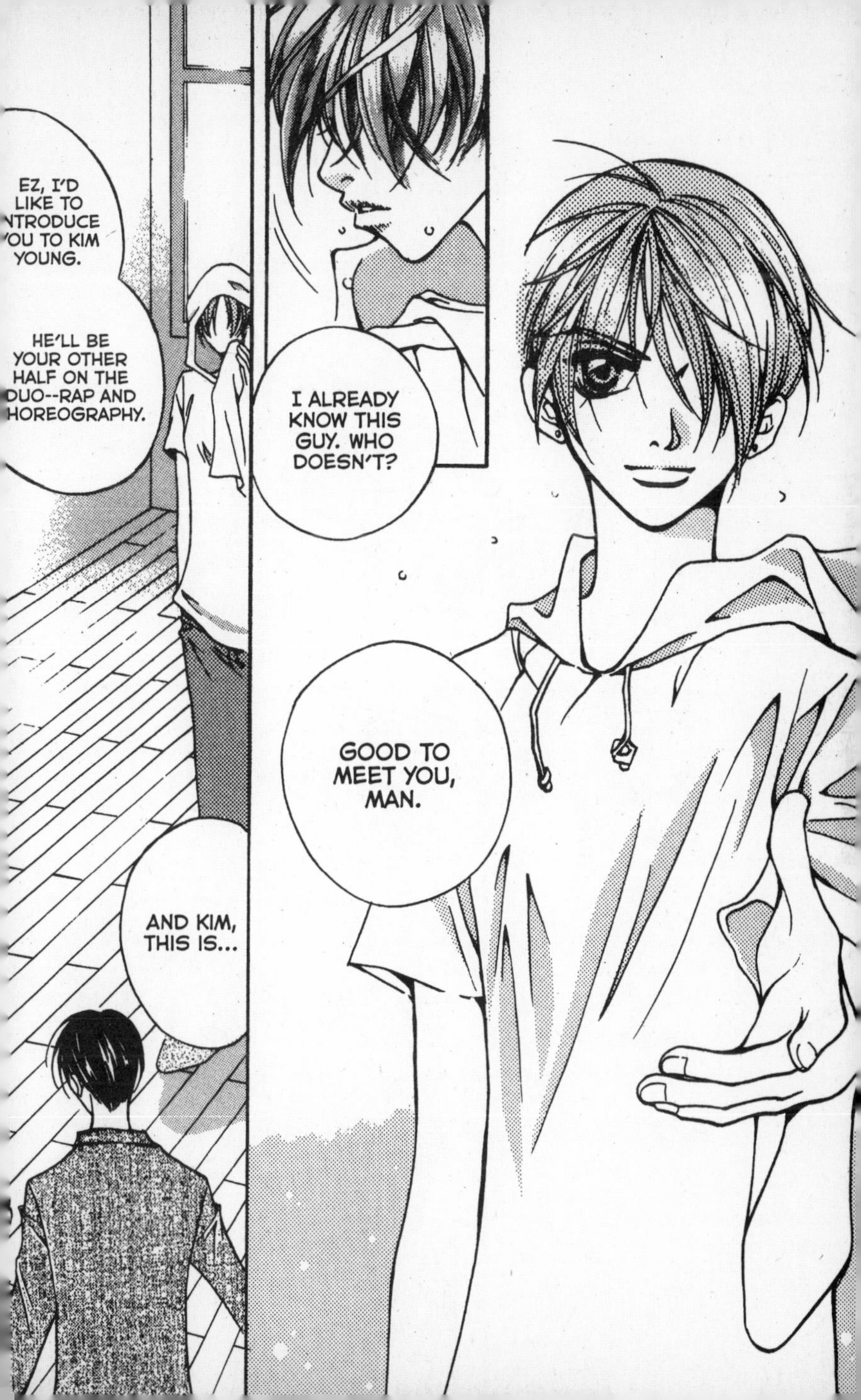
EZ, I'D LIKE TO NTRODUCE 'OU TO KIM YOUNG.
HE'LL BE YOUR OTHER HALF ON THE DUO--RAP AND HOREOGRAPHY.
AND KIM, THIS IS...
I ALREADY KNOW THIS GUY. WHO DOESN'T?
GOOD TO MEET YOU, MAN.

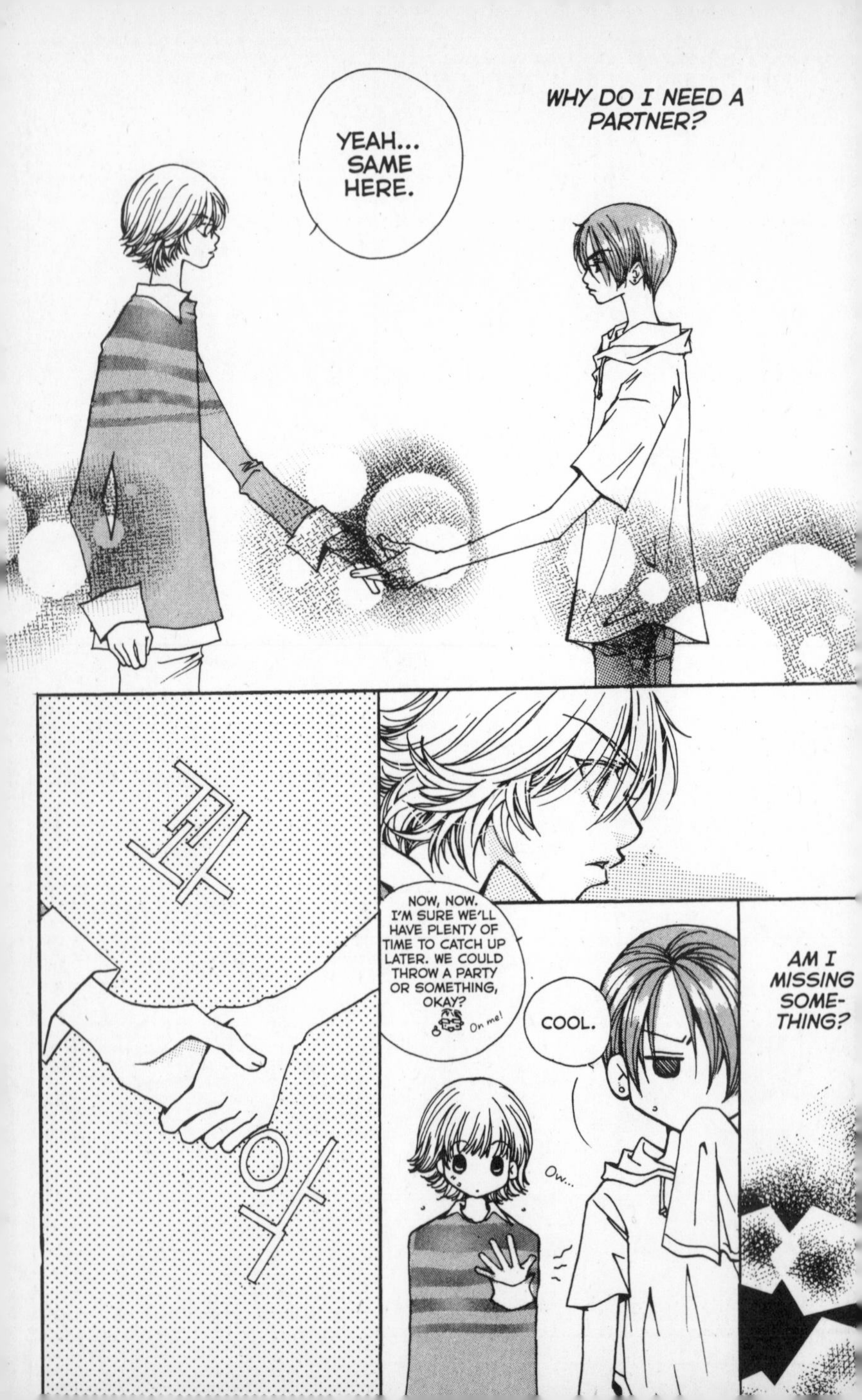
YEAH... SAME HERE.
WHY DO I NEED A PARTNER?
NOW, NOW. I'M SURE WE'LL HAVE PLENTY OF TIME TO CATCH UP LATER. WE COULD THROW A PARTY OR SOMETHING, OKAY?
On me!
COOL.
Ow...
AM I MISSING SOME-THING?

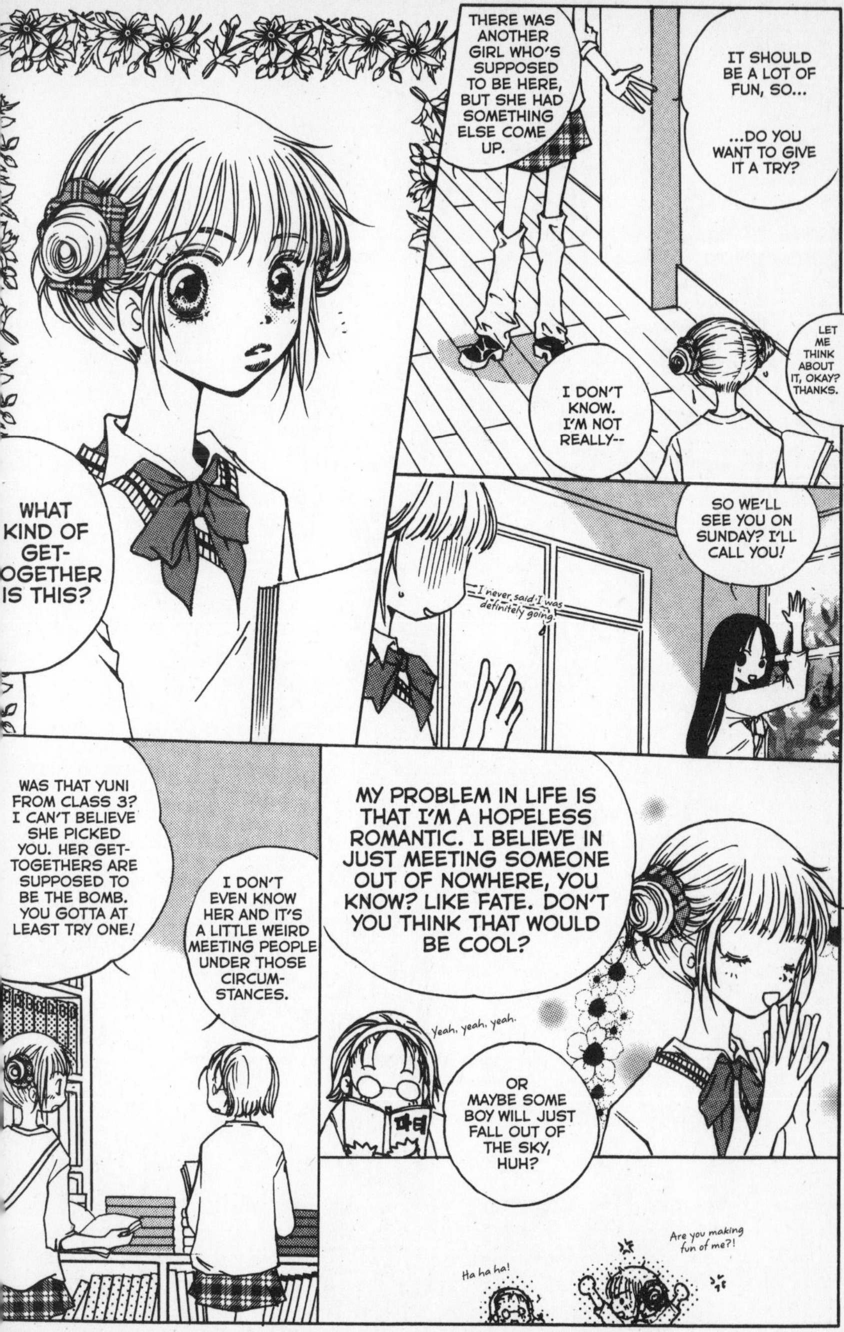
WHAT KIND OF GET-TOGETHER IS THIS?
THERE WAS ANOTHER GIRL WHO'S SUPPOSED TO BE HERE, BUT SHE HAD SOMETHING ELSE COME UP.
IT SHOULD BE A LOT OF FUN, SO...
...DO YOU WANT TO GIVE IT A TRY?
I DON'T KNOW. I'M NOT REALLY--
LET ME THINK ABOUT IT, OKAY? THANKS.
SO WE'LL SEE YOU ON SUNDAY? I'LL CALL YOU!
I never said I was definitely going.
WAS THAT YUNI FROM CLASS 3? I CAN'T BELIEVE SHE PICKED YOU. HER GET-TOGETHERS ARE SUPPOSED TO BE THE BOMB. YOU GOTTA AT LEAST TRY ONE!
I DON'T EVEN KNOW HER AND IT'S A LITTLE WEIRD MEETING PEOPLE UNDER THOSE CIRCUM-STANCES.
MY PROBLEM IN LIFE IS THAT I'M A HOPELESS ROMANTIC. I BELIEVE IN JUST MEETING SOMEONE OUT OF NOWHERE, YOU KNOW? LIKE FATE. DON'T YOU THINK THAT WOULD BE COOL?
Yeah, yeah, yeah.
OR MAYBE SOME BOY WILL JUST FALL OUT OF THE SKY, HUH?
Ha ha ha!
Are you making fun of me?!

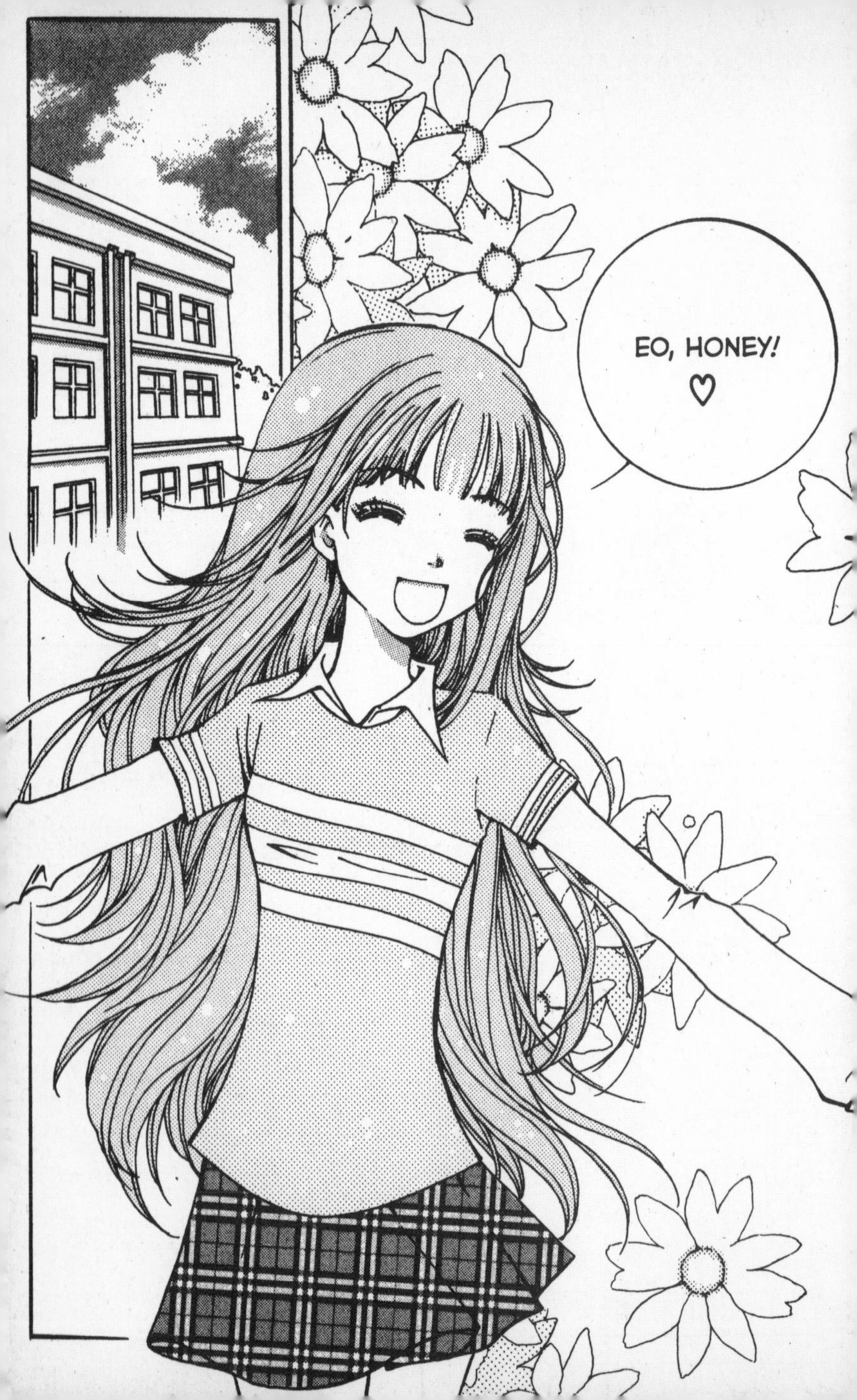
EO, HONEY! ♡

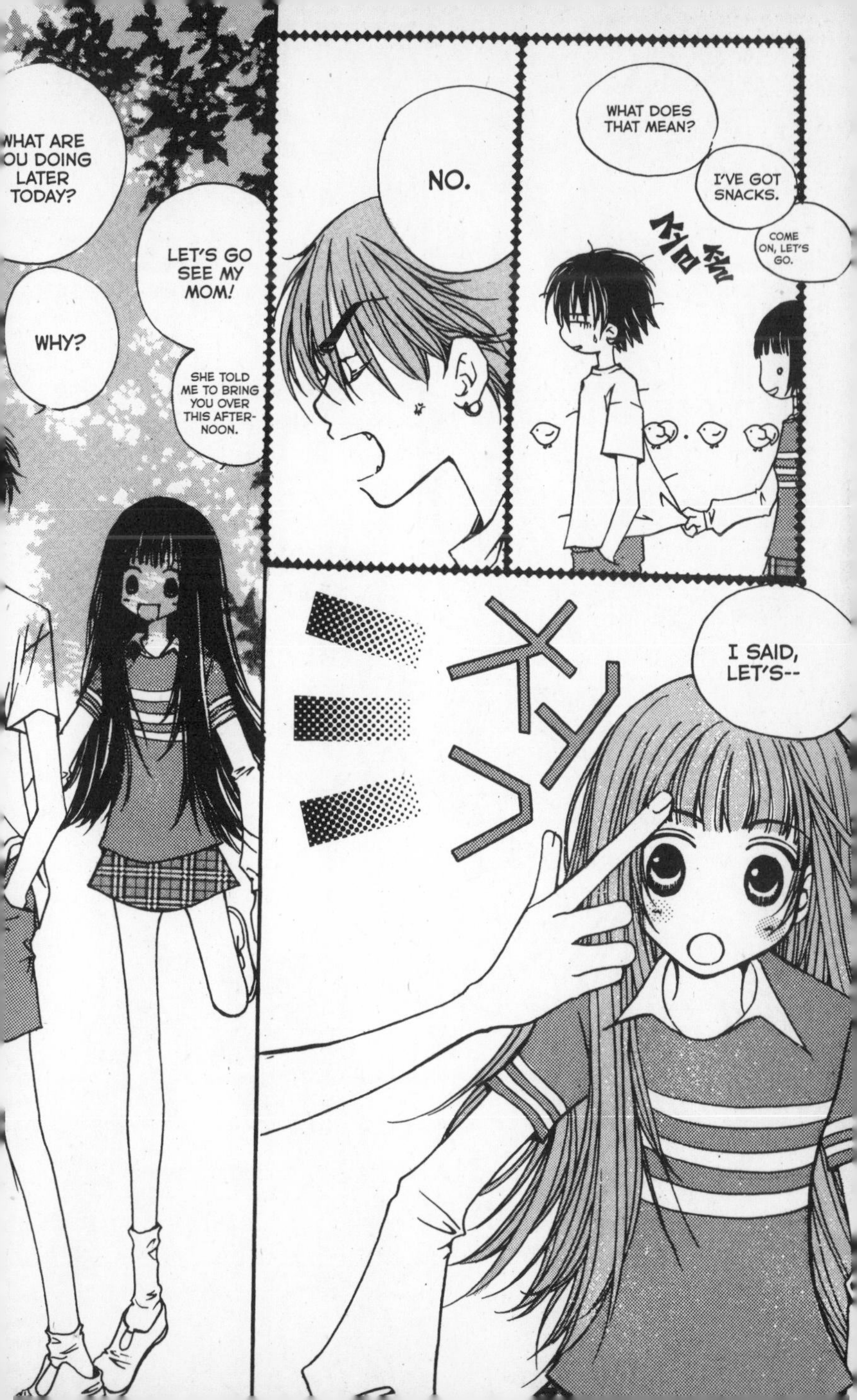

WHAT ARE OU DOING LATER TODAY?
LET'S GO SEE MY MOM!
WHY?
SHE TOLD ME TO BRING YOU OVER THIS AFTER-NOON.
NO.
WHAT DOES THAT MEAN?
I'VE GOT SNACKS.
COME ON, LET'S GO.
I SAID, LET'S--

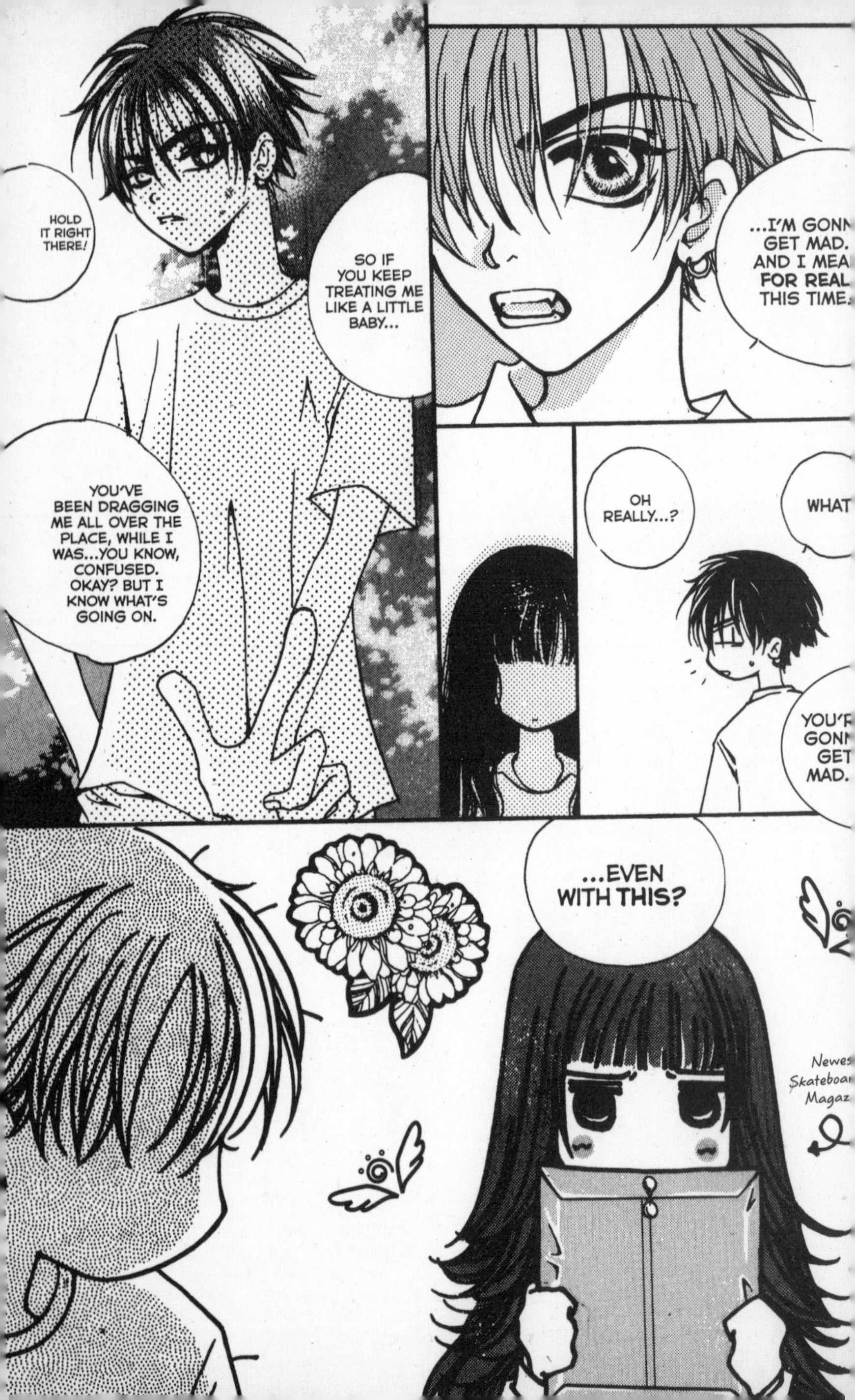
HOLD IT RIGHT THERE!
SO IF YOU KEEP TREATING ME LIKE A LITTLE BABY...
YOU'VE BEEN DRAGGING ME ALL OVER THE PLACE, WHILE I WAS...YOU KNOW, CONFUSED. OKAY? BUT I KNOW WHAT'S GOING ON.
...I'M GONN GET MAD. AND I MEA FOR REAL THIS TIME.
OH REALLY...?
WHAT
YOU'R GONN GET MAD.
...EVEN WITH THIS?
Newes Skateboar Magaz

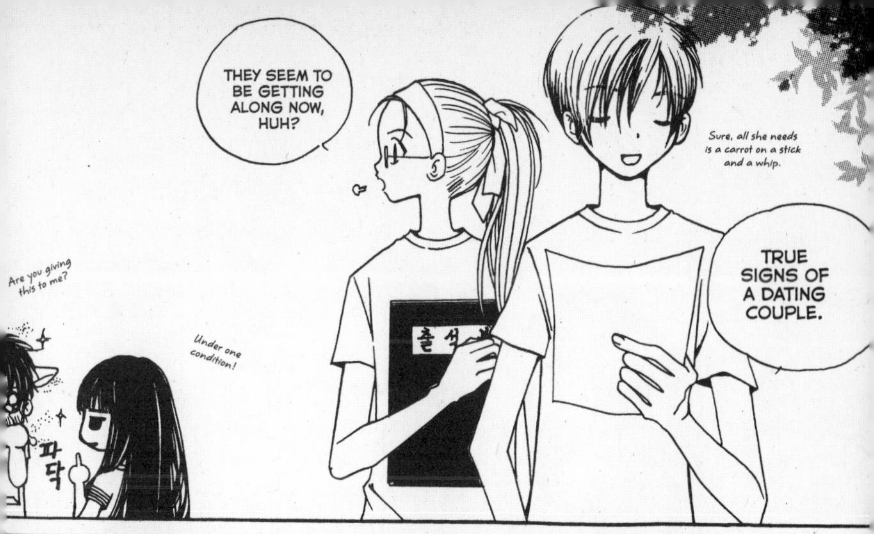
THEY SEEM TO BE GETTING ALONG NOW, HUH?
TRUE SIGNS OF A DATING COUPLE.
Sure, all she needs is a carrot on a stick and a whip.
Are you giving this to me?
Under one condition!
파닥
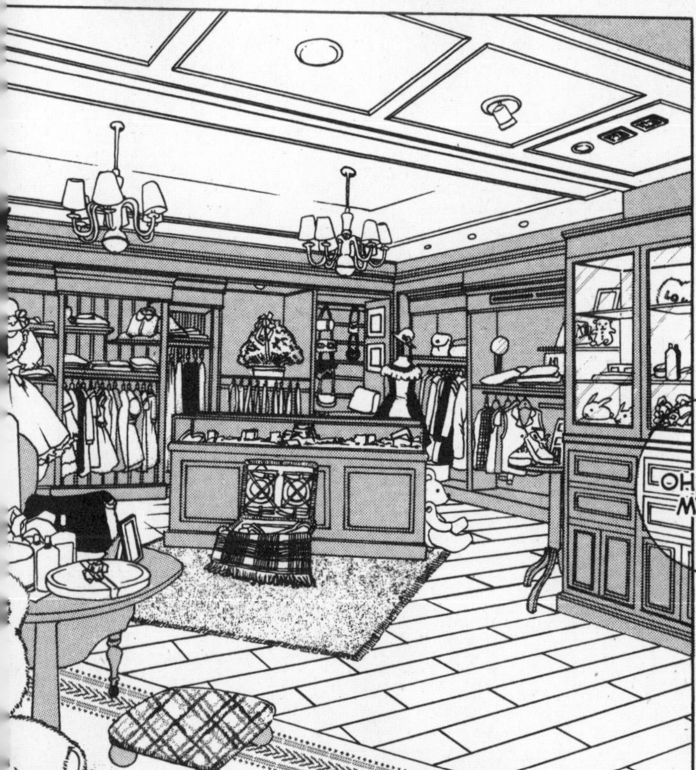
OH, MY, ♡ MY...

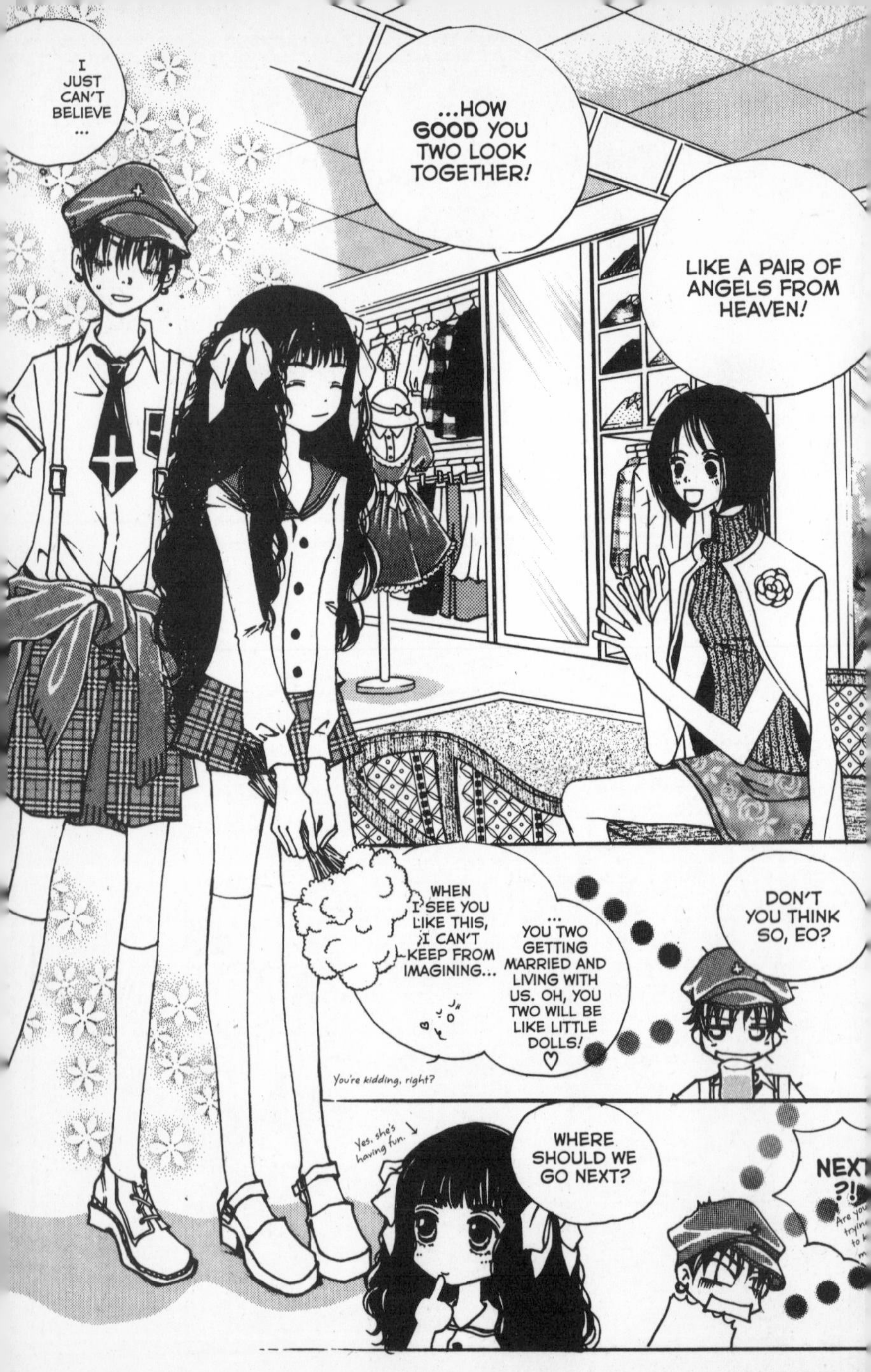
I JUST CAN'T BELIEVE ...
...HOW GOOD YOU TWO LOOK TOGETHER!
LIKE A PAIR OF ANGELS FROM HEAVEN!
WHEN I SEE YOU LIKE THIS, I CAN'T KEEP FROM IMAGINING...
... YOU TWO GETTING MARRIED AND LIVING WITH US. OH, YOU TWO WILL BE LIKE LITTLE DOLLS! ♡
You're kidding, right?
DON'T YOU THINK SO, EO?
Yes, she's having fun.
WHERE SHOULD WE GO NEXT?
NEXT ?!

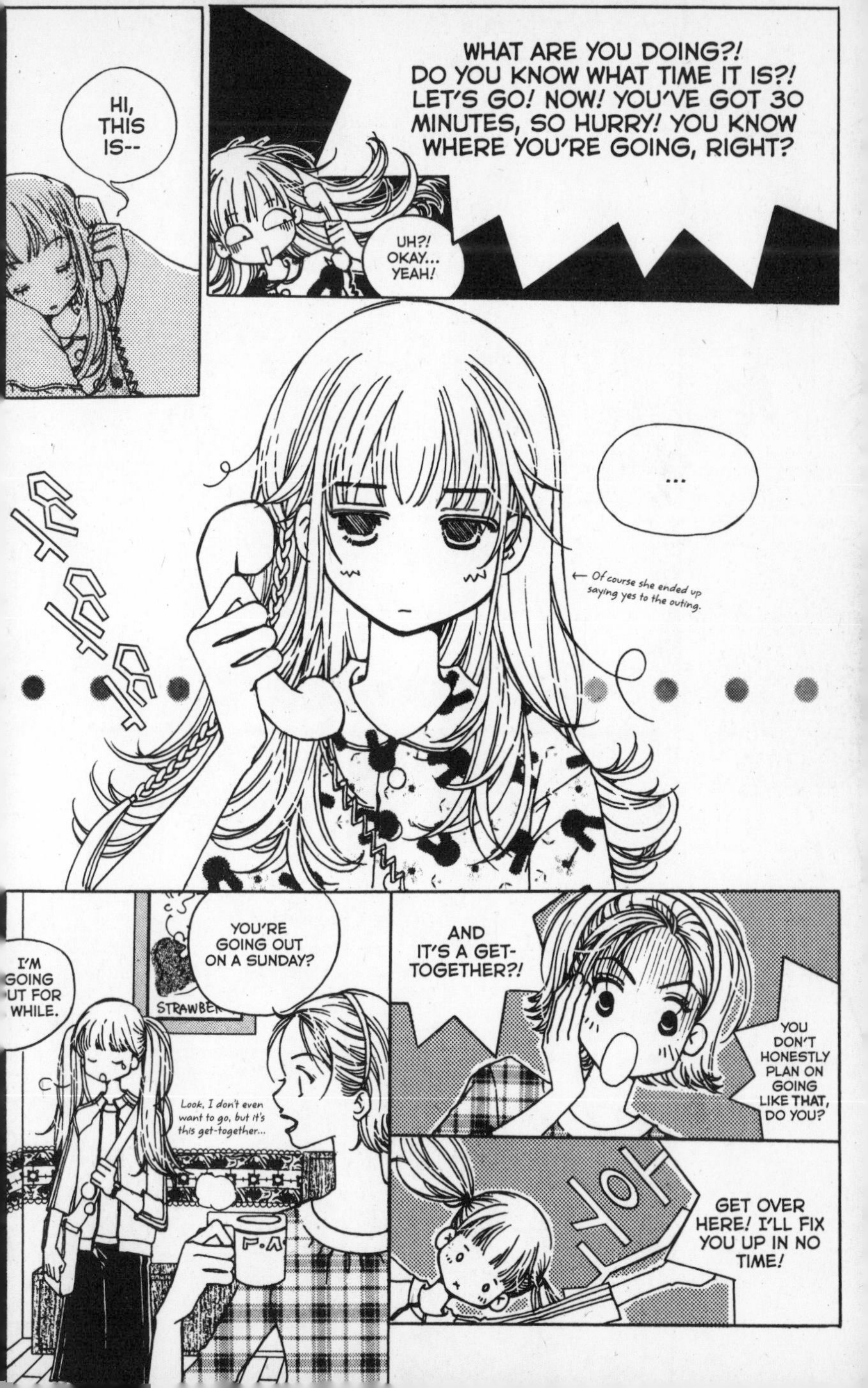
HI, THIS IS--
WHAT ARE YOU DOING?! DO YOU KNOW WHAT TIME IT IS?! LET'S GO! NOW! YOU'VE GOT 30 MINUTES, SO HURRY! YOU KNOW WHERE YOU'RE GOING, RIGHT?
UH?! OKAY... YEAH!
...
← Of course she ended up saying yes to the outing.
I'M GOING UT FOR WHILE.
STRAWBER
YOU'RE GOING OUT ON A SUNDAY?
Look, I don't even want to go, but it's this get-together...
AND IT'S A GET-TOGETHER?!
YOU DON'T HONESTLY PLAN ON GOING LIKE THAT, DO YOU?
GET OVER HERE! I'LL FIX YOU UP IN NO TIME!

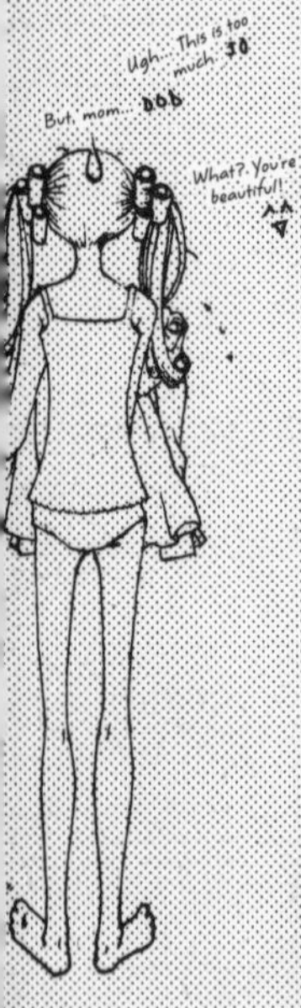

Ugh... This is too much.
But, mom...
What? You're beautiful!

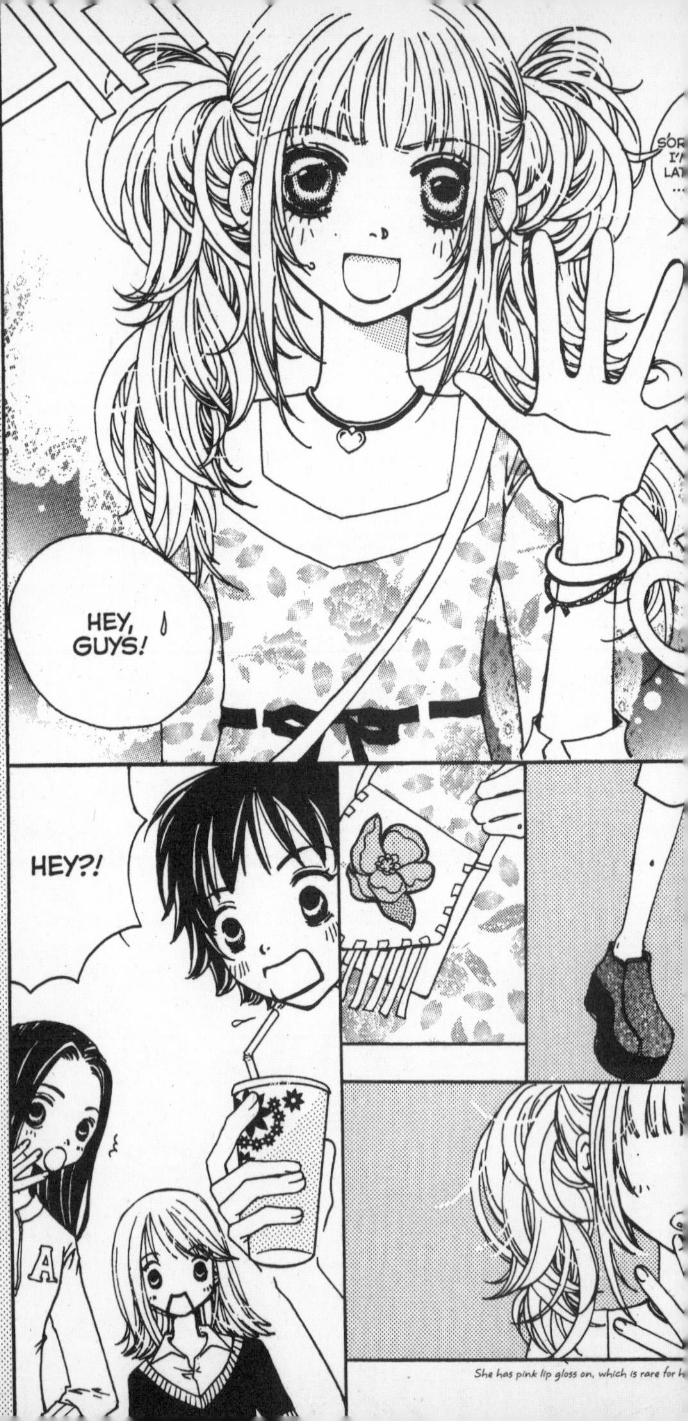

HEY, GUYS!
HEY?!

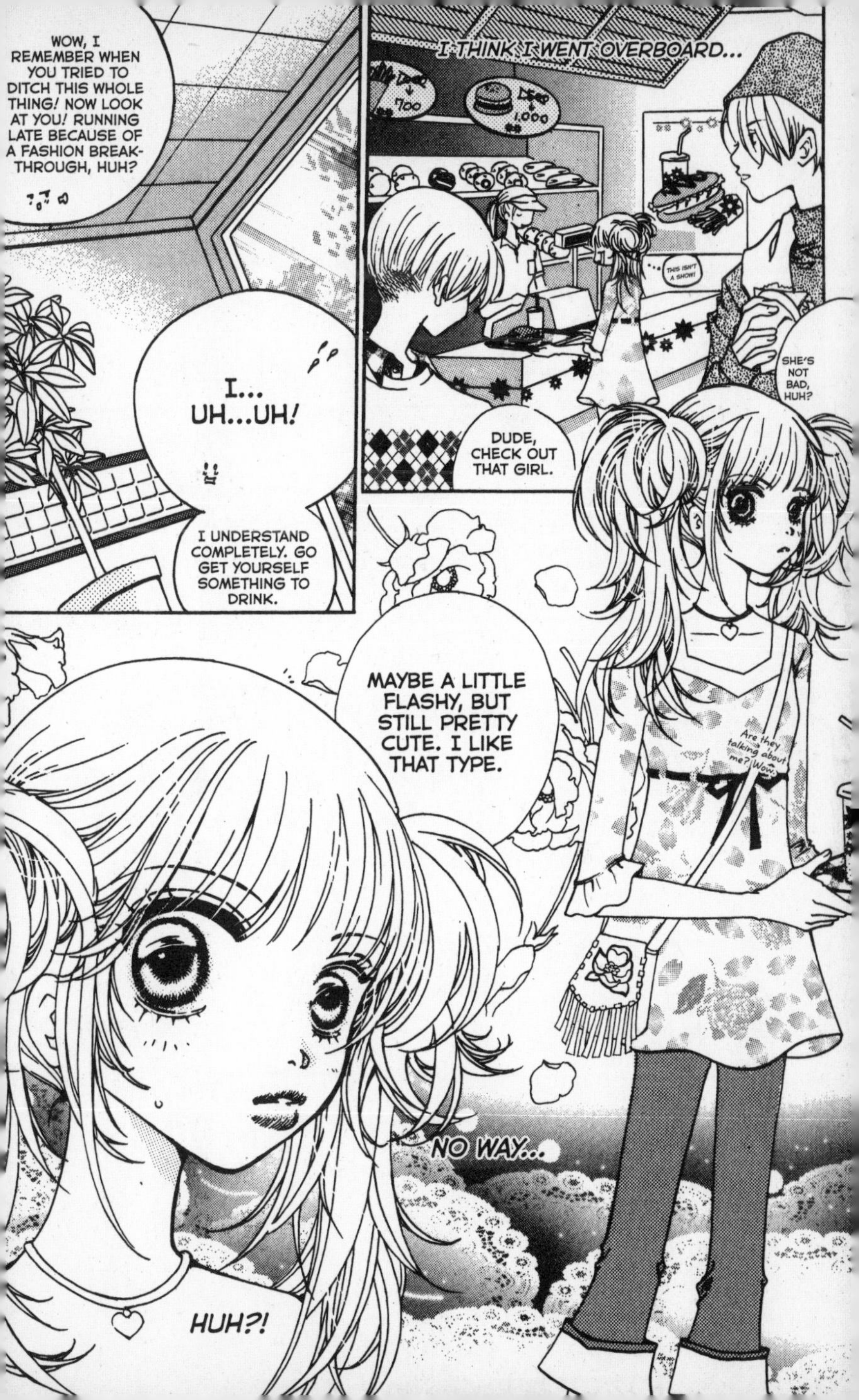
WOW, I REMEMBER WHEN YOU TRIED TO DITCH THIS WHOLE THING! NOW LOOK AT YOU! RUNNING LATE BECAUSE OF A FASHION BREAK-THROUGH, HUH?
I... UH...UH!
I UNDERSTAND COMPLETELY. GO GET YOURSELF SOMETHING TO DRINK.
I THINK I WENT OVERBOARD...
THIS ISN'T A SHOW!
DUDE, CHECK OUT THAT GIRL.
SHE'S NOT BAD, HUH?
MAYBE A LITTLE FLASHY, BUT STILL PRETTY CUTE. I LIKE THAT TYPE.
Are they talking about me? Wow.
NO WAY...
HUH?!

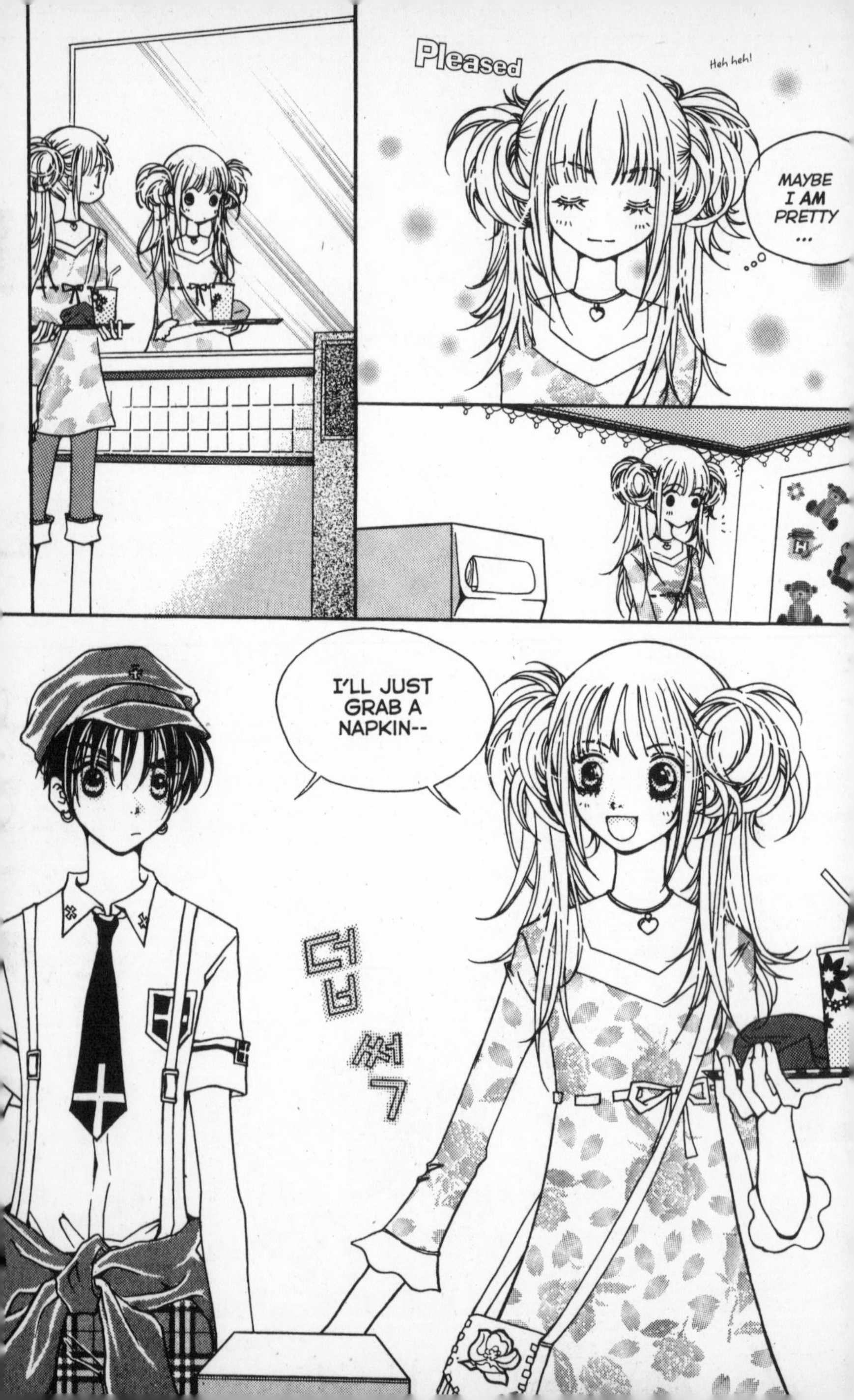
Pleased
Heh heh!
MAYBE I AM PRETTY ...
I'LL JUST GRAB A NAPKIN--
덥석

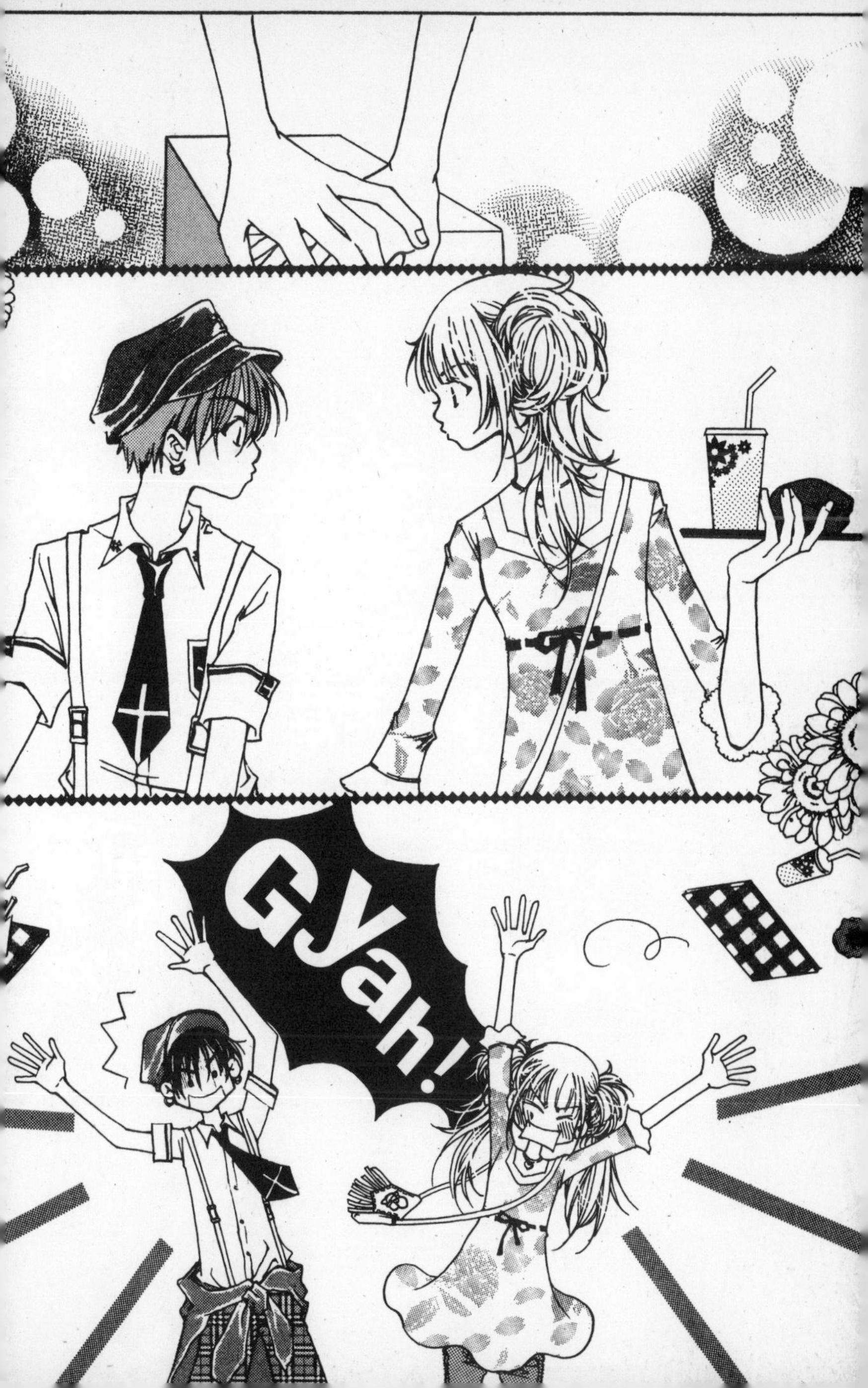
GYah!

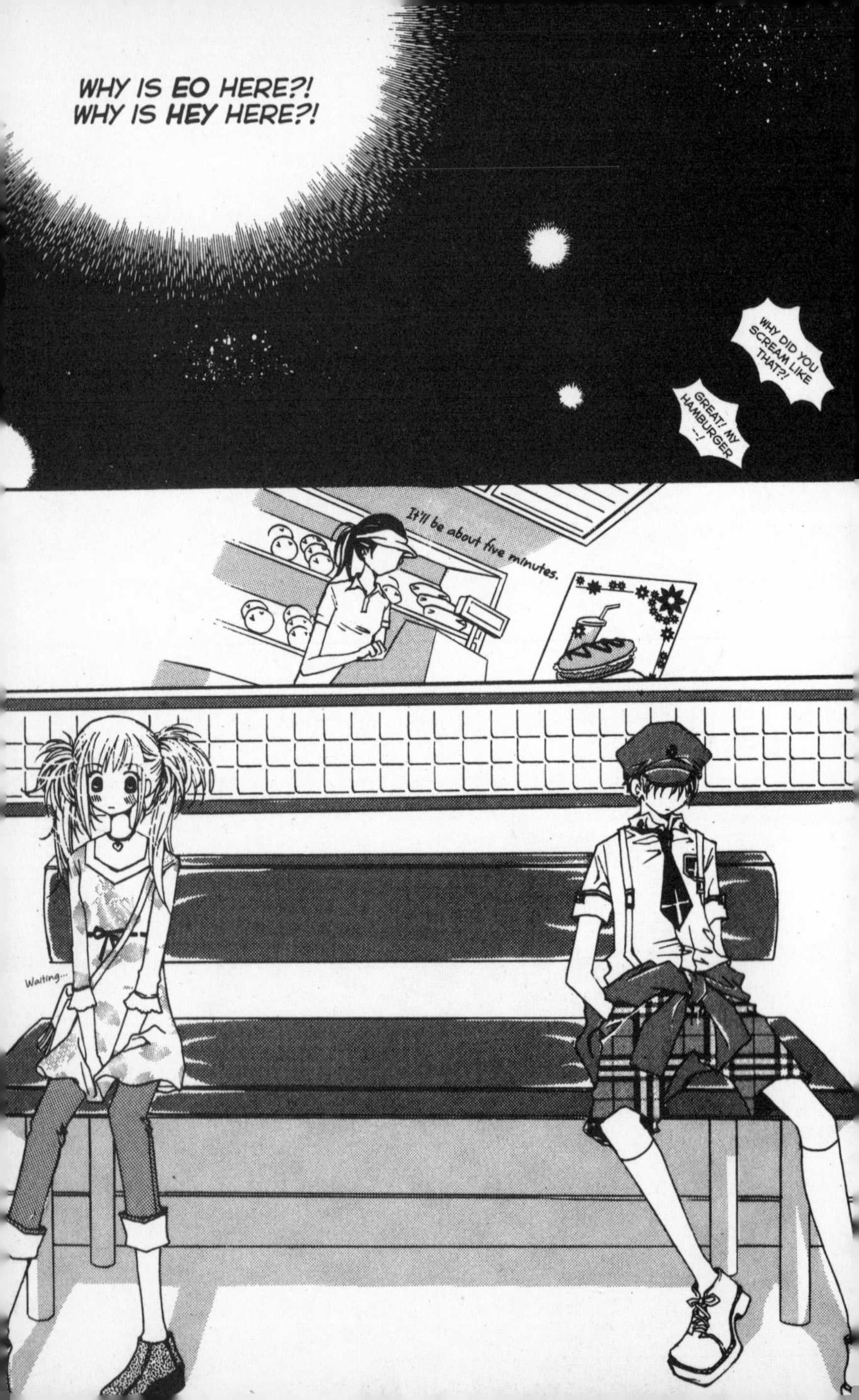
WHY IS EO HERE?!
WHY IS HEY HERE?!
WHY DID YOU SCREAM LIKE THAT?!
GREAT! MY HAMBURGER~!
It'll be about five minutes.
Waiting...

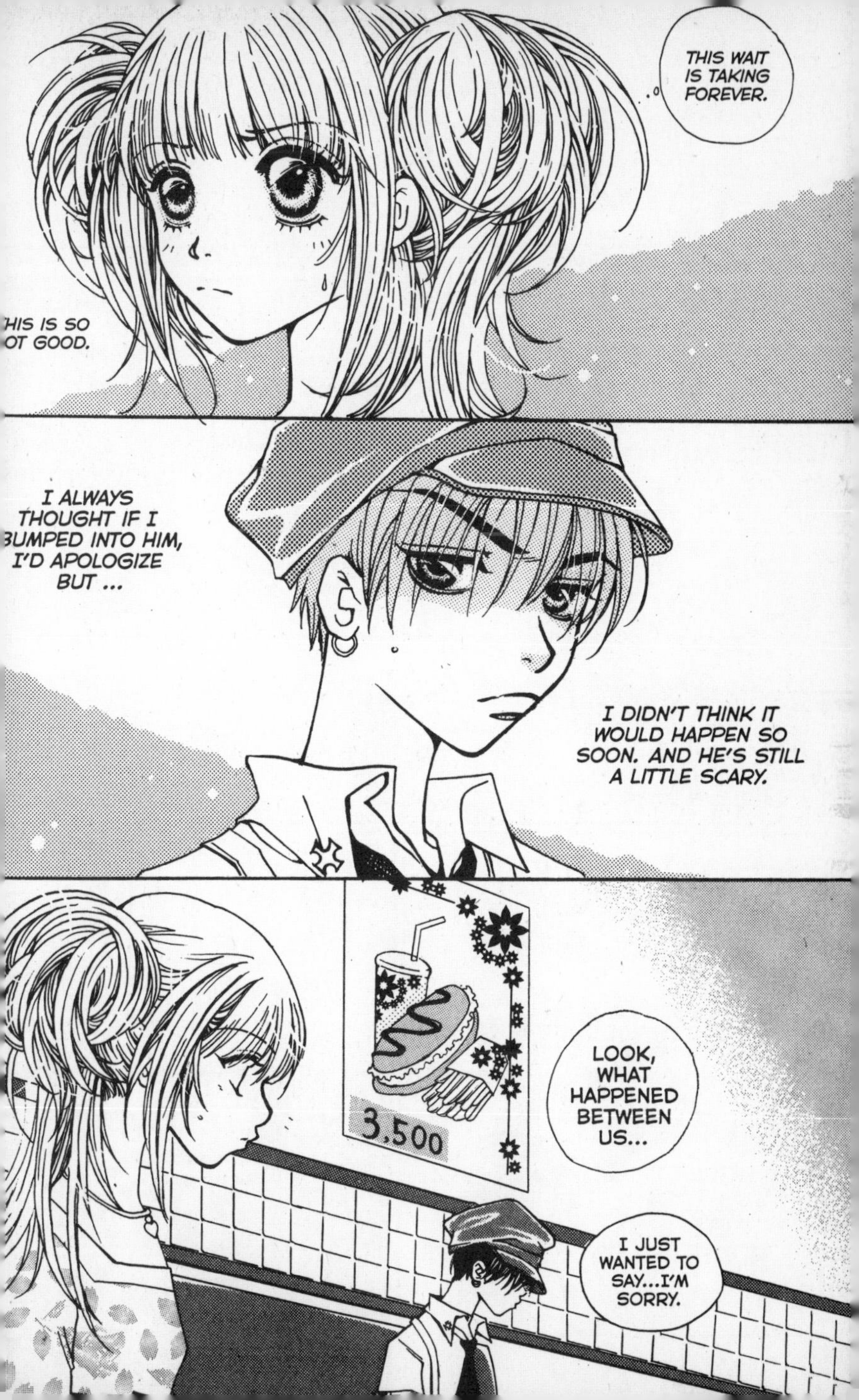

THIS WAIT IS TAKING FOREVER.
HIS IS SO OT GOOD.
I ALWAYS THOUGHT IF I BUMPED INTO HIM, I'D APOLOGIZE BUT ...
I DIDN'T THINK IT WOULD HAPPEN SO SOON. AND HE'S STILL A LITTLE SCARY.
3,500
LOOK, WHAT HAPPENED BETWEEN US...
I JUST WANTED TO SAY...I'M SORRY.

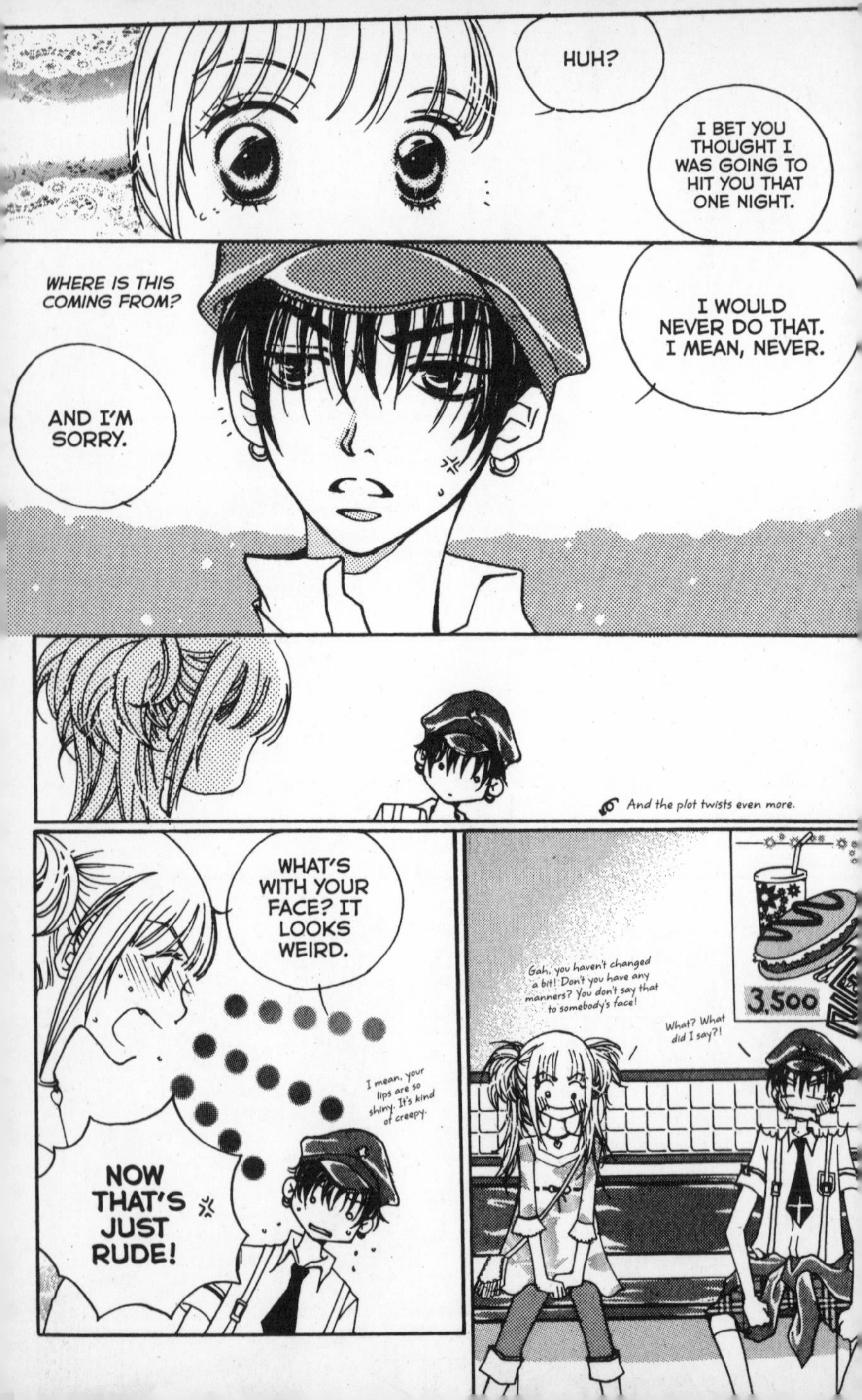
HUH?
I BET YOU THOUGHT I WAS GOING TO HIT YOU THAT ONE NIGHT.
WHERE IS THIS COMING FROM?
I WOULD NEVER DO THAT. I MEAN, NEVER.
AND I'M SORRY.
And the plot twists even more.
WHAT'S WITH YOUR FACE? IT LOOKS WEIRD.
I mean, your lips are so shiny. It's kind of creepy.
NOW THAT'S JUST RUDE!
Gah, you haven't changed a bit! Don't you have any manners? You don't say that to somebody's face!
What? What did I say?!
3.500

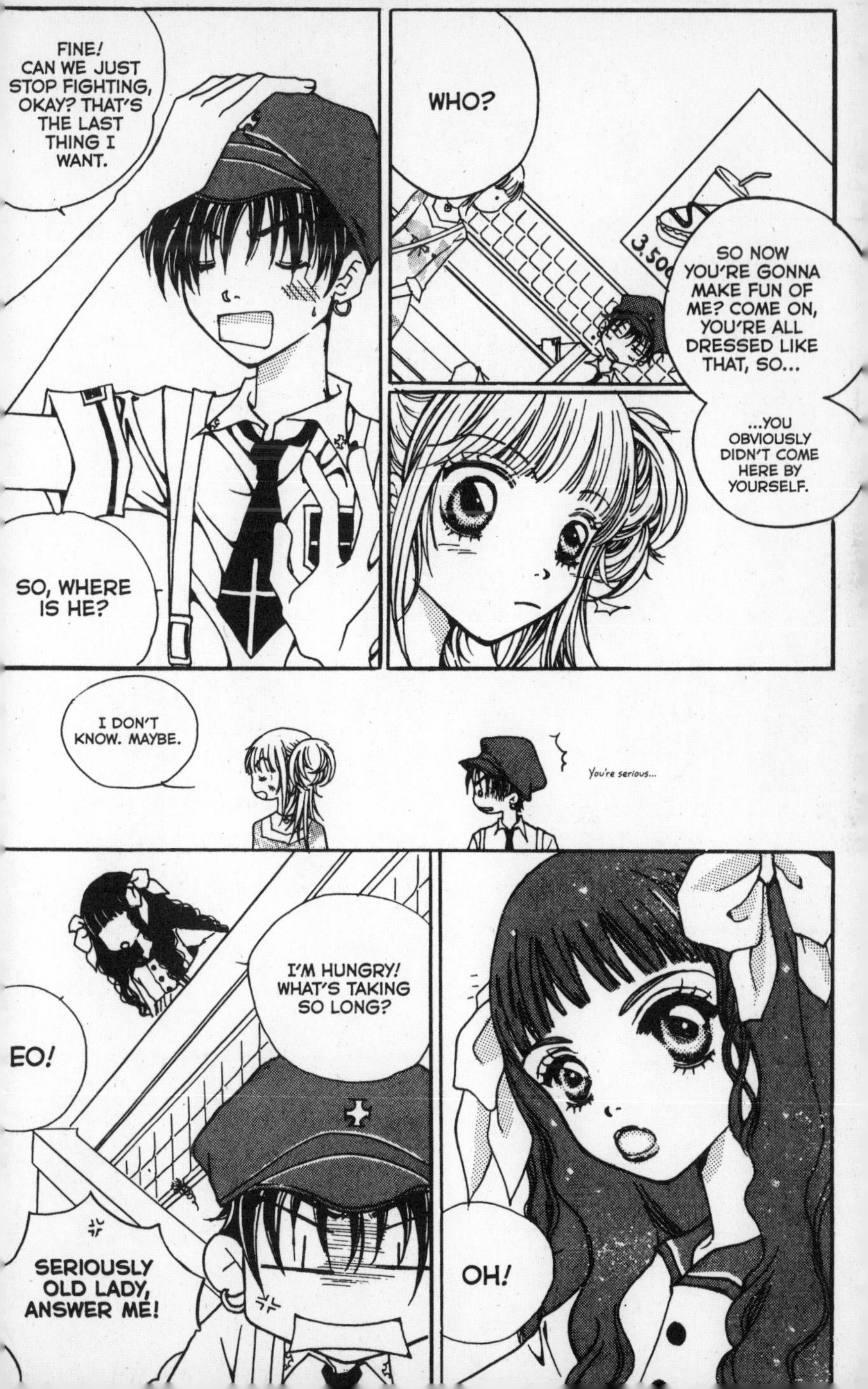
FINE! CAN WE JUST STOP FIGHTING, OKAY? THAT'S THE LAST THING I WANT.
SO, WHERE IS HE?
WHO?
3,500
SO NOW YOU'RE GONNA MAKE FUN OF ME? COME ON, YOU'RE ALL DRESSED LIKE THAT, SO...
...YOU OBVIOUSLY DIDN'T COME HERE BY YOURSELF.
I DON'T KNOW. MAYBE.
You're serious...
EO!
I'M HUNGRY! WHAT'S TAKING SO LONG?
SERIOUSLY OLD LADY, ANSWER ME!
OH!

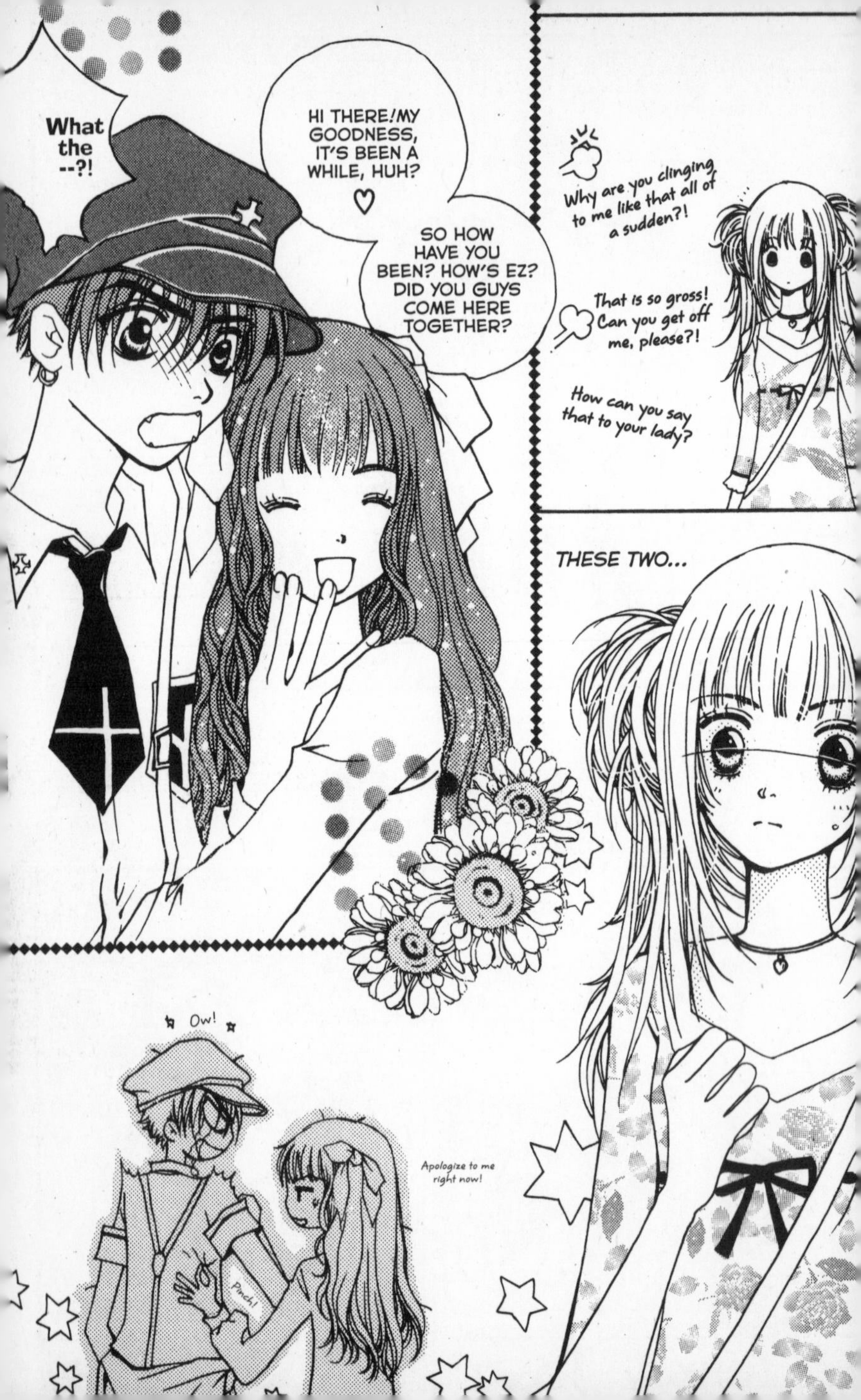
What the --?!
HI THERE! MY GOODNESS, IT'S BEEN A WHILE, HUH? ♡
SO HOW HAVE YOU BEEN? HOW'S EZ? DID YOU GUYS COME HERE TOGETHER?
Why are you clinging to me like that all of a sudden?!
That is so gross! Can you get off me, please?!
How can you say that to your lady?
Ow!
Apologize to me right now!
Pinch!
THESE TWO...

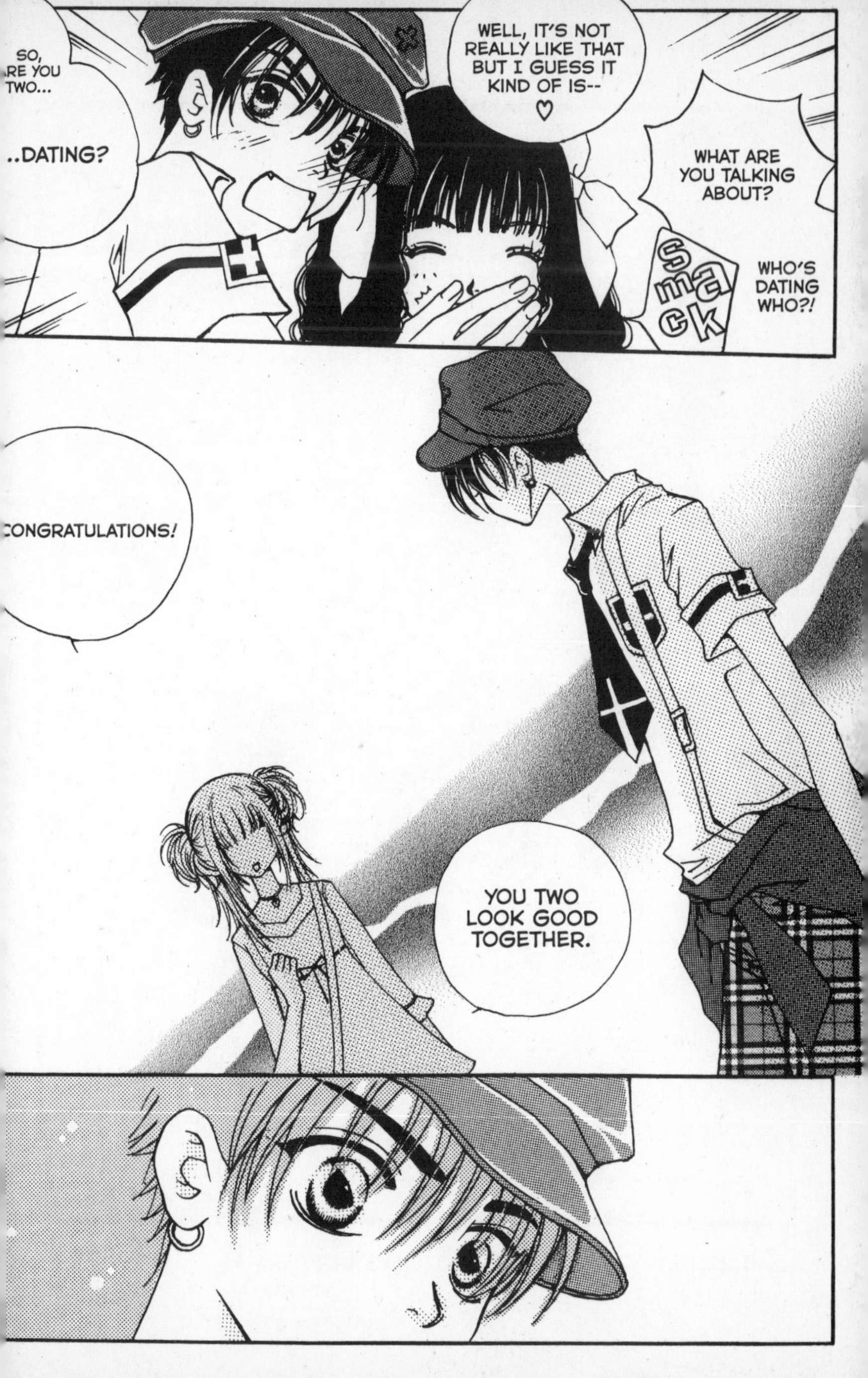

SO, ARE YOU TWO...
..DATING?
WELL, IT'S NOT REALLY LIKE THAT BUT I GUESS IT KIND OF IS-- ♡
WHAT ARE YOU TALKING ABOUT?
smack
WHO'S DATING WHO?!
CONGRATULATIONS!
YOU TWO LOOK GOOD TOGETHER.

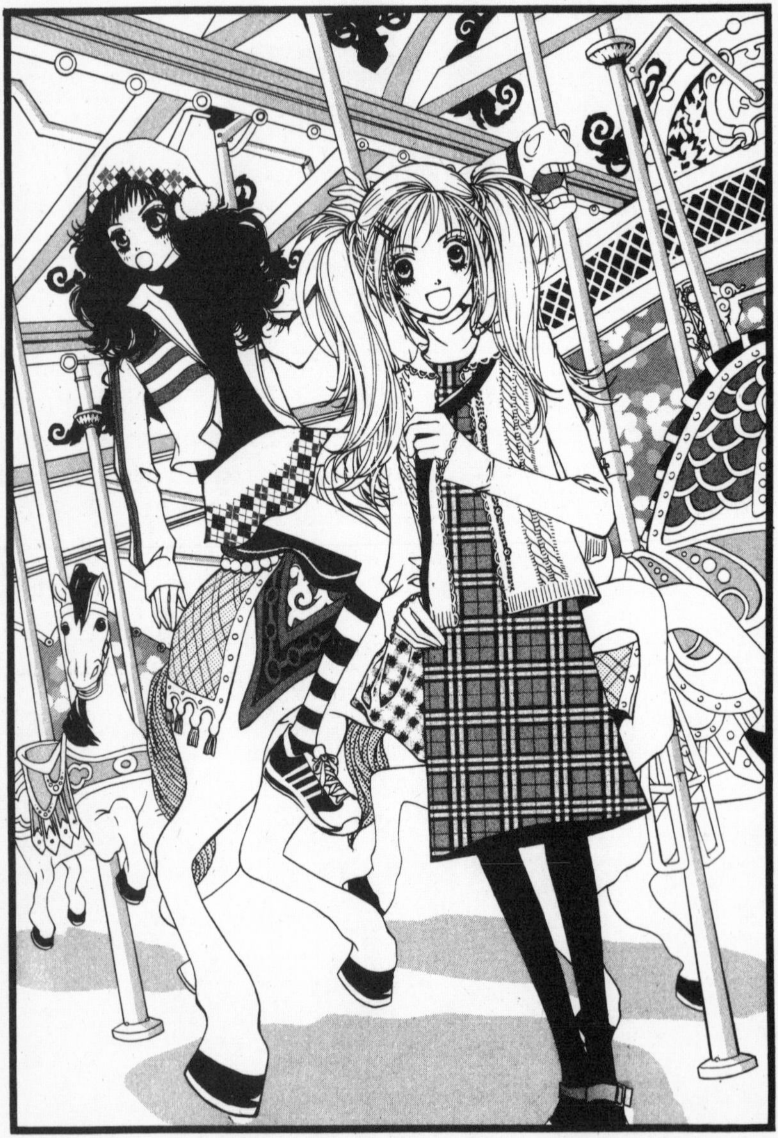

Chatper 5: Their Circumstances II

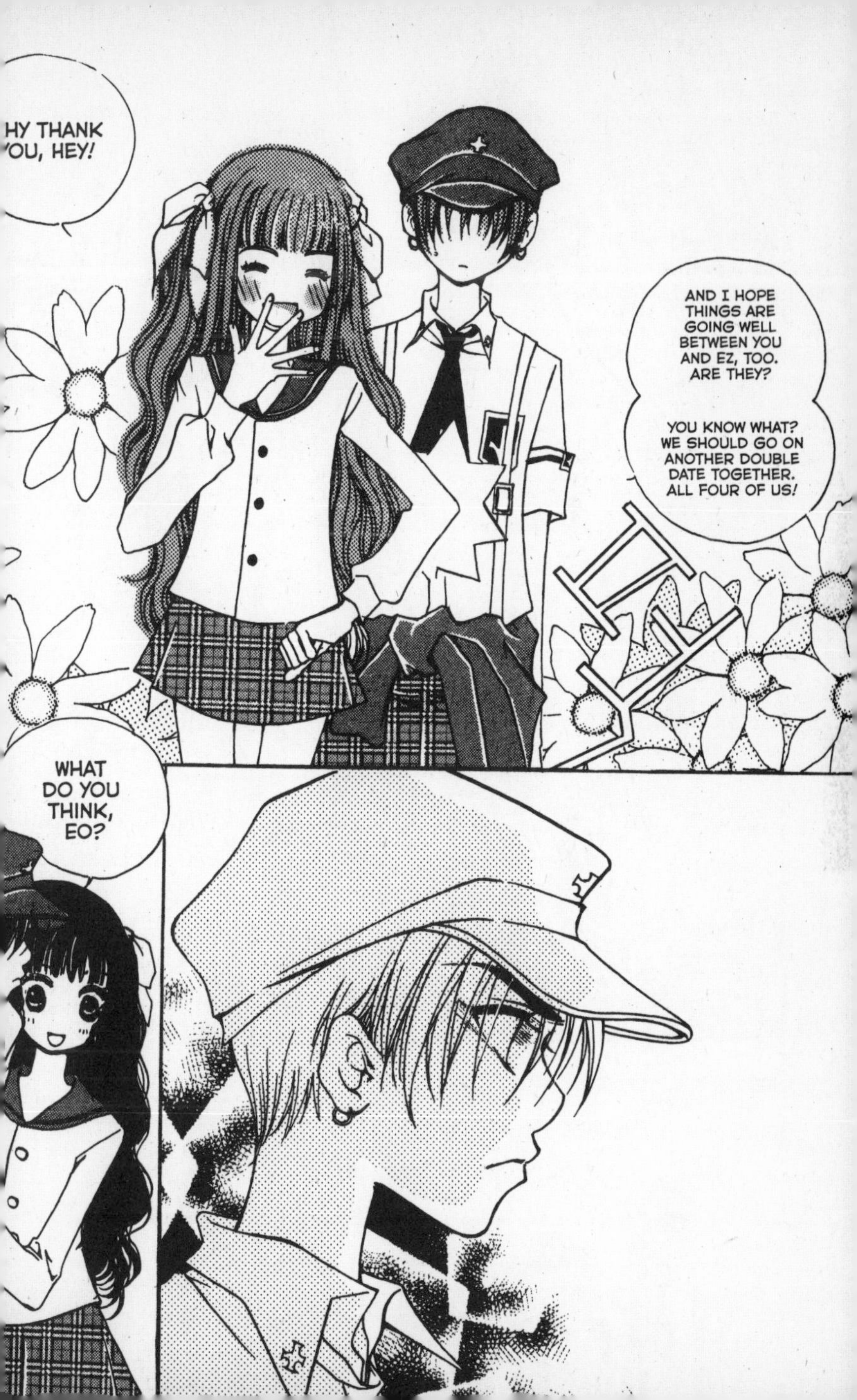
HY THANK
YOU, HEY!
AND I HOPE THINGS ARE GOING WELL BETWEEN YOU AND EZ, TOO. ARE THEY?
YOU KNOW WHAT? WE SHOULD GO ON ANOTHER DOUBLE DATE TOGETHER. ALL FOUR OF US!
WHAT DO YOU THINK, EO?

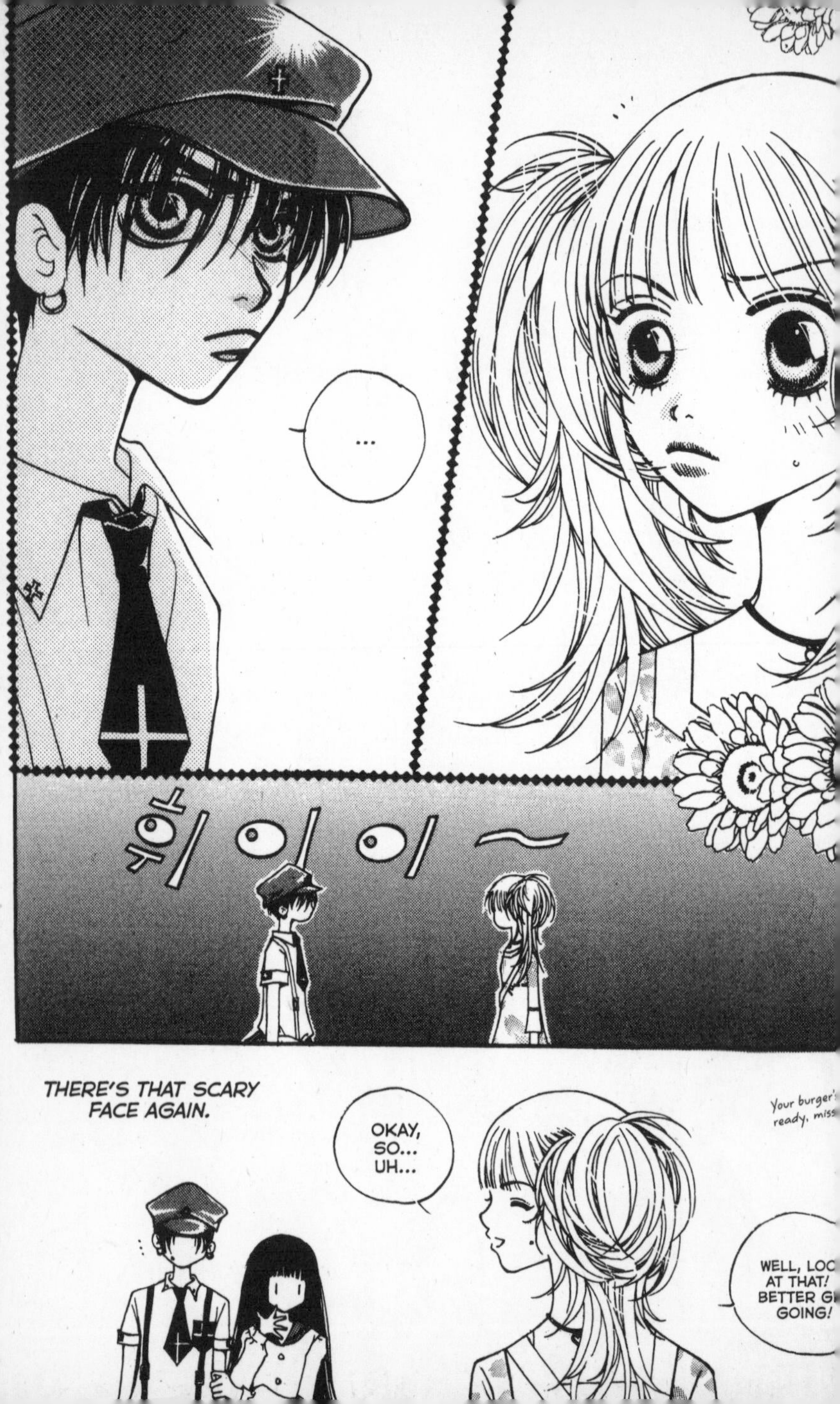
...
THERE'S THAT SCARY FACE AGAIN.
OKAY, SO... UH...
Your burger's ready, miss
WELL, LOO AT THAT! BETTER G GOING!

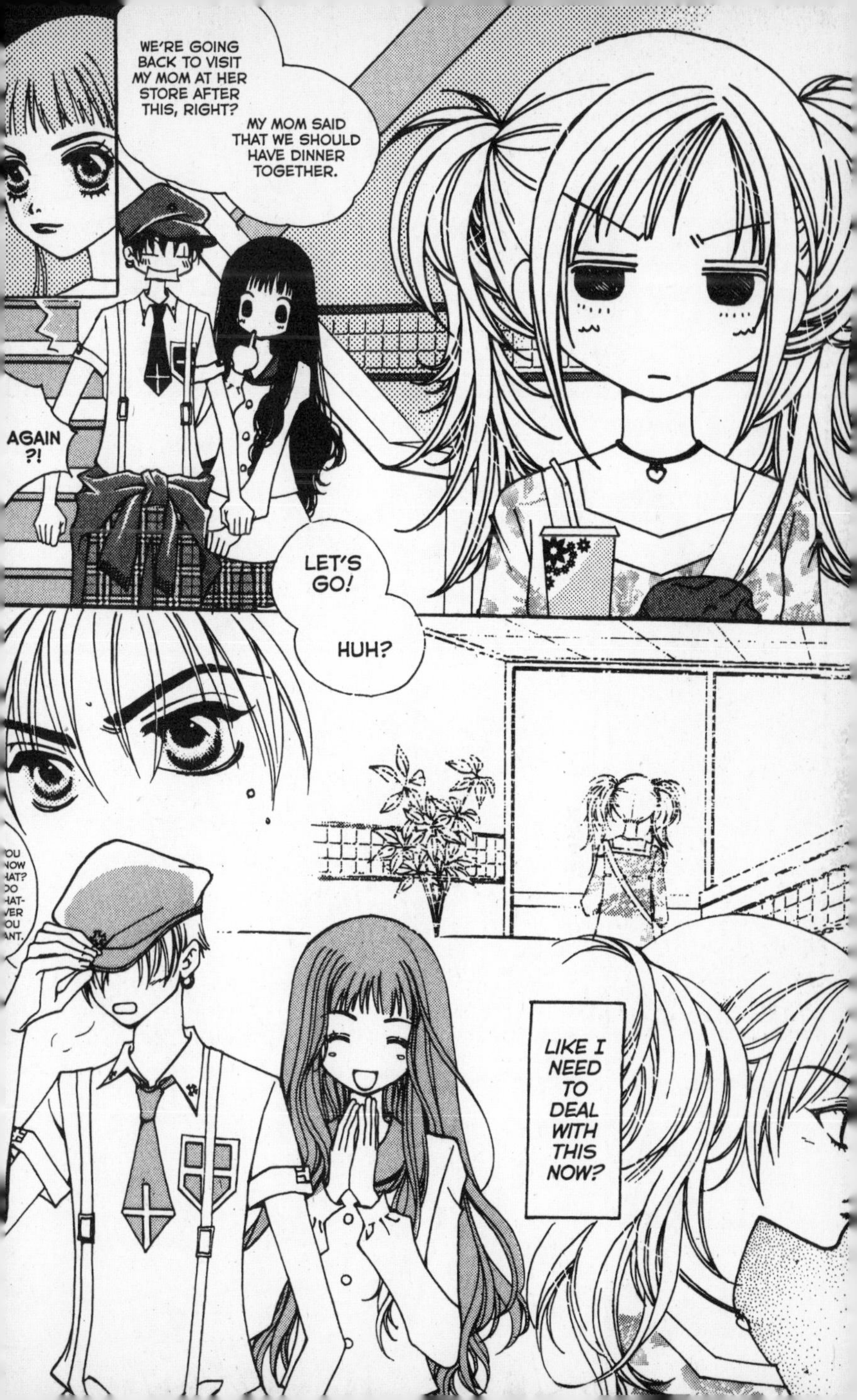
WE'RE GOING BACK TO VISIT MY MOM AT HER STORE AFTER THIS, RIGHT?
MY MOM SAID THAT WE SHOULD HAVE DINNER TOGETHER.
AGAIN ?!
LET'S GO!
HUH?
LIKE I NEED TO DEAL WITH THIS NOW?

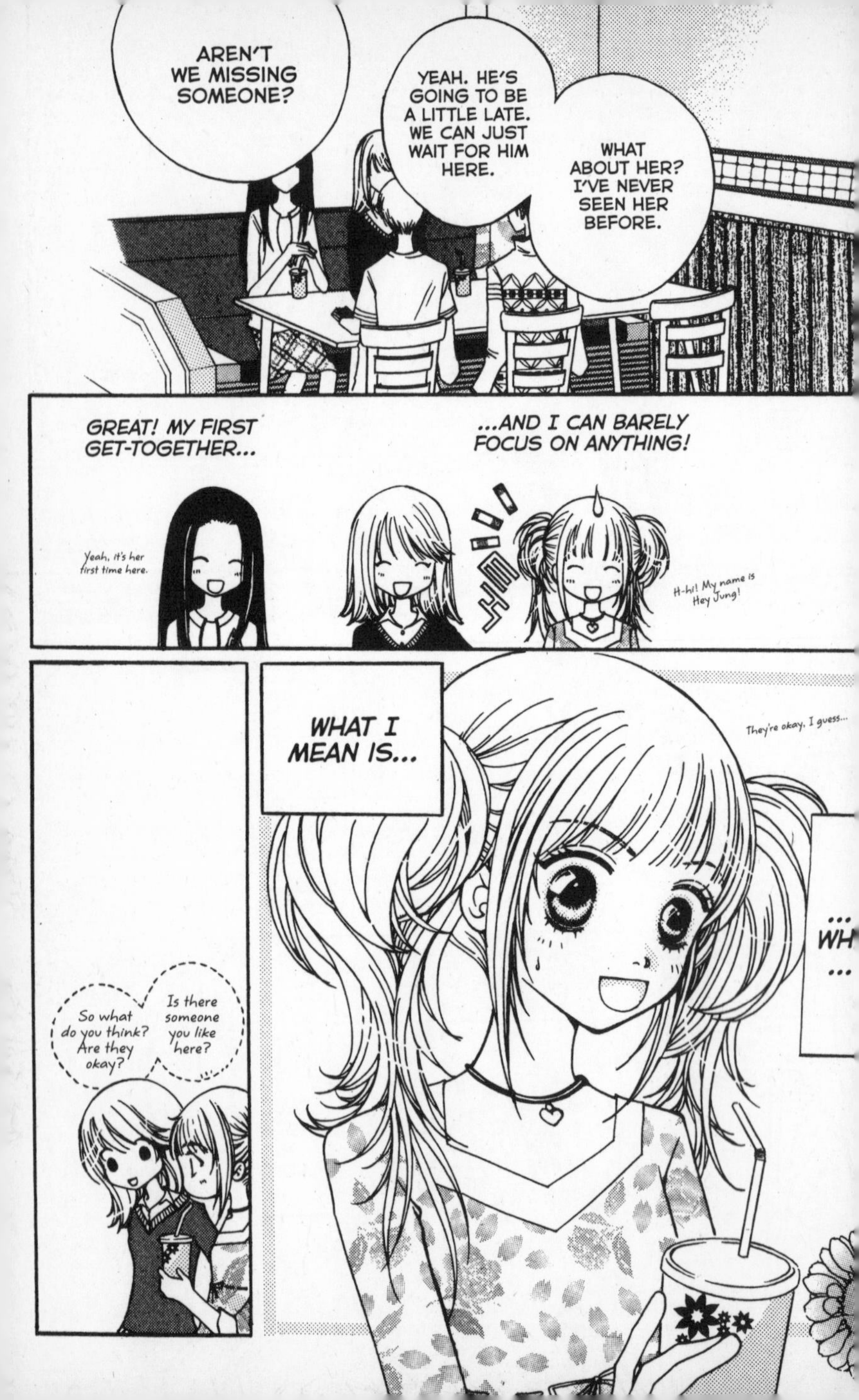
AREN'T WE MISSING SOMEONE?
YEAH. HE'S GOING TO BE A LITTLE LATE. WE CAN JUST WAIT FOR HIM HERE.
WHAT ABOUT HER? I'VE NEVER SEEN HER BEFORE.
GREAT! MY FIRST GET-TOGETHER...
...AND I CAN BARELY FOCUS ON ANYTHING!
Yeah, it's her first time here.
H-hi! My name is Hey Jung!
So what do you think? Are they okay?
Is there someone you like here?
WHAT I MEAN IS...
They're okay, I guess...

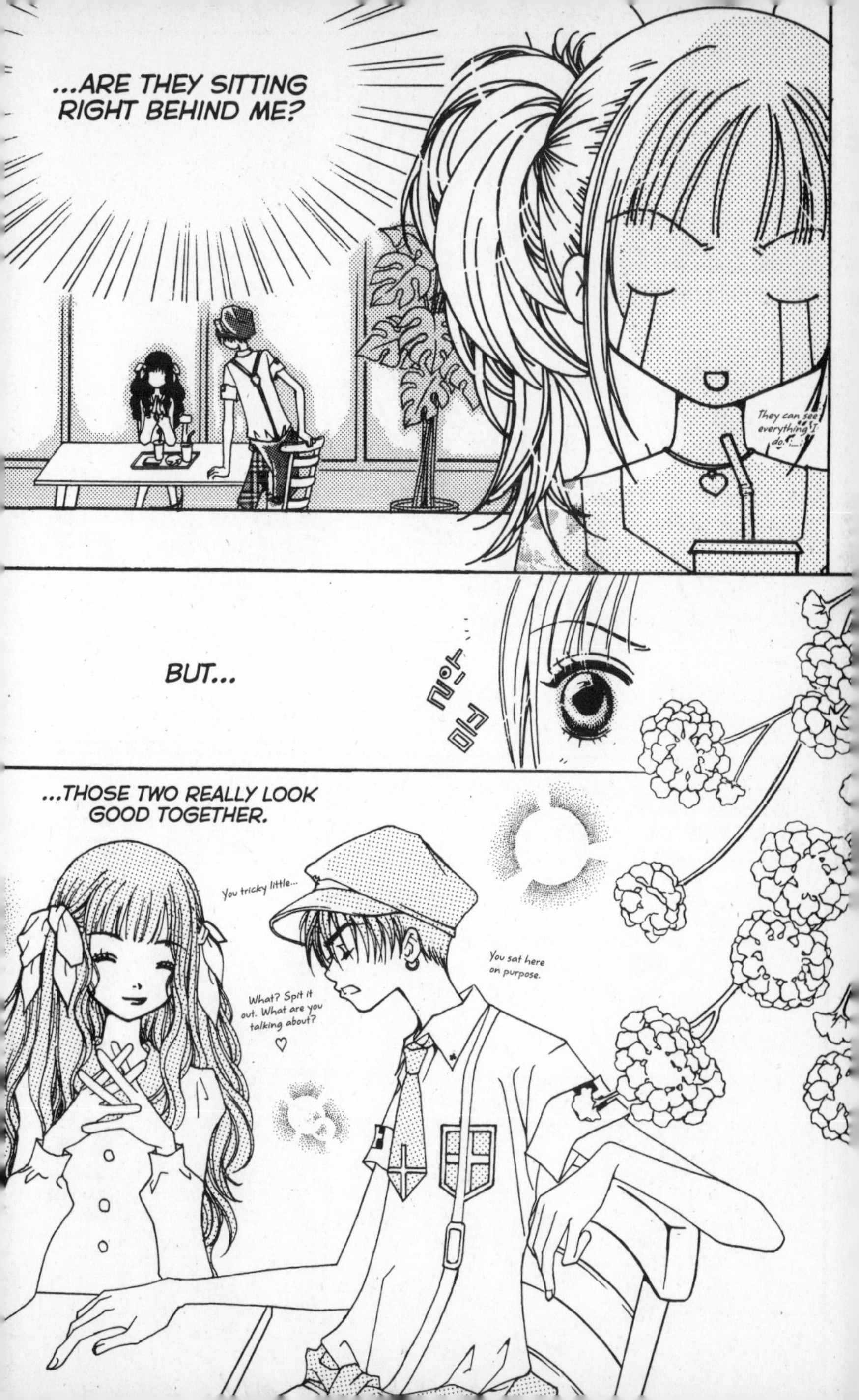
...ARE THEY SITTING RIGHT BEHIND ME?
They can see everything I do......
BUT...
...THOSE TWO REALLY LOOK GOOD TOGETHER.
You tricky little...
What? Spit it out. What are you talking about? ♡
You sat here on purpose.

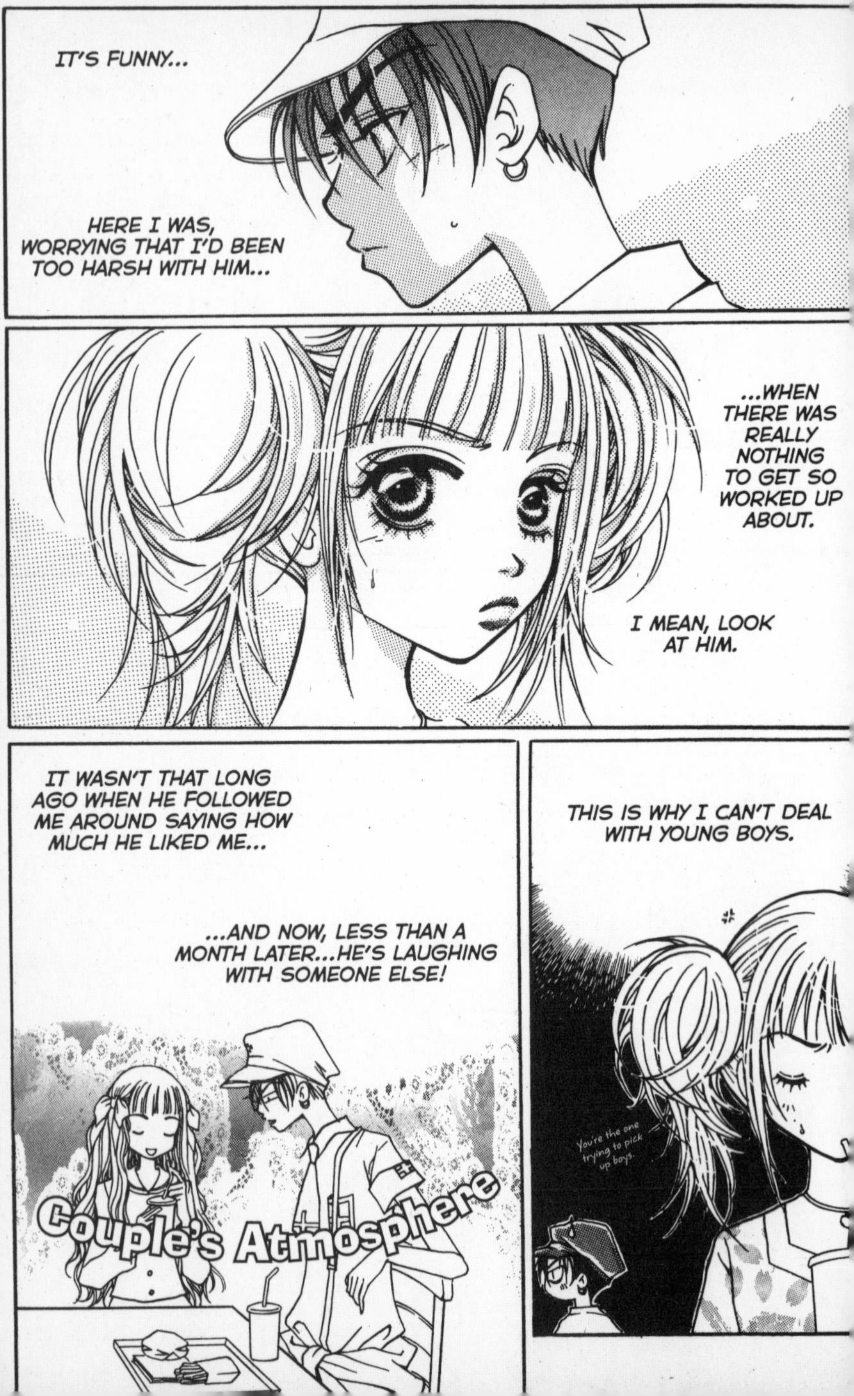
IT'S FUNNY...
HERE I WAS, WORRYING THAT I'D BEEN TOO HARSH WITH HIM...
...WHEN THERE WAS REALLY NOTHING TO GET SO WORKED UP ABOUT.
I MEAN, LOOK AT HIM.
IT WASN'T THAT LONG AGO WHEN HE FOLLOWED ME AROUND SAYING HOW MUCH HE LIKED ME...
...AND NOW, LESS THAN A MONTH LATER...HE'S LAUGHING WITH SOMEONE ELSE!
Couple's Atmosphere
THIS IS WHY I CAN'T DEAL WITH YOUNG BOYS.
You're the one trying to pick up boys.

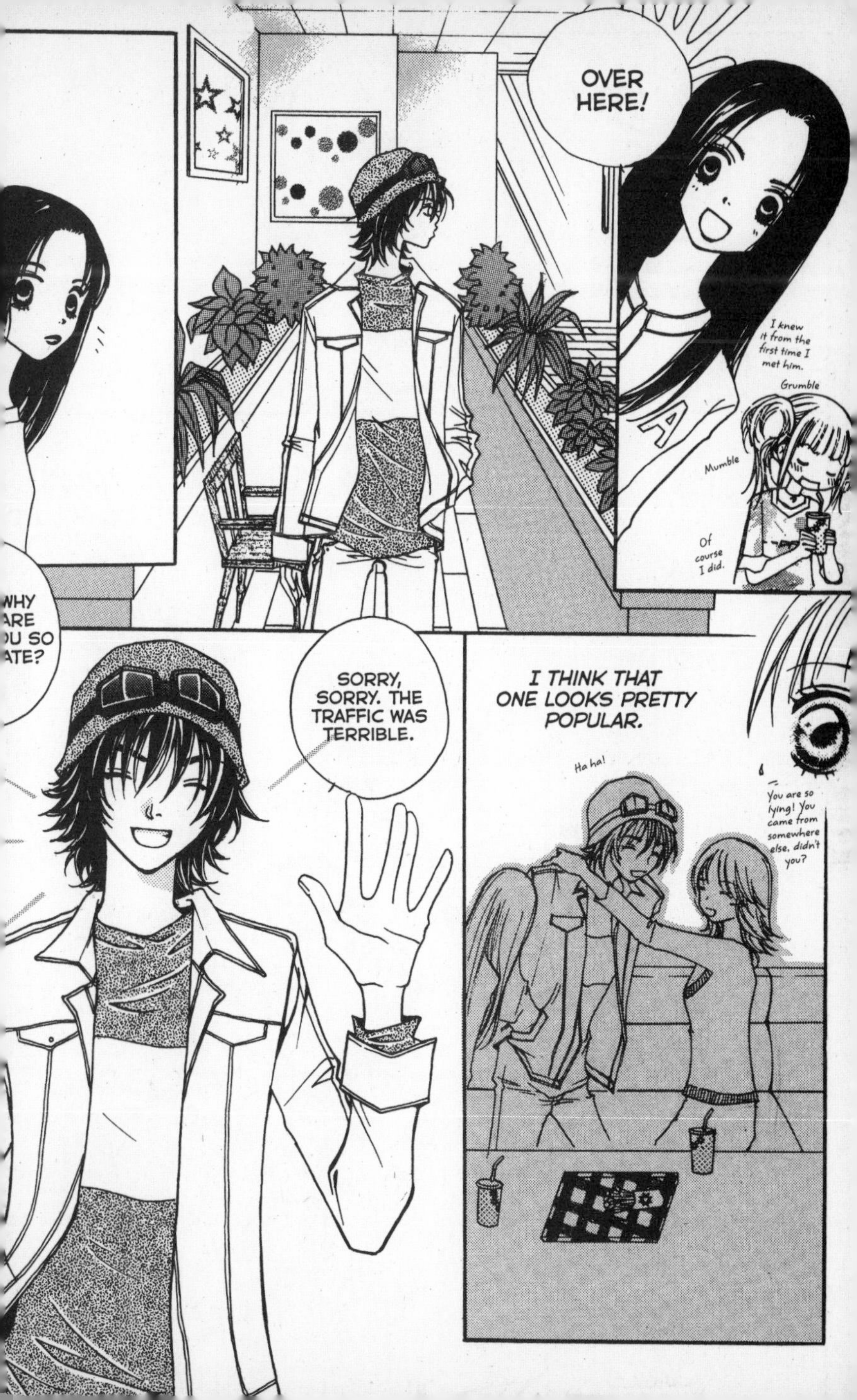
OVER HERE!
I knew it from the first time I met him.
Grumble
Mumble
Of course I did.
WHY ARE OU SO ATE?
SORRY, SORRY. THE TRAFFIC WAS TERRIBLE.
I THINK THAT ONE LOOKS PRETTY POPULAR.
Ha ha!
You are so lying! You came from somewhere else, didn't you?

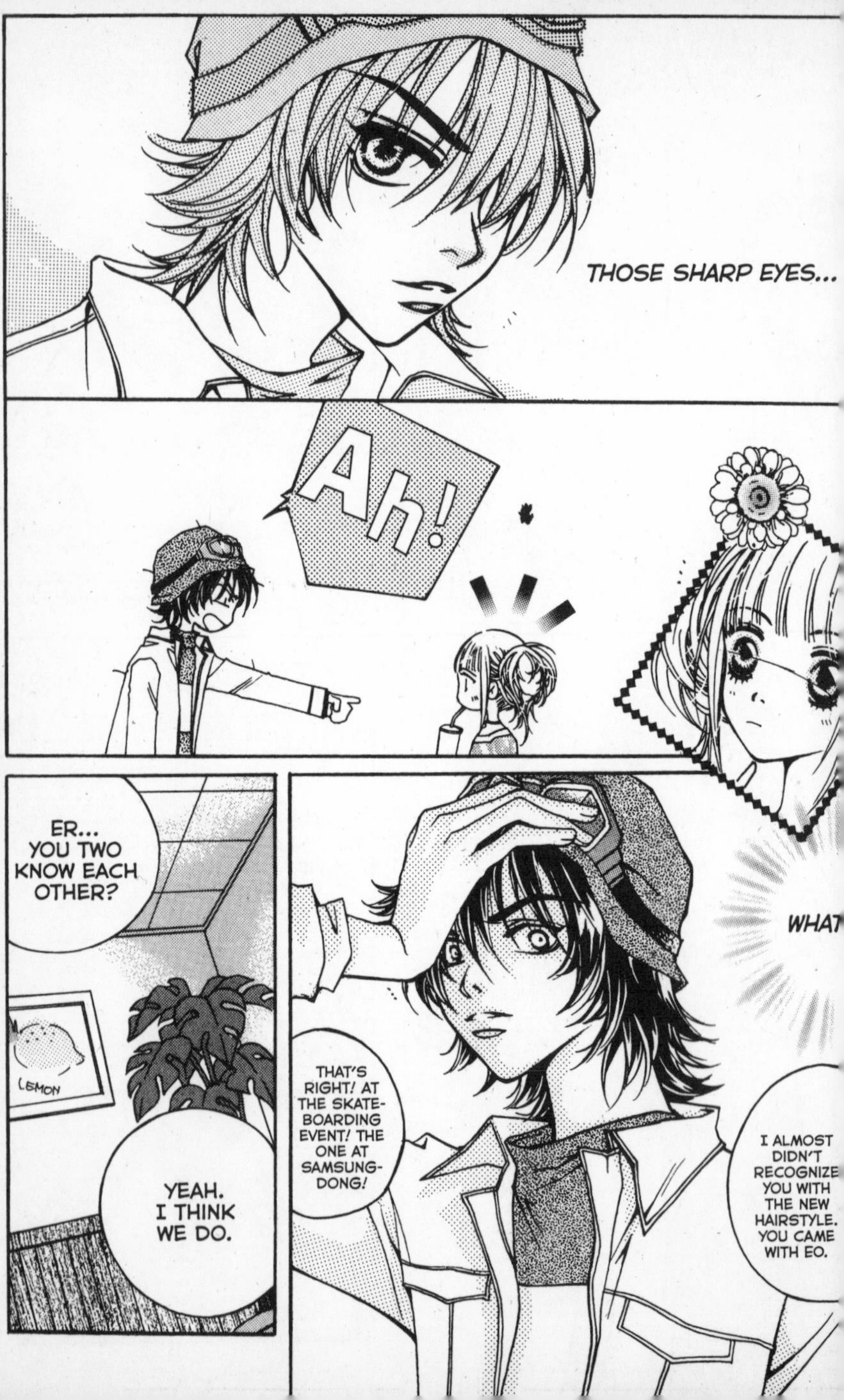
THOSE SHARP EYES...
Ah!
ER... YOU TWO KNOW EACH OTHER?
LEMON
YEAH. I THINK WE DO.
WHAT
THAT'S RIGHT! AT THE SKATE-BOARDING EVENT! THE ONE AT SAMSUNG-DONG!
I ALMOST DIDN'T RECOGNIZE YOU WITH THE NEW HAIRSTYLE. YOU CAME WITH EO.

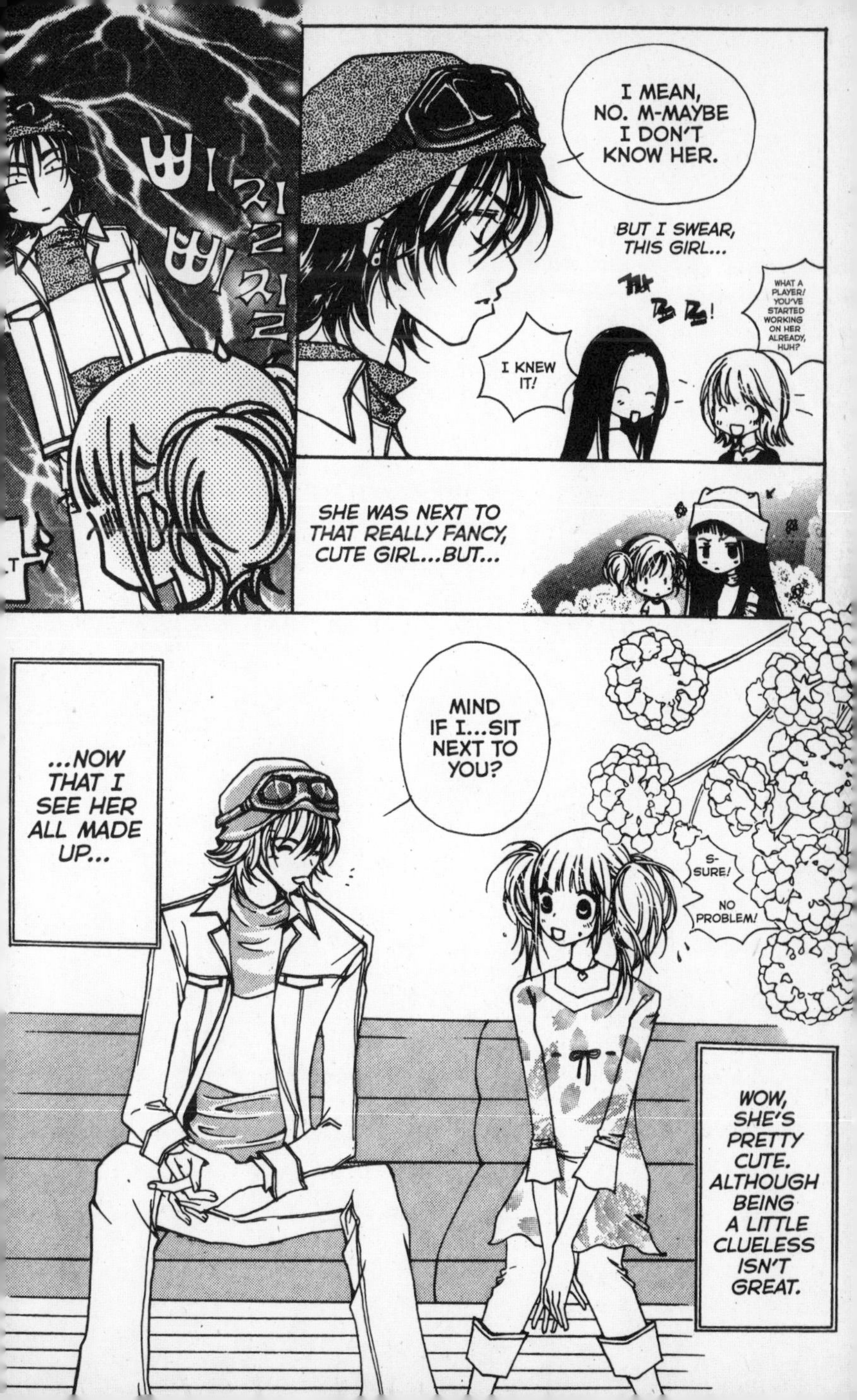
I MEAN, NO. M-MAYBE I DON'T KNOW HER.
BUT I SWEAR, THIS GIRL...
I KNEW IT!
WHAT A PLAYER! YOU'VE STARTED WORKING ON HER ALREADY, HUH?
SHE WAS NEXT TO THAT REALLY FANCY, CUTE GIRL...BUT...
...NOW THAT I SEE HER ALL MADE UP...
MIND IF I...SIT NEXT TO YOU?
S-SURE!
NO PROBLEM!
WOW, SHE'S PRETTY CUTE. ALTHOUGH BEING A LITTLE CLUELESS ISN'T GREAT.

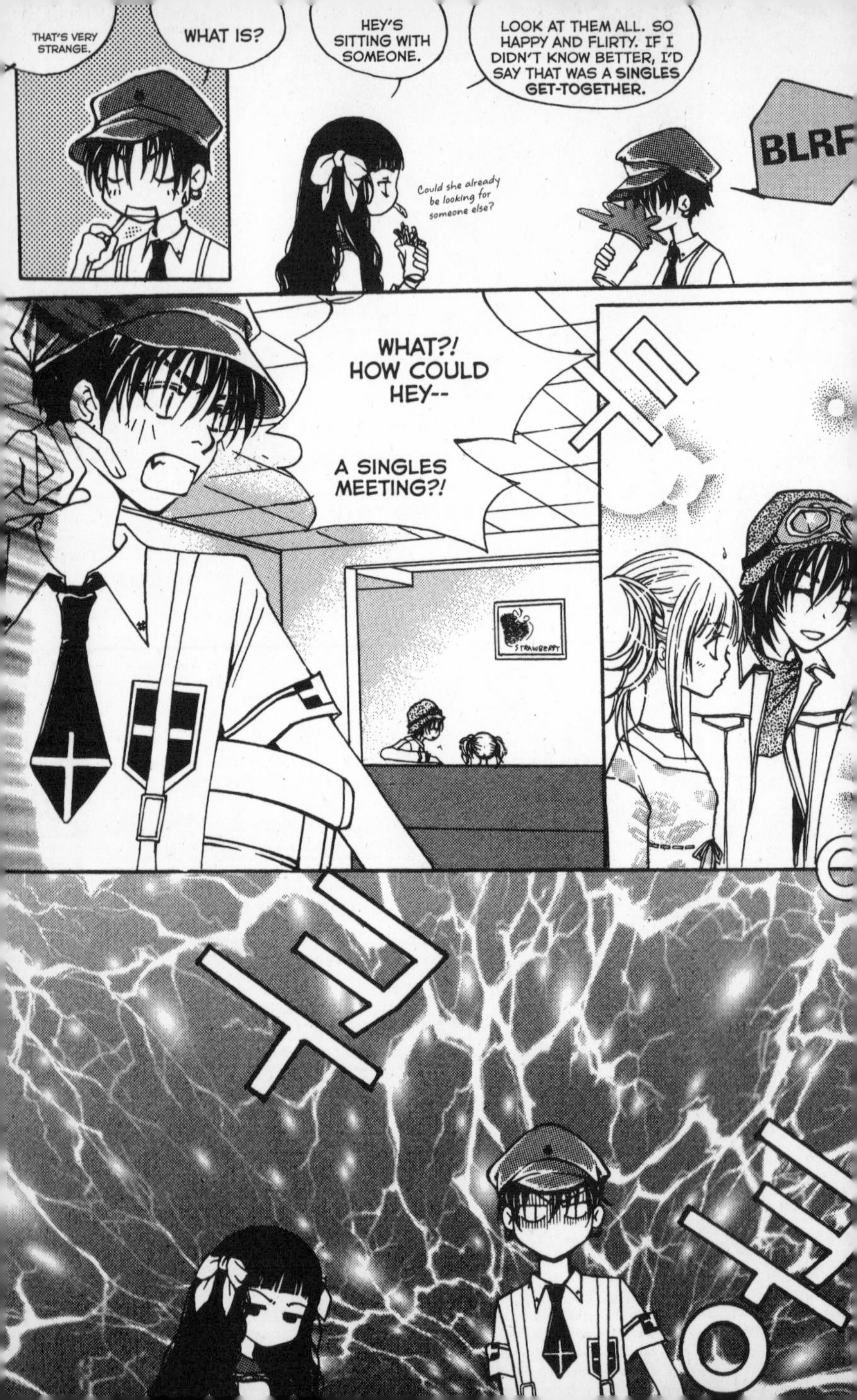
THAT'S VERY STRANGE.
WHAT IS?
HEY'S SITTING WITH SOMEONE.
LOOK AT THEM ALL. SO HAPPY AND FLIRTY. IF I DIDN'T KNOW BETTER, I'D SAY THAT WAS A SINGLES GET-TOGETHER.
Could she already be looking for someone else?
BLRF
WHAT?! HOW COULD HEY--
A SINGLES MEETING?!
STRAWBERRY

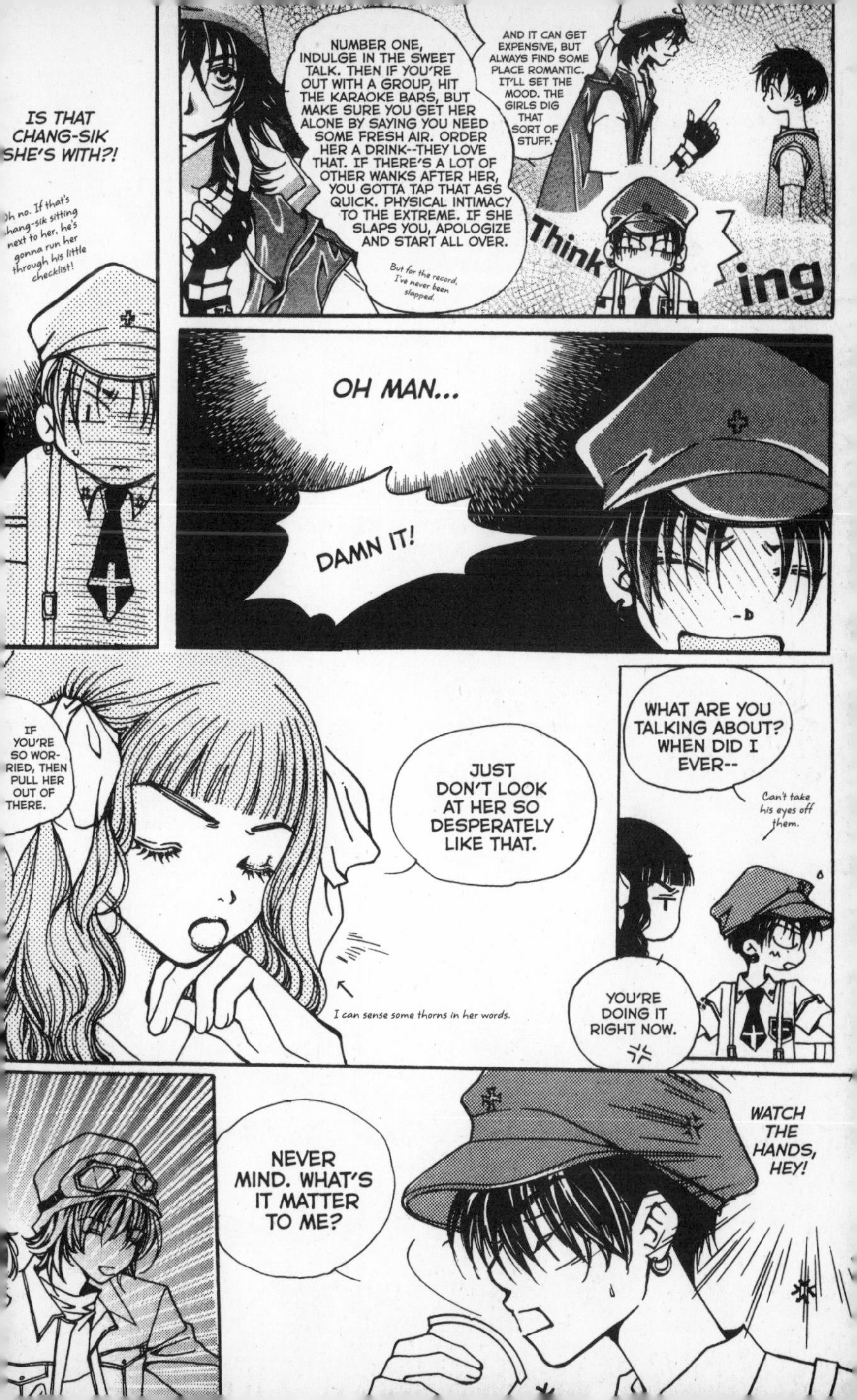
IS THAT CHANG-SIK SHE'S WITH?!
h no. If that's hang-sik sitting next to her, he's gonna run her through his little checklist!
NUMBER ONE, INDULGE IN THE SWEET TALK. THEN IF YOU'RE OUT WITH A GROUP, HIT THE KARAOKE BARS, BUT MAKE SURE YOU GET HER ALONE BY SAYING YOU NEED SOME FRESH AIR. ORDER HER A DRINK--THEY LOVE THAT. IF THERE'S A LOT OF OTHER WANKS AFTER HER, YOU GOTTA TAP THAT ASS QUICK. PHYSICAL INTIMACY TO THE EXTREME. IF SHE SLAPS YOU, APOLOGIZE AND START ALL OVER.
But for the record, I've never been slapped.
AND IT CAN GET EXPENSIVE, BUT ALWAYS FIND SOME PLACE ROMANTIC. IT'LL SET THE MOOD. THE GIRLS DIG THAT SORT OF STUFF.
Think ing
OH MAN...
DAMN IT!
IF YOU'RE SO WOR-RIED, THEN PULL HER OUT OF THERE.
JUST DON'T LOOK AT HER SO DESPERATELY LIKE THAT.
I can sense some thorns in her words.
WHAT ARE YOU TALKING ABOUT? WHEN DID I EVER--
Can't take his eyes off them.
YOU'RE DOING IT RIGHT NOW.
NEVER MIND. WHAT'S IT MATTER TO ME?
WATCH THE HANDS, HEY!

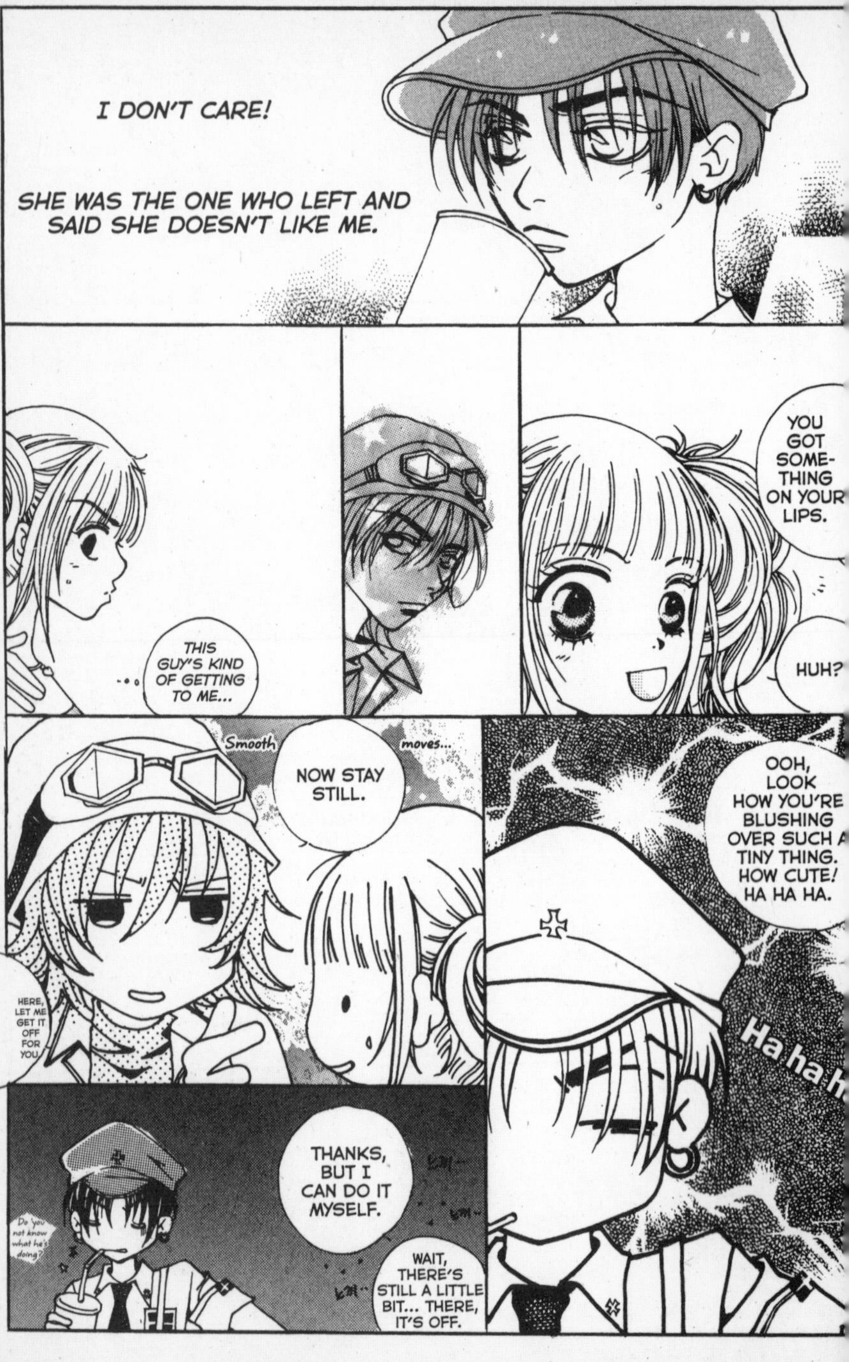
I DON'T CARE!
SHE WAS THE ONE WHO LEFT AND SAID SHE DOESN'T LIKE ME.
...
THIS GUY'S KIND OF GETTING TO ME...
YOU GOT SOME-THING ON YOUR LIPS.
HUH?
Smooth moves...
NOW STAY STILL.
HERE, LET ME GET IT OFF FOR YOU.
Do you not know what he's doing?
THANKS, BUT I CAN DO IT MYSELF.
WAIT, THERE'S STILL A LITTLE BIT... THERE, IT'S OFF.
OOH, LOOK HOW YOU'RE BLUSHING OVER SUCH A TINY THING. HOW CUTE! HA HA HA.
Ha ha h

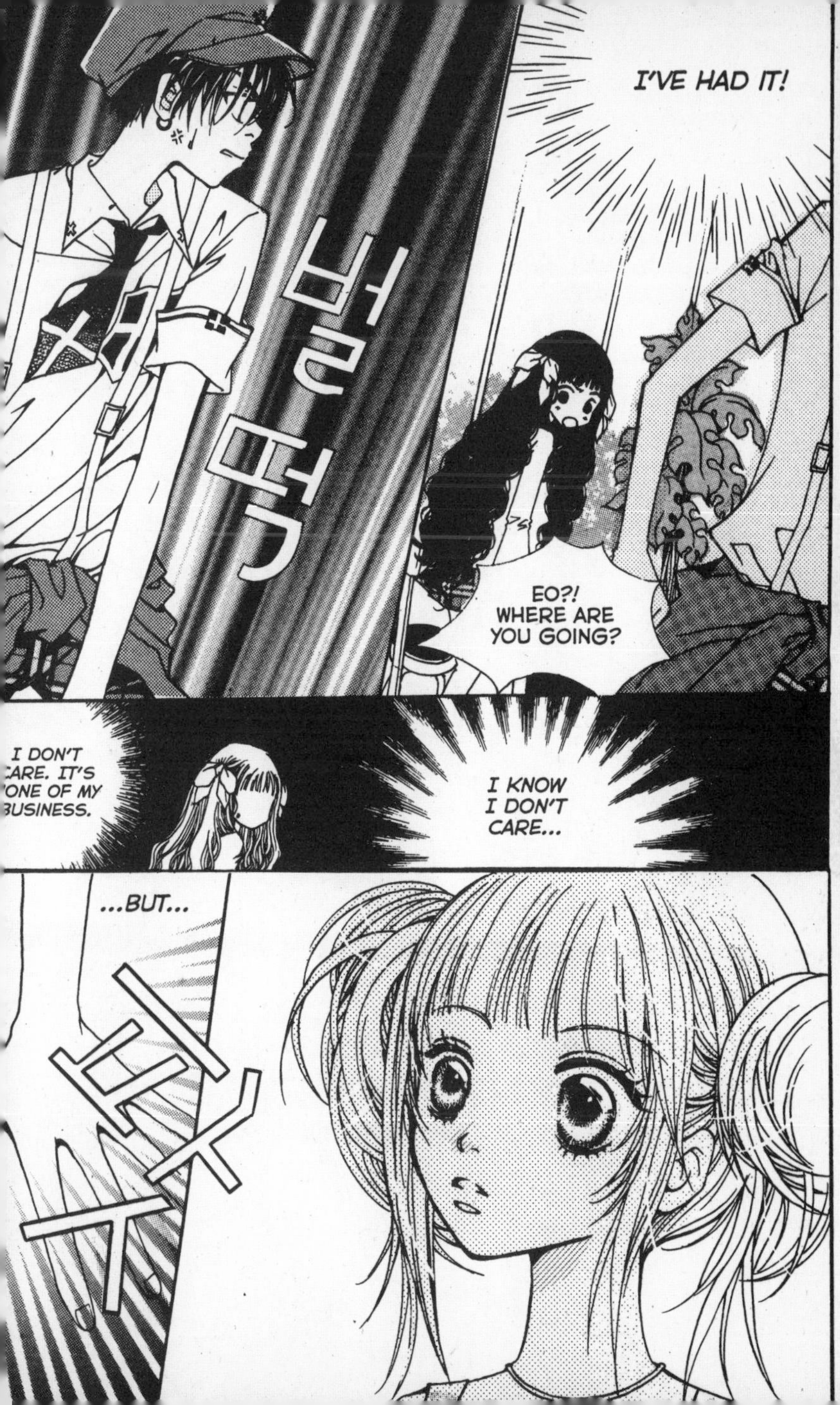
I'VE HAD IT!
EO?! WHERE ARE YOU GOING?
I DON'T CARE. IT'S NONE OF MY BUSINESS.
I KNOW I DON'T CARE...
...BUT...

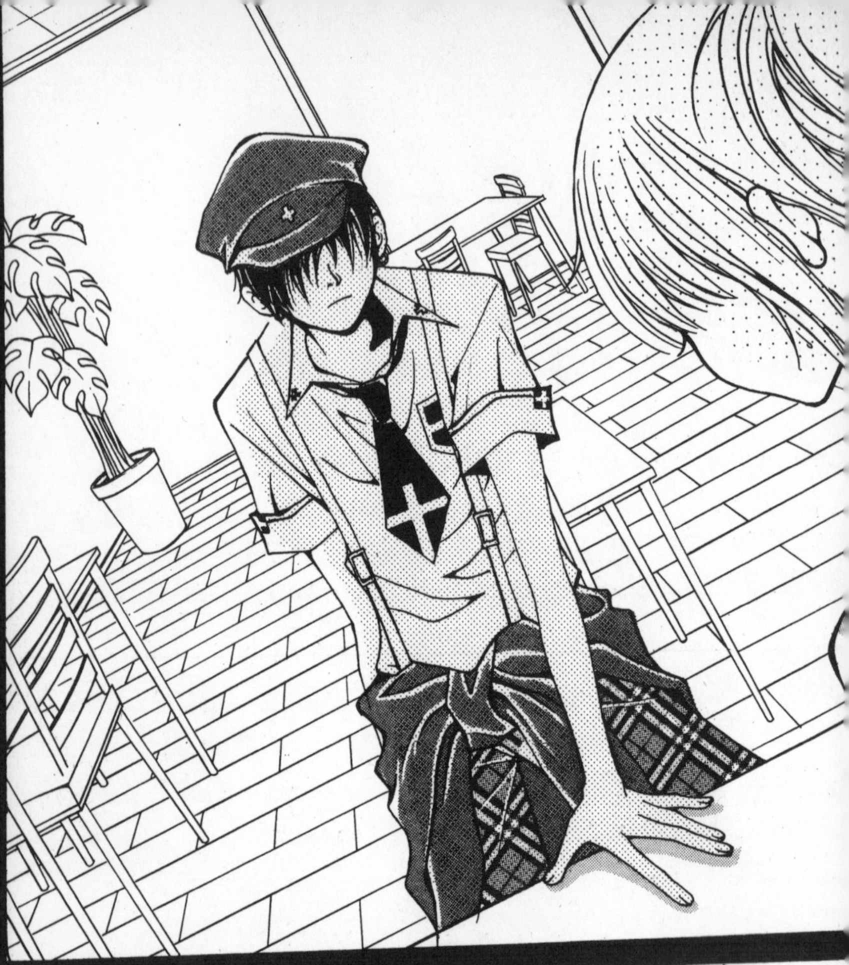

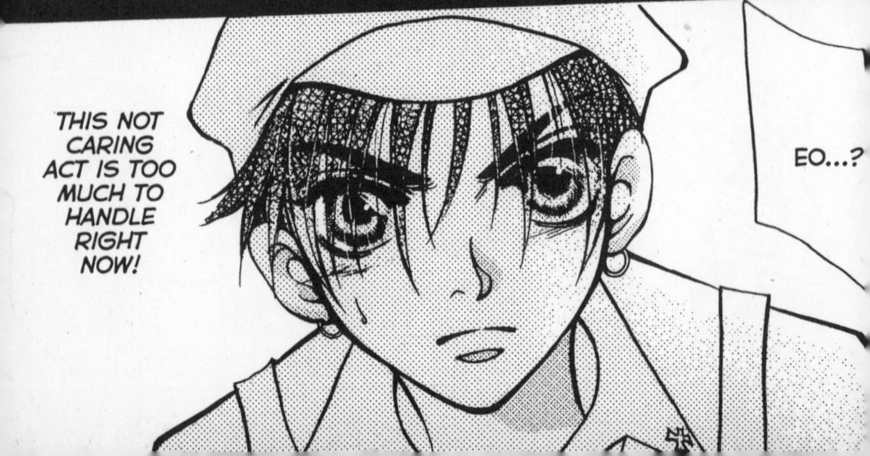
THIS NOT CARING ACT IS TOO MUCH TO HANDLE RIGHT NOW!
EO...?

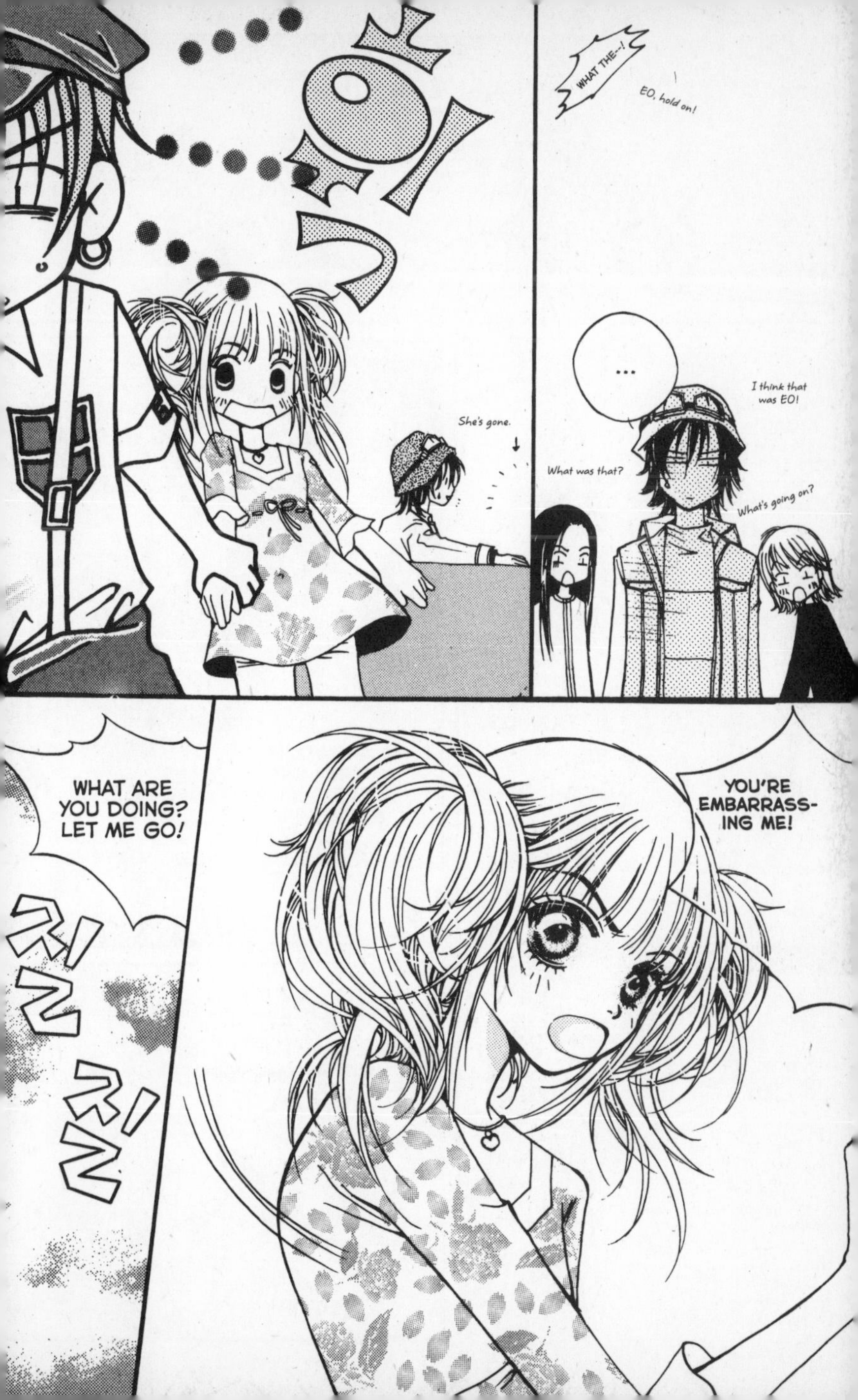
She's gone.
WHAT THE--!
EO, hold on!
...
I think that was EO!
What was that?
What's going on?
WHAT ARE YOU DOING? LET ME GO!
YOU'RE EMBARRASS-
ING ME!

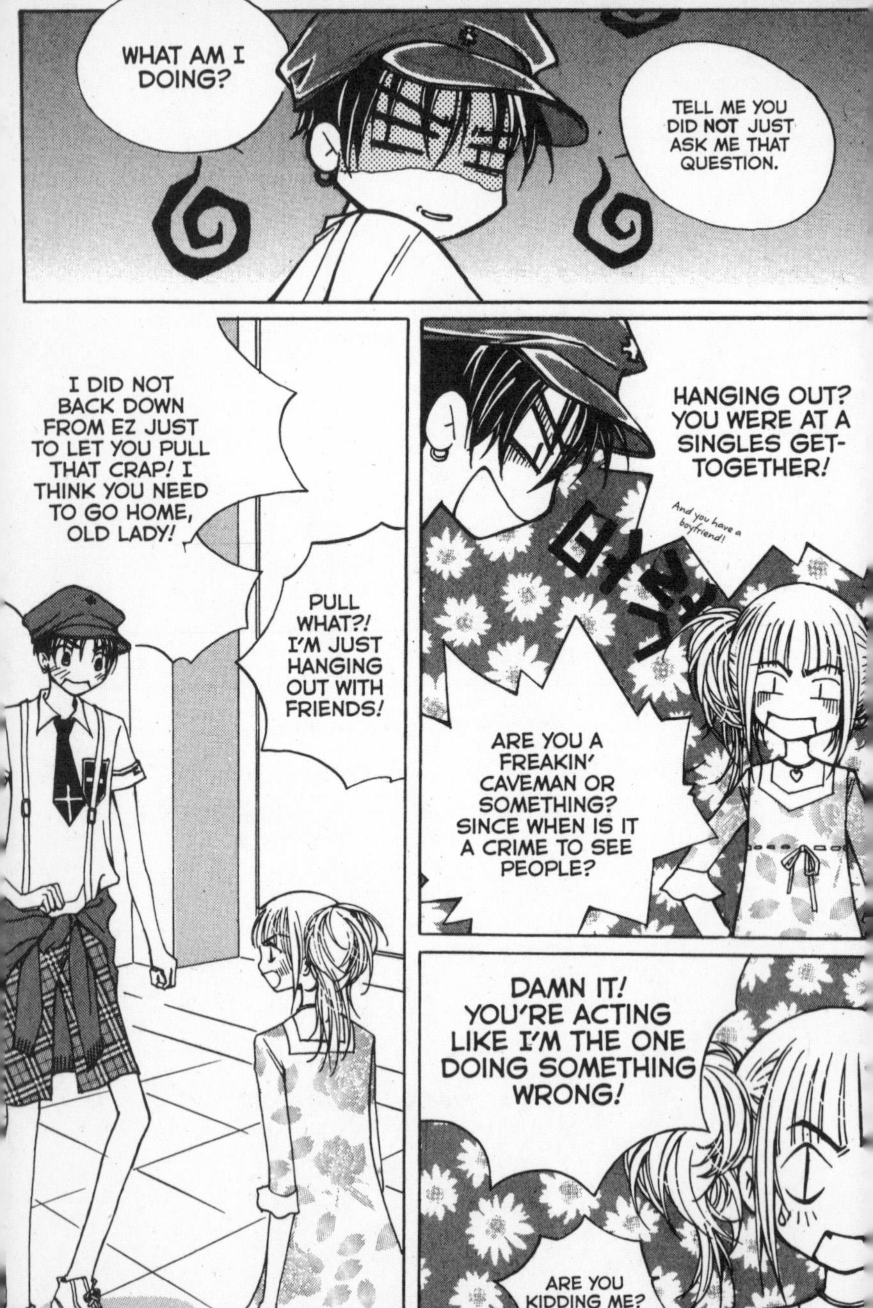
WHAT AM I DOING?
TELL ME YOU DID NOT JUST ASK ME THAT QUESTION.
I DID NOT BACK DOWN FROM EZ JUST TO LET YOU PULL THAT CRAP! I THINK YOU NEED TO GO HOME, OLD LADY!
PULL WHAT?! I'M JUST HANGING OUT WITH FRIENDS!
HANGING OUT? YOU WERE AT A SINGLES GET-TOGETHER!
And you have a boyfriend!
ARE YOU A FREAKIN' CAVEMAN OR SOMETHING? SINCE WHEN IS IT A CRIME TO SEE PEOPLE?
DAMN IT! YOU'RE ACTING LIKE I'M THE ONE DOING SOMETHING WRONG!
ARE YOU KIDDING ME?

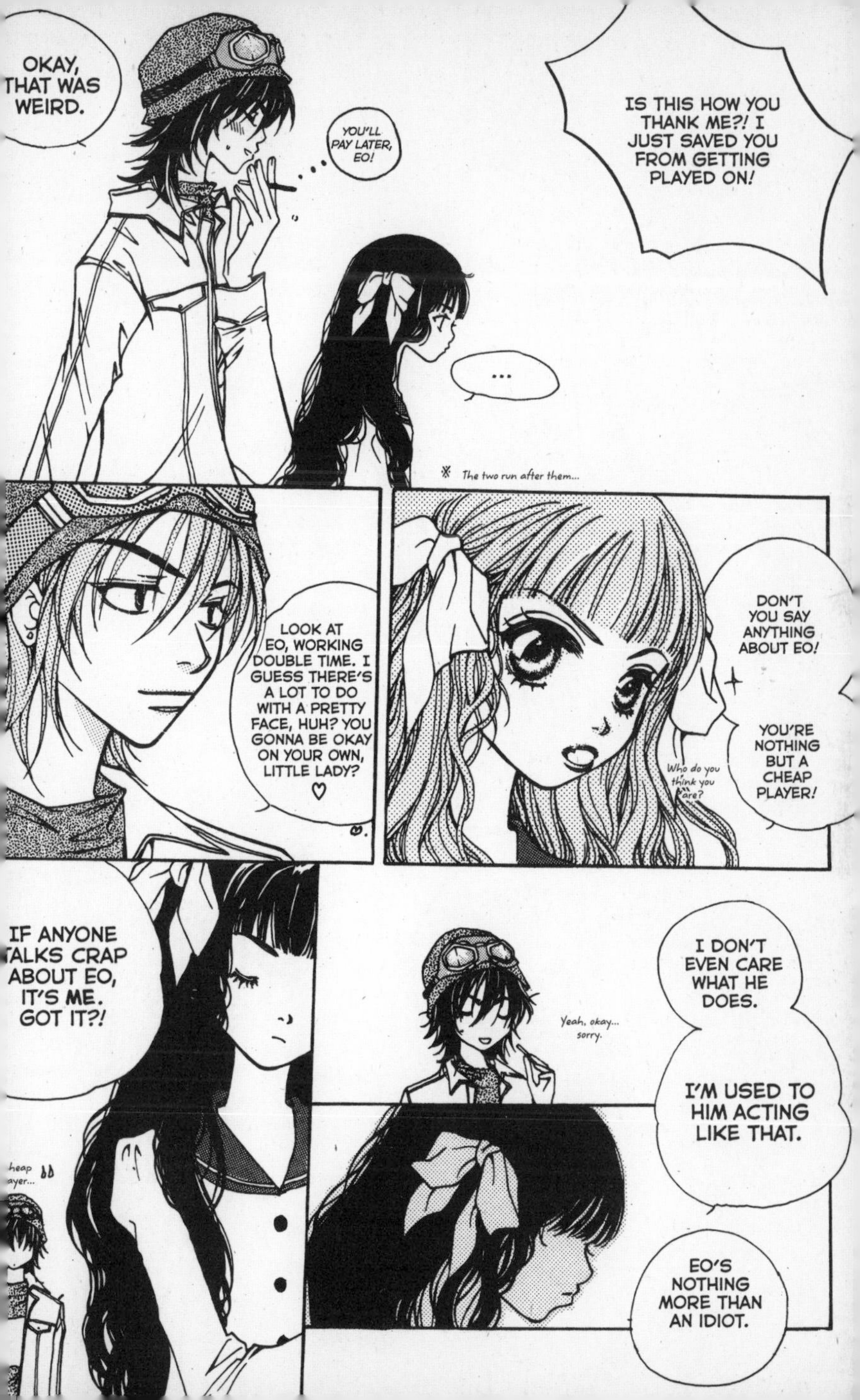
OKAY, THAT WAS WEIRD.
YOU'LL PAY LATER, EO!
IS THIS HOW YOU THANK ME?! I JUST SAVED YOU FROM GETTING PLAYED ON!
...
※ The two run after them...
LOOK AT EO, WORKING DOUBLE TIME. I GUESS THERE'S A LOT TO DO WITH A PRETTY FACE, HUH? YOU GONNA BE OKAY ON YOUR OWN, LITTLE LADY? ♡
DON'T YOU SAY ANYTHING ABOUT EO!
Who do you think you are?
YOU'RE NOTHING BUT A CHEAP PLAYER!
IF ANYONE TALKS CRAP ABOUT EO, IT'S ME. GOT IT?!
Yeah, okay... sorry.
I DON'T EVEN CARE WHAT HE DOES.
I'M USED TO HIM ACTING LIKE THAT.
EO'S NOTHING MORE THAN AN IDIOT.

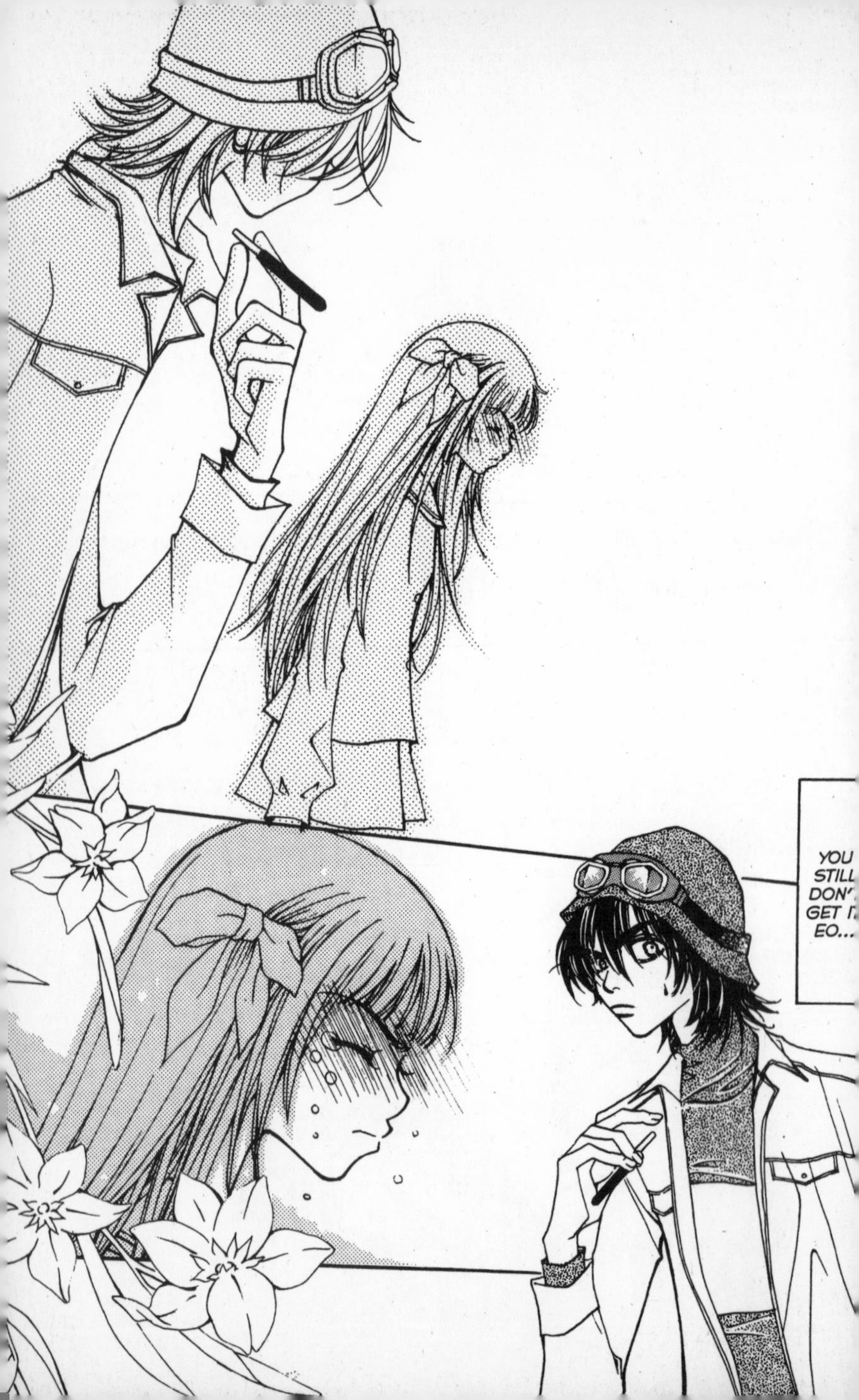
YOU STILL DON' GET I EO...

LOOK, YOU ARE **NOT** MY BOYFRIEND SO JUST STAY OUT OF MY BUSINESS!

OH!

Y-YOU HEAR ME?

BUT WHAT HAPPENS TO YOU **DOES** MATTER TO ME.

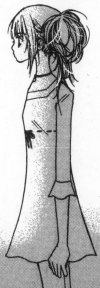

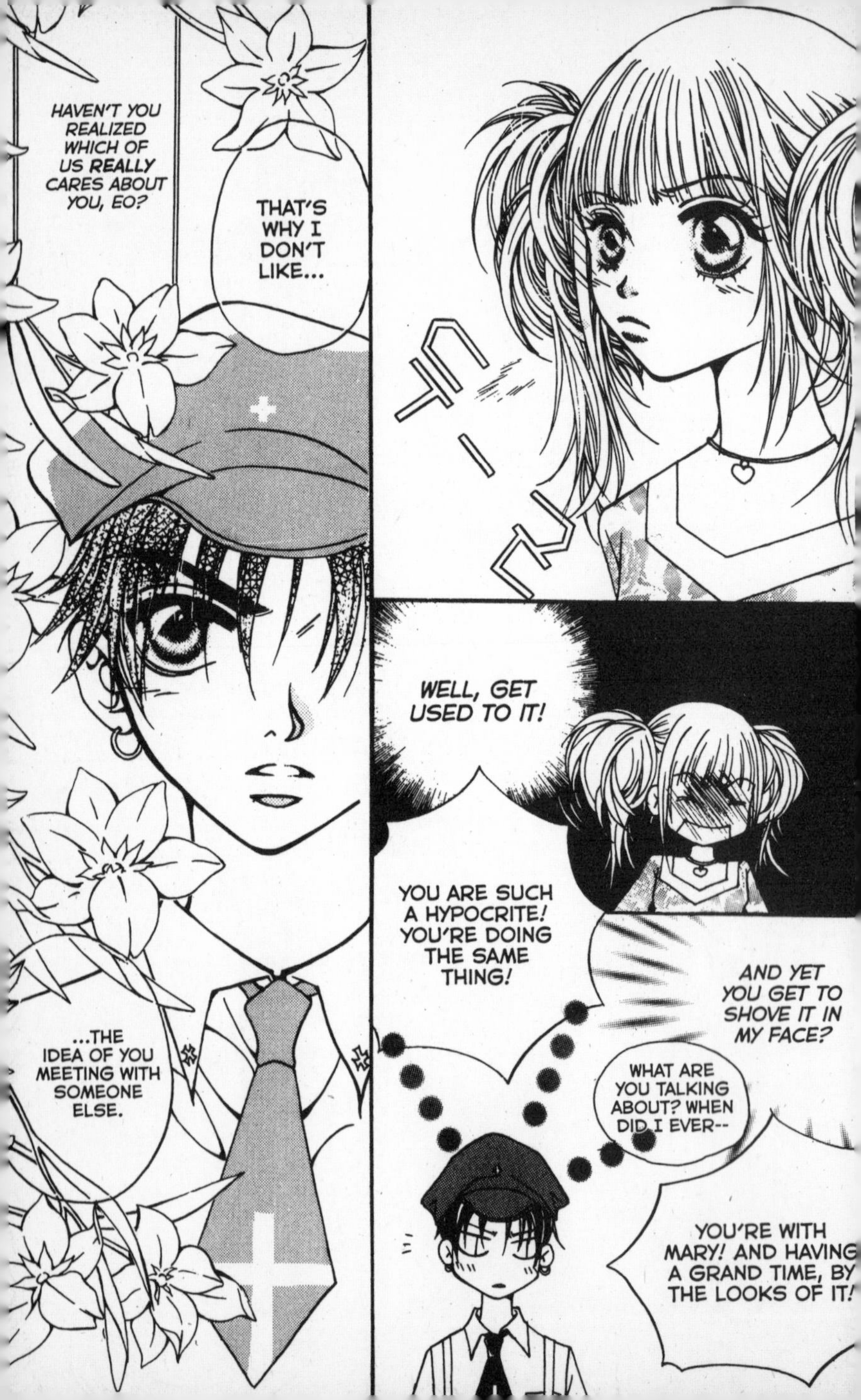
HAVEN'T YOU REALIZED WHICH OF US REALLY CARES ABOUT YOU, EO?
THAT'S WHY I DON'T LIKE...
...THE IDEA OF YOU MEETING WITH SOMEONE ELSE.
WELL, GET USED TO IT!
YOU ARE SUCH A HYPOCRITE! YOU'RE DOING THE SAME THING!
AND YET YOU GET TO SHOVE IT IN MY FACE?
WHAT ARE YOU TALKING ABOUT? WHEN DID I EVER--
YOU'RE WITH MARY! AND HAVING A GRAND TIME, BY THE LOOKS OF IT!

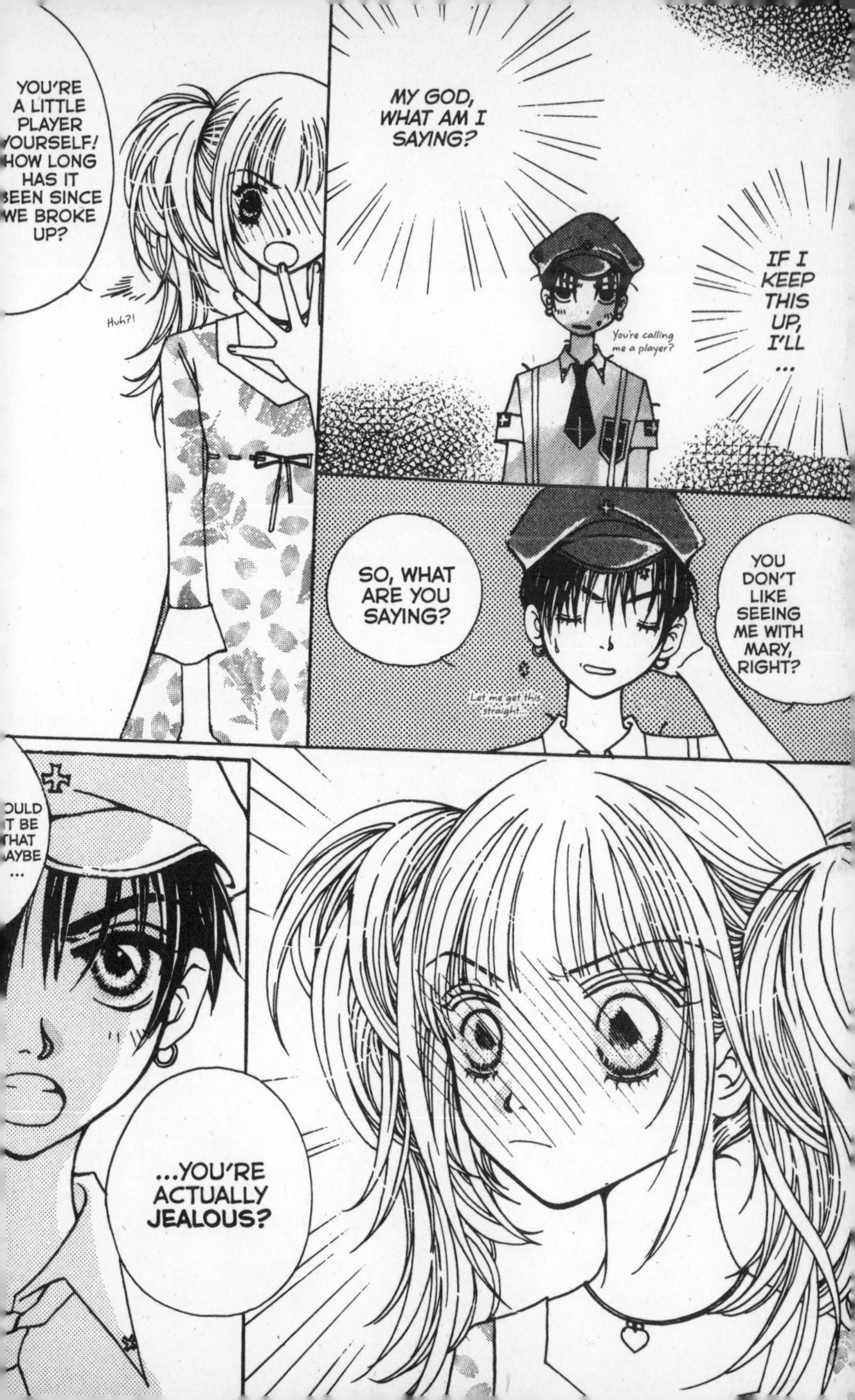

YOU'RE A LITTLE PLAYER YOURSELF! HOW LONG HAS IT BEEN SINCE WE BROKE UP?
Huh?!
MY GOD, WHAT AM I SAYING?
You're calling me a player?
IF I KEEP THIS UP, I'LL ...
SO, WHAT ARE YOU SAYING?
Let me get this straight...
YOU DON'T LIKE SEEING ME WITH MARY, RIGHT?
OULD T BE THAT AYBE ...
...YOU'RE ACTUALLY JEALOUS?

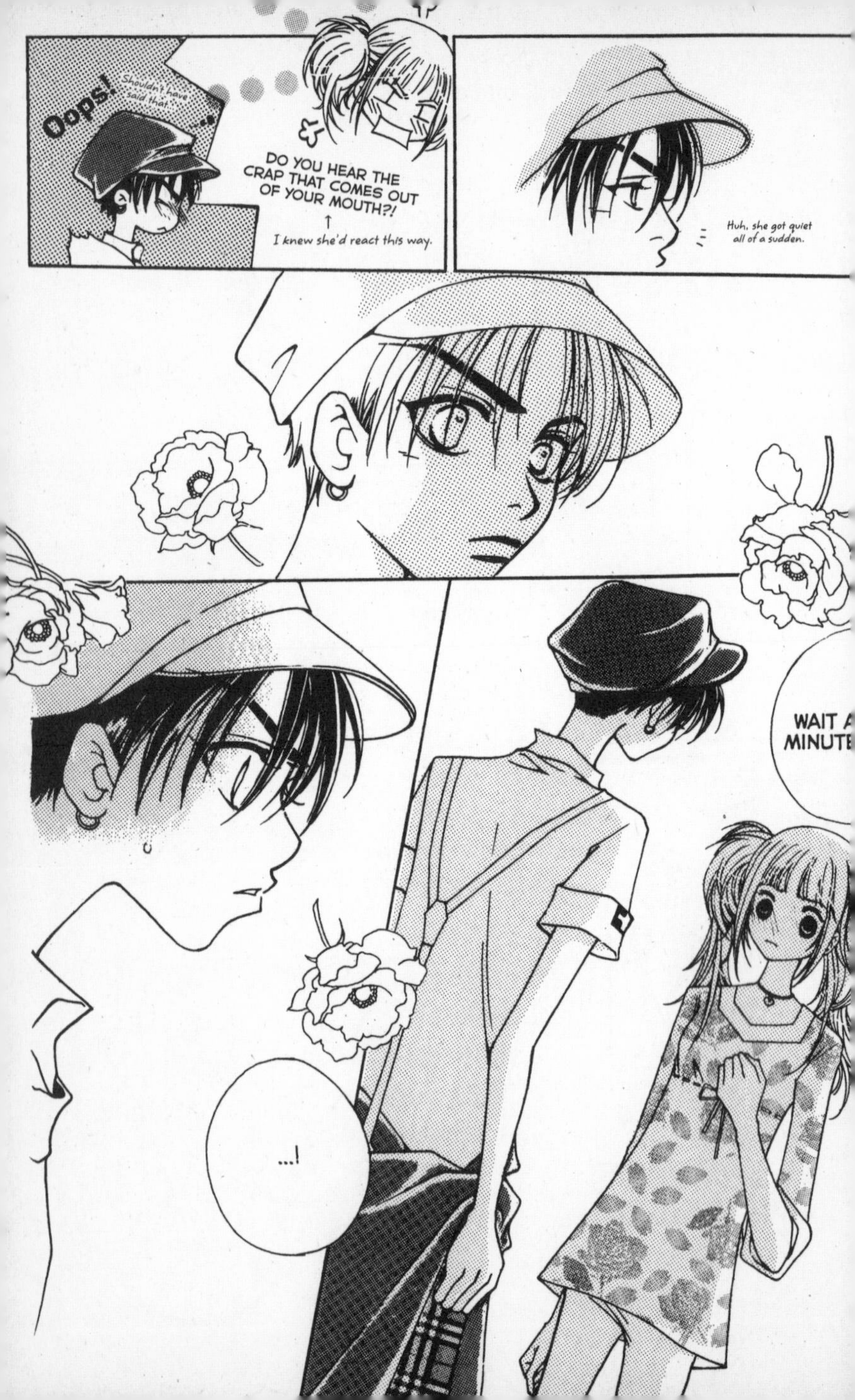
Oops!
Shouldn't have said that...
DO YOU HEAR THE CRAP THAT COMES OUT OF YOUR MOUTH?!
I knew she'd react this way.
Huh, she got quiet all of a sudden.
...!
WAIT A MINUTE

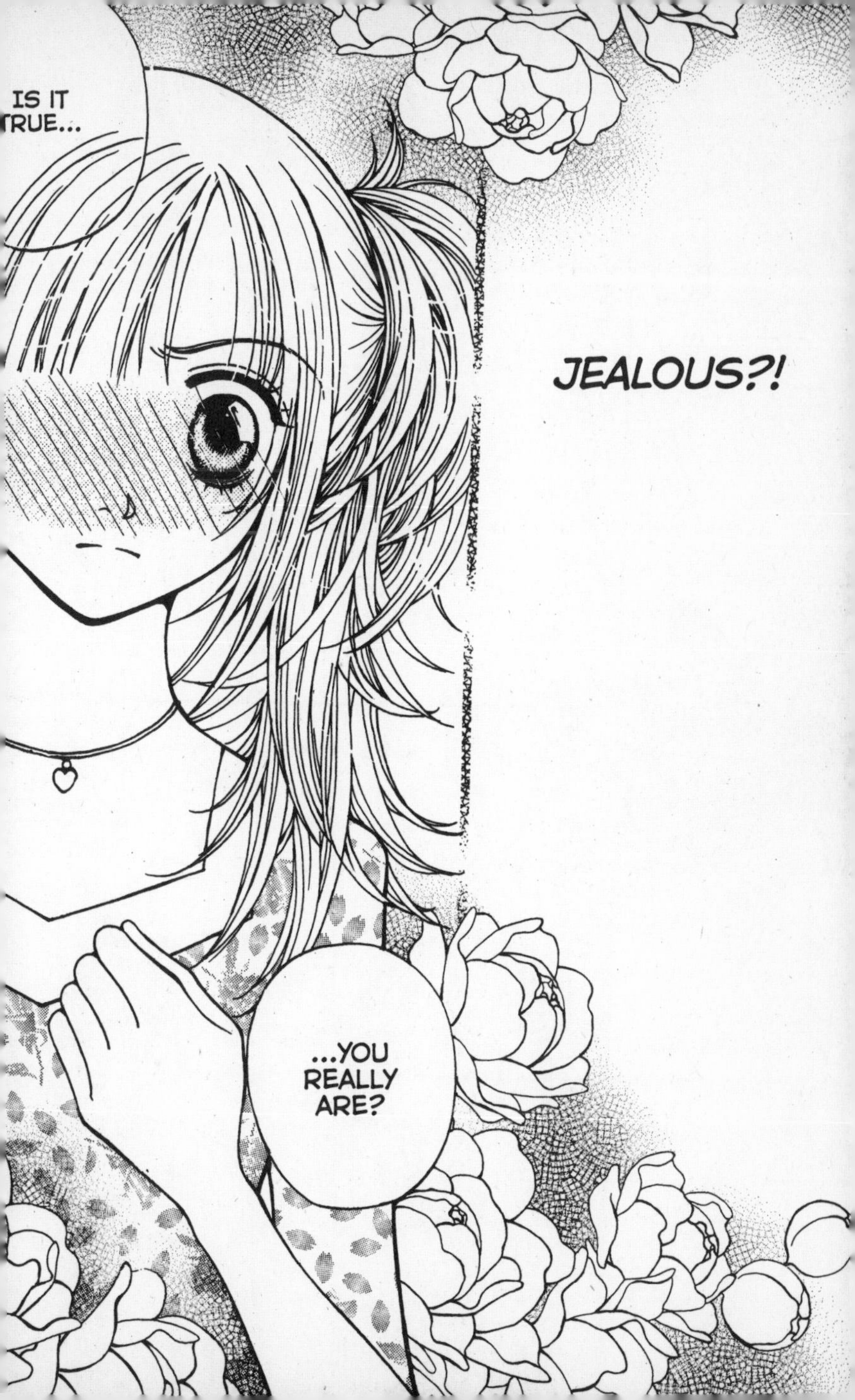
IS IT TRUE...
...YOU REALLY ARE?
JEALOUS?!

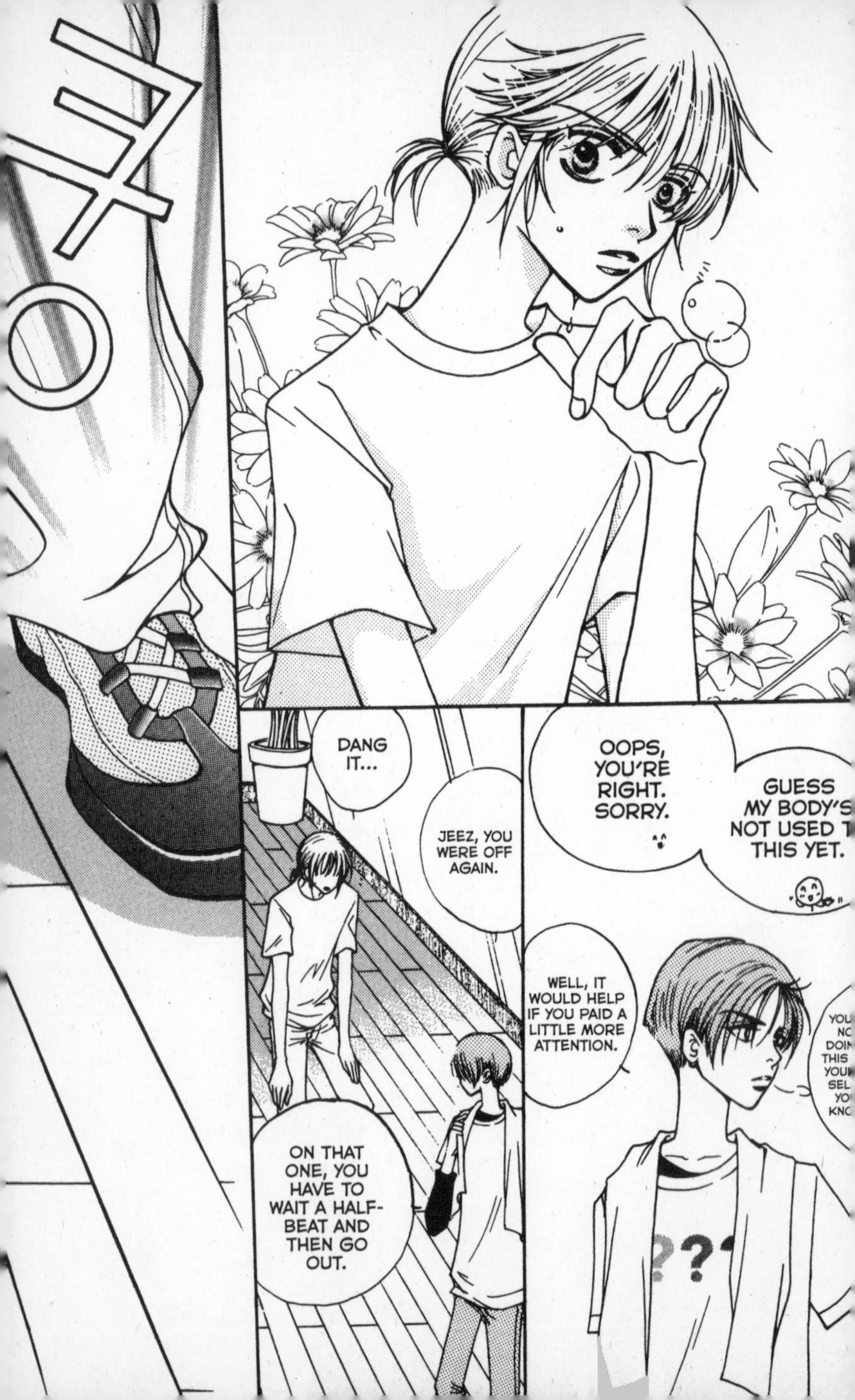
DANG IT...
JEEZ, YOU WERE OFF AGAIN.
ON THAT ONE, YOU HAVE TO WAIT A HALF-BEAT AND THEN GO OUT.
OOPS, YOU'RE RIGHT. SORRY.
GUESS MY BODY'S NOT USED T THIS YET.
WELL, IT WOULD HELP IF YOU PAID A LITTLE MORE ATTENTION.
YOU NO DOIN THIS YOUR SEL YO KNO

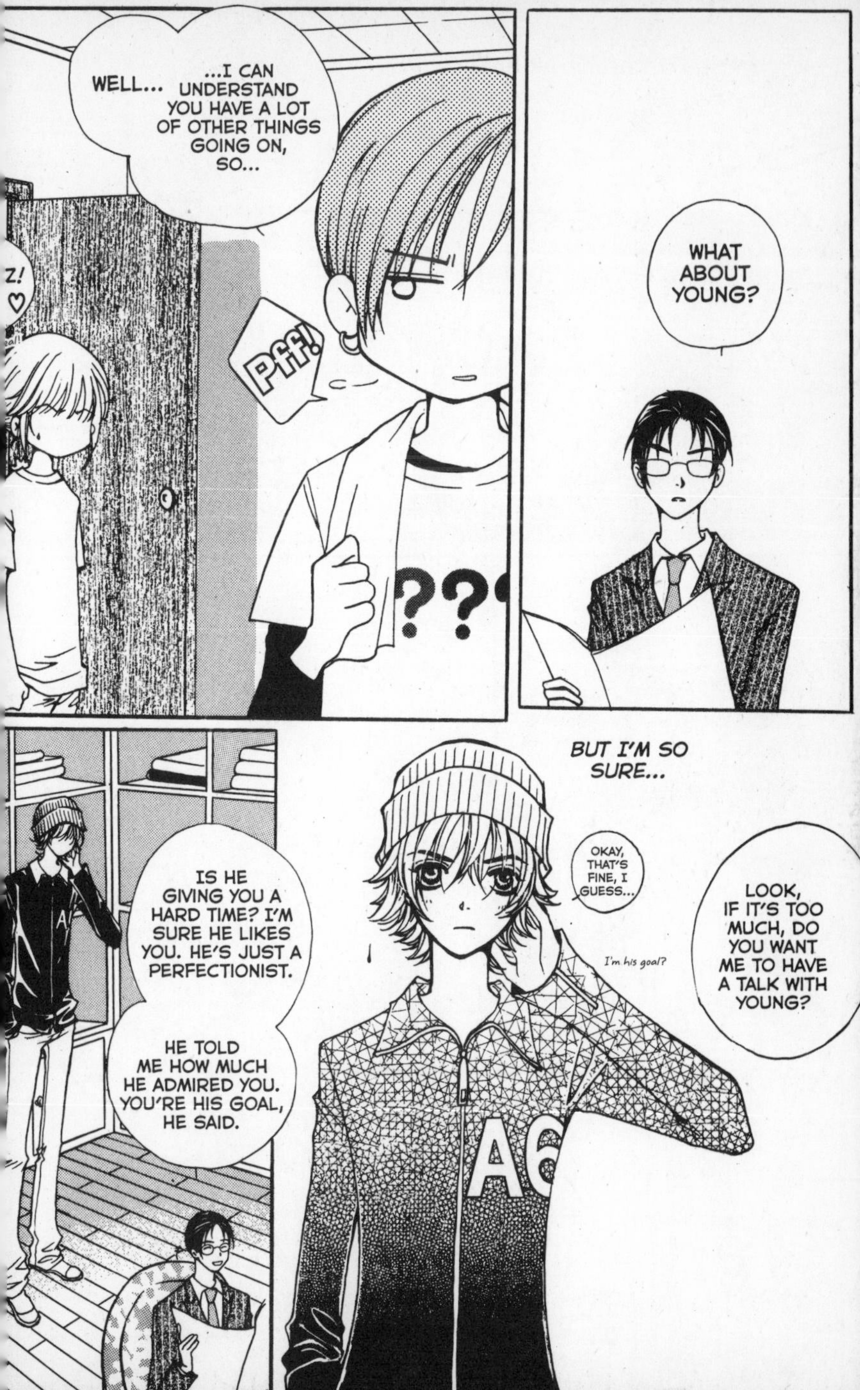
WELL... ...I CAN UNDERSTAND YOU HAVE A LOT OF OTHER THINGS GOING ON, SO...
Pff!
WHAT ABOUT YOUNG?
IS HE GIVING YOU A HARD TIME? I'M SURE HE LIKES YOU. HE'S JUST A PERFECTIONIST.
HE TOLD ME HOW MUCH HE ADMIRED YOU. YOU'RE HIS GOAL, HE SAID.
BUT I'M SO SURE...
OKAY, THAT'S FINE, I GUESS...
I'm his goal?
LOOK, IF IT'S TOO MUCH, DO YOU WANT ME TO HAVE A TALK WITH YOUNG?

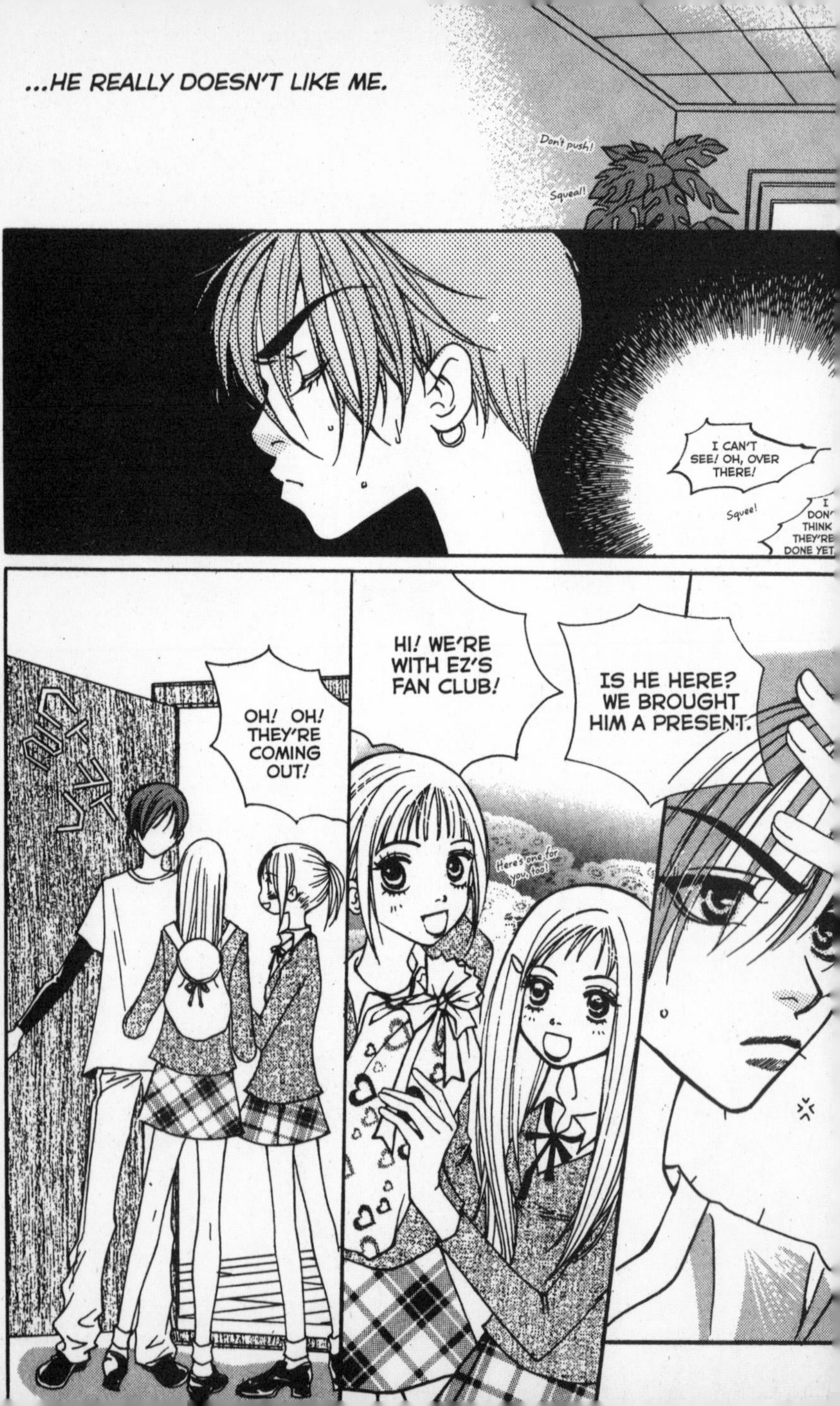
...HE REALLY DOESN'T LIKE ME.
Don't push!
Squeal!
I CAN'T SEE! OH, OVER THERE!
Squee!
I DON' THINK THEY'RE DONE YET.
OH! OH! THEY'RE COMING OUT!
HI! WE'RE WITH EZ'S FAN CLUB!
Here's one for you, too!
IS HE HERE? WE BROUGHT HIM A PRESENT.

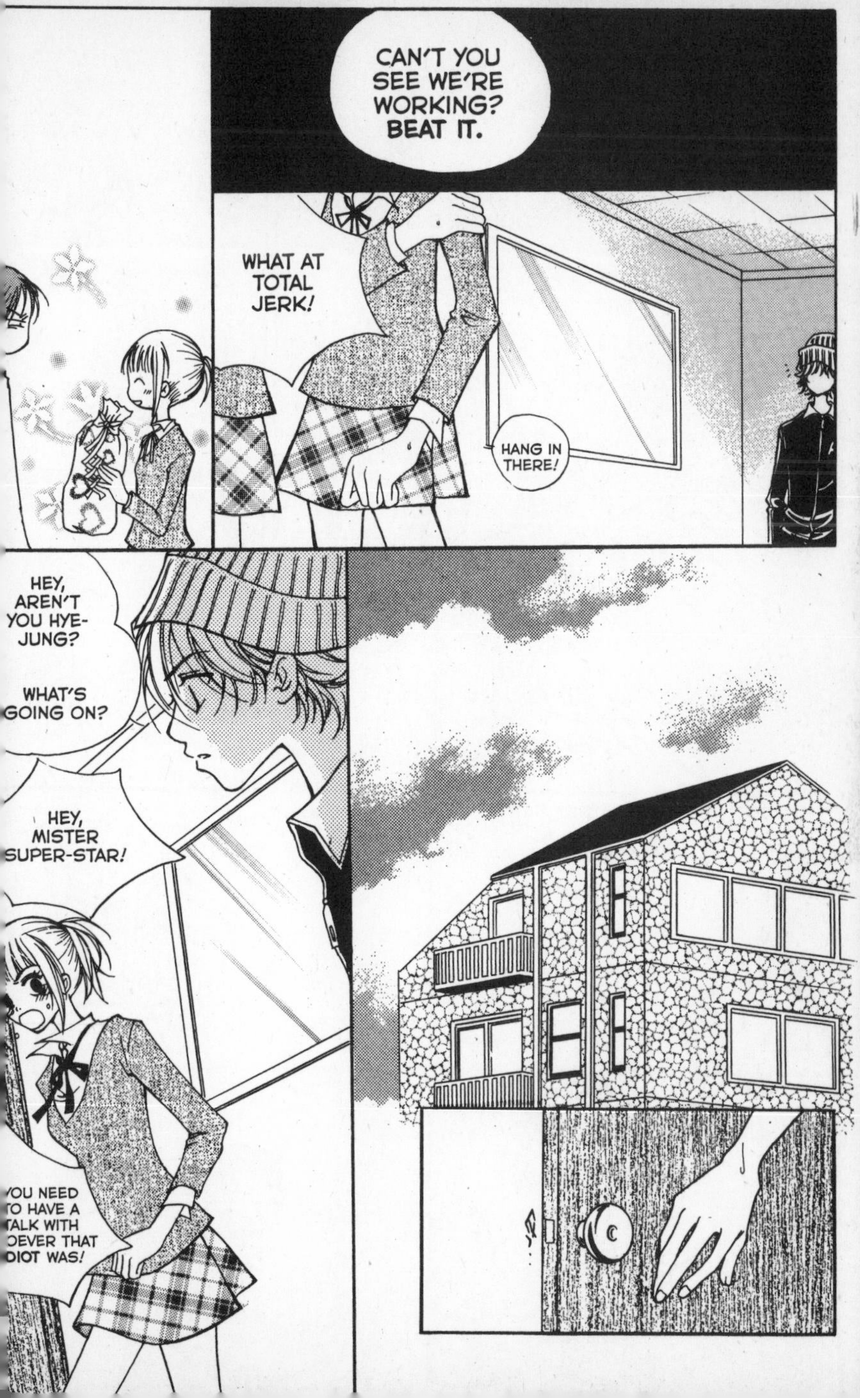
CAN'T YOU SEE WE'RE WORKING? BEAT IT.
WHAT AT TOTAL JERK!
HANG IN THERE!
HEY, AREN'T YOU HYE-JUNG?
WHAT'S GOING ON?
HEY, MISTER SUPER-STAR!
YOU NEED TO HAVE A TALK WITH OEVER THAT DIOT WAS!

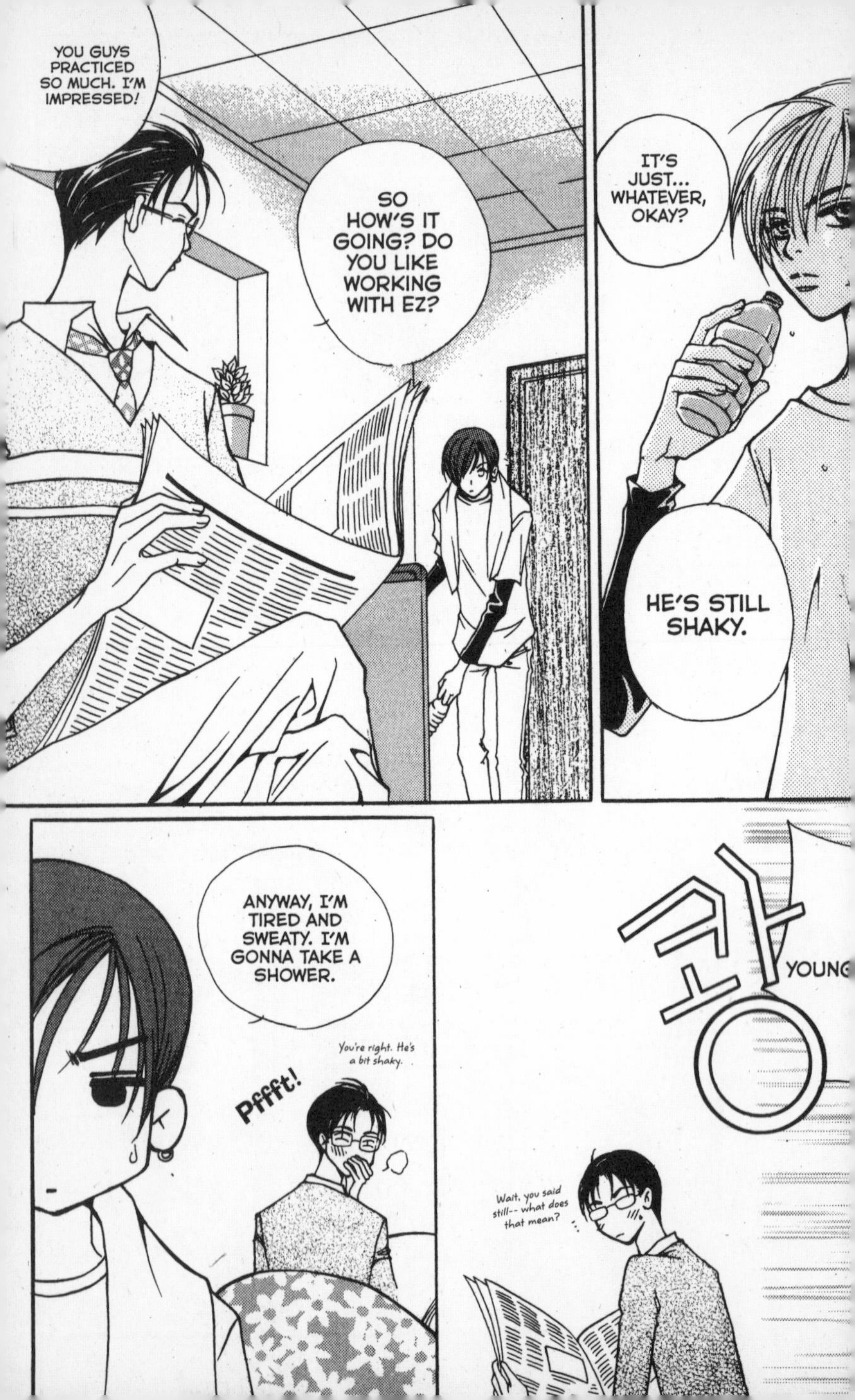
YOU GUYS PRACTICED SO MUCH. I'M IMPRESSED!
SO HOW'S IT GOING? DO YOU LIKE WORKING WITH EZ?
IT'S JUST... WHATEVER, OKAY?
HE'S STILL SHAKY.
ANYWAY, I'M TIRED AND SWEATY. I'M GONNA TAKE A SHOWER.
You're right. He's a bit shaky.
Pffft!
YOUNG
Wait, you said still-- what does that mean?

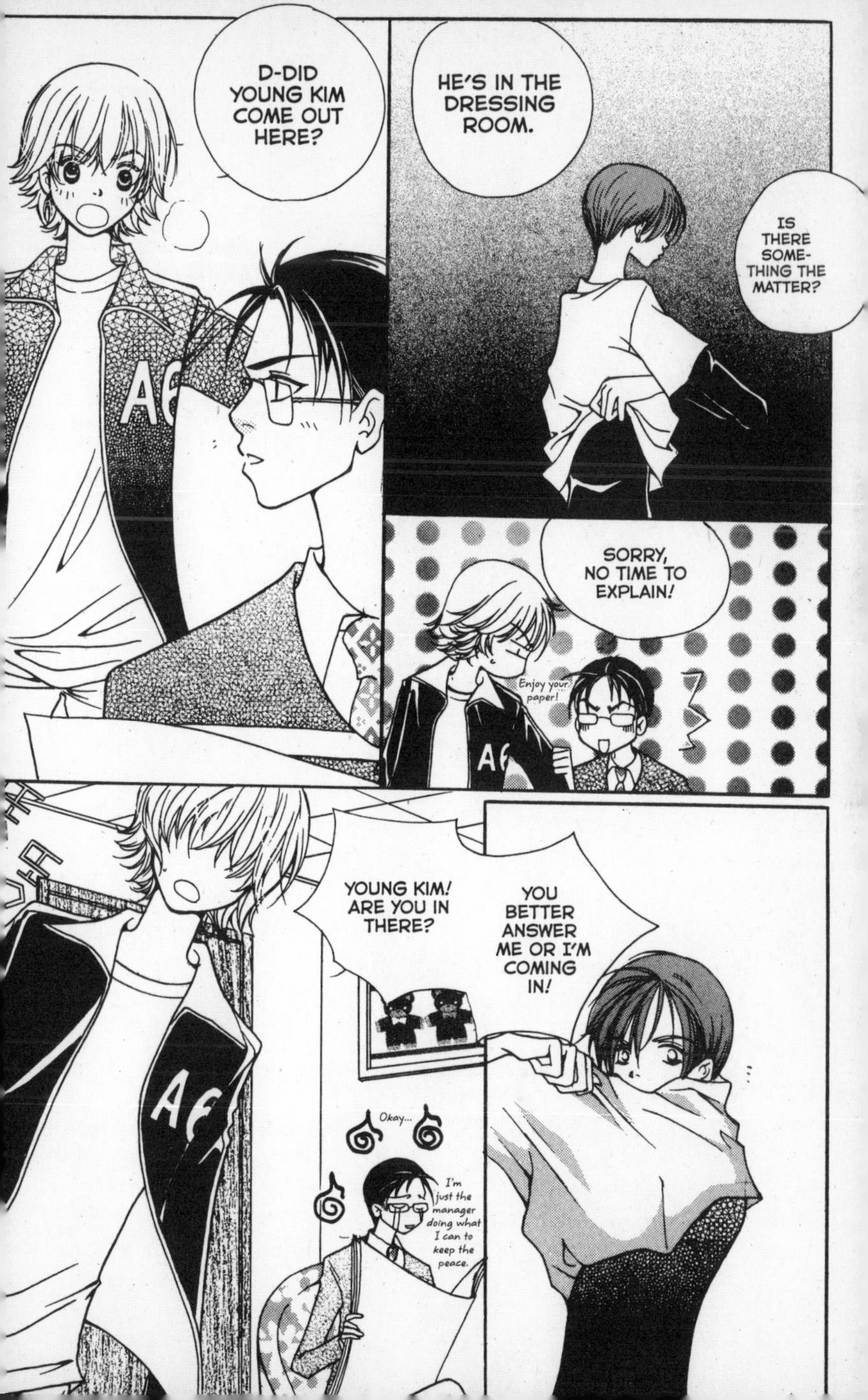
D-DID YOUNG KIM COME OUT HERE?
HE'S IN THE DRESSING ROOM.
IS THERE SOME-THING THE MATTER?
SORRY, NO TIME TO EXPLAIN!
Enjoy your paper!
YOUNG KIM! ARE YOU IN THERE?
YOU BETTER ANSWER ME OR I'M COMING IN!
Okay...
I'm just the manager doing what I can to keep the peace.

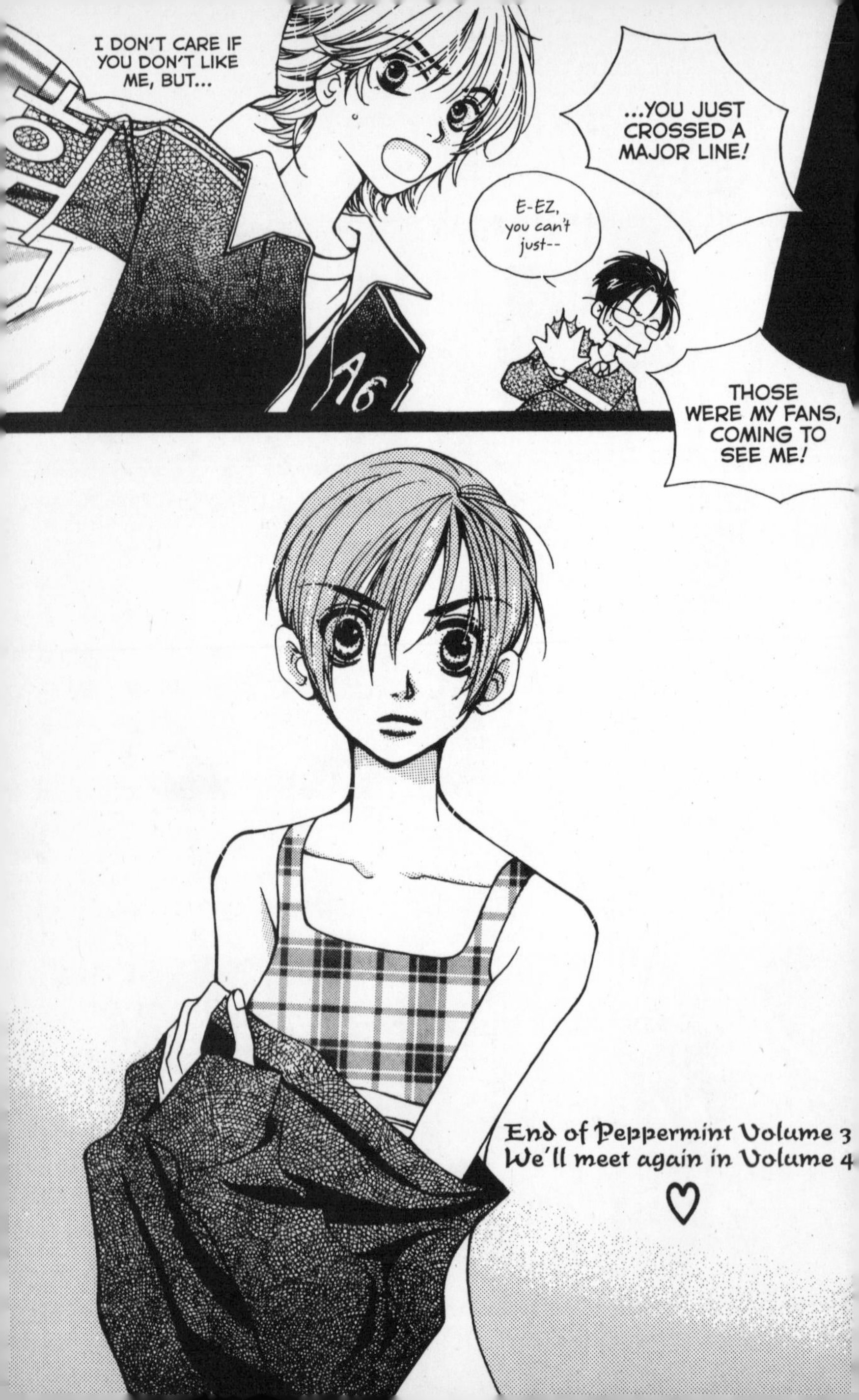
I DON'T CARE IF YOU DON'T LIKE ME, BUT...
...YOU JUST CROSSED A MAJOR LINE!
E-EZ, you can't just--
THOSE WERE MY FANS, COMING TO SEE ME!
End of Peppermint Volume 3
We'll meet again in Volume 4
♡

In the final volume of...

Peppermint

EZ and Young's duo shocks the music market with their whole new hardedge image. And music isn't the only thing turning over a new leaf in Hey's life. While misunderstandings and hurt feelings put a damper on her and EO's chance at romance, time may be all that's needed to heal their wounds.

WHAT DO YOU THINK WILL HAPPEN NEXT?

Anything goes in the last installment of this minty fresh romantic-comedy!

Peppermint

Author's Corner

Eun Jin Seo

IF YOU LOOK TOO CAREFULLY, YOU'LL SEE THAT THIS COMIC
IS FULL OF BLACK HOLES. THINGS JUST VANISH. HEY LOSES
THINGS WAY TOO EASILY. LIKE WHEN SHE GOES ON THE DATE
AND FORGETS HER BAG. AND THEN WHEN SHE FIGHTS WITH EO,
SHE LEAVES HER BAG BEHIND AGAIN, BUT THIS TIME IT'S GONE
FOR GOOD. HOW DID THIS HAPPEN? NO WORRIES, THERE ARE MANY
MORE BAGS IN THE SEA. BE STRONG, HEY!

•

ARIES AND BLOOD TYPE O.
DEBUT: 1995 COLOR ILLUSTRATOR ON *BANSIN*.
WORKS INCLUDE: *PSYCHE, SALAD DAYS,* ETC.
CURRENTLY IN "PARTY" WITH *PEPPERMINT*
AND IN "JUTI" WITH *TRUMPS!*

♥ SEND ALL FAN LETTERS TO ♥

PEPPERMINT FANMAIL
C/O TOKYOPOP
5900 WILSHIRE BLVD, SUITE #2000
LOS ANGELES, CA 90036

kkkamelki@hanmail.net

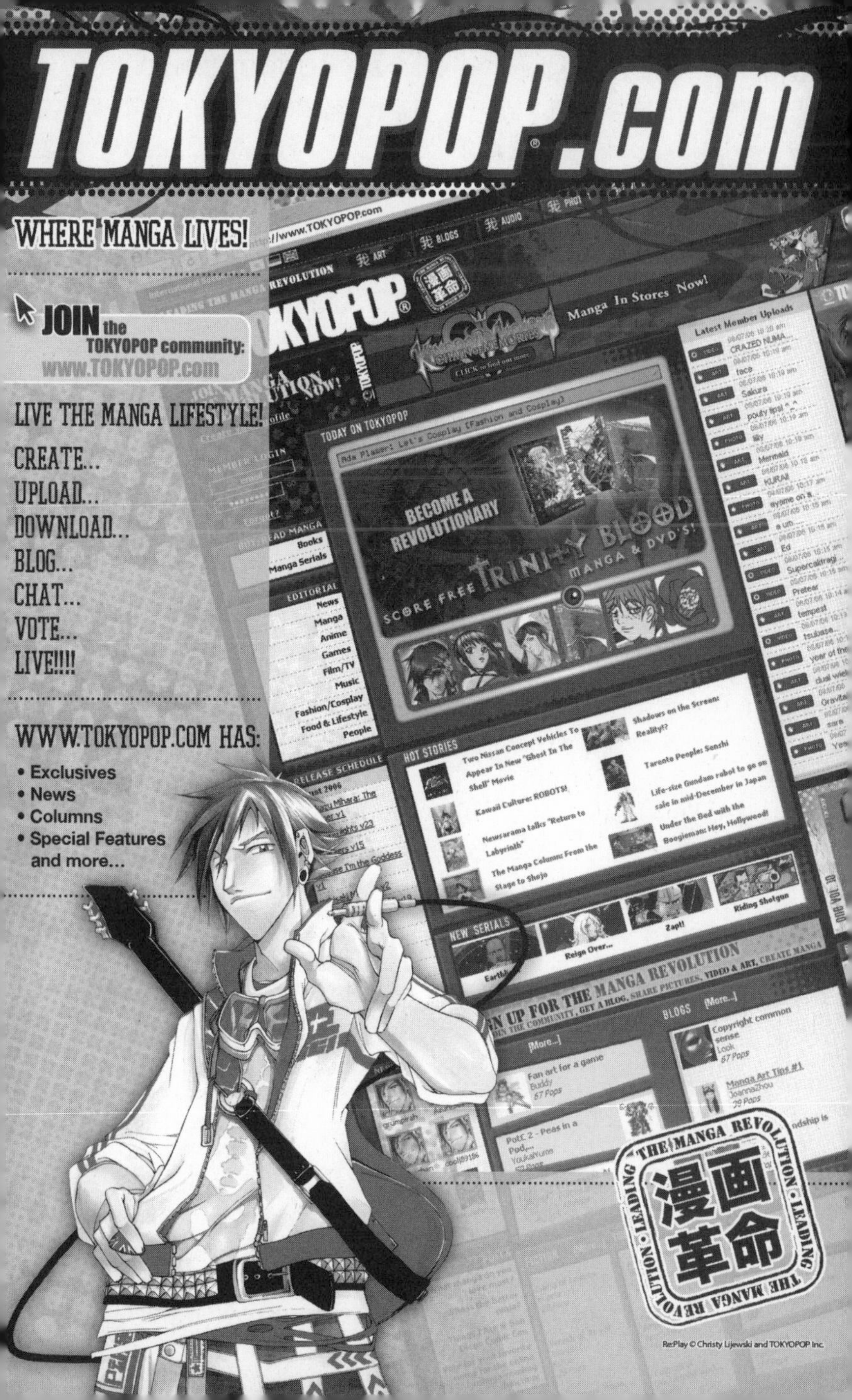
TOKYOPOP.com
WHERE MANGA LIVES!
JOIN the TOKYOPOP community: www.TOKYOPOP.com
LIVE THE MANGA LIFESTYLE!
CREATE...
UPLOAD...
DOWNLOAD...
BLOG...
CHAT...
VOTE...
LIVE!!!!
WWW.TOKYOPOP.COM HAS:
• Exclusives
• News
• Columns
• Special Features
and more...
THE MANGA REVOLUTION • LEADING
漫画革命
Re:Play © Christy Lijewski and TOKYOPOP Inc.

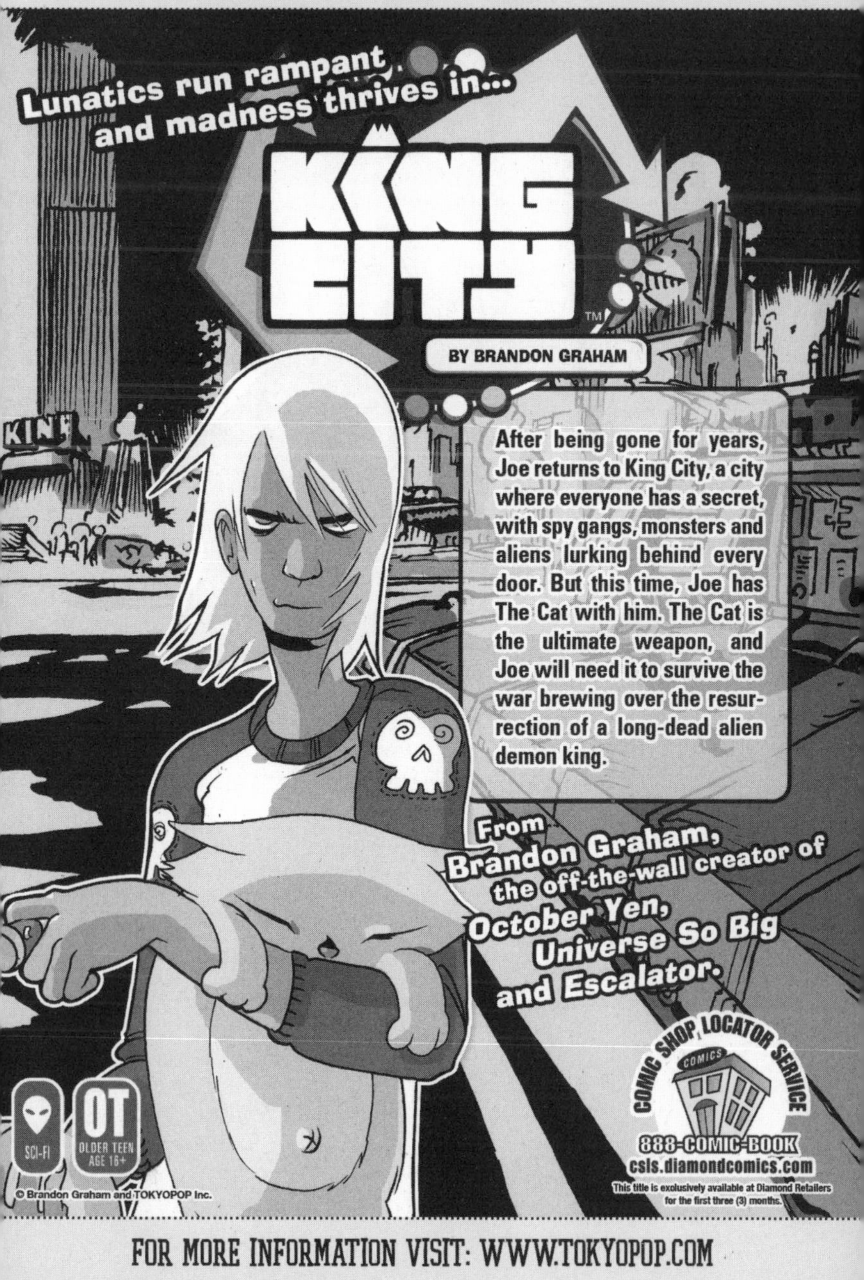
Lunatics run rampant and madness thrives in...
KING CITY™
BY BRANDON GRAHAM
After being gone for years, Joe returns to King City, a city where everyone has a secret, with spy gangs, monsters and aliens lurking behind every door. But this time, Joe has The Cat with him. The Cat is the ultimate weapon, and Joe will need it to survive the war brewing over the resurrection of a long-dead alien demon king.
From Brandon Graham, the off-the-wall creator of October Yen, Universe So Big and Escalator.
SCI-FI
OT OLDER TEEN AGE 16+
© Brandon Graham and TOKYOPOP Inc.
COMIC SHOP LOCATOR SERVICE
COMICS
888-COMIC-BOOK
csls.diamondcomics.com
This title is exclusively available at Diamond Retailers for the first three (3) months.

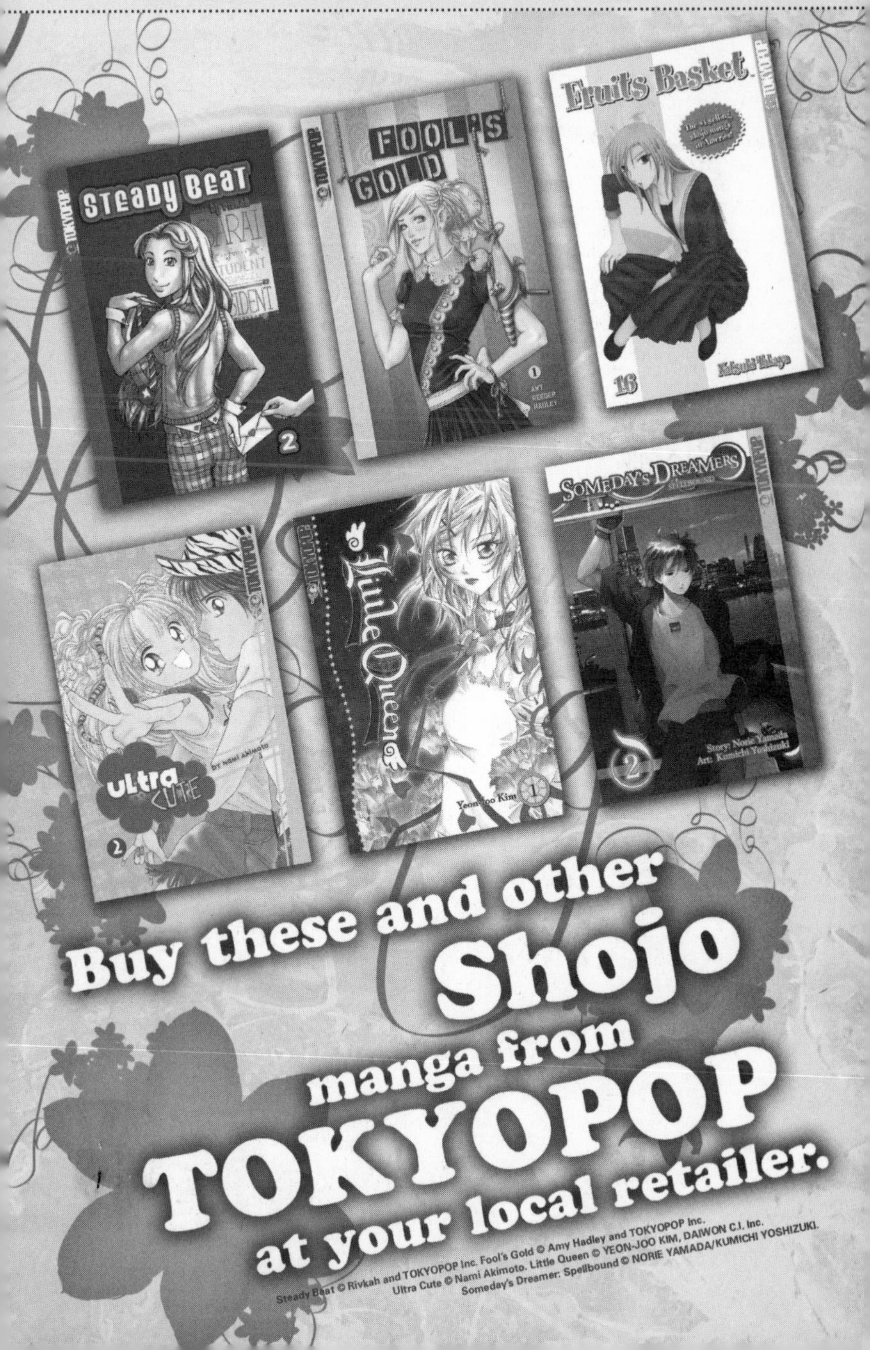
STEADY BEAT
2
FOOL'S GOLD
1
AMY REEDER HADLEY
Fruits Basket
16
SOMEDAY'S DREAMERS
SPELLBOUND
Story: Norie Yamada
Art: Kumichi Yoshizuki
2
ultra CUTE
BY NAMI AKIMOTO
2
Little Queen
Yeon-Joo Kim
1
Buy these and other
Shojo
manga from
TOKYOPOP
at your local retailer.
Steady Beat © Rivkah and TOKYOPOP Inc. Fool's Gold © Amy Hadley and TOKYOPOP Inc.
Ultra Cute © Nami Akimoto. Little Queen © YEON-JOO KIM, DAIWON C.I. Inc.
Someday's Dreamer: Spellbound © NORIE YAMADA/KUMICHI YOSHIZUKI.

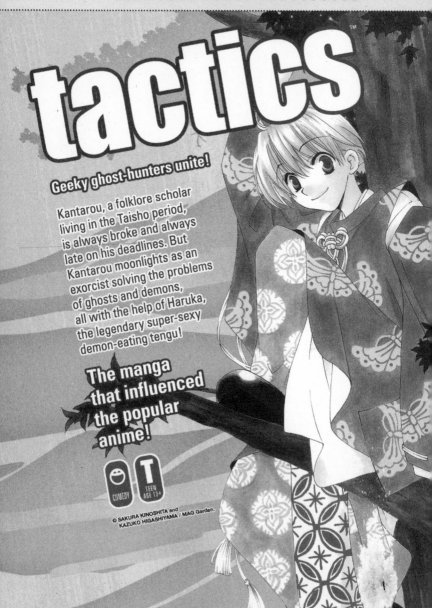